THE
Big Book
of Kids
Activities

PAGE STREET
PUBLISHING CO.

First published in 2021 by
Page Street Publishing Co.
27 Congress Street, Suite 105
Salem, MA 01970
www.pagestreetpublishing.com

Distributed by Macmillan, sales in Canada by The Canadian Manda Group.

25   24   23   22   21   1 2   3   4   5

ISBN-13: 978-1-64567-324-8
ISBN-10: 1-64567-324-3

Library of Congress Control Number: 2020948807

Cover and book design by Molly Kate Young for Page Street Publishing Co.
Photography by Tamara Lee-Sang, Melissa Lennig, Ashlee Hamon, Charlotte Dart, Holly Homer, Jamie Harrington, Brittanie Pyper and Tonya Staab

Printed and bound in the United States

500 Projects
That Are the Bestest, Funnest Ever

THE
Big Book
of Kids
Activities

Holly Homer, Jamie Harrington, Brittanie Pyper,
Rachel Miller, Colleen Kessler, Emma Vanstone,
Amanda Boyarshinov, Kim Vij
and Tonya Staab

PAGE STREET
PUBLISHING CO.

THE BIG TABLE OF CONTENTS

- - - - - - - - - - - - - - - - -

part three

SCIENCE | 212

part four

BACKYARD ACTIVITIES | 293

Introduction

The thing about kids is they grow up. They start out inquisitive, adventurous and wildly participatory. They find thrill in activities, silly games and simple crafts. Somewhere along the way a governor gets placed that says that inquiry can only be serious, adventures should be within a specific path and participation needs a leader.

Why is play constrained?

Why do adults look both ways before joining in?

Why isn't play the first thing on the family calendar?

Modern life has filled our schedules with things that we have to do. Modern life has filled our schedules with things our kids have to do. Modern life has held us captive indoors.

We *want* to play.

We *long* for time together.

We *seek* fun.

The good news is that play is waiting on us. It sits quietly giggling at the dining room table, under the bed, behind the curtains, in the kitchen junk drawer, in the trunk of the car, between the couch cushions and peeking through the door to the backyard.

Play doesn't mind if you stop by for just a moment. It is fine with being added to the situation at the last minute. It loves occupying those little moments between the scheduled ones and then sneaking into the rest of the day.

Play can take an ordinary day and make it a favorite day. It doesn't require equipment, money or planning. It can fill a moment. It can fill a day. And when intentionally sought out, it can fill a life.

We want to value time over toys. We want our kids to keep play close as they grow and weave it into their future. We want them to remember the times we played *together*.

Our fondest memories of childhood are those filled with play. Our bedrooms weren't filled with toys, they were chock-full of possibilities. Our play wasn't fancy or structured, it followed us around like an imaginary friend.

There were homemade wooden blocks in the living room and a rag doll on the bed. There were woods to explore and sketches of tree house plans waiting to be built. There were fireflies in a jar on the bedside table and a mysterious cocoon taped upright to the bookshelf. We had collections of rocks and a stack of homemade games created with items from the kitchen junk drawer. There was a garden outside that attracted sneaky rabbits and a swing whose arc was never-ending. There were diaries that held novels in progress and frozen containers of yogurt to eat on the back porch. There were distant travels on a magical throw rug and craft projects that required broken crayons and scraps of yarn. There were orchards that smelled like cider and snow that was shoveled into games of fox and hound. Stairs doubled as slides and bicycles rode faster than the wind. There were books to read and reread and blanket tents large enough for a revival. There were plays to write, act and direct with an audience of stuffed animals and card games that ended in playful boasts. There were endless trees to climb and imaginary friends to visit.

We hope that this book inspires you to find play in big and small moments every day. We hope it is an imagination boost that launches childhood memories beyond these pages.

We believe that you don't need the latest gadgets or an elaborate plan to engage children. Play meets everyone right where they are with what they have in their hand.

Sure, play is fun, but children will learn life skills that will stay with them forever. Finding joy, acting with diligence, teamwork, gratitude, mindfulness of others, patience, compassion, sportsmanship and respect are all play companions.

Play is family glue.

Let's play!

Unless otherwise specified, each of these activities may be enjoyed by one or more participants. Often, our activities include optional modifications to take the age of the kid(s) into greater consideration. The suggested modifications for younger kids are more suitable for ages one to three; those for older kids are more suitable for ages four to ten. And of course, many of these activities are truly for "kids of all ages," so feel free to join in the fun!

Part One

CRAFTS

Slime 48

Playdough 71

(one)

SUPER FUN CRAFTS

Making something with a child is about the process, not the product. The memories are made from the collective energy of creation. The finished craft is an experience souvenir.

Holly's Pick: I adore the Shake-It-Up Ink (page 26) because over time, markers become very dear to me and this is a way to use them all the way up!

Rachel's Pick: Kick the Can Art (page 22) is a great way for kids to be active while creating art! The finished product looks a bit like Pollock's works. We have several on our walls.

Bubble Prints

Bubbles and childhood are a perfect match. They require a surprising amount of concentration to create. The perfect bubble is one that is a bit bigger or elongated or has a particularly bright rainbow or holds together longer. Actually, the perfect bubble seems to be the current one!

This activity uses bubbles to create art prints. It includes our favorite bubble recipe and a fun use of recycled water bottles to create a bubble rainbow.

- - - - - - - - - - - - - -

Materials
(to make one bubble shooter)

+ 9 to 12 drinking straws
+ Rubber band
+ Broad plastic cup
+ Multiple sheets of paper

Strongest Bubbles
(to make about 1½ cups [360 ml] bubble solution)

+ 1 cup (235 ml) water
+ ⅓ cup (80 ml) liquid dish detergent (not concentrated; if concentrated, use slightly less)
+ 3 tbsp (45 ml) corn syrup
+ 10 to 15 drops food coloring

It is best to stir the ingredients to mix them, not shake. Let it sit overnight for the best results. We split our recipe into multiple baby food jars and then added food dye for our printing craft.

Grab a handful of straws and secure them together with a rubber band. We found that five or six straws worked best.

Dip one end into the bubble solution placed into a plastic cup broad enough to accommodate the straw bundle. Blow lots of bubbles!

Hold the end of the shooter over a piece of paper and see what happens on the paper as the colored bubbles pop. Let dry.

Modifications for Younger Kids
Instead of using dish detergent to create the bubbles, make them pain-free by using tear-free baby wash. This way, if your child gets a bubble in an eye it won't sting.

Younger kids who might inhale with the straw in their mouth vs. exhale should continue to use a bubble wand until the coordination is mastered. No one wants a mouthful of bubbles!

Modifications for Older Kids
Cut the bottom off a water bottle. Put a dish rag over the opening and use a rubber band to secure that to the bottle. Dip the rag into the bubble juice and blow on the "mouth" of the bottle. The result should be a "snake" of bubbles.

Use your bubble-printed paper to write a card to a friend or family member you haven't seen in a long time—you can also use bubble prints on butcher paper to create your own wrapping paper for gifts.

*See photo insert page 1.

Craft Stick Puzzles

In my room, under my bed was a shoebox full of treasures. I collected tiny things that I found or purchased with cherished allowance dollars. There was a set of nested paper boxes where the largest one was no bigger than 2 inches (5 cm) across that a friend made and decorated. There was a tiny clay teapot that was given to me for my birthday. There was one of those plastic mazes with a ball bearing. Each held value much bigger than its size.

I believe if I had made something like these craft stick puzzles back then, it would have been added to that box. Create a puzzle using craft sticks and then place a rubber band around them for storage—the perfect fit for any treasure box.

– – – – – – – – – – – – – – – – – – – –

Materials
(to make one puzzle)

+ 6 to 8 wide craft sticks
+ Wide painter's or masking tape
+ Markers or paint

Place craft sticks next to one another on a table, making a blank canvas as wide as you want your puzzle to be. Using a piece of painter's tape, secure them together. Turn over and decorate with markers or paint.

When done with the puzzle decor, release the sticks from the tape. Try to put the puzzle back together, restoring the picture you drew.

Modifications for Younger Kids
The simpler the picture, the easier it will be to put together. Consider making one gigantic geometric shape that your toddler or preschooler needs to put together.

Modifications for Older Kids
Have older kids repeat the process on the blank side of the puzzle with the same colors they used in the original picture. This will make it more difficult to put together either side as a complete picture. You can also make multiple puzzles and mix the sticks together.

*See photo insert page 1.

TIP
Make a quiet-time bag for naps-on-the-run. We have all had to do an errand at the worst time of day—naptime. Calming activities are a great alternative when naps are unavailable. Consider adding these puzzle sticks, the Dry-Erase Doodles (page 110) and the Baggie Maze (page 109) to your "quiet" bag.

Bathtub Art with Recipe

There are two types of people in the world: those who take baths and those who don't. I don't mean the latter are unwashed, but they certainly don't appreciate the luxury of a good tub bath. Kids who enjoy a bath will love this project and those who don't might just be converted.

This art project uses DIY bathtub paint and a large tub tile canvas to create art.

– – – – – – – – – – – – – – – – – – – –

Materials

+ Several colors of Homemade Bathtub Paint (page 15)
+ Paintbrush(es)
+ Bathtub

Homemade Bathtub Paint
(to make about 1½ cups [360 ml] paint)

+ Medium-size bowl
+ ½ cup (80 g) cornstarch
+ ½ cup (120 ml) boiling water
+ 1 cup (235 ml) dish detergent
+ Liquid food coloring

In the bowl, stir the cornstarch into the hot water until it is dissolved and has a pasty consistency. Add the detergent and stir until there are no chunks. Add the desired color of food coloring. Store in an airtight container. Stir well before use.

This paint is easy enough to use with both brushes and fingers, depending on the artist's preference.

It can be washed away when bathtime is over and the mess will just go down the drain.

Modifications for Younger Kids
Just painting in the tub without a picture goal in mind is fun. Kids can even use the paint to paint themselves.

Modifications for Older Kids
Paint tub tiles different colors to create a very large pixel art installation. This can be planned ahead of time, using graph paper.

TIP
If you are worried about your child having a reaction to the dish detergent in the paint, you can replace the dish detergent with any clear shampoo that your family prefers.

No-Sew No-Glue Tutu

One of the best things about being a girl is that accessorizing can be an art form. There is no reason to step out into the world with ordinary clothes when tiaras, tutus and princess attire are at your fingertips. Dressing isn't for warmth and protection. Dressing is for expression.

What we love about this homemade tutu is that it is perfect for those of us who haven't developed sewing skills. A simple slipknot attaches the tutu fluff for a custom look.

Materials
(to make one tutu)

+ Scissors
+ Elastic long enough to fit around the child's waist
+ Fabric and ribbon scraps—lots of them!
+ Tulle strips—cut 4 inches (10 cm) wide

Cut a piece of elastic long enough to wrap around your child's waist. Knot it. Make sure it is tight enough that the skirt won't fall off but loose enough to pull on and off easily. If you leave a "tail" on the knot, you can retie it to make the skirt bigger as your kids grow.

Take a fabric or ribbon scrap and create a slipknot over the waistband to attach it. The tails of the scrap can be even, or if you want more of a free-form look, they can be staggered. Repeat until you have the desired skirt fullness.

Have fun planning the different fabrics and ribbons to make your skirt. You can do a theme—like green or tan strips to make a luau skirt, or tie small jingle bells to the bottom of the strips for a musical dress.

(continued)

Modifications for Younger Kids

Younger kids will love watching the tutu grow as each fabric strip is added. Have them choose which scrap is added next.

Modifications for Older Kids

Have your child create the knots. Older girls may find that this slipknot technique can be used for crafting custom headbands, bracelets and ponytail holders.

Painting on Crayons and Gel Paint

Painting and coloring are often thought about as separate projects, but this activity combines the two for a delightfully colorful two-step art process. The fun thing about this activity is that it is well suited for artists of all ages. Even the youngest kids can get involved with some crayon banging on paper that is transformed into a masterpiece with a simple homemade gel paint recipe.

- - - - - - - - - - - - -

Materials

+ White construction paper
+ Light or brightly colored crayons
+ Paintbrush or sponges

Gel Paint
(to make about ¼ cup [60 ml] of paint)

+ 4 tbsp (60 ml) hair gel
+ 5 to 15 drops food coloring

Start with a plain piece of paper and create a crayon drawing, using different colors and filling in different areas with crayon strokes. It is best to use contrasting crayons from the color of the paint. For example, if you are going to paint the background with dark paint, color with light, bright colors. Mix the hair gel and food coloring together.

After your children have filled the pages with the crayon drawing, have them wipe the project with a single color of gel paint. Lightly buff the artwork afterward to watch the crayon coloring "pop" out. Beautiful!

The ratio of dye to hair gel can be altered to get a more colorful paint result. This paint will keep for months in an airtight container.

We love the ease of making this paint—and cleanup is a breeze. Even if the paint has dried on, it will wash off the brushes easily. It is perfect for group events!

Modifications for Younger Kids

Please be aware that this recipe is not edible, so close supervision may be required. To make this into an edible recipe, use plain gelatin mix instead of the hair gel. Gelatin paint is not smooth, so it's better for finger painting; also, note that it does not store as well.

Modifications for Older Kids

Explore color theory with your kids. Kids can make choices on color combinations that will be complementary, based on the color wheel, or choose to work on a monochromatic masterpiece.

> **TIP**
> We prefer using lighter colors of crayon and darker colors of paint over the crayon, for the best effect.

Decorated Dishes

The kids in our house all have their own mugs. Having something in the kitchen that is "just theirs" is a special treat. Each child designed and created the custom mugs. It makes it easier to set the table or figure out who might have left a dish on the kitchen counter.

Having a special plate, bowl or mug makes mealtime more fun. This activity personalizes a mug or dish. These are treasured at home or make great gifts for family and friends.

- - - - - - - - - - - - - -

Materials

+ Scissors
+ Piece of paper
+ Crayons or markers
+ Clear ovenproof mugs or dishes
+ Rubbing alcohol
+ Permanent oil markers

Cut pieces of plain paper slightly smaller than the surface of the mug you will be decorating. We used an 8½ x 11-inch (20.5 x 28-cm) piece of paper folded into four sections. Have the kids draw/color/paint/doodle on the paper, creating the design that will be traced onto the mug. Kids can create several designs and then choose the best one.

Prepare the mug's surface by wiping with rubbing alcohol to remove any oil. Even a greasy fingerprint will cause the paint to not set properly.

Secure the paper on the inside of the mug and then trace the design with permanent oil markers on the outside.

Leave the mugs overnight for the paint to fully dry. Then put them in a cold oven and set the temperature for 350°F (180°C or gas mark 4) and bake for an hour. Turn off the oven and let the mugs slowly cool before removing them. If exposed to rapidly changing temperature, many mugs will crack.

Modifications for Younger Kids

Keep younger kids away from permanent oil markers because they can stain the skin. Have them draw the original and have an adult transfer the art to the mug for the children.

Modifications for Older Kids

Let them draw directly onto the surface of the mugs or dishes. If they make a mistake, encourage them to incorporate that mistake into the artwork.

TIP

If you are using white mugs or dishes, have the children lightly color their outline with a crayon. Don't have them color it in; use the oil markers to color in the picture. Keep in mind that the oil markers will not color on top of crayon.

Clay Recipe for Bead Making

You can create your own ceramic-like clay—it is great for molds, for sculpting and for making beads—using ingredients commonly found in the kitchen! This is better than a trip to the ceramics studio.

- - - - - - - - - - - - -

Materials

Air-Dry Clay
(to make 3½ cups [about 700 g] clay)

+ 1 cup (160 g) cornstarch
+ 2 cups (442 g) baking soda
+ 1½ cups (355 ml) water
+ 1 tbsp (15 g) cream of tartar

Bracelet or Necklace

+ Air-dry clay
+ Toothpick
+ Metallic acrylic paint
+ 12- to 18-inch (30.5- to 45.5-cm)-long piece of strong string (bracelet or necklace length)
+ Plastic sewing needle

Mix the clay ingredients in a medium-size saucepan over medium heat on the stovetop. Stir constantly. It is finished cooking when the clay pulls away from the sides of the pan (it should be the consistency of dough). Try to use it the day you make the dough; in a pinch you can store in an airtight container and revitalize it with a spray of water prior to use.

Take small equal portions and roll them into spheres. Use a toothpick to create a hole through the middle of the sphere. Roll the newly formed beads in metallic paint. Let air-dry overnight.

String the dried beads onto the string (the string can be doubled to strengthen it) in the pattern of choice. Tie the ends together a little bigger than wrist circumference so that the bracelet can be pulled on over the hand and a little bigger than neck circumference so that the necklace can be pulled over the head.

Modifications for Younger Kids
Use a plastic needle (a dull one) for younger kids to use to aid in stringing the beads.

Modifications for Older Kids
Letting kids get creative with bead size, shape and color allows them to make a unique accessory.

TIP
Substituting elastic for string makes it easier to wear, but just a bit more challenging to string.

DIY Roll-Up Crayons

A special treasure in your school pencil box is a reminder from home throughout the day that you are part of a family that loves you. This fancy school supply is something that likely no one else at school will have—it will give your kids a smile and remind them of the fun time they had making it at home.

All you need is used glue stick containers and old crayons to create a twist-up crayon that is sure to make kids smile. Or upcycle extra-wide straws—they are super hard to fill, but the finished product of an ultralong crayon is awesome! Medicine bottles make perfectly sized crayons for toddlers (be sure to wash thoroughly before recycling).

- - - - - - - - - - - - -

Materials

+ Empty clean glue stick tubes
+ Tape
+ Sheet of paper
+ Muffin tin
+ Cupcake liners
+ Old broken crayons
+ Paper to wrap the finished sticks (optional, if gifting)

Clean out the inside of the empty glue stick with soap and water and let dry. Tape paper around the glue stick container to cover the label. Our kids love making their roll-up crayons pretty.

Line a muffin tin with the cupcake liners. Use each wrapper for a different color. Peel the crayons and place in the cupcake liners with like-colored crayons.

Preheat your oven to 350°F (180°C or gas mark 4). Leave the muffin tin in the oven for 8 to 10 minutes, until the crayons are fully melted. Pour the melted color from the cupcake liner into the empty glue container. Let cool.

Modifications for Younger Kids

Obviously, any step that has anything to do with oven use or hot melted wax crayons needs to be completed by an adult. Younger kids can design colors to go into each glue container by combining primary colors. Have younger kids decorate construction paper wrappers for the glue containers.

Modifications for Older Kids

Older kids can make swirled colors by adding different colors of crayons together and lightly swirling the colors together as it cools.

*See photo insert page 1.

Freezer Paper Stencils

One Christmas I made decorated pillowcases for each of my relatives. Each pillowcase was stretched over a piece of cardboard and painted, using fabric paint and stencils. I set them in a row on the floor, propped up against the wall to dry. That was when the next-door neighbor's cat showed up. The cat proceeded to walk along the wall, dragging his tail through my works of art while I screamed and started planning new presents.

So put out the cat, because we are painting pillowcases, or T-shirts, dish towels, tote bags and so on—the options are endless! This simple craft uses freezer paper to create stencils for kids to use to customize fabric items.

Materials

+ Pencil or pen
+ Roll of freezer paper
+ Scissors
+ Cardboard
+ T-shirt or other fabric like a pillowcase
+ Fabric paint and paintbrushes

Trace a shape onto freezer paper. The simpler the design, the better the outcome will be. Cut out the stencil.

Out of cardboard, create a flat surface to place under the first layer of fabric. Place the stencil on the fabric and outline it with crazy strokes of fabric paint.

Allow the paint to dry a bit before removing the stencil, to prevent seepage and drips. Pull off the stencil and admire the transformation.

(continued)

If you are making a pillowcase, consider painting with glow-in-the-dark paint over your artwork. Your kids will love to look at their pillow art as they go to sleep.

Modifications for Younger Kids

Let kids choose the design for older participants to create a stencil. Younger kids can help outline and pull off the stencil after the paint has dried.

Squeezing a bottle of paint is a good fine-motor exercise. Finding a fabric paint bottle that is a good size for your child's hand will aid in coordination of painting.

Modifications for Older Kids

Older kids can be let loose on this project to design and create as they wish. Creating a set of matching pillowcases for an upcoming slumber party or gifting their best friend with a matching pillow can be a lot of fun!

TIP
Why use paper gift wrap that is just discarded? Consider wrapping your gift in a decorated pillowcase the next time you are going to a birthday party.

Homemade Paint Recipe for Mask Making

One of my kids dressed as a Blue Power Ranger for eight months. Each morning he would get up and put on blue clothing (only blue clothing) and then cover it with the Power Ranger costume. The mask was a flat plastic circle with an elastic band that usually sat on top of his head, ready to pull down for any necessary superhero actions.

Some kids need to dress up. It is part of developing who they are growing to be. I can report that I haven't seen the Power Ranger costume for years, but occasionally he still wears blue.

This activity upcycles cereal boxes into handmade masks painted with a homemade paint recipe that's known to be used by the masters.

– – – – – – – – – – – – – – –

Materials
(to make one mask)

+ A variety of chalk sticks (great use of leftover scraps from sidewalk chalk)
+ Bowl
+ Resealable plastic bag
+ Hammer
+ 1 or 2 egg yolks
+ Scissors
+ A large cereal box
+ A variety of lid sizes to trace (we used four sizes)
+ Ruler
+ Paintbrushes

Soak the bits of chalk in a bowl of water for several minutes to soften them. Put them into a resealable plastic bag, to contain the mess, and pound them lightly with a hammer to break up the chalk into a powdery paste. Mix the chalk paste with the egg yolk until it is the consistency of paint. Be sure to wash your hands thoroughly and clean up any spills promptly and properly. Also, as this paint contains raw egg, you will want to discard any unused paint.

Cut the cereal box into a giant circle using a lid as a template. Measure the distance between your child's eyes. Make the eye holes. Using small lids, create the eye circles around the holes. Use a giant lid to create the lower lip outline. Paint the back of the box—the blank brown side—and embellish.

Modifications for Younger Kids

Instead of using homemade egg paint, have your child finger paint. If you don't have finger paint or are working with a child who puts everything in his/her mouth, add some food coloring to vanilla pudding and use that as "paint."

Modifications for Older Kids

Ask the children to describe their personality or appearance. After they have told you what is distinctive about them, have them try to draw a superhero mask based on the characteristics they described.

Homemade Sidewalk Chalk

The world is our canvas—or at least our driveway! Our kids enjoy tracing their body, creating never-ending hopscotch boards and playing our homemade game of chalk tangle. Some of the best chalk we have used is homemade. Toddlers prefer the chunky sticks. Homemade chalk can be customized for color and color intensity. We think the brighter and more layers of color, the better!

This activity makes sidewalk chalk from scratch. Make extra. Your kids will love to give these sticks to their friends as gifts.

Materials

+ Disposable bowls and spoons or wooden sticks for mixing
+ ½ cup (80 g) cornstarch
+ Water
+ 1 lb (455 g) plaster of Paris
+ Multiple colors of tempera paint
+ Empty toilet paper rolls
+ Waxed paper
+ Rubber band(s)

Use disposable bowls to mix in and plastic spoons or wooden stir sticks that you can throw away. Because you are using plaster of Paris, you do not want to wash anything because it will clog your drain. Small children should not be involved in this first step and we recommend it be done outside.

Mix the cornstarch and water first, and then add the plaster of Paris slowly while continuing to stir. It will be the consistency of pancake batter. Once mixed, separate into smaller bowls and add the desired tempera paint color and mix.

Line the empty toilet paper tubes with waxed paper (both inside the tube and underneath where the tube will stand). Spoon the color mixture into the lined toilet paper tubes. If you use a rubber band to bunch a group of rolls, it will make it easier to keep them standing upright.

Let the sticks dry fully, roughly 24 to 48 hours, before removing the paper tubes and heading to the driveway.

Modifications for Younger Kids

Younger kids can direct color coordination and work as an assistant, going and getting things as needed.

Modifications for Older Kids

Have your older kids layer the colors inside each tube to create rainbow sticks. As you draw a line on the sidewalk, it will change colors!

*See photo insert page 1.

> **WARNING**
> Do not allow your children to touch the plaster with their hands, as it can cause burns. Throw away any unused plaster. Do not rinse out the containers in the house, because the plaster can solidify inside pipes.

Kick the Can Art

One of the reasons that we are so passionate about kids' activities is that there is no excuse not to play. It doesn't take money or special equipment. Anything can be turned into a game. Kids have known this since the beginning of time. Adults have been known to forget this.

The existence of games like Kick the Can prove this. You play with what you have. The fun in this activity is that you can also create art during your next game.

— — — — — — — — — — — — — —

Materials

(to make one can)

+ Scissors
+ Sheets of paper
+ Large, empty, clean coffee can with a lid
+ 2 or 3 colors of paint
+ 3 or 4 marbles of various size
+ Tape

Cut the paper to be just a little shorter than the height of the can, so that you can line the entire inside of the can with the paper. Squirt paint into the can. Drop the marbles in, then secure the lid with tape.

Kick the can.

It is best to only use two colors of paint, ones that when they mix create a pleasing color—if you use lots of colors, the finished product tends to look more gray or brown, instead of vibrant.

Keep Away

One child is given the can to try to keep it away from a designated home base by kicking it. The other participants attempt to intercept the can and kick it back home. Whenever the can successfully lands on home base, the art project is removed and a new one started. The participant who kicked the can to the goal gets to choose the colors of the new art piece.

Can Soccer

Traditional soccer rules can be modified to accommodate a can (no head butting allowed!) and each time a goal is scored, the art can be reset.

Modifications for Younger Kids

The magical sound of shaking marbles in a tin can may be enough entertainment for the very young. If younger participants want to play, give them special rules that allow them to pick up the can and throw it. Set up an invisible "personal space barrier" of 3 feet (92 cm) so they don't end up in the middle of a kick.

Modifications for Older Kids

If the majority of participants are older, just add one marble to the can. Older kids tend to kick the can more between art resets and fewer marbles will make a more distinctive pattern.

TIP

To help kids with communication and to keep frustration levels low when kids are not equally matched (say a four-year-old is playing with an eight-year-old), have a "freeze phrase" that younger participants can use once a round that freezes the other players and allows them a chance to get close and kick the can.

Paper Bag Game Portfolio

I was introduced to the dot game (where you try to complete squares against an opponent) while in kindergarten, when I was on a big yellow school bus en route to a field-trip destination. The time flew by as the games continued. It still seems mysterious to me how one line can cause a chain reaction of squares.

Despite handheld video games and portable video consoles, there is a tactile satisfaction to traditional two-person games battled on paper. This craft creates a safe place to keep and transport a variety of paper games.

- - - - - - - - - - -

Materials
(to make one paper bag book)

+ Scissors
+ 3 or 4 paper lunch bags
+ Hole punch
+ Yarn
+ Copy or construction paper
+ Markers/crayons/paint

Cut the bottom off the bag to create a paper sleeve. Fold the bag in half. Repeat three to five times for each portfolio.

Stack the bags together, making sure the folded sides are aligned. Hole punch six holes equidistant from one another down the folded side. Secure by lacing and tying yarn through each hole.

Now there are pockets to keep each paper game. Cut paper to fit snugly in the portfolio and outline the game (or leave the paper blank). Some games we love:

- Tic-tac-toe
- Hangman
- Dots
- Shut the Box
- Finish the Picture

Modifications for Younger Kids
Fill the portfolio with coloring activities and blank paper for doodles.

Modifications for Older Kids
Older kids can choose how to design their portfolio and which games to include. They could also include blank sheets ready for origami, along with the directions for folding.

> **TIP**
> Laminating the paper game inserts and using dry-erase markers can keep the games going and going.

People Sticks

When I read a book, the characters are vividly brought to life as I see them. I think that is why watching a movie adaptation of a favorite book can be so disappointing. Everything doesn't look right!

Kids can create their favorite characters on craft sticks as they see them. Then use these companions as bookmarks, for impromptu puppet shows or for a game of Who Am I?

- - - - - - - - - - -

Materials

+ Craft sticks—1 per character
+ Paint pens

(continued)

Decorate the craft sticks, using paint pens to transform it into a favorite book character. It can be as simple or as elaborate as the child imagines.

Modifications for Younger Kids

Cut up a magazine or coloring book and glue the faces or entire bodies onto the sticks.

Modifications for Older Kids

Have them create a complete cast of book characters—even obscure ones—and act out the story, using the upright book as a stage. If they are in a group, have them play a game of Who Am I? with the stick people. Pick a stick from the pile and without looking at it, hold it up to your forehead. The other kids at the table give one clue at a time, describing the character without using the character's name, until the correct character is guessed.

*See photo insert page 2.

> ### TIP
> Have kids retell a favorite story, using puppets (or sticks). It will help them with reading comprehension and story sequencing, even if they aren't reading yet.

Woven Upcycled Container

Roughly a year and a half ago, we spent some time in Ethiopia, where we adopted our sons. One of my memories of Ethiopia includes a family that wove beautiful hats from wool. This weaving craft is inspired by those industrious kids we met. It is a simple activity using a recycled take-out container and some yarn that can create art and stir memories.

Materials

+ Scissors
+ Square styrofoam take-out container
+ Various balls of yarn
+ Tape

Cut the top off of the take-out container. Wrap one color of yarn around and around the bottom half of the container, leaving ¼ inch (6 mm) or so between strands over the opening. Once you have the desired loom width, tape the end of the yarn to the underside of the makeshift loom. While on the underside, stretch a large piece of tape across all the yarn loops to increase stability on the other side.

Tape around the end of a piece of yarn to create an easily handled "tip." Weave the yarn back and forth over and under the stationary yarn assembled in the loom. Use different colors and different over/under patterns for a unique and colorful creation.

Modifications for Younger Kids

Space the stationary loom strands out farther. Consider using a thicker yarn or craft fabric strands. Make sure the color of the yarn used for weaving is different from the stationary loom yarn to make it easier for kids to see the weaving process.

Modifications for Older Kids

Older kids can have the freedom to create an intricate design based on how they use the loom. Finished squares can be sewn together to create scarves, blankets and many other things.

> ### TIP
> This is a great pre-math activity to help preschoolers learn pattern making and develop fine motor skills.

TP Tube Stamping

Kids love to give gifts, but often they are not in a position to do so. That is why we love this activity so much. It gives children the ability to be involved in giving almost any gift by creating the wrapping. It makes them part of the gift team.

Using recycled household items to create a stamp, kids can customize gift bags for recipients in a special way.

- - - - - - - - - - - - - - - - - -

Materials
(to make one rolling stamp)

+ Foam sticker sheet or stickers
+ Scissors
+ Empty toilet paper roll
+ Paint
+ Paper plate
+ Paper bag

Cut the foam sticker sheet or stickers into the desired shape. We cut ours into simple geometric shapes. Peel off the backing and adhere to the toilet paper roll in a pattern. Rows of similar shapes work really well.

Spread paint in a thin layer on a paper plate and roll the toilet paper stamp through it until all the shapes are covered with color. Place the stamp at one end of the bag and roll it down the length. Let dry and then repeat on the other side of the bag.

Modifications for Younger Kids
Use finger paint so younger kids can accent the rolled pattern with some additional hands-on design; the mess can be cleaned up easily.

Modifications for Older Kids
Older kids can create custom tubes with multiple patterns on each tube for stripes of shapes. They can use a paintbrush to apply color to each shape individually for a more precise paint distribution.

TIP
Is your gift too large to fit in a bag? Try stamping plain white or brown package paper for custom gift wrap!

Rubber Band Splatter

On a boring afternoon when there is "nothing to do," there is no better way to reverse the melancholy mood than with a messy activity. Kids making a mess are usually smiling! It must have something to do with throwing oneself into a task and feeling the paint fly. Even kids who don't like to get messy have a hard time resisting this activity.

This artistic process uses rubber band snapping to paint a modern art masterpiece (for supervising adults see the tips for containing the mess).

- - - - - - - - - - - - - - - - - -

Materials

+ Construction paper—cut to fit the bottom of the box
+ Small box or tub
+ 3 to 5 rubber bands
+ 2 or 3 colors of tempera paint
+ Paintbrush

Place a piece of paper in the bottom of your box. Stretch the rubber bands across the top of the box. Paint the rubber bands with a variety of colors.

Pull on the bands to watch the paint splatter onto the paper below.

(continued)

Modifications for Younger Kids

For smaller children, use edible paint. Kids who are prone to putting their fingers into their mouth can enjoy the activity, too.

Modifications for Older Kids

Older kids can work toward a more predictable end result through organized color coordination and rubber band snapping.

TIPS

This activity should be done with kids wearing old clothes. If creating art inside, consider using a drop cloth or old towels or use it as a pre-bath activity in the tub.

If you don't want a mess at all, remove the idea of paint and let the kids create a rubber band instrument. They will enjoy the noises it makes.

Shake-It-Up Ink

I love a new set of markers. The colors are so bright and the lines they create are crisp. The problem with markers is that over time, they lose their markerness. Opening up a marker that doesn't work is a big disappointment. This activity uses those underachieving markers to create ink that gives them a leading role in a splotch art masterpiece.

- - - - - - - - - - - - - -

Materials

+ Empty, clean small glass jars with lids
+ Old dried-out markers—5 or so for each color
+ Bottle of rubbing alcohol
+ Kitchen pan
+ Multiple syringes or medicine droppers
+ Paper

Use a separate glass jar for each color you want to create. Open up the old markers and place the colorful core in the jar for that desired color. When all the marker cores are distributed, pour rubbing alcohol over them with enough liquid to cover.

Place the lids on the jars and let the kids shake the odd concoction. Let the jars sit overnight to allow the ink to fully form.

Fill a kitchen pan with water and slide a piece of paper through it to dampen the page. Use the water for color changes and cleanup. Then fill a syringe or medicine dropper with the newly formed ink and drop onto the damp paper.

Watch how the colorful drops start small and seep out into colorful bursts.

Modifications for Younger Kids

Children who have difficulty controlling a syringe or medicine dropper can be given a filled ear bulb, which uses more gross vs. fine motor coordination.

Modifications for Older Kids

Have older kids experiment with creating new colors by combining marker core colors. They can also try this project on dry paper to see what a difference the dampness can make.

TIPS

Using a medicine dropper can help develop fine motor skills, which can help strengthen little hands for tasks like writing and picking up small objects. This can help prewriters more easily control their pencil grasp, and strength in older kids can translate into better coordination.

Looking to give a fun and unique gift? Replace the paper with ceramic tiles and watch your kids create one-of-a-kind coasters for friends and family. Glue felt to the back of the tiles.

Shrinking Cup Flower Sculptures

While growing up, I was mesmerized by Shrinky Dinks. Because they were out of my allowance range, it was a rare occurrence to be able to draw something on a thin plastic sheet and then bake it into a magically appearing keychain. The whole process was awesome.

These flower sculptures use a similar concept to transform plain clear plastic cups into colorful art. The good news is that the allowance can stay in the jar!

— — — — — — — — — — — — — —

Materials

+ Clear plastic cups
+ Colorful permanent markers
+ Scissors
+ Baking sheet and oven (use with adult supervision)

Decorate the clear plastic cups with various colors and patterns. Use scissors to cut slits every inch (2.5 cm) or so around the rim of the cups, leaving the bottom of the cups intact.

Place the colorful cups on a baking sheet. Place in an oven at 350°F (180°C or gas mark 4) for a minute. Watch carefully so as not to overmelt.

Let the flower cool before touching.

Try using a deeper clear plastic cup and leaving the bottom two-thirds unslit, to create a usable vase.

Modifications for Younger Kids

Younger kids can help decorate and design flowers, while saving the cutting and baking for adults.

Modifications for Older Kids

Older kids can plan what the finished project will look like through several trials of flower making. Petals could be shaped more specifically with scissors and colors coordinated to imitate real flowers.

*See photo insert page 2.

Soap Surprises

Cracker Jack and cereal packagers knew the secret to captivating a kid audience. Promise a secret treat buried in the box and watch kids unearth the treasure at the expense of perfectly good food. In my house there is a rule that the prize cannot be reached for. It has to fall out on its own. In some cases, this caused a week of eating cereal with no reward. It can be brutal.

It isn't that the actual treat is so amazing. It is the waiting. It is the hunt. This soap activity exploits the hunt into wash time. Hide secret treasures in soap that can only be revealed through washing. It is a win-win for both kids and parents.

— — — — — — — — — — — — — —

Materials
(to make five Soap Surprises)

+ Kitchen grater
+ 2 soap bars
+ 2 bowls
+ Blue or other food coloring
+ Microwave-safe bowl
+ Microwave
+ Spoon
+ Small, inexpensive treasures

(continued)

Using a kitchen grater on the largest hole size, grate the soap into one bowl. In a second bowl, change the color of half of the batch with your desired color of food coloring. Place a handful each of the colored gratings and the plain gratings in the microwave-safe bowl. Add a tablespoon (14 ml) or so of water and microwave at full power for 10 seconds. Remove from the microwave and stir. If the soap is a moldable texture, then proceed to the next step. If not, add a bit more water and repeat the microwaving process.

Mold the soap around a treasure, making sure to cover all its edges. Create a soap ball or bar with your hands. Let the ball set overnight before use.

Modifications for Younger Kids

Give your kids a spoon. Young children love to stir, and stir and stir. You can't over- or undermix your soap shavings. Do this on your kitchen floor and some of the bits are guaranteed to fall on the floor. Let your tots mop up the floor in their socks when you are finished.

Modifications for Older Kids

Have older kids try to push the soap into large cookie cutters for molding at the end. Create a soap bath set for a sibling or friend as a gift.

TIP

Add a science experiment to your soap-making activity. Watch water and air molecules literally expand by leaving Ivory soap (has to be Ivory soap) in the microwave. Watch the soap grow and expand as the air inside the soap expands.

Solar Oven Crayon Art

Sometime this summer, the kids are going to say it is too hot to play outside. My kids have been known to say this on a breezy April Texas day, causing my automatic lecture about how an additional 20°F (5.6°C) and more is in store over the next few months and they should enjoy this perfect weather.

This activity is one to save for when you hear the complaint. Showing kids how to harness the sun for their enjoyment is much more effective than my automatic lecture.

— — — — — — — — — — —

Materials

+ Shoe box
+ Tinfoil
+ Old crayons
+ Scraps of thick cardboard

Line the box with tinfoil and set it in the sun. Send the kids on an expedition.

Peel off the crayon wrappers and get the colors ready for use. Place the crayon bits on the cardboard. Place the cardboard in the solar box. As the crayons melt, they will seep into the cardboard for an interesting puddle effect.

Depending on the weather, the crayon bits should melt within 30 minutes. If the sun is not strong enough to melt the crayon bits, due to the time of year or climate in your area, you can transfer this activity to your kitchen oven. Line a cookie sheet to avoid any waxy spills. Set the oven temperature at 170°F (77°C, or gas mark less than 4).

Modifications for Younger Kids

Keep in mind that the melting crayon bits are hot, and from experience we can warn you: melted crayon wax stains everything. Plan accordingly.

Modifications for Older Kids

Older kids could modify the oven design, try it at different times of day and chart how long it takes to melt the crayon bits. Do different colors melt at faster rates than others?

*See photo insert page 2.

Story Layers

Story sequencing is key to communication. Kids learn this innately through telling their own stories, creating flip books and adding layers to their story as in this activity. We use clear plastic lids upcycled from take-out containers to create a blank canvas to tell a multidimensional story.

- - - - - - - - - - - -

Materials

+ Multiple clear plastic containers or lids
+ Scissors
+ Permanent marker
+ Tape or glue
+ Craft sticks
+ Blank construction or copy paper for theater background

If using the clear clamshell-type takeout container, cut through the lid attachment so there are two separate pieces. Create a group of similarly sized clear canvases for artwork.

Show the kids how they will be able to layer the elements on top of one another so each lid only needs to show part of the story.

Start with the setting. Have kids draw what the surroundings of the story look like on the first clear lid.

Then on the next lid, have them add a character and any details surrounding that character. The next lid can introduce another character and story parts that the character might change. Another lid can wrap up the story with a conclusion or solution to the characters' problems.

Tape or glue craft sticks to the bottom of each of the clear plastic lids and number them.

Set up a theater with a plain paper background. Have the child start telling his/her story with the first layer and then continue the story by adding the other layers one by one.

Challenge kids to pick up a friend's or sibling's story and come up with a different story, using the same sequence of scenes.

Modifications for Younger Kids

Have kids tell you a story that you help them draw. When they are telling the story, ask questions to encourage more thought and detail.

Modifications for Older Kids

Have older kids create longer stories with more than one series of scenes. They could also create an additional layer by decorating the backdrop to complement their unique story.

This activity helps older kids learn story sequencing, but also reinforces scale and space when drawing. The planning required for placing a story element to be seen through several scenes as the story continues is a challenge even for older children.

*See photo insert page 2.

Tinfoil Relief

My kids' first exposure to the art concept of relief, where part of the picture is raised from the background, was with pencil rubbings at church. One of my standard quiet activities is to place the church bulletin over the embossed front cover of the songbook and show them how a pencil can be used to transfer the word hymnal to the paper.

This art project uses this common household item for a sunk-relief masterpiece. Using a bit of yarn and some paint, your child can transform a piece of tinfoil into something really, really cool.

– – – – – – – – – – – – – –

Materials

+ Sticky yarn (or yarn and glue)
+ Piece of cardboard
+ Tinfoil
+ Masking tape
+ Spray paint
+ Scrubbing pad (as for dishes)

Create shapes with the sticky yarn on the cardboard. We created geometric shapes. The possibilities are endless.

After you have the yarn design laid out, press the yarn down lightly to make sure it won't move.

Cover your yarn with the foil. Tape the foil down to the back of the cardboard.

Rub the foil to make the yarn "bump," or become raised.

Go outside and spray paint the foil-covered cardboard.

Let the paint fully dry before lightly buffing the yarn relief with the dish scrubber. Buffing will remove the paint, showing the design of the yarn through the paint.

Modifications for Younger Kids
Let younger kids help with all the steps, excluding the spray painting, or skip the spray paint altogether.

Modifications for Older Kids
Encourage older kids to create a series of related relief works to display together.

TIP
Do you have leftover tinfoil? Consider watching your tots create a ball with it. They will enjoy feeling the foil crinkle as they form the ball.

Toilet Paper Roll Spy Decoder

Why send a regular message when you could use a code and send it in secret? Kids know that any statement can be elevated in its fun status through the magic of decoding. There are tons of different ways to create a code. It is a balance of making it easy for the recipient, but too tough to crack if it should fall into the wrong hands. A decoder machine is the perfect solution. This activity recycles a toilet paper roll into a code tool. Once the decoder is in the right hands, the secret code is easily solved.

– – – – – – – – – – – – – –

Materials
(to make one decoder)

+ Scissors
+ Paper
+ Empty toilet paper roll
+ Marker
+ Tape

Cut a strip of paper so it will wrap around the toilet paper tube snugly with a ¼-inch (6-mm) overlap. Then cut that strip in half. On each half write the letters of the alphabet along the margin. Space the letters out equally. One piece will have the letters written on the right edge and the other will have the letters written on the left edge.

Using tape, secure the ends to each other to create a sleeve that will slip onto the toilet paper tube. Tape both papers in this manner and slip them onto the toilet paper tube so that they can rotate on the tube.

Rotate the letter sleeves until the letters line up. Write down the key position for the recipient— something like G = I or H = J. Then keeping the decoder in that position, write out the coded message on another piece of paper. Once finished, rotate the letter sleeves so no one sees the original position.

Roll up your coded message and place inside the tube. Send it to the recipient and see whether they can crack the code.

Modifications for Younger Kids

Tape one of the sleeves to the tube so only one rotates. Color the stationary sleeve in a different color and write the code with that same color so it is easier to decode.

Modifications for Older Kids

Older kids can create a series of code tumblers that sequence letters in different ways, coding each letter sleeve in a different way with a color or symbol. That requires the recipient to use several sleeves to fully decode.

TIP
Secret codes are a great way to practice reading and writing skills. Kids get so involved in the process, they don't even notice they are learning.

Water Bottle Bangles

I once made a craft that I had seen on a TV DIY show. It required a trip to the local craft supply store for materials. When it was completed, I realized it had taken a full day and the supplies cost three times what it was worth. On top of that, I wasn't skilled at the craft and my final project didn't quite look right. The whole thing was a mess!

That is one of the things that inspired crafts like this DIY bracelet. It requires no trip to the local craft store for materials and the final project will look great no matter the skill level of the crafter.

Materials
(to make two or three bangles)

+ Empty water bottle
+ Colorful permanent markers
+ Scissors

Decorate the empty water bottle with markers. You can use the indented rings in many commercial water bottles to create color stripes and blocks. Cut the water bottle into 1½- to 3-inch (4- to 7.5-cm)-wide rings.

Modifications for Younger Kids

If little arms are too small for wearing bracelets, this project makes the perfect size ring toy. Check scissor-cut areas for any sharp or rough edges and smooth with sandpaper or cover with a durable tape.

Modifications for Older Kids

Kids can design their own bracelets of different widths and decorations for a planned stacked fashion statement.

Paper Bag Puppet People

Paper bag puppets are the perfect pretend play activity. Transform a brown paper lunch bag with materials from around the house such as scraps of fabric, yarn, ribbons and paper. The possibilities are endless.

Host a puppet show for friends and family no matter where you are.

- - - - - - - - - - - - - - -

Materials

+ Paper lunch bag
+ Markers
+ Googly eyes
+ Pom-poms
+ Scrapbook paper
+ Yarn
+ Ribbon
+ Tools: glue and scissors

Keeping your paper bag flat, create faces for your puppets using markers, googly eyes, pom-poms and paper. We love the idea of colorful pom-poms for puppet noses, but you are the artist! Think outside the box when adding yarn for hair. Your puppet might have pigtails, spiky hair, or look just like you. Once you've decided how you want your puppet to look, use glue to attach all of the features.

Dressing your puppets up is just as fun as giving their faces some character. Use scrapbook paper to create shirts, pants, skirts or overalls. Then use ribbon for belts, collars and pockets! Glue everything into place. You can even add accessories to your puppets such as neckties, glasses, hats or necklaces.

*See photo insert page 3.

TIP
Create paper bag puppets of your whole family.

Paper Roll Train

We love making toys from items found in the recycling bin. Not only is it great for the environment, but it also inspires creative ways to repurpose ordinary items! This train is a fun and unique upcycling activity.

- - - - - - - - - - - - - - -

Materials

+ 7 (4½-inch [11.5-cm]) toilet paper rolls
+ Craft paint
+ 20 lids (from sports drink bottles or milk jugs)
+ Yarn, ribbon or cord
+ Tools: scissors, paintbrushes, a hot glue gun and a single-hole punch

To create the upper parts of the engine and caboose, cut one of your paper rolls in half widthwise. Pinch one end of one half together and cut out a half circle shape in the end, making it concave so it will fit onto the convex surface of the roll. Repeat with the second paper roll half. You will glue these to the top of the engine and caboose later. Finding a smaller roll in your recycling bin or crafting one of the rolls into a smaller diameter roll can make a nice smokestack on the front of the engine. You will want to cut a half circle shape at the end of it as well.

Paint all of your paper rolls and set them aside to dry. You may choose to paint each train car a different color or make it look more uniform. You will probably want to paint the concave pieces you cut the same color as the engine or caboose.

Once dry, ask an adult to help you attach the tops to the engine and caboose with hot glue, and then glue the lids onto each of the paper rolls for wheels. Never use a hot glue gun without an adult's help.

Use the hole punch to make holes in the sides of each of your tubes. Thread yarn through each hole and tie the carriages, engine and caboose together.

*See photo insert page 3.

TIP

Make paper roll scenery for your train to travel past, such as houses and trees.

Coffee Filter Owls

Coffee filters have always been a magical mystery to me. How does something so simple help turn water and coffee grounds into coffee? The magical transformation of turning coffee filters into owls is no less amazing.

Paint a background on construction paper for your owls, and then add sticks from the backyard for them to perch on.

- - - - - - - - - - - - -

Materials

+ Coffee filters
+ Paper plate
+ Watercolor paints
+ Construction paper
+ Googly eyes
+ Tools: paintbrushes, scissors and glue

Flatten a coffee filter and place it on a paper plate for painting. Use watercolor paints to color your coffee filter owl and set it aside to dry on top of a second filter. Owls are usually brown, but we love making our owls pink and purple with a dash of green.

Once all your painted filters have dried, they are ready to fold into owls. Fold in the sides of each filter toward the center, making sure the top section is a little wider than the bottom. Press the sides down. Now, fold over 1½ inches (4 cm) of the top section and glue it into place.

Add some personality to your paper owls by cutting beaks and feet out of construction paper and attaching them, along with some googly eyes, using glue.

*See photo insert page 3.

TIP

You can make this same craft with cupcake liners. The ones with colorful patterns will make the most fun owls.

Paper Cup Farm Animals

Our kitchen cabinet has a shelf with a collection of mismatched paper cups. I love the idea of grabbing a few and creating an entire barnyard scene. Turn your leftover party cups into these cute animals!

Make a farm scene for the animals by painting grass and a pond on a piece of construction paper. Then make a fence out of wooden craft sticks.

- - - - - - - - - - - - -

Materials

+ Paper cups
+ Craft paint (we used pink, white, black, yellow and red)
+ Pipe cleaners
+ Tools: a pencil, paintbrushes and scissors

Turn a paper cup upside down and paint it with the main color of the farm animal you're making.

Sketch the facial features onto each cup, and then paint those too. This is easier than you think because you can use simple shapes: circles for the eyes, a rectangular oval shape with dot nostrils for a pig or cow nose and a triangle for a chicken beak with an upside-down heart for a wattle.

Poke small holes where you want to add pipe cleaners for pig and cow ears or a rooster comb. Shape the pipe cleaners and then secure them in place by twisting them together on the inside of the cup.

*See photo insert page 3.

> **TIP**
> We've shown you how to make a pig, cow and rooster. Can you make a duck, sheep and horse too?

Cupcake Liner Jellyfish

The ocean is closer than you might think with this simple and fun craft. Make a smack of jellyfish from cupcake liners. And don't we all feel a little smarter now that we know a group of jellyfish is called a smack?

- - - - - - - - - - - - -

Materials

+ Crepe paper streamers in assorted colors
+ Cupcake liners in assorted sizes and colors
+ Googly eyes
+ Tools: scissors and glue

Cut the crepe paper streamers into thin strips about ¼ inch (6 mm) wide and between 3 to 5 inches (7.5 to 12.5 cm) in length. You'll want shorter strips for smaller cupcake liners and longer ones for the jumbo-sized liners.

Glue the crepe paper strips to the inside of the cupcake liners and set aside to dry.

Turn your cupcake liners upside down so the crepe paper "tentacles" hang down. Glue googly eyes onto the outside of the cupcake liners.

*See photo insert page 4.

> **TIP**
> Remove one side of a cardboard box and paint the inside blue to display your cupcake liner jellyfish.

Paper Straw Beads

Have you noticed that paper straws come in such fun colors and patterns? You can use any leftovers you might have from a party, or choose a coordinating set at the store. We love the simplicity and endless creative possibilities of this craft.

- - - - - - - - - - -

Materials

+ Paper straws in assorted colors and patterns
+ String
+ Tools: scissors

Using scissors, cut your straws into ½-inch (1.3-cm) pieces.

Thread them onto string to make necklaces and bracelets. Don't forget to tie the ends of the string together so the beads don't slide off. You will need one straw to make a bracelet and at least two straws to make a necklace.

*See photo insert page 4.

TIP
Host a crafting party with friends to make paper straw bead friendship bracelets to exchange.

Craft Stick Caterpillars

Yarn-wrapped caterpillars are perfect for kids of all ages. This craft will help younger kids develop their fine motor skills, and older kids will love trying to make patterns. Play with assorted colors to make artful creations.

- - - - - - - - - - -

Materials

+ Wooden craft sticks
+ Yarn
+ Pipe cleaners
+ Googly eyes
+ Tools: scissors and glue

Ask an adult to cut a craft stick into three pieces and glue the pieces together so they look like small mountain peaks.

Wrap your craft stick caterpillar with yarn, gluing the ends of the yarn so it doesn't unravel. Make sure to leave about ½ inch (1.3 cm) unwrapped for the head

Cut short pieces of pipe cleaners to twist around the caterpillar for legs and antennae. You can bend them to fashion exactly the right shapes for the legs and antennae.

Wind one more pipe cleaner around and around the unwrapped portion of the craft stick for the head, and then attach googly eyes with glue.

*See photo insert page 4.

TIP
Attach even more craft stick pieces together to make an extra-long caterpillar with a hundred legs.

Paper Bag Town

As kids, we created our own town with blocks, sticks and toys, but we never thought of this really simple idea. Create a town from paper bags! Your town can be the place for stuffed animals, dolls and action figures to hang out, work and live.

- - - - - - - - - - - - - -

Materials

+ Paper lunch bags
+ Craft paint
+ Markers
+ Scrap paper and recycling materials
+ Scrapbook paper
+ Tools: paintbrushes, scissors and a stapler

Keeping your paper bags flat, use paint and markers to create shops, houses and buildings in your town. Each bag will be a different building in your town. The open part of the bags will be the top of the buildings. You could use traditional neutral colors or make your town super colorful with bright pinks, reds, yellows, purples and oranges.

Once the paint is dry, open up each paper bag and stuff them with scrap paper and recycling materials so that your buildings will stand up and not be easily knocked over.

Cut a square of scrapbook paper a little wider than your building. Fold the paper in half, and staple it over the top of a paper bag to make the roof. Repeat with the remaining paper bags.

*See photo insert page 4.

TIP

Make a short movie about your town and the people and animals in it.

Paper Plate Fishbowl

One magical holiday, my parents went to a white elephant gift exchange and came home with a goldfish. A real live goldfish. I was thrilled. My mom was not. She was overheard saying, "Who takes a LIVE pet to a gift exchange?" This craft would have solved everything.

- - - - - - - - - - - - - -

Materials

+ White paper plate
+ Watercolor paints
+ Scrapbook paper
+ Googly eyes
+ Tools: scissors, paintbrushes, a pencil and glue

Cut a small semicircle out of the top of the plate and save this piece to use later as a fishbowl stand.

Paint your fishbowl shades of green and blue with watercolor paints. Paint the fishbowl stand piece brown or black.

Draw fish and seaweed on scrapbook paper. Cut the shapes out and glue them onto your fishbowl. Add googly eyes to your fish with glue too.

Let's finish the fishbowl stand by turning it upside down and gluing it to the bottom of the plate. Use scissors to make the bottom edge straight so you don't have a wobbly fishbowl!

*See photo insert page 5.

TIP

What other sea creatures could you put in your fishbowl? How about a sea turtle, starfish or jellyfish?

Glow-in-the-Dark Galaxy Jar

Think of this craft as an indoor starry sky. If you live in the city, don't have a good view of the night sky or your bedtime is before dark, this is a perfect solution. We have also found that kids who are anxious or don't like the dark find it relaxing to keep a galaxy jar in their room.

- - - - - - - - - - - - - -

Materials

+ Clear hair gel (enough to fill the jar)
+ Glitter paint (we used blue, purple and pink)
+ Glow-in-the-dark paint
+ Water (optional)
+ Large canning jar or clear plastic bottle
+ Glow-in-the-dark stars
+ Tools: 3 bowls and a spoon

Divide the hair gel between three separate bowls. We added half to one bowl, and then divided the other half between two bowls. Add just a little glitter paint and glow-in-the-dark paint to each bowl and mix until combined into your desired galaxy colors. You can always add more if you want the color to be a little brighter. If the consistency is too thick, add water one teaspoon at a time until the consistency is a little thinner. This will ensure you will be able to see the stars.

Pour one bowl of colorful gel into the jar, and then add stars along the inside wall of the jar. Add the second bowl of colorful gel and then more stars. Then add just a little of the third bowl of gel at a time while adding stars to the jar.

*See photo insert page 5.

TIP
If you have a young child who will be left alone with this jar, glue the lid on so that they cannot open it.

Butterfly Suncatcher

Butterflies flying in the sunshine of a summer afternoon always make me smile. These colorful butterfly suncatchers capture that magic. Make as many as you can and display them in a window that gets lots of sunlight.

- - - - - - - - - - - - - -

Materials

+ Tissue paper in assorted colors
+ Wooden craft stick
+ Black craft paint
+ Clear contact paper
+ Black twine
+ Scrap paper or construction paper
+ Tools: scissors, a paintbrush, a marker, a hot glue gun and double-sided tape

Cut the tissue paper into 1-inch (2.5-cm) squares.

Paint the craft stick with black paint, and set it aside to dry.

Cut a rectangle out of the contact paper that is taller than the craft stick. Remove the backing and have the sticky side facing toward you. Add the tissue paper squares all over the sticky side of the contact paper, arranging them in a unique butterfly wing design.

Draw a butterfly on a piece of paper and cut it out to use as a stencil. Place the paper butterfly over the contact paper, trace around it using the marker and cut it out.

Ask an adult to attach the craft stick to the center of the butterfly with hot glue. Cut small pieces of black twine for feelers and also have an adult hot glue these to the top of the craft stick. Never use a hot glue gun without an adult's help.

Use double-sided tape to attach your butterfly to a window.

*See photo insert page 5.

Paper Plate Snail

Snails are so cool. Their spiral home rides with them everywhere they go. Kids won't even notice that they are developing fine motor skills while crafting this adorable project. We love that you can use different sizes of paper plates to create a whole family of snails.

Materials

+ White paper plates
+ Craft paint (we used hot pink, neon green, orange, bright blue and black)
+ Cotton balls
+ Googly eyes
+ Tools: scissors, glue and a marker

On one of the white plates, add a little of each color of paint to dab the cotton balls in.

Use a separate cotton ball for each color. Put a cotton ball into the paint, and then dab paint onto the paper plate. Repeat with your other colors too.

Once your paper plate is dry, beginning from the outside, carefully cut a spiral. On the outside part of the spiral, cut two antennae for the eyes, called tentacles, into the top. Attach the googly eyes to the tentacles with glue, and then use your marker to give your snail a big smile.

*See photo insert page 5.

> ### TIP
> Use cotton balls to paint a scene on construction paper for your paper plate snail.

Glow-in-the-Dark Firefly

Chasing fireflies in the summertime is a childhood tradition. This glow-in-the-dark craft will bring back those memories. Keep your firefly next to your bed and watch it light up after dark!

Materials

+ Wooden spoon
+ Black and yellow craft paint
+ Black and white construction paper
+ Googly eyes
+ Black twine
+ Glow-in-the-dark paint
+ Tools: paintbrushes, a pencil, scissors and a hot glue gun

Paint the handle of the wooden spoon black and the head of the spoon yellow. Set aside to dry.

Draw two sets of wings on the white and black construction paper and cut them out. Once the spoon is dry, ask an adult to attach the wings to your firefly with hot glue. Never use a hot glue gun without an adult's help.

Glue on the googly eyes, and paint on a happy smiley face. Glue small pieces of black twine onto the top of the spoon for the firefly antennae.

Paint over the yellow section of the spoon and the white wings with glow-in-the-dark paint.

*See photo insert page 6.

> ### TIP
> Make a whole lot of these glow-in-the-dark fireflies, attach fishing line to them and hang them under a patio to watch them flying at night.

Clothespin Pirates

Ahoy, matey! Sail the seven seas with these clothespin pirates. These peace-loving pirates are fun as action figures, puppets or Christmas ornaments. Add a small eye screw and string to hang them on the Christmas tree.

- - - - - - - - - - - - - - -

Materials

+ Googly eyes
+ Wooden clothespins
+ Markers
+ Felt
+ Tools: a hot glue gun and scissors

Ask an adult to attach the googly eyes to the top of a clothespin with hot glue. Never use a hot glue gun without an adult's help.

Draw pirate clothes onto your clothespin using the markers. You can even draw a bandana on your pirate, too, if you like.

If you prefer your pirate to wear a pirate hat, cut out two identical pieces from the felt. Use a marker to draw a skull and crossbones onto the hat. Glue the top and sides of the hat together, and then glue it to the top of the clothespin.

You can use more felt to make a belt or eye patch too.

*See photo insert page 6.

TIP
Every pirate needs a parrot. Make a clothespin parrot for your pirate too.

Mosaic Paper Plate Rainbow

This mosaic paper plate rainbow is the perfect activity for little fingers. Not only will it teach them the colors of the rainbow, but it will also help with their fine motor skills, scissors skills and creating patterns.

- - - - - - - - - - - - - - -

Materials

+ Paper plate
+ Scrapbook paper in all the colors of the rainbow
+ Tools: scissors, a drinking glass, a pencil and glue

Cut your paper plate in half. Now you can make two rainbows. On the straight edge of one plate half, center a drinking glass so that you can draw a semicircle in the center. Cut it out to make an arched rainbow shape.

Cut the scrapbook paper into ½-inch (1.3-cm) squares, and glue them onto the plate in the colors of the rainbow—red, orange, yellow, green, blue, indigo and violet.

*See photo insert page 6.

TIP
Add a wooden craft stick or dowel to your rainbow and take fun photographs of your rainbow outside. Can you see where the pot of gold is?

Paper Roll Octopus

This octopus is adorable, and it holds a secret . . . shhh! Your paper roll octopus is the perfect place to keep your tiniest treasures safe. Pop the octopus on top of them, and your treasures will be kept safe and hidden so you don't lose them.

- - - - - - - - - - - - - - - -

Materials

+ Scrapbook paper
+ 1 (4½-inch [11.5-cm]) toilet paper roll
+ Ribbon
+ Googly eyes
+ Tools: scissors, glue, a single-hole punch and a marker

Cut a piece of scrapbook paper the same height as the paper roll. Wrap it around the paper roll and secure it with glue.

Cut four slits in one end of the paper roll to create flaps that are long enough to cover the end of the roll when folded over. Fold the flaps over each other and glue them down to make the top of your octopus.

Use the hole punch to make eight holes around the open end of the paper roll. Poke ribbon through the holes, loop it over and glue it back onto the top of the ribbon closest to the hole. Repeat this for all eight holes.

Attach googly eyes to your octopus with glue, and then draw on a happy face with a marker.

*See photo insert page 6.

TIP

Now is the perfect time to learn the "Octopus's Garden" song by the Beatles and have a sing-along with your family using your paper roll octopus as a puppet.

Cupcake Liner Flowers

Next time you need a homemade gift for Grandma, a teacher or Mom, think of these adorable cupcake liner flowers. Make several to create a beautiful bouquet for someone you love. Kids of all ages can make this craft, and the flower variations are so fun to explore.

- - - - - - - - - - - - - - - -

Materials

+ Cupcake liners in assorted sizes and colors
+ Buttons
+ Paper straws
+ Tools: scissors, glue and tape

Turn all of your cupcake liners inside out so that the pattern or color is on the inside.

Cut slits all the way around the edge of the regular-sized liners to make petals.

Glue a mini cupcake liner inside each regular liner, and then glue a button in the center of each mini liner.

Attach a straw to the back of each flower with tape.

*See photo insert page 7.

TIP

If you have jumbo cupcake liners, you can add an extra layer of petals to your flowers.

Craft Stick Birds

For this project, start outside with some bird watching. Take as many bird photos as you can as "research." Use them as inspiration to create stick birds that represent your local flock. When you're done, put them in a houseplant or put on a puppet show.

- - - - - - - - - - - - -

Materials

+ Craft paint
+ Jumbo wooden craft sticks
+ Feathers
+ Googly eyes
+ Yellow construction paper
+ Scrapbook paper and doll accessories
+ Tools: paintbrushes, glue and scissors

Paint your craft sticks the base color of the bird you want to make. Once dry, glue feathers to the back, and then add googly eyes and a construction paper beak to the front. Get creative with your feather arrangements! You may have birds with a few feathers or a lot.

Now it's time to dress up your bird. Use scrapbook paper or doll accessories to add a fancy hat, a scarf, jewelry, a bow or a tie.

*See photo insert page 7.

TIP
If you want to display your birds in the garden or a fairy garden outdoors, make them with craft supplies that can be protected with a layer of outdoor sealant. Try to keep them in a covered area out of the harsh sun and rain.

Paper Plate Marble Maze

Mazes have always been a favorite at my house. I love the 3D version you can make with a paper plate. The larger your plate, the more maze you can build on it. Marble mazes are the perfect rainy day activity, plus they help develop hand-eye coordination and fine motor skills.

- - - - - - - - - - - - -

Materials

+ Paper plate
+ Paper straws
+ Construction paper
+ Tools: a pencil or marker, scissors and glue

Using a pencil or marker, draw the maze on the paper plate and mark the beginning and the ending with the words "start" and "finish."

Cut the paper straws into a variety of lengths to fit the sections of the maze that you sketched onto the plate.

Cut strips of construction paper ½ to 3 inches (1.3 to 7.5 cm) wide and 2½ inches (6.5 cm) long to make tunnels for your marble to travel through.

Bend the ends of your tunnel and glue them into place on your plate. Now you can glue your straws into place, too, as the sides of the maze trail.

*See photo insert page 7.

TIP
Cut an opening at one end of your marble maze plate. Cut a matching section in a second paper plate and join your plates together. How big can you make your marble maze?

Water Bottle Flowers

Water bottle flower art is a great way to repurpose water bottles before they head to the recycling bin. The simplicity of this craft makes it a perfect activity for even the youngest crafter. Frame your flower art to hang on the wall or make homemade greeting cards.

- - - - - - - - - - - -

Materials

+ Craft paint
+ Paper plates
+ Plastic bottles
+ Construction paper
+ Tools: paintbrushes

Pour a little paint onto a paper plate. Dip the bottom of a plastic bottle into the paint and stamp it onto the construction paper. You can even mix paint colors a little so your flowers have different colors in them.

Use your paintbrush to make a center for each flower, and then to make a stem and leaves.

*See photo insert page 7.

> ## TIP
> Collect plastic bottles in different sizes to make big and small flowers.

Crayon Scratch Art

Crayon scratch art provides endless possibilities for creativity. Whether you scratch your name, make a picture of your family or your house, or scratch a message to a friend, this is a craft that everyone will love.

- - - - - - - - - - - -

Materials

+ Heavy construction paper
+ Crayons
+ Black craft paint
+ Toothpicks
+ Tools: a paintbrush

Color your entire piece of construction paper with all different colors of crayons.

Paint over the crayon with black paint until you can't see any color peeking through. You don't need to wait until the paint is dry to start scratching your design with a toothpick, but it's less messy if you do.

As you scratch away the paint, your picture will reveal the bright crayon colors hiding underneath.

*See photo insert page 8.

> ## TIPS
> Use different items such as a bamboo skewer or fork to create different patterns. You will notice that wider tools reveal more color than toothpicks do.
>
> The smaller the sheet of construction paper, the easier it will be for little hands to color the whole sheet with crayons.

Ping-Pong Ball Monsters

A cuter monster has never been sighted! Sing "Monster Mash" while you make these fun Ping-Pong Ball Monsters. The best part is that their arms and legs can move so they can dance along to the music too.

- - - - - - - - - - - -

Materials

+ Ping-pong balls
+ Craft paint
+ Empty egg carton
+ Pipe cleaners
+ Googly eyes
+ Tools: a paintbrush, scissors, a hot glue gun and a marker

The first step is to paint your ping-pong balls. This can get messy, but you can do it in two parts. Paint the top half of your ping-pong balls and place them on top of the egg carton to dry. Once dry, turn them over and paint the other side.

While your ping-pong balls are drying, turn the pipe cleaners into crazy hair, legs and arms for your monster. Ask an adult to hot glue these into place along with the googly eyes. Never use a hot glue gun without an adult's help. You can use a marker to add other facial features to your monster too.

*See photo insert page 8.

> ## TIP
> What else can you make with ping-pong balls and pipe cleaners? How about a person, an octopus or a spider?

Yarn Pumpkins

Be advised that creating yarn pumpkins can lead to an obsession with yarn art! That is what happened to me. I started innocently with a pumpkin, and before I knew it, I was trying to figure out how to make nearly every shape out of yarn!

- - - - - - - - - - - -

Materials

+ Cotton crochet yarn
+ White glue
+ Balloons
+ Pin
+ Tree branch
+ Felt
+ Tools: scissors, a bowl and a hot glue gun

Cut several 3-yard (2.5-m) lengths of yarn. This makes it easier to work with.

In a bowl, mix three parts glue to one part water. If it feels too thick, add just a little more water to it, but you don't want it to be too watery.

Add your yarn to the glue and water mixture and make sure the strands are soaked.

Blow up a balloon, but stop when it hits a round shape. The smaller your balloon, the better the shape and the sturdier your pumpkin will be.

As you lift the yarn strands out of the glue, gently squeeze some of the excess glue off and wrap the strands around the balloon. You can arrange the strands from top to bottom in an orderly manner or get crazy with swirls and twists. Make sure that it all sits flat on the balloon when you are finished.

Hang it somewhere to dry for one to two days.

Once dry, ask an adult to pop the balloon with a pin, and then carefully remove it through one of the holes in the yarn.

(continued)

Break off a small section from a thick tree branch and cut a leaf shape out of felt. Ask an adult to attach both to the top of the pumpkin with hot glue. Never use a hot glue gun without an adult's help

*See photo insert page 8.

Snowman Paper Cups

These snowman paper cups are not only a fun craft project, but if you leave off the pipe cleaner, you can add hot cocoa to your cup and enjoy a cool weather treat. The felt scarf will stop your hands from getting too hot when holding the cup.

- - - - - - - - - - - - - -

Materials

+ Orange felt, plus any color of your choice
+ White paper cups
+ Pipe cleaners
+ Pom-poms
+ Tools: scissors, glue and a marker

From felt in the color of your choice, cut a section about ¾ inch (2 cm) wide and long enough to wrap around one of the cups. Cut slits on each end to make a fringe. Wrap the scarf around a cup and glue it in place.

Cut out a triangle from the orange felt and glue it on for the carrot nose. Draw on buttons, eyes and a mouth for your snowman.

Cut a section of pipe cleaner to form an arch over the top of the cup. Glue the ends to the sides of the cup, and then glue a pom-pom on each side to fashion snowman earmuffs.

*See photo insert page 8.

Paper Bag Octopus

This adorable paper bag octopus is a quick and easy craft that's perfect for little hands. You can't just make one!

- - - - - - - - - - - - - -

Materials

+ Paper lunch bag
+ Craft paint (we used yellow, green and red-orange)
+ Scrap paper and recycling materials
+ Yarn
+ Googly eyes
+ Tools: paintbrushes, scissors, glue and a marker

Open up a paper lunch bag and paint all of the sides. Putting one hand inside the bag makes it easier to paint. Stand it up with the open side on a surface to dry.

Once dry, add scrap paper and recycling materials to the bag until it's half full. Cinch the bag together just above the stuffing and tie it shut with yarn.

Cut slits in the unstuffed portion of the bag to make eight tentacles for your octopus.

Turn your octopus right side up so the head is on top and the legs dangle down below. Attach googly eyes with glue, and then draw on a mouth with a marker.

*See photo insert page 9.

TIP

For older kids wanting to do a little more to their octopus, add glitter paint, draw rings on the tentacles and curl up the ends.

Chomping Alligator Clothespins

Making these alligator clothespins is a great fine motor skill activity for younger kids. Just be careful that these cheeky gators don't chomp down on your finger. I have one that sits on my desk, and every time I look down, it makes me giggle.

- - - - - - - - - - -

Materials

+ White paper
+ Wooden clothespins
+ Green craft paint
+ Googly eyes
+ Tools: scissors, a paintbrush, glue and a marker

Cut the white paper into four strips of teeth and glue them to the top and bottom of the part of the clothespin that opens and closes.

Now paint your alligator clothespin green, including just a little along the top of the teeth.

Glue googly eyes on the top of your alligator, and then, using a marker, add two dots for the nose and a squiggly line down the back.

*See photo insert page 9.

TIP

Put tiny magnet strips on the back of your alligator to hold notes on the refrigerator or white board.

Plastic Bottle Whirligigs

These plastic bottle whirligigs will look so pretty hanging up on the porch and swinging in the breeze. Their dance in the wind can be mesmerizing. Watch as the light catches off of them and casts rainbows across the floor.

- - - - - - - - - - -

Materials

+ Plastic sports drink bottles (lids and labels removed)
+ Fishing line
+ Glass baubles or gems with a hole in the top
+ Tools: scissors and a single-hole punch

Ask an adult to help you cut the bottom off a bottle, and then cut a 1-inch (2.5-cm) spiral all the way up to the top of the bottle in one piece.

Make a hole in each end of your spiral with the hole punch.

Using fishing line, attach a glass gem to one end of the spiral so it will hang down and make rainbows in the breeze. Tie a loop onto the other end of the spiral to hang the whirligig from.

*See photo insert page 9.

TIP

Use permanent markers to decorate your whirligig with lots of color for the sun to shine through.

Paper Plate Watermelon Suncatchers

Summer and watermelon just go hand in hand! These paper plate watermelon suncatchers will bring summer into your home no matter the season. The sun shining through the pink tissue paper will fill the room with warm colors.

– – – – – – – – – – – – – – –

Materials

+ White paper plates
+ Green craft paint
+ Pink and black tissue paper
+ Clear contact paper
+ Tools: scissors, a paintbrush and tape

Cut the center out of the paper plates, leaving only the textured rims. To make two watermelon slices, cut a rim in half.

Paint the rims of the plates green.

Cut the pink tissue paper into 1-inch (2.5-cm) squares, and cut small circles from the black tissue paper for seeds. Then cut a square from the contact paper that's large enough to fit two plate rims inside.

Remove the backing of the contact paper and have the sticky side facing toward you. Place two green plate rims on the sticky side of the contact paper and add pieces of black and pink tissue paper to fill the empty space between the rims.

Secure the rims in place with tape and trim the excess contact paper around the watermelon slices. Tape them to a sunny window for display.

*See photo insert page 9.

TIP
Cut teardrop shapes in a circle around the center of your paper plate to make orange, lemon or lime slice suncatchers.

Coffee Filter Watercolor Roses

Although this is a kid-friendly craft, the finished roses are absolutely gorgeous and totally acceptable for every age! Make bouquets of these coffee filter watercolor roses to hand out to family and friends. They will love receiving such a thoughtful handmade gift.

– – – – – – – – – – – – – – –

Materials

+ Coffee filters
+ Paper plates
+ Watercolor paints (we used reds, pinks and light purples)
+ Wooden stir sticks
+ Tools: paintbrushes, scissors and glue

Flatten the coffee filters and place them on separate paper plates. Brush each coffee filter with watercolor paints and set them aside to dry.

Once dry, cut each coffee filter into a spiral. Glue one end to just below the top of a wooden stir stick and start wrapping it around, keeping the base tight against the stick while keeping the top loose to make the petals look full. Once you've finished wrapping the filter, secure the outside end with glue.

*See photo insert page 10.

Happy Sunshine Clothespins

Science has shown that the sun can boost your mood and help you feel calm and focused. These sunshine clothespins are sure to brighten your day. Clipping and unclipping the clothespins is so much fun that this project is half craft, half sensory activity!

- - - - - - - - - - - - - -

Materials

+ Wooden clothespins
+ Yellow craft paint
+ Yellow construction paper
+ Googly eyes
+ Tools: paintbrushes, a drinking glass, a pencil, scissors, glue and a marker

Paint your clothespins with yellow paint and set them aside to dry. If you clip them to the edge of a cardboard box, it's easier to paint both sides without waiting for one side to dry.

Place a drinking glass on a sheet of yellow construction paper and trace around it. Cut the circle out, and then glue on googly eyes. Use a marker to add a smiley face.

Once your clothespins are dry, clip them all the way around the construction paper face.

*See photo insert page 10.

(two)

SLIME

It wiggles, it jiggles and it slithers in your hands. It's the perfect combination of fun and science. The crazy thing about slime is that when you start, everything is separated, but then the ingredients come together and activate each other to form something you've never felt before.

Slime can be gooey and gross, like frog's vomit (page 52) or a sack of spiders (page 55). Or it can be super-silly, like a melted snowman (page 51) or cronch (page 57). You never know what you're going to slime together!

Magnetic Slime

Adult Supervision • Do Not Eat

Magnetic slime might just be the most awesome thing you've ever played with! It is a slimy, black goo that seems to eat and crawl toward magnets! Can you really make this right in your own home? Yes!

- - - - - - - - - - - -

Ingredients

+ 1 (4-oz [118-ml]) bottle white school glue
+ ¼ cup (60 ml) water
+ ¼ cup (60 ml) liquid starch
+ 2 to 4 tsp (8 to 16 g) black iron oxide powder (you can find this online)

Equipment

+ Bowl
+ Spoon
+ Neodymium magnet (a cylindrical magnet that is magnetized on the ends)

Add the school glue to a bowl and stir in the water using the spoon. Once it's fully mixed, add the liquid starch and stir until it starts to come together like slime. Remove the slippery goo from the bowl and knead it with your hands, stretching it to make it more slime-ish. At this point, you have a bunch of white goo.

Now it's time to add the iron oxide powder. This is what makes the slime magically magnetic! Use your thumbs to make a small indentation in the slime. With an adult's help, add a teaspoon of iron oxide powder to the dent in your slime. Fold the slime over the powder and knead it with your hands to make the powder mix into the goop. The slime will turn black. Repeat until you've added enough powder to the slime to make it react to the neodymium magnet. The slime should pull up toward the magnet when it is held above the slime. It will also appear to "eat" the magnet when it is placed in the center of the slime. So cool! You will want to play with this "magic" slime for hours!

Ectoplasm

Do Not Eat

Otherwise known as ghost slime, this boogery substance is as easy to make as its name is fun to say! With ooey, gooey goodness that's equally gross in the light or the dark, you can pretend to hunt ghosts like a professional.

- - - - - - - - - - - -

Ingredients

+ 1 (16-oz [454-g]) box cornstarch
+ 1½ cups (360 ml) water
+ 15 drops neon green food coloring
+ 2 tbsp (30 ml) green glow-in-the-dark paint (optional)

Equipment

+ Bowl

In a bowl, mix the cornstarch and water into a goo with your hands. Add the food coloring until your desired color is reached. This really could not be easier!

To make it glow-in-the-dark, squish in the green glow-in-the-dark paint for a cool effect. Make sure you hold the concoction up to a bright light for about 2 minutes to activate it.

Pudding Slime

Adult Supervision • Edible

Pudding Slime? Can you taste it? Yes, you can! Gross out your friends by tasting this crazy creation in front of them, then tell them your secret ingredient. You are sure to get giggles and have your friends begging to play with Pudding Slime, too.

- - - - - - - - - - - - - - - -

Ingredients

+ 2 (3.4-oz [96-g]) packets of instant pudding in your favorite flavor
+ 1 packet of matching flavor powdered drink mix
+ 1 cup (160 g) cornstarch, divided
+ ½ cup (120 ml) hot water

Equipment

+ Bowl
+ Spoon

Add the pudding, drink mix and ½ cup (80 g) of the cornstarch to a bowl. Start mixing. Ask an adult to help you stir in the hot water slowly, mixing the whole time. Be careful! Remember the water is hot! Add the remaining cornstarch slowly. Stir it all together. It will be very sticky at first, but like with any slime, the more you work with it, the better it will get. If it is too wet, add a teaspoon more of cornstarch at a time. If it is too dry, add a teaspoon more of warm water at a time.

TIPS

Want to experiment? Add different flavors of drink mix to see what colors you end up with!

Store in an airtight container. Refresh with water.

Pomegranate Slime

Adult Supervision • Do Not Eat

Have you ever tasted a pomegranate? With an adult's permission, taste some of the seeds before you add them to this gooey mixture. You will get a tangy, sweet and sour taste. Not only are the seeds yummy, they add bumpy fun to your goopy slime concoction.

- - - - - - - - - - - - - - - -

Ingredients

+ 1 large pomegranate
+ 1 cup (240 ml) water
+ 1 (5-oz [147-ml]) bottle clear liquid school glue
+ ¾ cup (180 ml) liquid starch (you can find this in the laundry aisle)

Equipment

+ Large bowl
+ Spoon (optional)

Have an adult cut open the pomegranate. Pick out as many seeds as you can. Put the seeds in your bowl. Be very careful! Even small amounts of pomegranate juice can stain! Add the water, glue and liquid starch to the bowl. Smoosh and goosh it all up with your hands (or a spoon if you prefer) until it's a red glob of textured, slimy goo.

TIPS

Have a roll of paper towels on hand. This can get messy and can stain.

Store in an airtight container. Limited shelf life. Refresh with water.

Sludge Monster

Adult Supervision • Do Not Eat

Have you seen a sludge monster? A sludge monster is a slimy glob of goo who isn't very smart. We don't know what his feet look like, or if he even has feet, because he is always covered in gloop. He lives in the sewers of the city, and eats the dirtiest of dirty garbage. Make your own gooey Sludge Monster, and let your imagination fly.

- - - - - - - - - - -

Ingredients

+ 1½ cups (360 ml) warm water, divided
+ 1 (4-oz [118-ml]) bottle white school glue
+ 1 tsp of food coloring in your favorite monster color
+ 1 tsp borax
+ 2 figurines that will be used just for the Sludge Monster slime

Equipment

+ 2 bowls
+ Spoon

In one bowl, mix ½ cup (120 ml) of warm water with the bottle of glue and food coloring. Mix this up well with a spoon.

In the second bowl, using the spoon, mix 1 cup (240 ml) of warm water with the borax until dissolved. Pour the bowl of borax water into the bowl of colorful glue water. Count out loud to twenty and watch the gooey science magic happen! Then stir the mix with the spoon. Use your hands to hold the goo back, then pour out the extra water so you have just the goo. It will be very sticky. Knead it, pound it with your fist, squish it and push it. Pour out the extra water one more time. Play with the goo until it is no longer sticky. Now grab those figurines! Cover them in the goo, and you have instant sludge monsters.

Melted-Snowman Slime

Adult Supervision • Do Not Eat

You loved your snowman when you made him on that ice-cold day, but then he was gone. Not now! This creation lets you keep your snowman all year long! Although he may be a little melted, he will always be your snowman friend. (And maybe "he" will be a "she"!)

- - - - - - - - - - -

Ingredients

+ ½ cup (120 ml) water
+ ½ cup (120 ml) washable white glue
+ ½ cup (120 ml) liquid starch

Equipment

+ Bowl
+ Spoon or craft stick
+ Snowman parts (googly eyes, buttons and colored foam sheets cut into a scarf, a hat and a nose)

Mix the water and glue in a bowl. Use a spoon or craft stick and mix it well. Pour in the liquid starch. Watch closely as the slime forms right before your eyes. It will be pretty sticky at first, but mix that goo up with your hands. You will feel it become less watery and more slimy. This is what you want. The more you play with it, the more like real slime it becomes. After about 15 minutes of playing with it, kneading it, punching it and rolling it, you will have a perfect melted-snowman consistency. If you have excess liquid after the slime forms, just discard it.

(continued)

You can do two things with the slime. You can make the snowman stand up and quickly add the snowman parts, then watch him melt away before your eyes. Or you can flatten out the goo and place the snowman parts on top. It will look like you have a perfectly melted snowman.

*See photo insert page 10.

Frog's Vomit Slime

Adult Supervision • Do Not Eat

Here's the deal: there's nothing ooier or gooier than frog's vomit. Frog's Vomit Slime is crazy stretchy, and it's even got a little gross surprise inside! Don't be scared though, no actual frogs are involved.

— — — — — — — — — — — —

Ingredients

+ 1 cup (240 ml) clear school glue
+ 2 cups (480 ml) warm water, divided
+ 2 drops green food coloring
+ 3 drops yellow food coloring
+ Lime essential oil (optional)
+ 1 tsp borax powder (you can find this in the laundry aisle)
+ Mini-fly toys

Equipment

+ Large bowl
+ Spoon or craft stick
+ Plastic cup

Measure out the clear glue into the large bowl. Add 1 cup (240 ml) of warm water, the food coloring and the optional lime essential oil. Stir the mixture until it all comes together.

Mix the remaining 1 cup (240 ml) of warm water and the borax powder together in the plastic cup. Slowly pour the contents of the plastic cup into the glue mixture and stir until the slime starts to form. You might end up kneading the slime with your hands for a few minutes to get it to form. Sprinkle your mini-flies into the Frog's Vomit and get them squished all in the slime. Now it's time to play!

Unicorn Snot

Adult Supervision • Do Not Eat

Why? Because, unicorns are magical. Everything about them just screams . . . CUTE! Even their glittery boogers are sparkly and fun.

— — — — — — — — — — — —

Ingredients

+ 1 (5-oz [147-ml]) bottle clear school glue
+ 2 tbsp (30 ml) water
+ A few drops of food coloring (What colors would a unicorn sneeze?)
+ 2 tbsp (48 g) glitter (silver, pink or purple works great)
+ ½ cup (120 ml) liquid starch

Equipment

+ Large bowl
+ Spoon
+ 2 or 3 small clear jars with lids (optional)

First of all, cover your work surface. Glitter is one of those things that likes to multiply and get in areas you didn't know existed.

Now, dump your glue, water, food coloring and glitter into a bowl. Stir that up well with the spoon. Add the liquid starch. You will see it start to form the slime. Squeeze, squish and squash the slime all over the bowl. You will have water and starch drip away from the slime and into the bowl. This is okay! You are making your snot! Now, take the slime and knead it for about 15 minutes to get the right texture.

TIPS

If 2 tablespoons (48 g) of glitter isn't enough for you, go wild! Add another tablespoon (24 g).

Store in a clear jar as a room decoration!

Store in an airtight container.
Refresh with water.

I Spy Slime

Adult Supervision • Do Not Eat

You know those cool *I Spy* books? This slime is like that, but in gooey, slithery form! You can play with this slime with your friends and make it a game! See who can find the most items the fastest.

Ingredients

+ 1 batch of Clear Slime (page 70)
+ ½ cup (120 g) of spangle mix and beads

Equipment

+ Large bowl
+ Spoon

Once the clear slime is made, it's time to add your mix-ins. Squish your spangle mix and beads into your slime. Now pick up the slime and squish it in your hands. Are you able to spy all your trinkets?

TIPS

Store in an airtight container.
Refresh with water.

Pillow Slime

Adult Supervision • Do Not Eat

Want a slime that is as soft and fluffy as a pillow? This slime is sure to do the trick. It's from our friend Avery Ivanovsky of BoJo Slime. Just beware: it is so soft, it might even put you to sleep!

Ingredients

+ 2 tsp (6 g) instant snow
+ 1 cup plus 2 tbsp (270 ml) water, divided
+ 1 cup (240 ml) clear school glue
+ Food coloring (optional)
+ Essential oils for smell (optional)
+ 1 tsp borax

Equipment

+ 2 bowls
+ Spoon
+ Food storage container

(continued)

First add the instant snow into one bowl and then add enough water to make it resemble slush (about 2 tablespoons [30 ml]). Next, pour the glue into your slushy mixture. Add the optional color and scent, if you like.

In a separate bowl, mix 1 cup (240 ml) of warm water and borax until the borax is dissolved. Slowly pour the borax solution into the glue mixture until the slime is thick enough to stretch slightly, but not sticky. Set it in a clear airtight container for at least 3 days. This allows your Pillow Slime to clear up and sets the texture. Once it's ready, play and have fun!

*See photo insert page 10.

TIPS
Store in an airtight container.
Refresh with water.

Avalanche Slime

Adult Supervision • Do Not Eat

This is the coolest thing ever. The two slimes together look like ice and snow. The colors seem to fall and slide, creating your own avalanche. Take it out to play, and you will have a marble-looking goo. Don't be scared by the long directions. It's really easy to make!

- - - - - - - - - - -

Ingredients

+ ½ cup plus 1¼ tsp (126 ml) saline solution (make sure it says buffered on the package), divided
+ 1 tsp baking soda, divided
+ 1 (5-oz [147-ml]) bottle clear school glue
+ 1 (4-oz [118-ml]) bottle white school glue
+ 2 colors of gel food coloring

Equipment

+ 1 jar or drinking glass
+ Spoon
+ Bowl
+ Clear 1-cup (240-ml) food storage container
+ Wooden craft stick

Squeeze ½ cup (120 ml) saline solution into the jar or glass. Add ½ teaspoon of the baking soda. Stir until it is dissolved. Dump your whole bottle of clear glue into the solution. Do not stir! Let it sit. Go to the next step.

Pour your bottle of white glue into the bowl. Add ½ teaspoon of baking soda and stir it up using the spoon. Now, squirt about 1 teaspoon of the saline solution into the white-glue mixture (just eyeball it). Start to stir. Add about ¼ teaspoon of the saline solution until the slime starts to form. The more saline solution you add, the stiffer it will become. It is ready when it starts to pull away from the sides of the bowl.

Take the white slime out of the bowl. Stretch and play with this goop in your hands until it's not sticky anymore.

Now, go back to the clear mixture. Slowly stir it up with a spoon until a stiff slime forms. Take the clear slime out of the jar or glass. Squeeze it a bit to get the extra solution out, then place it in the bottom of the food storage container. Using the wooden craft stick, "paint" one color of food coloring on half of the clear slime. Use the other color for the other half of the slime, painting it on with the wooden craft stick. Place the white slime on top of your colorful masterpiece, filling up the rest of the food container. Put the lid tightly on the container, and turn the container upside down. Let it sit for about 24 hours. When the time is up, look at your beautiful creation! It will look like the color slid into the white slime! You can now take it out and play with it. It will create a beautiful marbled color as you play with it.

Fishbowl Slime

Adult Supervision • Do Not Eat

Spending time at the ocean is fun. Don't you just wish you could scoop some of it up and take it with you when the vacation is over? Now you can make your very own slime that looks just like the ocean. It is an instant mini-vacation!

▬ ▬ ▬ ▬ ▬ ▬ ▬ ▬ ▬ ▬ ▬ ▬ ▬

Ingredients

+ 1 large (9-oz [266-ml]) bottle clear school glue
+ ½ tsp baking soda
+ 10 to 15 drops blue food coloring
+ ¼ cup (60 ml) clear acrylic vase filler (you can get this at any craft store)
+ About 2 tbsp (30 ml) saline solution (make sure it says buffered on the package)
+ Small plastic sea creatures (optional)

Equipment

+ Small clear fishbowl or large bowl
+ Spoon

Empty the bottle of glue into the fish bowl. Stir in the baking soda, food coloring and vase filler. Mix it all up with the spoon. Add about 1 teaspoon of saline solution and stir well. Keep adding a teaspoon at a time of the saline solution. Stir for about 15 seconds each time you add the saline solution. You know it is ready when it holds together well but is still a loose slime. Now you can optionally stick the plastic sea creatures down into the goo. It will look like they are "swimming" in the "water." You can also take the slime out of the bowl and squish this crunchy goop in your hands. It has a fun, crunchy, beachy feel!

*See photo insert page 11.

TIPS

For extra fun, add glitter in with the acrylic vase filler before you stir it all up.

Store in an airtight container.

Spider Egg Sack

Adult Supervision • Do Not Eat

Have you ever seen a spider egg sack? They are white, sticky things full of baby spiders! Creep out your best friend or favorite adult with this terrifying gooey mix of hidden spiders. Don't worry. You will know they are totally fake.

▬ ▬ ▬ ▬ ▬ ▬ ▬ ▬ ▬ ▬ ▬ ▬ ▬

Ingredients

+ 1 Melted-Snowman Slime recipe (page 51), without the accessories
+ 1 packet of plastic baby spiders (you can find these online or at a party shop)

Make the Melted-Snowman Slime, leaving it undecorated. Form the slime into a ball. Here is the fun part. Stick the baby spiders up into the goo far enough that they can't be seen. Hand the goo to a friend, and tell them they can play with it. Hear them scream when they find the nest of spiders!!

TIPS

You can put a big spider on top of the goo, like it's protecting its eggs. You can also gross people out by leaving the "egg sack" out where people can see it. You might start a prank war with this one!

Store in an airtight container.

Toothpaste Slime

Do Not Eat

This slime is made with two ingredients that you probably already have at home. It has a different texture, but is easy, breezy and fun.

– – – – – – – – – – – – –

Ingredients

+ ½ cup (120 ml) thick, creamy shampoo
+ 2 tbsp (30 ml) white toothpaste
+ 1 tbsp (24 g) glitter (optional)
+ 1 tbsp (4 g) gelatin mix in your favorite color (optional)

Equipment

+ Bowl
+ Spoon

Put the shampoo in a bowl. Add the toothpaste to the bowl. Now is when you can add the glitter if you want, but let's get real. It's glitter. Who doesn't want to add it?! You can now also add your favorite color of gelatin mix if you desire. Stir it together with a spoon for about 90 seconds. If it is too stiff, add more shampoo. If it is too runny, add more toothpaste. Stir for 30 more seconds. Place the bowl of slimy goo in the freezer for about 30 minutes. When you take it out, the slime should be thick, but not too sticky. Squish and squeeze the slime until it is normal temperature again. Now it's ready!

TIPS
Store in an airtight container.
Limited shelf life.

Butter Slime

Adult Supervision • Do Not Eat

This slime gets its name not only because it uses butter, but also because of how buttery soft it feels when you squish it between your fingers. Kind of a combination between a slime and a dough, this goo is stretchy, but spreadable like butter should be.

– – – – – – – – – – – – –

Ingredients

+ ¼ cup (40 g) cornstarch
+ ¼ cup (33 g) baby powder
+ ½ cup (120 ml) creamy, thick shampoo
+ 1 (4-oz [118-ml]) bottle white school glue
+ 2 tbsp (30 ml) hand lotion
+ 7 drops yellow food coloring
+ About ½ cup (60 g) shaving cream (eyeball it)
+ 1 tbsp (15 ml) baby oil
+ 1 cup (230 g) softened butter
+ 1 tsp baking soda
+ 2 tbsp (30 ml) saline solution (make sure it says buffered on the package)

Equipment

+ Bowl
+ Spoon

Put the cornstarch, baby powder and shampoo in a bowl. Stir it with the spoon until it forms a sticky dough. Add the glue, lotion, food coloring, shaving cream, baby oil and butter, and stir it all together. Now, stir in the baking soda.

Next is the tricky part. You want to add the saline solution a little bit at a time. If you use too much, the slime will be too hard. Keep stirring. If it is a little on the sticky side, add a little more baby powder. When it's right, take it out of the bowl. Squish and knead it in your hands until the buttery perfection is achieved. This is so buttery smooth, you won't want to put it down!

Cronch Slime

Adult Supervision • Do Not Eat

What is cronch? It's like crunch, but so much better! Hear the crackle when you whip up a batch of this cool Cronch Slime. Your friends will be super jealous! They'll be begging you to make them some too!

- - - - - - - - - - - - - -

Ingredients

+ 2 (5-oz [147-ml]) bottles clear school glue
+ 1 tsp baking soda
+ 1 cup (240 ml) warm water
+ 1 (12-oz [355-ml]) bottle saline solution (make sure it says buffered on the package)
+ Bag of colored foam balls (bean-bag filler)

Equipment

+ Large glass mixing bowl
+ Spoon
+ Plastic craft tub

In the bowl, mix the two bottles of glue, the baking soda and the warm water. Mix until it's fully combined. Squirt about ½ teaspoon of the saline solution at a time into the glue mixture. Stir it vigorously, and give the solution time to react. Keep adding solution and stirring vigorously until the mixture starts to pull away from the sides of the bowl.

Now, mix for about 2 more minutes with the spoon. By this time, it should be ready to take out and knead, stretch and pull in your hands. Next, dump the bag of foam balls into the craft tub. Place the slime you made into the container with the little balls. Squish and mush everything up until it is incorporated together. When you stretch and play with the slime, it should make a crunching sound.

*See photo insert page 11.

Candy Slime

Adult Supervision • Edible

A better name for this might be Laughing Slime. That's because it's made with Laffy Taffy® candy! Make a batch and bring on the rainbow giggles.

- - - - - - - - - - - - - -

Ingredients

+ 1 bag of bite-size Laffy Taffy® candy (we used about 8 pieces of each color)
+ Water

For each color of candy

+ ¼ tsp coconut oil
+ 3 tbsp (24 g) powdered sugar
+ 3 tbsp (30 g) cornstarch

Equipment

+ Bowls (for each color of candy)
+ Pot
+ Spoon
+ Plate

(continued)

Unwrap and separate the Laffy Taffy® candy into the bowls by color. Get an adult to help you with the next part. Place a pot with 3 inches (8 cm) of water on the stove on medium-high heat. Place one of the bowls of candy into the water (basically using the double-boiler method), being careful not to get water on the candy so it doesn't seize. Heat up the candy until it is melted, stirring frequently. Once the candy is almost entirely melted, add the coconut oil and stir well.

While the adult is heating up the candy, place the powdered sugar and cornstarch on a plate. When the candy is done, have an adult take the bowl out of the water and pour the candy onto the plate with the cornstarch and sugar. Be careful. It will be hot. When the candy on the plate cools down enough to touch, knead and squish the candy into the cornstarch and sugar. Repeat with the remaining candy colors. You now have a rainbow of edible slimy goodness that smells great too!

TIP

If the candy gets too tough again, have an adult pop it in the microwave and heat it for about 10 seconds. It will soften it up again. Save the wrappers to tell the jokes while you play with your candy slime.

Edible Gummy Worm Slime

Adult Supervision • Edible

Let's make worm slime! Eww. How about gummy worm slime? This recipe is going to wiggle its way right into your play (and tummy) when you make this edible slime!

- - - - - - - - - - -

Ingredients

+ 1½ cups (273 g) gummy worms
+ 1 tsp vegetable oil
+ 2 tbsp (20 g) cornstarch
+ 2 tbsp (16 g) powdered sugar

Equipment

+ Microwave-safe bowl
+ Spoon

Make a pile with all the gummy worms inside your microwave-safe bowl. Ask an adult to microwave the bowl on high for 15-second increments until all of the gummy worms are melted. Stir with the spoon after each 15-second increment. Be careful. The bowl and candy will be hot. Add the vegetable oil and stir until combined. Mix the cornstarch and powdered sugar into the candy mixture until well combined. Allow the slime to cool. Now you have a smushy, tasty, stretchy treat you can nibble on while you play.

TIPS

If you find your slime sticky, you can add more cornstarch.

Store in an airtight container.

Fluffy Slime

Adult Supervision • Do Not Eat

This slime is so fluffy, it's almost like playing with pillowy billows of whipped cream. You'll be tempted to taste a bit of this soft cream. Resist the urge! Your taste buds won't love it as much as your hands do.

— — — — — — — — — — — —

Ingredients

+ 1 (11-oz [311-g]) can shaving cream
+ 1 packet powdered drink mix in your favorite color
+ 1 (4-oz [118-ml]) bottle white school glue
+ 1 tsp baking soda
+ 1½ tbsp (23 ml) saline solution (make sure it says buffered on the package), divided

Equipment

+ Plastic tub
+ Spoon

Dump the shaving cream, drink mix and glue into a plastic craft tub. Fold this together with a spoon. Add the baking soda to the mix and keep folding.

Add a tablespoon (15 ml) of the saline solution to the mix, and start whipping it up! You might need an extra ½ tablespoon (8 ml) of saline solution if it is not coming together properly. Add a small amount of saline solution to your hands and knead the fluffy mixture on a flat surface. Have fun playing with this billowy soft, slimy goo!

TIPS

What is folding? Folding something together means mixing it up carefully by bringing the bottom of the mix up to the top and repeating.

Store in an airtight container.

Edible Red Licorice Slime

Adult Supervision • Edible

Red licorice is one of those timeless candies that everyone has tried at least once. This classic sweet berry flavor is just screaming to get its turn as a slime. At last! Your imagination, and taste buds, will jump for joy.

— — — — — — — — — — — —

Ingredients

+ 1 cup (182 g) cut red licorice
+ 1 tsp coconut oil
+ 1 tsp raspberry gelatin powder
+ 1 tbsp (8 g) powdered sugar
+ 1 tsp cornstarch

Equipment

+ Kitchen scissors
+ Microwave-safe bowl
+ Spoon
+ Small bowl

With an adult's help, use the kitchen scissors to cut the red licorice into small pieces. Place the pieces of candy in the microwave-safe bowl. Add the coconut oil to the candy. Microwave in 20-second intervals, stirring after each interval using the spoon. When the mixture is melted, have an adult take the bowl out of the microwave. Be careful! It will be hot. Let the mixture cool down a bit. In a small bowl, mix together the gelatin, powdered sugar and cornstarch. Add it to the bowl of melted licorice. Stir vigorously with the spoon until well combined. After the mixture is completely cool, you can pick it up. Throw it down on a flat surface. Knead it, stretch it, eat it. This has a limited shelf life, so be sure to store it in an airtight container.

Red Hot Tamale Slime

Adult Supervision • Do Not Eat

Red, glittery slime is taken to an entirely new level with the scent of red-hot cinnamon. Easy to make, and so good to smell, this goop just might be the perfect slime. Even though it smells good and includes candy, this project isn't for eating!

- - - - - - - - - - - - - - - -

Ingredients

+ ½ cup (99 g) Hot Tamale® candy
+ ½ tsp coconut oil
+ 1 (5-oz [147-ml]) bottle clear school glue
+ 5 drops red food coloring
+ 1 tbsp (24 g) red glitter
+ ¼ cup (60 ml) hot (not boiling) water
+ ½ tsp baking soda
+ 1 tbsp (15 ml) saline solution (make sure it says buffered on the package)

Equipment

+ Microwave-safe bowl
+ Spoon

Put the candy and the coconut oil into your bowl. With an adult's help, put the bowl in the microwave. Microwave it for 20 seconds at a time, stirring well each time it's done. Be careful! It will get hot! It is done when it is a thick liquid mixture. Let it cool down for 3 minutes.

Add the bottle of glue, your food coloring and the glitter to the candy. Mix well with the spoon. Add the water and the baking soda. Add the saline solution, a little at a time, to the mixture. Stir well the entire time. It is done when the mixture starts to pull away from the sides of the bowl. Take out your goo. Knead it, poke it and stretch it until it is not as sticky. You now have a delicious-smelling red slime!

TIPS

Store in an airtight container. Limited shelf life.

Spiderweb Slime

Adult Supervision • Do Not Eat

Real spiderwebs start as a simple thread made by a spider. They turn this plain little piece of thread into uberfancy works of spider art. You do not need the creepy-crawly spider to make your supercool spiderweb! You just need this webby slime.

- - - - - - - - - - - - - - - -

Ingredients

+ 1 (4-oz [118-ml]) bottle white school glue
+ 1 cup (240 ml) foaming hand soap
+ ½ tbsp (8 ml) creamy shower gel or shampoo
+ ½ tbsp (8 ml) hand lotion
+ ½ tbsp (8 ml) baby oil
+ 2½ heaping cups (300 g) shaving cream, plus more for spreading
+ 1 to 2 tbsp (15 to 30 ml) liquid starch (you can find this in the laundry aisle)

Equipment

+ Large mixing bowl
+ Spoon
+ Airtight container

Fold the glue, soap, gel or shampoo, lotion, baby oil and shaving cream together in a bowl. Add the liquid starch a little at a time, folding it together the entire time. Now, get in there with your hands and knead, squeeze and fold that goo. It will be very sticky at first, but will eventually start to pull away from the sides of the bowl.

Now, take out that slime, and put it on a clean, flat surface. Play with, poke and knead this semi-sticky substance for about 15 minutes. It should be the consistency of a puffy slime. Put the slime in an airtight container. Using your hands, spread a thin layer of shaving cream over the top of the slime. Cover the container tightly with a lid. Let it sit for 2 to 3 days. When you take off the lid, the slime will look like spiderwebs and be crackly and crunchy. Push, poke and fold the slime in the container. This slime is so much fun!

TIPS

Add 6 drops of food coloring in the first step to give the slime a pop of color.

To make it foamier, add ½ cup (60 g) more of shaving cream in the first step.

Store in an airtight container.

Limited shelf life.

Snow Cone Slime

Adult Supervision • Do Not Eat

Did you say snow cone? Yes, please! What's better than chilling with a deliciously colorful snow cone on a hot summer day? Why, making one that doesn't melt of course!

Ingredients

+ 1 (5-oz [147-ml]) bottle clear glue
+ 1½ tsp (8 ml) liquid starch (you can find this in the laundry aisle)
+ 2 cups (400 g) polypropylene plastic pellets (you can find them at a craft store)
+ Food coloring (optional)
+ Food extract (optional)

Equipment

+ Small bowl
+ Spoon
+ Airtight container
+ Mixing bowl
+ Paper cones found at party stores (optional)

Mix the glue and starch in a small bowl very gently. You might want to let the mixture sit in an airtight container for about 3 to 4 days to become completely clear. When it's ready, place the slime in a mixing bowl. Add the plastic pellets ¼ cup (50 g) at a time, squishing them into the slime. The slime will eventually turn crackly and it will become harder to add the pellets. When you are done, you will have what looks like a crunchy snow cone.

*See photo insert page 11.

TIPS

Add your favorite color of food coloring to make it look like your favorite snow cone.

Add your favorite-smelling food extract to make it smell yummy.

Squish the mixture into paper cones to really give it that snow cone look.

DO NOT EAT THIS SNOW CONE. It looks amazing, but is not edible.

Store in an airtight container.

Holographic Slime

Adult Supervision • Do Not Eat

Three-dimensional rainbows of color you can hold in your hand: that is what this slime is all about! Get hypnotized by the color spectrum you'll create with this slimy masterpiece.

-- -- -- -- -- -- -- -- --

Ingredients

+ 1 (5-oz [147-ml]) bottle clear school glue
+ ½ cup (120 ml) water
+ 2 tbsp (48 g) holographic powder or glitter
+ 1 tbsp (15 ml) white acrylic paint
+ ½ tsp baking soda
+ 2 tbsp (30 ml) saline solution (make sure it says buffered on the package)

Equipment

+ Bowl
+ Spoon

Pour the glue, water, powder or glitter, paint and baking soda into a bowl, and mix up the solution until it is well combined. Add the saline solution a little at a time, stirring with each addition, until the mixture starts to pull away from the bowl. Take out the goopy, shiny slime, and place it on a flat surface. Okay, now you can play with your holographic slime!

TIPS

Use glow-in-the-dark paint instead of white paint to see the sparkles even when it's dark. It's such a fun way to play with this slime.

Store in an airtight container.

Laundry Soap Slime

Adult Supervision • Do Not Eat

Can slime really be this easy? Yes! You probably already have these ingredients in your home. This is a good slime to start with if you are new to the slime game. It is so simple!

-- -- -- -- -- -- -- -- -- -- --

Ingredients

+ 1 (5-oz [147-ml]) bottle clear school glue
+ ½ cup (120 ml) liquid laundry soap (Tide® works best)

Equipment

+ Bowl
+ Spoon

Pour the glue into the bowl. Add a teaspoon at a time of laundry soap, stirring well each time you add it. Keep adding detergent and stirring until the mixture pulls away from the sides of the bowl. Voila! You have Laundry Soap Slime.

TIPS

Add 1 tablespoon (24 g) of your favorite color of glitter if desired.

Add 2 drops of food coloring to change the color.

Store in an airtight container.

Contact Slime

Adult Supervision • Do Not Eat

This is another easy slime recipe, and it also doubles as a science experiment! What makes the contact solution turn the baking soda and glue into squishable slime? It has to do with how the polymers bond to one another. I bet you didn't think you were going to be a scientist today!

- - - - - - - - - - - - - -

Ingredients

+ 1 (4-oz [118-ml]) bottle white school glue
+ 1 tsp baking soda
+ 1 tbsp (15 ml) saline solution (make sure it says buffered on the package)

Equipment

+ Bowl
+ Spoon

Put the glue in your bowl. Add the baking soda and stir the mixture together. Add the contact solution (also known as saline) a little at a time, stirring while you add. When the slime starts to pull away from the sides of the bowl, it is ready. You can now take it out and play! The more you squish it with your hands, the better it will become.

TIPS

Add 2 drops of food coloring for fun, colorful play.

Add 2 teaspoons (16 g) of glitter for some sparkly amazingness.

Store in an airtight container.

Coke® Slime

Adult Supervision • Do Not Eat

Some call it Coke®. Some call it soda pop or just soda. Whatever you call it, this fizzy beverage will make an awesome-smelling slime that is hard to resist.

- - - - - - - - - - - - - -

Ingredients

+ 1 cup (240 ml) Coca-Cola®
+ 1½ tsp (14 g) borax powder
+ 1 (5-oz [147-ml]) bottle clear school glue

Equipment

+ Bowl
+ Spoon

Mix the Coca-Cola® and borax powder in the bowl. Be careful, the borax will make the Coca-Cola® fizzy. Add the glue and stir the mixture together. Keep stirring until the slime pulls away from the sides of the bowl. Now, get your hands in there and mix it together. The more you play with it, knead it, roll it and fold it with your hands, the less sticky it will be.

TIPS

Add a tablespoon (24 g) of glitter to the mix as you stir it. This will give your slime a pop of bling.

Try this with different soda pops to get different yummy scents.

Store in an airtight container.

Glitter Glue Slime

Adult Supervision • Do Not Eat

When you think of glitter glue, you probably think of fun crafts that involve adding a sparkle to your art. This same glue can be used to make a twinkling slime. With just a few ingredients, you can turn a bottle of crafty glitter glue into an ooey, gooey slime that you can stretch, pull and play with.

- - - - - - - - - - - - - -

Ingredients

+ 1 (6-oz [177-ml]) bottle glitter glue
+ 5 drops matching food coloring (optional)
+ ¼ tsp borax powder
+ ½ cup (120 ml) warm water

Equipment

+ 2 bowls
+ Spoon

Pour the glitter glue into a bowl. Mix in the food coloring, if desired, to give your slime a more vibrant color.

In the second bowl, mix the borax powder into the warm water until it dissolves. Fold this mixture into the glue a bit at a time. It is ready when the slime pulls away from the sides of the bowl. Get your hands ready, and grab the glob of goo out of the bowl. Smoosh it between your fingers, pull it apart with your hands and play with it on a flat surface. The more you play with it, the less sticky it will become.

TIPS

You may not use all of the borax-water solution. Discard any unused solution.

Store in an airtight container.
Refresh with water.

Kinetic Slime

Adult Supervision • Do Not Eat

This slime has a jiggle and feels snotty, like the goo you know and love. It also holds itself together unlike any slime you've ever played with. Just wait until you feel this mix for yourself! You will become an addict of the kinetic craze.

- - - - - - - - - - - - - -

Ingredients

+ 1½ cups (551 g) play sand (you can find this at a craft or hardware store)
+ 2 tbsp (20 g) cornstarch
+ 1½ tbsp (23 ml) of your favorite liquid hand soap
+ ½ tbsp (8 ml) coconut oil
+ 1 (4-oz [118-ml]) bottle white school glue
+ ½ cup (120 ml) liquid starch (you can find this in the laundry aisle)

Equipment

+ Plastic craft bin
+ Bowl
+ Spoon

Pour the play sand, cornstarch, soap and coconut oil into the plastic bin. Mix it all up with your hands. Set it aside.

Pour the bottle of glue into the bowl. Add a little bit of the liquid starch at a time. Keep stirring the entire time. When the mixture starts to pull away from the sides of the bowl, it's done.

Take it out of the bowl, and mix and knead it with your hands until it isn't so sticky and you have a good slime. Add the slime into the sand mixture in the plastic bin. Using your hands, squish the whole thing into one big blob of kinetic slime. This may take some time, but be patient. This slime is amazeballs!

TIP

Store in an airtight container.

Puffy Cloud Slime

Adult Supervision • Do Not Eat

Look up at the sky and what do you see? Clouds you wish you could grab and squish in your hands. With this superfoamy slime, it's almost like you are plucking those billowy puffs right out of the sky. Grab some and squish away!

Ingredients

+ 1 cup (240 ml) white school glue
+ 3 pumps of hand lotion
+ 2 pumps of foaming hand soap
+ 1 tbsp (10 g) cornstarch
+ ½ tsp borax
+ 1 cup (240 ml) water

Equipment

+ 2 bowls
+ Spoon

Mix the glue, lotion, soap and cornstarch in a bowl until combined. You should have a foam-like mixture.

In a separate bowl, dissolve the borax in the water. Add the borax solution to the glue a little at a time, stirring, until your slime starts to form and pull away from the sides of the bowl.

Knead it and play with it until it is slimy but doesn't stick to your hands. Now you have your super excellent cloud slime.

TIP

Store in an airtight container.

Iceberg Slime

Adult Supervision • Do Not Eat

What is an iceberg? It is a ginormous piece of ice, sometimes as big as an island, that has broken off a glacier. This hard piece of giant ice floats around in the open ocean. Make a bit of "iceberg" in your own home using this slime recipe that hardens as it sits.

Ingredients

+ 1 (4-oz [118-ml]) bottle white school glue
+ 1 (11-oz [311-g]) can shaving cream
+ 2 tbsp (30 ml) hand lotion
+ 2 tbsp (16 g) baby powder
+ 1 packet powdered drink mix in your favorite color
+ 1 tsp borax powder
+ 1 cup (240 ml) hot (not boiling) water

Equipment

+ Spoon
+ Large plastic mixing bowl or plastic bin
+ Smaller bowl
+ Rubber mallet or hammer

Using a spoon, mix the glue, shaving cream, lotion, baby powder and drink mix together in the large mixing bowl until fully combined. Mix the borax powder and water together in the smaller bowl using a spoon. Add the borax-water solution into the large bowl of goo, a little at a time, stirring each time to fully incorporate. When you are finished, it should nicely pull away from the sides of the bowl.

Dump the poufy goo onto a clean, flat surface. Knead it, fold it, poke it and play with it for about 15 minutes. Drop the puff of play goo back into the large bowl. Put the bowl in a safe place. Let it sit, uncovered, for 3 days.

(continued)

When the time is up, feel the top. It should be hard and crunchy. With the help of an adult, use the mallet or hammer to crack the surface of your homemade "iceberg." When you are done breaking up the surface, you can fold and play with the goo until it is all soft and fluffy again. Now you can put it back in the bowl, and start hardening your "iceberg" again!

Cloud Slime

Adult Supervision • Do Not Eat

You know how in the winter it sometimes just feels like snow? You can tell it is up there in the clouds, but it hasn't fallen to the ground yet. That is exactly how this slime is! It is a puffy cloud full of "snow" that you can actually have fun with in your hands!

Ingredients

+ 3 tbsp (36 g) instant snow powder (you can find this at a craft store or online)
+ 3 cups (720 ml) water, divided
+ 1 tsp borax
+ 1 (4-oz [118-ml]) bottle white school glue
+ 6 drops of your favorite food coloring (optional)
+ 3 drops peppermint oil (optional)

Equipment

+ Large craft tub
+ Cup
+ Spoon
+ Bowl

Dump the snow powder into your craft tub. Add about 2 cups (480 ml) of water. This "snow" will grow as you add the water. Set that aside.

Now, grab your cup. Add 1 cup (240 ml) of water and your borax to the cup. Stir this mixture until it is completely dissolved. Empty your bottle of glue into the bowl. Next, mix your food coloring and peppermint oil in with the glue if you desire. Slowly add your borax mixture, about a teaspoon at a time, to the glue. Mix well after each time you add the borax mixture. The goo is ready when it starts to pull away from the sides of the bowl.

Take it out of the bowl, and knead, stretch and pull it until it isn't quite so sticky anymore. Now, throw this goo into your tub of snow. Knead the snow into the slime really well. Play with it until the slime is full of the snow, and none of it is falling out. You will not use all of the snow. Now you have made your perfect cloud slime!

> **TIP**
> Store in an airtight container.

Gummy Bear Slime

Adult Supervision • Edible

Yum. Squish. Yum. Squish. Stretch. Play. Repeat. This slime is made with completely edible ingredients, and you won't find a tastier glob to stretch your imagination.

Ingredients

+ 1½ cups (273 g) gummy bears
+ 1 tsp vegetable oil
+ 1 tsp gelatin in your favorite flavor
+ 2½ tbsp (20 g) powdered sugar
+ 2½ tbsp (25 g) cornstarch

Equipment

+ Microwave-safe bowl
+ Spoon

Pile the gummy bears into the bowl. Drizzle the vegetable oil over the gummy bears. With an adult's help, put the bowl into the microwave. Microwave in 20-second increments, stirring after each time. When the gummy bears have turned to a liquid consistency, have an adult take the bowl out of the microwave. Be careful. It will be hot. Let it cool down a little, then stir in your flavored gelatin, the powdered sugar and the cornstarch with a spoon. If it's too runny, add more sugar. If it's too firm, add a bit more oil. When it's done, it should be stretchy, tacky and edible!

TIPS

Store in an airtight container.
Limited shelf life.

Fuzzy Slime Monster

Adult Supervision • Do Not Eat

Not all monsters are scary. They can be cute, ooey and gooey too. What will your monster become once you finish this supercool recipe? It's your monster. You decide!

— — — — — — — — — —

Ingredients

+ 1 (4-oz [118-ml]) bottle white school glue
+ 2 tbsp (30 ml) liquid starch
+ 2 tsp (10 ml) acrylic paint in your favorite color
+ 2 tbsp (48 g) glitter (optional)
+ 4 cotton balls, shredded
+ Googly eyes (different sizes are fun)
+ A few colorful play feathers (optional)
+ 1 pipe cleaner, cut in 6 pieces (optional)

Equipment

+ Large bowl
+ Spoon

Pour the bottle of glue into the bowl, and slowly add in the starch while stirring. You may not need all 2 tablespoons (30 ml). You want the slime to just release from the sides of the bowl. Add your acrylic paint and, if you like, glitter, and continue squishing the slime up until it is an even color.

Now, take the shredded cotton balls one at a time, and squeeze and fold them into the slime. When you are done, take your blob of "fuzzy" slime out of the bowl. Shape it into a glob monster. Add as many googly eyes as you want. If you desire, stick the colorful feathers in the top for hair. Use the pipe cleaners for arms, horns, a nose or whatever else your imagination creates. It's your Fuzzy Slime Monster!

TIPS

The pipe cleaners can be a bit pokey once cut. Use with care.

Store in an airtight container.

Googly Eye Slime

Adult Supervision • Do Not Eat

What's that you see peering at you through a haze of goo? Could it be your squishy, slithery slime? It just might be! The more eyes, the more fun with this glob of superjiggly fun.

- - - - - - - - - - - - - -

Ingredients

+ 1 cup (240 ml) hot water
+ 1 tbsp (27 g) borax
+ 1 (5-oz [147-ml]) bottle clear school glue
+ 2 tbsp (30 ml) water
+ ¼ cup (50 g) googly eyes

Equipment

+ 2 bowls
+ Spoon

Ask an adult to help you mix the hot water and the borax in a bowl with a spoon until the borax is completely dissolved. Set it to the side. Pour the glue into the second bowl. Gently mix in the water to thin the glue out. Try not to get too many air bubbles into the mix. Pour the glue mixture into the borax mixture. Slowly stir the glue around in the water for about 30 seconds. Let the mixture sit for about 5 minutes.

When the time is up, take the slime out of the water. Flatten it out with your hands on a clean, dry surface. Add the googly eyes to the center of the slime. Fold the slime up around the googly eyes. Now, squish it all together until it's combined. When the eyes are peering in all directions out of the slime, you know it's ready!

*See photo insert page 11.

TIP

Store in an airtight container.

Color-Changing Slime

Adult Supervision • Do Not Eat

Is it pink? Is it black? It just might be both! With the thermochromic pigment found in this recipe, temperature can determine the color of your slime. How does that even work?!

- - - - - - - - - - - - - -

Ingredients

+ 1 (4-oz [118-ml]) bottle white school glue
+ 2 to 3 tsp (30 to 46 g) thermochromic pigment (you can find this online)
+ ½ tsp baking soda
+ 1 cup (120 g) shaving cream
+ 1 tbsp (15 ml) hand lotion
+ 1 tsp baby powder
+ 1 tbsp (15 ml) saline solution (make sure it says buffered on the package)

Equipment

+ Bowl
+ Spoon

Add the glue to the bowl. Sprinkle in the thermo-chromatic pigment. Be careful: This can be messy. Once it is all mixed up, stir in the baking soda.

To make it fluffy, add the shaving cream, folding it into the mixture until it is all incorporated. Now, fold in the lotion and baby powder. Add the saline solution in small amounts, stirring vigorously after each addition. You may not need the full amount, or you might need a little more. The more you add, the more tough the mixture will become. Now, take out the blob of goo. Knead it in your hands until it is no longer sticky. You will want to play with this one forever!

TIPS

Warm your hands up by blowing on them or rubbing them together before you play with the slime. More heat equals more color change.

Rub ice along the surface of the slime. Colder temperatures equal more color change.

Store in an airtight container.

Glossy Slime

Adult Supervision • Do Not Eat

Isn't all slime a bit glossy? This slime is extra glossy. It almost shines with a blingy luster as you squeeze, pull, twist and play.

- - - - - - - - - - - - - -

Ingredients

+ 1 (4-oz [118-ml]) bottle white school glue
+ 2 tbsp (30 ml) baby oil
+ 2 tsp (6 g) baby powder
+ 2 tsp (10 ml) water
+ 6 drops food coloring (optional)
+ ¼ cup (60 ml) liquid laundry detergent

Equipment

+ Bowl
+ Spoon

Put the glue and baby oil in the bowl and mix well. Add the baby powder and water. Mix up the ingredients until a soft dough forms. Add the food coloring, if desired, and mix until it's evenly blended. Now, add the laundry detergent a little at a time, stirring vigorously each time you add more detergent. The slime will be ready when it pulls away from the sides of the bowl. Take the slime out of the bowl. Knead and stretch it until it is no longer sticky.

TIPS

Put a tiny bit of baby oil on your hands before you play with the slime. This will keep it from sticking.

Store in an airtight container.

Cheetah Slime

Adult Supervision • Do Not Eat

What's black and orange and super fast? A cheetah, of course. So is this slimy mixture. Fast to make, that is. Have your own cheetah fun in under 10 minutes!

— — — — — — — — — — — —

Ingredients

+ 1 (5-oz [147-ml]) bottle clear school glue
+ 2 tbsp (30 ml) liquid starch (you can find this in the laundry aisle)
+ 10 drops orange food coloring (or mix yellow and red)
+ ¼ cup (200 g) small black sequence beads

Equipment

+ Bowl
+ Spoon

Empty the entire bottle of glue into a bowl. Gently stir the liquid starch into the glue. Try not to "whip" the mixture. You want as little air in the mixture as possible. Add the food coloring and keep stirring. The slime is ready when it starts pulling away from the bowl. Add the sequence beads, squishing and kneading until the beads are evenly dispersed. Now you have cool Cheetah Slime!

TIP
Store in an airtight container.

Clear Slime

Adult Supervision • Do Not Eat

This clear slime recipe is a great base for so many slime recipes. Whether you add to it or play with it as is, this slime is wicked cool! It almost looks like you are playing with and shaping water. Your friends will be a bit confused, and totally amazed.

— — — — — — — — — — — —

Ingredients

+ ½ cup (120 ml) hot water
+ ¼ tsp borax
+ 1 (5-oz [147-ml]) bottle clear school glue
+ ½ cup (120 ml) room-temperature water

Equipment

+ 2 bowls
+ Spoon

Ask an adult to help you mix the hot water and the borax in a bowl until the borax is completely dissolved. Set it to the side.

Pour the glue in the second bowl. Gently mix in the room-temperature water to thin the glue out. Try not to get too many air bubbles into the mix.

Pour the glue mixture into the borax mixture. Slowly stir the glue around in the water for about 30 seconds. Let the mixture sit for about 5 minutes. When the time is up, knead the slime in the borax solution for about a minute more. Take the slime out. Stretch it out and hold it up. You should be able to see right through it!

TIPS
Be sure to throw out any unused borax solution.

Store in an airtight container.

(three)

PLAYDOUGH

These dough activities are all about the squish. They're fun to smoosh and moosh and you can even use them to sculpt and design. Some of these doughs are all natural, and some of them are made from cake frosting, but all of these doughs are ridiculously cool! You can mix different colors and textures together to make pretty much anything you want!

The Best Homemade Playdough

Adult Supervision • Do Not Eat

Want a smooshy, fun-to-make alternative to store-bought dough? You are bound to get hours of laughs and giggles from this fun dough. It is the world's best homemade playdough.

— — — — — — — — — — —

Ingredients

+ 2 cups (240 g) flour
+ ½ cup (137 g) salt
+ 2 tbsp (10 g) cream of tartar
+ 2 tbsp (30 ml) oil (any kitchen oil will do— coconut oil, vegetable oil, even olive oil)
+ 1½ cups (360 ml) boiling water
+ Food coloring (optional)

Equipment

+ Large bowl
+ Spoon

Pour the flour, salt and cream of tartar into a large bowl. Stir in the kitchen oil of your choice. Have an adult help you pour the boiling water very carefully into the bowl. Be careful! It will be very hot. Mix all the ingredients together with a spoon until you get dough. Let it cool completely, and then make a ball with the dough. Now, punch the middle of the ball to make a hole. Put a few drops of food coloring in the hole you made, if you like. Knead the ball with your hands until it is all mixed together. Now you have your homemade playdough!

TIPS

Gel food coloring makes more vibrant colors than regular liquid food coloring.

While you are kneading the color into the dough, it can stain your hands. Wear plastic gloves to prevent this. Keep the dough in the bowl to keep it from staining surfaces.

Store in an airtight container. Refresh with water.

Hot Chocolate Playdough

Adult Supervision • Do Not Eat

Hot chocolate is just one of those things that makes everyone feel happy, relaxed and ready to hang out. This hot chocolate playdough is just the thing to pull out on a cold winter day. For extra fun, pair it with our Marshmallow Playdough (page 73) and stick it in a mug to make it look like real hot chocolate!

— — — — — — — — — — —

Ingredients

+ 2 cups (480 ml) water
+ 1½ cups (188 g) flour
+ 4 (0.75-oz [21-g]) packets of hot chocolate mix
+ 1 cup (273 g) salt
+ 2 to 3 tbsp (30 to 45 ml) vegetable oil

Equipment

+ Saucepan
+ Spoon
+ Wax paper

Ask an adult to mix the water, flour, hot chocolate mix, salt and vegetable oil over low heat in a saucepan and stir for about a minute until the dough is formed. Let your dough cool and pull it out of the saucepan onto wax paper. Knead the dough together until it is fully mixed. This dough will make your whole home smell as good as hot chocolate tastes!

*See photo insert page 12.

*See photo insert page 12.

TIPS

If your dough is too oily, just add an extra packet of hot cocoa.

Store in an airtight container.
Limited shelf life.

Marshmallow Playdough

Adult Supervision • Edible

Making Marshmallow Playdough is as much fun as it sounds. It's even okay to put in your mouth! This can get sticky and gooey if you play with it for too long at one time, but that's half the fun!

▬ ▬ ▬ ▬ ▬ ▬ ▬ ▬ ▬ ▬ ▬ ▬

Ingredients

+ ¾ cup (35 g) miniature marshmallows
+ 2 tsp (10 ml) vegetable oil (or olive or coconut oil)
+ 6 to 7 drops food coloring (optional)
+ 5 to 6 tbsp (50 to 60 g) cornstarch

Equipment

+ Large microwave-safe bowl (a big one! Marshmallows expand when they're hot!)
+ Spoon

With an adult's help, put your marshmallows and oil into the microwave-safe bowl and heat for about 30 seconds. If you're using food coloring, you'll want to add it now. Stir well and return the bowl to the microwave. You're basically heating everything up until the marshmallows start to get big. When it's done, have an adult take the bowl out of the microwave and add some of the cornstarch. Stir, and keep adding until your playdough is not too sticky. This is going to make a stretchy playdough that is taste-safe!

TIPS

If your dough is too sticky, just add more cornstarch.

Store in an airtight container.
Limited shelf life.

Ice Cream Dough

Adult Supervision • Edible

This dough looks exactly like ice cream. One of our favorite ways to play with it is to get a couple of scoops and add it to some real waffle cones. If you want to make it even more fun, you can add in a few sundae toppings for a super treat!

▬ ▬ ▬ ▬ ▬ ▬ ▬ ▬ ▬ ▬ ▬ ▬

Ingredients

+ 1 (6.4-oz [181-g]) can premade frosting (get a fun color!)
+ 6 cups (720 g) powdered sugar
+ Waffle cones

Equipment

+ Mixing bowl
+ Mixer
+ Ice cream scoops

(continued)

Dump all of the frosting into the mixing bowl and start the mixer. Now, slowly pour in the powdered sugar and let the ingredients combine. Pull out your dough and scoop it onto the waffle cones for some silly, doughy fun!

Cracked-Egg Dough

Adult Supervision • Do Not Eat

Want to freak out your friends? This dough looks almost exactly like a real egg! You get to create a slimy, doughy, clear goo surrounding a yellow "yolk" of dough. Have your friends open one and hear them gasp and giggle!

- - - - - - - - - - - - - -

Ingredients

+ 1 ball of Clear Playdough (page 77)
+ 1 yellow ball of The Best Homemade Playdough (page 72)

Equipment

+ 2 bowls
+ 2 bags of plastic fillable Easter eggs

Place the Clear Playdough in one bowl. Make little balls about the size of egg yolks with the yellow Homemade Playdough. Do this by rolling the dough around in your hands. Place the yellow balls you create in your second bowl.

Open one of the plastic Easter eggs. Fill one half of the egg with Clear Playdough. Squish one of the yellow balls into the clear doughy goo. Fill the other half of the egg with Clear Playdough. Place the two halves of the egg together and close it. Repeat with all your plastic eggs.

Cake Batter Dough

Edible

Cake batter has a crazy feel to it that's hard to explain, but this dough looks and feels just like it! This is the perfect project to pull out when Mom or Dad is baking in the kitchen and wants to keep little hands busy!

- - - - - - - - - - - - - -

Ingredients

+ 1 cup (108 g) confetti cake mix
+ 2 tbsp (14 g) premade confetti frosting (with sprinkles)
+ 1 tbsp (10 g) cornstarch
+ 1 cup (176 g) sprinkles

Equipment

+ Bowl
+ Spoon

In a bowl, combine your cake mix and frosting. Stir well. Add the cornstarch a little at a time until it becomes less sticky. The more you knead it, the more it will become like dough. Once you reach the consistency you like, add in the sprinkles. You can then play with the dough and even use cookie cutters to cut out fun shapes!

Lavender Playdough

Adult Supervision • Do Not Eat

Sometimes you just need to chill out and squish something. This lavender playdough is exactly perfect for that. The smell is naturally calming, and the sprigs give it a textured crunchy feel!

- - - - - - - - - - - - - - - -

Ingredients

+ 1¼ cups (300 ml) water
+ 1 cup (273 g) salt
+ 2 tbsp (30 ml) vegetable oil
+ 2 tbsp (20 g) cream of tartar
+ 2 cups (250 g) flour
+ Sprigs of lavender

Equipment

+ Saucepan
+ Bowl
+ Spoon

With an adult's help, boil the water in a saucepan. While that is cooking, add the salt, oil, cream of tartar and flour to the bowl and mix them together. Have an adult help you pour the boiling water into the mixture and stir it with the spoon until it forms into a ball. Let it cool a bit. Once cool, pull the ball out of the bowl and drop it onto the counter. Knead it with your hands until the dough forms. Take your lavender and sprinkle the flower petals into the dough. Fold the petals into the mixture, and you have a nice calming dough for when you just need some chill time!

Softest Playdough

Do Not Eat

When you think of something being soft, you don't usually think of playdough, but this playdough is so soft and silky you won't ever want to play with anything else.

- - - - - - - - - - - - - - - -

Ingredients

+ 1 cup (240 ml) white lotion (can be scented or unscented)
+ 2½ cups (400 g) cornstarch
+ Food coloring

Equipment

+ Large bowl

(continued)

In a large bowl, mix together the lotion, cornstarch and a few drops of food coloring. Use your hands to knead the ingredients together until you form the softest, smoothest dough ever!

Naturally Dyed Playdough

Adult Supervision • Do Not Eat

Before there was ever food coloring in a tube or jar, people used natural things like fruits, flowers and spices to change the color of foods. We can do that same thing with playdough, changing its color without ever having to use any dye!

- - - - - - - - - - -

Ingredients

+ 30 blueberries
+ 1 cup (240 ml) water
+ ½ cup (63 g) flour
+ ¼ cup (68 g) salt
+ ½ tbsp (5 g) cream of tartar
+ ½ tbsp (8 ml) vegetable oil

Equipment

+ Saucepan
+ Paper towel
+ Bowl
+ Spoon

Have an adult put the blueberries and water into a saucepan on the stove and bring it to a boil. Reduce the heat and let the mixture simmer for 30 minutes, until it is a thick consistency. Leave it to cool for another 30 minutes, then place a paper towel over the bowl and pour the mixture through it and into the bowl, catching all the parts you don't want in your dough. This should leave you with a very deep blue-purple water. That is how you will dye your dough!

Next, combine the flour, salt, cream of tartar and vegetable oil in a saucepan with ½ cup (120 ml) of dyed water and ask an adult to stir it on low heat until the mixture rolls up into a ball. Let it cool just enough so that it won't burn your hands and drop it on your kitchen counter. Knead it together until it's fully formed into dough!

Feather Dough

Adult Supervision • Do Not Eat

This supereasy, feather-soft dough is a fun way for you to spend quality kitchen time with a grown-up. Whether you mold it, squish it, cut it or shape it, this four-ingredient dough is bound to bring you hours of fun.

- - - - - - - - - - -

Ingredients

+ ¼ cup (40 g) cornstarch
+ ½ cup (110 g) baking soda
+ ¼ cup plus 1 tbsp (75 ml) water
+ 1 tbsp (15 ml) baby oil
+ Food coloring (optional)

Equipment

+ Small saucepan
+ Spoon
+ Parchment paper

In a small saucepan, stir together the cornstarch, baking soda and water. With an adult's help, place the saucepan on the stove, and turn the heat to medium. Be very careful! Have the adult help you stir the mixture constantly. It will start to bubble and get a bit solid. Just keep stirring!

In about 3 minutes, a ball will form. With the adult's help, take the saucepan off the burner to cool. Make sure you turn off that burner! Have the adult spread the ball onto some parchment paper. (Be careful! It will be HOT!) When it is completely cool, you can knead in the baby oil and, if you like, a drop or two of food coloring to give it an extra touch of amazingness. You are now ready to play!

TIPS

Knead in a ½ teaspoon of scented shower gel or a drop or two of your favorite-smelling essential oil to make it uniquely yours.

Store in plastic wrap in an airtight container. Refresh with water.

Clear Playdough

Adult Supervision • Do Not Eat

This clear playdough is completely insane. You can mold it and shape it like real playdough, but it's clear. It's basically invisible!

- - - - - - - - - - - -

Ingredients

+ 1 tsp borax
+ 3 cups (720 ml) water, divided
+ 1 medium-size tube clear peel-off face mask
+ 10 tapioca balls

Equipment

+ Mixing bowl
+ Spoon
+ Microwave-safe bowl

In a mixing bowl, mix the borax with 1 cup (240 ml) of water. Squirt the tube of face mask into the bowl and stir together until the dough starts to form. Pull the dough out of the borax-water mixture, add another cup (240 ml) of water to the mixture and roll the dough around in it again until the dough is moldable.

Put the tapioca balls and remaining 1 cup (240 ml) of water into a microwave-safe bowl. With an adult's help, microwave it on high for about 30 seconds, until the water is cloudy. Now, dunk your dough into the tapioca water to give it a matte finish.

TIP

If you want your dough to have a shiny finish instead of a matte one, just skip the tapioca balls!

Glitter Playdough

Adult Supervision • Do Not Eat

This glitter dough has extra sparkle for those of you who need a little shine in your lives. For crazy fun, play with it outside and watch the sparkles dance on the table!

- - - - - - - - - - - -

Ingredients

+ 3 baby diapers
+ 1 cup (240 ml) water
+ 5 tbsp (120 g) glitter
+ 3 to 5 drops food coloring
+ 2 to 3 tbsp (20 to 30 g) cornstarch

Equipment

+ Bowl

Open up the baby diapers and pour the little balls that are inside into a bowl. Pour the water in to hydrate the balls, and you will have a sticky crystal-like substance. Now, add the glitter, food coloring and cornstarch, and mix with your hands. You'll have a cool, gooey dough!

*See photo insert page 12.

> ### TIP
> Depending on the size of diaper you use, you may need more or less water!

Textured Dough

Adult Supervision • Do Not Eat

Embrace the mess with this crazy, textured dough. It is full of lumpy, bumpy amazingness! Feel the different textures. Can you tell what they are with your eyes closed?

- - - - - - - - - - - -

Ingredients

+ 4 cups (500 g) flour
+ 1½ cups (410 g) salt
+ 3 tbsp (30 g) cream of tartar
+ 2 tbsp (30 ml) liquid coconut oil
+ 2 to 3 cups (480 to 720 ml) cold water
+ 3 drops of your favorite food coloring
+ ½ cup (181 g) play sand (you can find this at a craft or hardware store)
+ ¼ cup (50 g) dry rice
+ ¼ cup (53 g) dry lentils
+ ¼ cup (100 g) aquarium rocks (you can find these at the dollar store)

Equipment

+ Plastic bin (11 × 8 × 5 in [28 × 20 × 13 cm] works great)

Dump the flour, salt, cream of tartar, coconut oil and water in the plastic bin and mix together with your hands until a dough ball forms. Use your fist to punch a hole in the middle of the dough. Place the food coloring, play sand, rice, lentils and aquarium rocks in the hole you made. Knead and squish the dough together.

> ### TIPS
> Try substituting different textured items like dry kidney beans, macaroni noodles or beads. Let your imagination run wild!
>
> Store in an airtight container.

No-Cook Two-Ingredient Dough

Do Not Eat

Even just making this awesome two-ingredient dough is bound to bring giggles and smiles. It is messy fun.

- - - - - - - - - - - - - - -

Ingredients

+ 1 cup (125 g) all-purpose flour
+ 2 to 3 pumps of your favorite liquid hand soap or shower gel

Equipment

+ Large bowl

Dump the flour into a large bowl. Add the hand soap or shower gel. Mix and knead the mixture with your hands. If the mixture is too dry, add another pump of soap or gel. If it is too wet, add more flour. Get your hands good and messy with this one. Mix and knead until it is the consistency you want. Have fun!

TIP
Store in an airtight container.

Shaving Cream Dough

Adult Supervision • Do Not Eat

This dough is super fun to make outside on a warm summer day when you can get good and messy. Make sure you ask an adult before you raid the shaving cream stash to make this awesome light and fluffy dough. It's so fun, it almost bounces!

- - - - - - - - - - - - - - -

Ingredients

+ 1 (11-oz [311-g]) can shaving cream
+ 1 cup (160 g) cornstarch
+ Food coloring (optional)

Equipment

+ Large bowl or plastic tub

Dump the shaving cream into a large bowl or plastic tub. Add the cornstarch into the shaving cream ½ cup (80 g) at a time. Mix and squish it up each time you add the cornstarch. If you like, add a few drops of food coloring to get a cool color effect. Mix and knead the ingredients with your hands until the dough forms a squishy ball. If it is too crumbly, add a little more shaving cream. If it is too wet, add a little more cornstarch.

TIPS
Try different scented shaving creams.

Use cookie cutters to make fun and crazy shapes with the dough.

Glow-in-the-Dark Dough

Adult Supervision • Do Not Eat

This recipe uses The Best Homemade Playdough (page 72) as a base for this groovy, glowing mixture.

- - - - - - - - - - -

Ingredients

+ 1 batch of The Best Homemade Playdough (page 72)
+ Glow-in-the-dark paint

Leave the food coloring out of this batch of The Best Homemade Playdough. Once the dough is cooled and you have formed a ball, take your hands and smash that ball flat. Add about 1 teaspoon at a time of glow-in-the-dark paint. Knead the paint into the dough with your hands. Keep adding paint until it is the color and consistency you want.

If the mixture gets too runny, just add some flour. Hold the completed dough under a bright light for a few minutes. Now you're ready to turn out the lights and have some glowy, doughy fun.

TIPS

For even more vibrant fun, play under a black light!

To recharge the glow, just hold the dough up to a bright light for a few minutes. The glow will be restored, and the fun will continue.

Store in an airtight container.

Peanut Butter Playdough

Edible

You had me at peanut butter. This dough is as tasty as it is fun! Cut it, smoosh it, roll it, squish it and then eat it! This dough is twice the fun!

- - - - - - - - - - -

Ingredients

+ 1 (16-oz [454-g]) container creamy peanut butter
+ 2 cups (240 g) powdered sugar

Equipment

+ Large bowl

Combine the peanut butter and powdered sugar in a large bowl. Mix it and knead it with your hands until it forms a ball of peanut buttery goodness. Enjoy!

TIPS

Roll the ball in granulated sugar for a touch of texture.

Try crunchy peanut butter for even more texture.

Use 1½ cups (387 g) of peanut butter and ½ cup (148 g) of chocolate hazelnut spread for extra fun yumminess.

Store in an airtight container. Limited shelf life.

Jell-O® Dough

Adult Supervision • Do Not Eat

What is better than playing with colorful dough? Playing with yummy-smelling colorful dough! You might even be tempted to taste this incredible, edible playtime dough. Watch out, though! Things don't always taste exactly like they smell.

- - - - - - - - - - - - -

Ingredients

+ 2 cups (250 g) flour
+ ½ cup (137 g) salt
+ 2 tbsp (20 g) cream of tartar
+ 2 tbsp (30 ml) liquid coconut oil
+ 1 (3-oz [85-g]) flavored gelatin packet
+ 1 cup (240 ml) very hot water

Equipment

+ 2 bowls
+ Spoon

Put the flour, salt, cream of tartar and coconut oil into a large bowl. Mix it all together. With an adult's help, place the flavored gelatin into another bowl with the very hot water. Stir it with a spoon until the gelatin is all dissolved.

Now, have the adult pour the hot mixture into your bowl of mixed-up ingredients. Using the spoon, stir all the ingredients together to make a dough. Once the dough cools down, take it out of the bowl, and use your hands to knead it a little on a flat surface. If it is too dry, you can add a little more water. If it is too wet, you can add a little more flour. Time to have some smelly-good fun!

TIPS

Cream of tartar helps dough last a bit longer, but not forever!

Store in an airtight container. Limited shelf life.

Candy Playdough

Adult Supervision • Do Not Eat

Everybody loves candy! Mix it with a playdough, and you have instant rainbows of squishy, smooshy fun. Grab a friend, and you'll both be seeing rainbows of awesomeness.

- - - - - - - - - - - - -

Ingredients

+ 10 to 20 jelly beans in a color of your choice
+ 1 cup (240 ml) water
+ 2 cups (250 g) flour
+ ¼ cup (68 g) salt
+ 2 tbsp (20 g) cream of tartar
+ 1 tbsp (15 ml) liquid coconut oil

Equipment

+ Microwave-safe container
+ Large bowl
+ Spoon

Put the jelly beans into a microwave-safe container. Cover them with water and, with an adult's help, heat them in the microwave for 30 seconds. They will be hot.

When the time is up, remove the jelly beans from the water and place the colored water, flour, salt, cream of tartar and coconut oil into a large bowl. Mix it all up. Have an adult help you mix all the ingredients with a spoon until a dough ball forms. Put a good amount of flour on your hands, and clap them above the dough to lightly cover it. This will keep it from being too sticky. Once it is cooled completely, you're ready to play! Repeat with as many colors as you like!

Cookie Dough Dough

Edible

Have you ever made cookies at home? They smell tasty, are yummy to nibble and start with a dough much like this one! This fun, good-smelling recipe lets you shape, mold, pretend and, best of all, nibble while you play!

‒ ‒ ‒ ‒ ‒ ‒ ‒ ‒ ‒ ‒ ‒ ‒ ‒

Ingredients

+ 1 cup (80 g) quick-cooking oats
+ ½ cup (63 g) flour
+ 1½ tbsp (15 g) cream of tartar
+ 1½ tbsp (15 g) dry hot chocolate mix
+ 1½ tsp (6 g) brown sugar
+ 1 tsp vanilla extract
+ 2 tbsp (28 g) softened butter or margarine
+ 1 cup (240 ml) cold water

Equipment

+ Large bowl

Mix the oats, flour, cream of tartar, hot chocolate mix and brown sugar in a large bowl. Get in there with your hands! Add the vanilla, butter and cold water. Keep squishing it around. Make sure you squish it between your fingers to mix it up well. Once it's all mixed, you're ready to play!

TIPS

Use chocolate candies, raisins or sprinkles for texture.

Try adding ½ teaspoon of cinnamon to give the dough a yummy pop of flavor.

Store in an airtight container. Limited shelf life.

Homemade Butter Dough

Adult Supervision • Do Not Eat

Butter is a fun thing to make at home. You get to use your arm muscles, and a bit of your patience muscle. Once you make your own butter, you can add it to this easy dough recipe for amazing playtime fun.

‒ ‒ ‒ ‒ ‒ ‒ ‒ ‒ ‒ ‒ ‒ ‒ ‒

Ingredients

+ 1½ cups (360 ml) heavy whipping cream
+ ½ cup (137 g) salt, divided
+ 2 cups (250 g) all-purpose flour
+ 2 tbsp (10 g) cream of tartar
+ ¾ cup (180 ml) hot water

Equipment

+ Stand mixer or hand mixer
+ Large bowl
+ Spoon

Pour the heavy whipping cream and ¼ teaspoon of the salt into the stand mixer (or a large bowl) and mix until it becomes solid. You made butter!

Now, slowly add the flour, the rest of the salt, the cream of tartar and the hot water to the bowl. Stir it up with the mixer. Once it starts to form a dough, remove it from the bowl and knead it with your hands. You just made your own Homemade Butter Dough!

TIP

Instead of using a mixer, place the heavy whipping cream into a sealed container and shake until solid. This usually takes 8 to 10 minutes.

Galaxy Dough

Adult Supervision • Do Not Eat

Go outside at night, and look up at the sky. Do you see bright stars among the blackness with splashes of blue and purple? This shimmery dough gives you a bit of that galaxy in the palm of your hand.

- - - - - - - - - - - - - - -

Ingredients

+ 2 cups (250 g) flour
+ ½ cup (137 g) salt
+ 2 tbsp (20 g) cream of tartar
+ 2 tbsp (24 g) dry strawberry milk powder
+ 1 packet grape powdered drink mix
+ 1 activated charcoal capsule, opened up to get the powder
+ 2 cups (480 ml) water
+ 1½ tbsp (23 ml) liquid coconut oil
+ ¼ cup (96 g) glitter in your favorite color (we like purple or silver with this dough!)

Equipment

+ Large bowl
+ Saucepan
+ Spoon

First things first: get an adult. In a large bowl, mix the flour, salt, cream of tartar, milk powder, drink mix and charcoal. Add the water and coconut oil to a saucepan. With an adult's help, put the saucepan on the stove. Turn the burner to medium heat. Stirring continuously, cook the liquids for about a minute. Then add the dry ingredients to the saucepan. Stir, stir, stir. Keep stirring until a dough forms.

With the adult's help, take the saucepan off the burner and turn off the burner. Keep stirring the dough. Once it is completely cool, drop it onto a flat surface. Sprinkle in your glitter, and mush it all together. Now you have your own galaxy in your hand!

*See photo insert page 12.

TIPS

Add beads or marbles for texture, and to make the galaxy effect even more vibrant.

Store in an airtight container. Limited shelf life.

Coconut Playdough

Adult Supervision • Do Not Eat

This dough just screams summertime! It will smell like you are playing under a palm tree on a tropical island. Watch out for falling coconuts!

- - - - - - - - - - - - - -

Ingredients

+ 2 cups (250 g) flour
+ ½ cup (137 g) salt
+ 2 tbsp (20 g) cream of tartar
+ 2 tbsp (30 ml) liquid coconut oil
+ Yellow food coloring
+ 1½ cups (180 ml) very hot coconut water
+ ½ tsp coconut or pineapple extract (optional)

Equipment

+ Large bowl
+ Spoon
+ Microwave-safe container

In a bowl, mix together the flour, salt, cream of tartar, coconut oil and food coloring. With an adult's help, heat up the coconut water in the microwave for 90 seconds and carefully add it to the mixture. Stir it all up, using the spoon, until a dough forms. Once it is cool enough, you can turn the mixture out onto a play surface.

To add the optional extract, form the dough into a ball. Use your fist to smash a hole in the middle. Add the extract to the hole. Squeeze, smoosh and mush the dough until it's all mixed up. Now enjoy your yummy-smelling tropical dough.

TIPS

You can substitute regular water for the coconut water if you don't have it, the dough just won't smell as tropical.

Store in an airtight container. Limited shelf life.

Rock Salt Dough

Adult Supervision • Do Not Eat

You've seen rock salt. People use it to whip up homemade ice cream. It can also be used to melt icy roads in the winter. Now you can use it to make an awesome fun dough!

- - - - - - - - - - - - - -

Ingredients

+ 2½ cups (313 g) flour
+ 1¼ cups (341 g) rock salt (ice cream salt), divided
+ 3 tbsp (45 ml) vegetable oil
+ 1 packet of your favorite powdered drink mix (colored is optional)
+ ¾ cup (180 ml) very hot water

Equipment

+ Large bowl
+ Spoon

Mix the flour, 1 cup (273 g) of the rock salt, the vegetable oil and the drink mix in a large bowl. Have an adult help you add the very hot water to the bowl. Mix it up with a spoon until it forms a dough.

When it is cool enough to touch, turn it onto your play surface. Work it with your hands until you get a squishy ball. If it is too dry, add more water. If it is too wet, add more flour. Roll the completed dough in the rest of the rock salt. You will end up with a textured glob of fun to shape, mold, create and imagine.

Kool-Aid®
Playdough

Adult Supervision • Do Not Eat

Grape, cherry, orange, maybe lime? What is your favorite Kool-Aid® flavor? Now you can make your favorite flavors into a fabulous and fun playtime dough. It smells scrumptious, and is a blast to play with!

- - - - - - - - - - - - -

Ingredients

+ 1 cup (125 g) flour, plus a small handful
+ 1¼ cups (341 g) salt
+ 1 tsp cream of tartar
+ 1 tbsp (15 ml) vegetable oil
+ 2 Kool-Aid® packets
+ ¾ cup (180 ml) water

Equipment

+ Microwave-safe bowl
+ Heat-resistant spatula

Dump the flour, salt, cream of tartar, vegetable oil, Kool-Aid® packets and water into a bowl. Mix it all up until it's good and combined. With an adult's help, place the bowl into the microwave and heat it for 60 seconds. Be careful! It will be very hot! Have the adult stir up the mixture, making sure to scrape down the sides of the bowl. Let it sit for a minute to set. Add a small handful of flour to your play surface. Dump the dough onto it, and knead it until it is good and elastic. Smell the fruity goodness!

Color-Surprise Dough

Adult Supervision • Do Not Eat

This dough is fun to make for parties. The dry ingredients are mixed and put into baggies ahead of time. When you are ready to play, add the wet ingredients and, surprise! Magical colored-dough time!

- - - - - - - - - - - - - -

Ingredients

For each Baggie

+ Dry watercolor paints
+ 1 cup (125 g) flour, divided in half
+ ¼ cup (68 g) salt
+ 2 tbsp (20 g) cream of tartar

For Later

+ 4 tsp (20 ml) vegetable oil, divided
+ 1⅓ cups (320 ml) hot water, divided into ⅓ cup (80 ml) portions

Equipment

+ Bowl
+ 4 resealable sandwich bags
+ 4 cups or mugs

First, take your dry watercolor paints, crush them up individually and separate them by color. Mix together ½ cup (63 g) of flour with the salt and cream of tartar in a bowl. Open the sandwich bags, placing each bag in a cup or mug to keep it open. Carefully dump ¼ cup (32 g) of the dry mixture in each bag. Add about half of one of your crushed dry watercolor paints to the middle, being careful not to mix it in. Top with the reserved ½ cup (63 g) of flour, dividing it evenly among the 4 cups. Seal the bag, carefully squeezing the air out of the bag.

When ready to use, have an adult help you. Add 1 teaspoon of oil to each bag. Squish it around with your hands. Have an adult add ⅓ cup (80 ml) of hot water to each bag, and squish it around. By this time, you should see your dough color! When it is cool enough, dump it on a play surface. Knead, squish and squash it together with your hands. Add more flour if it's too wet. Add more water if it's too dry. Have fun!

TIP

These can be made ahead for "Mom, I'm bored" moments.

Washable Soap Playdough

Adult Supervision • Do Not Eat

Want to make that adult in your life smile? Try this Washable Soap Playdough. You get all the ooey gooey fun, but it's going to keep your hands super easy to wash when it's time to clean up.

- - - - - - - - - - - - - -

Ingredients

+ 3½ cups (438 g) flour
+ 1½ cups (410 g) salt
+ 2 tbsp (20 g) cream of tartar
+ 2 tbsp (30 ml) olive oil
+ 2 cups (480 ml) water
+ 1 cup (240 ml) of your favorite-smelling hand soap or shower gel
+ 5 drops each of 4 or 5 different food colorings

Equipment

+ Bowl
+ Spoon
+ Large saucepan

Mix the flour, salt and cream of tartar in a bowl. With an adult's help, place a saucepan on the stove on medium-low heat. Combine the oil, water and soap or shower gel in the saucepan. Stir it up. Heat until it steams, but not until it boils. Take the saucepan off the burner and turn the burner off. Add your dry ingredients to the saucepan. Mix it all up with a spoon. It will be sticky, but keep stirring.

Once it has cooled down, transfer the dough from the saucepan to a clean surface. Knead and squish it with your hands until it is your desired consistency. Squish it into about 4 or 5 pieces. Roll the pieces into balls. Make a dimple in the top of each of your dough balls using your fist. For each dimple, drop in about 5 drops of a food coloring. Knead each ball until the color is all mixed in. Now you can play with one color of dough alone, or you can mix them to create a rainbow of colors!

TIPS

If the dough is too sticky, add more flour. If it is too thick, add more soap or shower gel.

Store in an airtight container.

Dino-Dig Playdough

Adult Supervision • Do Not Eat

Greetings, junior paleontologists. Welcome to a hands-on adventure with "buried fossils." This dough is so easy and fun to make, and it will keep you busy for a Jurassic period (maybe not quite that long)!

Ingredients

+ 2 cups (480 ml) water
+ 1½ cups (187 g) flour
+ 1 packet hot chocolate mix
+ 1 cup (273 g) salt
+ 2 tbsp (30 ml) vegetable oil
+ ⅓ cup (37 g) ground flax seed
+ ⅓ cup (28 g) coffee grounds
+ Plastic dinosaur toys or bones

Equipment

+ Saucepan
+ Spoon
+ Wax paper
+ Craft stick

Over low heat in a saucepan, mix the water, flour, hot chocolate mix, salt and oil together and stir until the dough is formed. Let your dough cool and pull it out of the pan onto wax paper. Knead the dough together until it is fully mixed. Add in the ground flax seed and coffee grounds. This helps give it that "dirt" look! Then add in your dinosaur toys or bones. Bury them in and then "excavate" them using your hands or a craft stick. Have fun burying your dinosaur bones and excavating them over and over again like a real paleontologist!

*See photo insert page 12.

TIPS

If your dough is too oily, just add in some extra flour.

Store in an airtight container. Refresh with water.

Edible Playdough

Adult Supervision • Edible

Playing with playdough is one of our favorite activities. With this activity, I've figured out a way to get my kids to enjoy playdough and make our dinner at the same time! The secret is homemade pasta noodles. Egg-based pasta dough is perfect for molding and can be colored red or green with beet or spinach juice. The kids play while the dough is transformed into dinner.

- - - - - - - - - - - - -

Materials
(to make 3½ cups [about 400 g] playdough)

+ 3 cups (375 g) all-purpose flour
+ ½ tsp salt
+ 1 egg
+ ¼ cup (60 g) sour cream
+ ⅓ cup (80 ml) milk (see Tip)
+ 2 to 3 tbsp (30 to 45 ml) olive oil
+ Beet or spinach juice to dye the dough (optional; see Tip)

Equipment

+ Large mixing bowl
+ Strong wooden or metal spoon

To make the dough: In a bowl, mix the dry ingredients together well with your hands or a strong wooden or metal spoon. Add the egg, sour cream, milk and oil. Add the juice, if using. The dough will be incredibly stiff. Cover it and put it in the fridge for a few hours. I usually make the dough in advance and store it in an airtight container in the refrigerator.

After the dough has "sat" for a few hours, it becomes more elastic and less stiff. Knead and play with the dough. The more your dough is played with, the better your noodles will become!

Form noodles by making dozens and dozens of "little worms." This is my kids' favorite part. If you enjoy a variety of noodle shapes, consider making small balls of dough and then flattening them. Those are tasty when they become dumplings. You can also roll out the dough into a sheet and cut the noodles into thin strips.

After your kids have had fun creating worms and a variety of noodle shapes, bring a pot of water to a boil. Add some sea salt and the noodles to the water and boil until they are fully cooked. It usually takes 20 to 30 minutes, but if your noodles are thinner than ours your time could be shorter.

Modifications for Younger Kids

If children struggle making long worms with the dough, consider giving them a clean pair of safety or play scissors. They can cut up tiny bits of the dough into their own version of pastini!

Modifications for Older Kids

Older kids (under supervision) can use tongs to lift the noodles out of the water, being careful not to burn themselves. This is a great opportunity to practice motor skills as the noodles can be very slippery. Kids can also play chef by creating a sauce for the family's meal.

TIP
The amount of juice depends on how dark you want your noodles to be. We add roughly 2 tablespoons (30 ml) of juice dye to a cup of dough, but if your kids enjoy the taste of spinach you can add even more! You can replace the milk with the vegetable juice if you prefer.

(four)

OTHER MOLDABLES

It's not exactly a smooth dough, and it's not exactly a glossy slime. Mix science with play, and an occasional touch of sparkle, and you get these crazy concoctions of awesomeness. Who knew such simple ingredients could come together to make such an incredible playtime delight?

Use dish soap to make Dish Soap Silly Putty (page 96) or you can even go to the moon (page 91). It doesn't matter if you're letting Kinetic Sand (page 90) slip slowly through your hands or using clay to make Air-Dry Clay (page 103), this chapter is nothing but fun!

Kinetic Sand

Adult Supervision • Do Not Eat

Think of sitting at the beach and making sand castles. Sand is so fun. Make it a dough, and your sand turns into over-the-top amazingness! This sand makes the best sand castles and anything else your imagination can squish together.

▬ ▬ ▬ ▬ ▬ ▬ ▬ ▬ ▬ ▬ ▬ ▬ ▬

Ingredients

+ 2 cups (724 g) fine play sand (you can find this at a craft or hardware store)
+ 1 tbsp (10 g) cornstarch
+ 2 tsp (10 ml) dish soap
+ ½ tsp coconut oil
+ 3 drops of your favorite food coloring
+ ¼ cup (60 ml) water (you will probably not use it all)

Equipment

+ Large bowl

Dump the sand into the bowl. Add the cornstarch, dish soap, coconut oil and the food coloring if you desire. Squish it around with your hands. Add just enough water so it is not too hard. It should be firm, but moldable. Congratulations! You just made your very own kinetic sand!

*See photo insert page 13.

Crunchy Cloud Dough

Adult Supervision • Do Not Eat

We've all spent a lazy day staring up at the clouds, finding different shapes and thinking about what it would be like to actually touch them. Well, now you can! So stop daydreaming, and let's make some superfun, supermoldable Crunchy Cloud Dough!

▬ ▬ ▬ ▬ ▬ ▬ ▬ ▬ ▬ ▬ ▬ ▬ ▬

Ingredients

+ 4 cups (500 g) all-purpose flour
+ ½ cup (120 ml) vegetable oil
+ 1 tbsp (15 g) powdered food coloring (or food coloring that is oil-based)
+ 2 cups (96 g) mini Styrofoam balls (also known as faux snow)

Equipment

+ Large bowl
+ Plastic cup
+ Spoon or craft stick
+ Large tub
+ Toys and cookie cutters (optional)

Pour the all-purpose flour into the large bowl and set aside. Mix the vegetable oil and food coloring together in the plastic cup, making sure the powder totally dissolves into the oil. Slowly pour the colored oil mixture into the all-purpose flour and mix it all together until the flour is colored evenly. Now, pour the Styrofoam balls into the bowl and use your hands to mix it all together. Move your dough over to a big tub and throw some cookie cutters and toys in the mix for all sorts of fun!

*See photo insert page 13.

Moon Dough

Adult Supervision • Do Not Eat

Create supersoft mounds of billowy fluff. This dough is like no other. Watch out. This dough is supermessy, but it is a breeze to clean up!

- - - - - - - - - - - - -

Ingredients

+ 4 cups (500 g) flour or baby powder
+ ½ cup (120 ml) baby oil
+ 2 tbsp (30 ml) baby lotion

Equipment

+ Plastic craft bin

Pour the flour or baby powder into the plastic craft bin. Drizzle the baby oil on top of the flour. Add the baby lotion. Squish and squeeze it together with your hands. It will be soft and moldable. That's it!

Cold Porcelain Clay

Adult Supervision • Do Not Eat

This clay has been used by artists to make sculptures. You can do the same. Whip up a batch of this clay and build your masterpiece.

- - - - - - - - - - - - -

Ingredients

+ 1 cup (160 g) cornstarch
+ 1 (4-oz [118-ml]) bottle white school glue
+ 2 tbsp (30 ml) lemon juice
+ 2 tbsp (30 ml) baby oil
+ Handful of flour
+ Hand lotion (just enough to coat your hands)
+ Acrylic paints

Equipment

+ Microwave-safe bowl
+ Spoon
+ Plastic wrap
+ Airtight plastic container

Mix the cornstarch, glue, lemon juice and baby oil slowly in the bowl until they are combined into a paste-like substance. Stir for about 4 or 5 more minutes. You want to make sure you get all the clumps out and it is a smooth liquid. Have an adult help you put the mixture into the microwave. Here is the important part: you are going to microwave it in 15-second intervals, and stir it vigorously for 1 minute in between intervals. It will get thicker and thicker. You want to repeat this step until you get a sticky dough that can be formed into a ball with your spoon. You will still have a good amount sticking to the sides of the bowl. This may take 6 to 9 turns in the microwave.

(continued)

Now, take a handful of flour and shake it over a clean, flat work surface. Rub the lotion on your hands to coat them. When it's cool, take out the sticky blob from the bowl. Place it on your work surface, scraping the sides of the bowl to get all the goo out. Knead this slimy goo until it becomes a dough that is no longer sticky (about 10 minutes).

Here is the waiting part. Wrap it tightly in plastic wrap, and place it in your airtight container. Let it sit for a good 24 hours. When the time is up, you can sculpt this moldable clay. Let your creation air dry until it's completely hard. Once it's dry, you can paint it with acrylic paints.

Frozen Tundra

Adult Supervision • Do Not Eat

Year-round snow? This is just what is needed on a hot summer day or in celebration of a snow day. Frozen Tundra is a cold dough, perfect for making snowballs, snowmen or just chilling.

- - - - - - - - - - - - - - - - -

Ingredients

+ ½ cup (120 ml) unscented lotion
+ ⅔ to 1 cup (75 to 115 g) corn flour (also known as masa)
+ 1 tsp white minty toothpaste
+ 1½ tbsp (26 g) grated white sidewalk chalk (optional)

Equipment

+ Bowl
+ Spoon
+ Cheese grater (optional)
+ Plastic wrap

In a bowl, mix together the lotion and corn flour with the spoon. Stir in the toothpaste to give your mixture a kick of mint. If desired, with the help of an adult, grate in the white sidewalk chalk for a snowy color. Mix it well. The mixture should be a doughy consistency that forms easily into a ball shape. Tightly cover the dough ball in plastic wrap. Place it in the freezer. Take the ball out of the freezer after 45 minutes. Uncover it, and throw the plastic wrap away. There you have it! Cold snow.

TIPS

Play until the "snow" isn't cold anymore. You can always place it back in the freezer to recharge the cold.

Substitute colored sidewalk chalk to make your tundra more vibrant.

Fake Snow

Do Not Eat

Snow is cold, melts and appears only during certain times of the year. Not with this fake snow! It's uberfun, and you can make it anytime you want. Don't worry if it gets a bit messy. This snow is easy to sweep or vacuum right up!

- - - - - - - - - - - - - - - - -

Ingredients

+ 1 (8-oz [227-g]) box baking soda
+ 1½ cups (180 g) shaving cream (doesn't have to be exact—eyeball it)
+ 2 drops of your favorite essential oil (optional)

Equipment

+ Plastic tablecloth
+ Plastic craft tub

Cover your work area with a plastic tablecloth. Dump the entire box of baking soda into the craft tub. Squirt in your shaving cream. Mix all that up with your hands for about 30 seconds. Now you can add 2 drops of essential oil if you desire. Keep mixing with those hands. The "snow" will form pretty quickly. Shape it and mold it as desired.

*See photo insert page 13.

TIP
This is the perfect time to make a miniature "snow" man.

Oven Clay

Adult Supervision • Do Not Eat

Do you fancy yourself an artist? This classic clay recipe has been used by many artists. It's easy to make and dries in the oven rather quickly.

- - - - - - - - - - - -

Ingredients

+ 2 cups (250 g) flour
+ 1 cup (273 g) salt
+ 2 tbsp (30 ml) liquid coconut oil
+ ½ to 1 cup (120 to 240 ml) water
+ Acrylic paints

Equipment

+ Bowl
+ Spoon
+ Baking sheet
+ Paintbrush

Add the flour, salt and coconut oil to a bowl and mix well. Add the water a little at a time, stirring until you get a clay consistency (you may not use all the water). Take the clay out and make whatever shape your heart desires.

Preheat the oven to 250°F (121°C). Place your clay shapes on a baking sheet, and have an adult place the sheet in the preheated oven. Bake for 30 minutes to 1 hour. Keep an eye on your creations. You want them to get hard, but not burn (until the edges are slightly brown). The size and thickness of your creations will determine how long they need to bake. If you make them too thick, they will crack.

When they are hard, have an adult take them out of the oven. Let them cool completely. Once they are done, you can paint them with acrylic paints to finish them off.

Emotional Stress-Relieving Sack

Adult Supervision • Do Not Eat

Like the Stress Ball recipe (on the next page), this one is easier to make with two people. It feels totally cool, and keeps its squished shape when you squeeze it. You have to check it out!

- - - - - - - - - - - -

Ingredients

+ 2 (12-in [30-cm]) party balloons
+ ¼ to ½ cup (48 to 96 g) The Best Homemade Playdough (page 72)

Equipment

+ Scissors
+ Permanent marker (optional)

(continued)

Cut the neck off of one of the balloons. Have a friend open up this balloon as wide as they can. Fill this balloon with some of The Best Homemade Playdough. Have your friend open up the second balloon as wide as they can. Fit it over the first balloon, open end first. Tie off the second balloon so it is secure. If you desire, draw your current emotion (happy, sad, angry or excited) on the sealed balloon. Squeeze and watch the stress fade away!

*See photo insert page 13.

> ### TIP
> Glue on feathers for hair, googly eyes or buttons for a superspecial squeeze ball.

Stress Ball

Adult Supervision • Do Not Eat

First of all, this is a two-person job, so grab a friend. Double the recipe, and make one for each of you! You both can be squeezing your way to bliss in mere minutes.

- - - - - - - - - - - - - -

Ingredients

+ 3 colorful balloons
+ ½ cup (63 g) flour or ½ cup (181 g) play sand
+ White or clear school glue

Equipment

+ Funnel
+ 1 empty water or soda bottle
+ Wooden craft stick (or you can use a dull pencil)
+ Scissors

Lay your balloons out in front of you. Blow one of the balloons up two or three times, but then let the air out each time. This will stretch out the balloon and make it easier to fill.

Next, get your funnel. Use it to pour the flour or play sand into the empty bottle. Attach the neck of the stretched-out balloon onto the opening of the bottle. Turn the bottle upside down, and pour the flour or sand into the balloon. You may not have to use all of it. This is okay. Just fill the balloon up to its neck.

Carefully take the balloon off the bottle. Use the wooden craft stick to make sure the flour or sand is all packed down into the balloon. The more full it is, the stiffer a stress ball you will have. Carefully cut the neck off the balloon. Then cut the neck off the second balloon. Have a friend stretch open the second balloon as wide as they can get it. Fit it over the open end of the balloon filled with flour or sand. Then cut the neck of the third balloon. Have a friend stretch open the third balloon as wide as they can. Put it over the cut end of your balloon ball. Take your glue and run it along the inside opening of the third balloon. Use just a tiny bit of glue. This will keep the balloon from slipping. Now you have a stress ball you can squish around in your hand!

Dish Soap Silly Putty

Adult Supervision • Do Not Eat

What an easy craft to make when you are in need of some slimy, gooey fun! Grab these two ingredients and go for it. You'll whip this up in no time.

- - - - - - - - - - - -

Ingredients

+ ¼ cup (60 ml) dish soap
+ ½ cup (80 g) cornstarch

Equipment

+ Bowl
+ Spoon

Combine the dish soap and cornstarch in a bowl using the spoon. When the mixture starts to pull away from the bowl, use your hands to knead and squish it up. If it's too dry, add more soap. If it's too wet, add more cornstarch. That's it! Now you have Dish Soap Silly Putty.

TIPS

Add a few drops of food coloring to give the putty a zing of color.

Add a few drops of essential oil to make the putty smell scrumptious.

Store in an airtight container.

Edible Putty

Edible

It's not a meal, but it's certainly fun to nibble on while you play. It's hard to believe that just three ingredients can be so fun, but check it out! You can squeeze and squish this putty, but still manage to sneak a bite while you create.

- - - - - - - - - - - -

Ingredients

+ 2 (3-oz [85-g]) packets flavored gelatin
+ ¾ cup (120 g) cornstarch
+ ¼ cup (60 ml) water

Equipment

+ Bowl
+ Spoon

Add the gelatin and cornstarch to the bowl. Mix this up with a spoon. Add a teaspoon of water at a time, stirring continuously. Add just enough water to make the dough pull away from the sides of the bowl. Now you can play with it using your hands. So simple!

TIPS

Store in an airtight container.
Limited shelf life.

Fishnet Squish Ball

Adult Supervision • Do Not Eat

This is literally amazeballs. It is a squishy ball that changes its bubbly shape when you squeeze it. Then bubbles of rubbery slime poof out between the netting. You can do it!

- - - - - - - - - - - -

Ingredients
+ 1 batch of Laundry Soap Slime (page 62)
+ 1 disposable water bottle
+ 1 balloon
+ 1 pair fishnet stockings (you can find this in the hosiery aisle of most stores)

Equipment
+ Scissors
+ Chopstick or dull pencil

Make your Laundry Soap Slime. With an adult's help, cut the water bottle in half using the scissors. Be careful. It may be sharp on the cut edge. Recycle the bottom of the bottle. Fit the opening of the balloon over the mouthpiece of the bottle so it resembles a funnel. Put about ½ cup (120 ml) of the slime into the open water bottle. Shove the slime into the balloon using the chopstick or pencil. You should fill the balloon up to its neck with slime.

Take the balloon off the water bottle. Tie the balloon closed. Push the balloon all the way down into the foot of the fishnet stocking. It should be snug. Cut the fishnet stocking, leaving room to tie it. Tie the fishnet stocking to close it. Now, squish your Fishnet Squish Ball. Watch it bubble out between the holes of the fishnet stocking. Pretty cool, huh?!

Yogurt Putty

Do Not Eat

Yogurt and putty. Definitely two words you don't often see together. Pick your favorite flavor of yogurt and spend some quality time playing.

- - - - - - - - - - - -

Ingredients
+ 1 cup (235 g) smooth yogurt (no fruit chunks)
+ Food coloring (optional)
+ 2 cups (320 g) cornstarch

Equipment
+ Bowl
+ Spoon

Dump the yogurt into a bowl. If you want color, add a few drops of food coloring to the yogurt and mix well. Stir in the cornstarch about a tablespoon (10 g) at a time. Stir each time you add cornstarch. You want the mixture to start to pull away from the sides of the bowl when you stir it. Now, get in there with your hands! Knead and stretch this cool mixture until it's not sticky anymore.

> **TIP**
> This putty does NOT store. Throw it away when you're done, and make a new batch the next time you want to play.

Forever Bubbles

Adult Supervision • Do Not Eat

Everyone loves bubbles. They make people cheer and giggle with glee as they dance and float in the air. They are even better when they are difficult to pop! Adding two ingredients to your bubble solution turns into infinite soapy fun.

— — — — — — — — — — — — —

Ingredients

+ 1 cup (240 ml) dish soap
+ 1 cup (240 ml) light corn syrup
+ ¼ cup (60 ml) bubble solution

Equipment

+ Bowl
+ Spoon
+ Bubble wand

Mix the dish soap, corn syrup and bubble solution in a bowl with a spoon. Use the bubble wand to blow bubbles. That's it!

*See photo insert page 14.

TIP

Use different water-safe toys to experiment with blowing different bubbles.

Kool-Aid® Foam

Adult Supervision • Do Not Eat

Watch it grow and change its frothy shape as you create this supercool foam. Then bury your hands in it. Try to squeeze it. Make tunnels in it. Play until it loses its foamy shape.

— — — — — — — — — — — — —

Ingredients

+ ½ cup (120 ml) water
+ 2 tbsp (30 ml) dish soap
+ 2 Kool-Aid® packets

Equipment

+ Large bowl
+ Spoon
+ Electric mixer (handheld is okay)
+ Plastic craft tub

Combine the water, dish soap and Kool-Aid® packets in a large bowl. Stir with a spoon until it's evenly mixed. Get out your mixer and, with an adult's help, start whipping up the mixture on medium speed. The more you whip it, the bigger the foam will get. When you are done, dump the mixture into your craft tub. Have fun!

TIPS

Use plastic, water-safe toys to play in the foam.

When the foam starts to shrink, you can ask an adult to help you regrow the bubbles by using the electric mixer again.

Squishy Fuzz Ball

Adult Supervision • Do Not Eat

Little fuzzy balls suspended in jelly-like goo. This just sounds superincredible. It's even more wild when you figure out you can hold this glob in your hands. Your friends are about to be jealous!

- - - - - - - - - - - - -

Ingredients

+ Water (about ½ cup [120 ml], depending on size of water bottle)
+ Clear school glue (about ½ cup [120 ml], depending on size of water bottle)
+ ¼ cup (12 g) fuzz balls
+ Transparent latex balloon

Equipment

+ Empty disposable water bottle

Get your empty water bottle. Fill it about halfway with water and halfway with glue, leaving some room at the top. After the glue has settled, drop in the fuzz balls.

Blow up the transparent balloon about halfway. Twist the neck of it a couple times so the air does not escape, but do not tie it yet. Fit the open end of the balloon on the open mouth of the bottle. Turn the bottle upside down. Dump the contents of the water bottle into the balloon. Carefully separate the balloon and the bottle. Don't let the liquid come out of the balloon! Tie the balloon. Now you have a squirmy, wormy, colorful, clear balloon that you can play with! Don't bounce this ball. It will pop!

TIP

For extra sparkle, add 2 tablespoons (48 g) of your favorite glitter to the water bottle before you transfer the contents into the balloon.

Fizzy Dough

Adult Supervision • Do Not Eat

It's dough. That erupts. You read that right! First you play with your cool homemade dough, then you transform it into erupting fizz!

- - - - - - - - - - - - -

Ingredients

+ 1 cup (120 g) flour
+ 1 (8-oz [227-g]) box baking soda
+ ¼ cup (60 ml) liquid coconut oil
+ ¼ cup (60 ml) white vinegar

Equipment

+ Plastic craft tub
+ Spoon

Mix together the flour, baking soda and coconut oil in your plastic tub, using the spoon. You can play with this like Moon Dough (page 91) until you want to move on to the next step. When you are ready for a change, slowly pour the vinegar over the mixture. Watch it fizz, fizz, fizz. Feel the different texture once the vinegar reacts to the baking soda.

TIP

Try different utensils to pour the vinegar. Try an eye dropper, spoon, baby syringe or whatever your imagination can think of. The more vinegar you drop at one time, the more foam you will create.

Oobleck

Adult Supervision • Do Not Eat

Is it a solid? Is it a liquid? Yes and yes. This is just about the coolest science-experiment-turned-craft ever! Move it, and it's solid. Stop moving it, and it's a liquid.

Ingredients

+ 1 cup (160 g) cornstarch
+ ⅓ cup (80 ml) water
+ 2½ tbsp (38 ml) thick liquid laundry detergent (Tide® works well)
+ 3 drops food coloring

Equipment

+ Bowl
+ Spoon

Mix the cornstarch, water, laundry detergent and food coloring in the bowl using the spoon. The mixture will get very hard to stir. At this point, get your hands in there. Try to squish the mixture between your fingers. You know it has turned into Oobleck when you can squeeze it into a solid ball shape in your hands, but when you release pressure, the mixture falls like a liquid back into the bowl. This is so cool to make!

Lemon Oobleck

Adult Supervision • Do Not Eat

Why do you think these ingredients together make Oobleck? The acid in the lemons is what helps activate this liquid . . . or solid . . . or liquid gooey substance. You become a scientist with a lemon-smelling lab.

Ingredients

+ 1 cup (160 g) cornstarch
+ 2 good-size lemons
+ 1½ cups (360 ml) water

Equipment

+ Bowl
+ Juicer
+ Spoon

Dump the cornstarch into a bowl. Using a juicer, add the juice of the 2 lemons into the bowl, and stir, stir, stir. Add the water a little bit at a time. Stir it up really well with the spoon each time you add water. It is done when you have a solid substance if you try to stir it, but a thick liquid if you leave it alone. How cool is that? You just made Lemon Oobleck using all-natural kitchen ingredients!

TIP
Add 4 drops of yellow food coloring if you want your Oobleck to have a more lemony color.

Magic Mud

Adult Supervision • Do Not Eat

Let's make potato Magic Mud! Wait. Stop. Does that say potatoes? Yes! Potatoes have supercool properties that can be transformed into magic mud! It is much like Oobleck (page 99), but it's purely made with potatoes and water.

- - - - - - - - - - -

Ingredients

+ 1 (5-lb [2.25-kg]) bag baking potatoes
+ 2 qt (2 L) hot water (or enough to cover the potatoes)
+ 2 cups (480 ml) room-temperature water

Equipment

+ Food processor or food chopper (optional)
+ 2 very large bowls
+ Spoon
+ Strainer
+ Large jar that seals (a large Mason jar will work)

Wash the potatoes under cold water until clean. Dice the cleaned potatoes. Use the food processor or food chopper with an adult's help to make the job easier. Put the diced potatoes into one of the bowls. Add the hot water, just enough to cover the diced potatoes. Stir continuously for 5 minutes. You will notice the water turn reddish-brown. This is normal. Strain the potato water into the second bowl. Let this sit for about 15 minutes. After a few moments you will see a cream-colored mixture at the bottom of the bowl. It will grow larger over the 15 minutes.

Now, pour the water out. Don't worry, the white mixture will stay in the bottom of the bowl. You now need to clean this mixture. Pour the room-temperature water in with the white residue. Mix this with a spoon until it is combined. Pour the mixture into the jar, and seal the jar. Shake the jar for 3 minutes, and then let the jar sit for another 15 minutes. Quickly pour the water out, and you will be left with a clean, white substance. Pour this substance into a bowl. You now have your magic mud. Try to squish it and move it around. It acts much like Oobleck. Do you know why this is? It acts much like Oobleck in that it's both a liquid and a solid gooey mixture!

TIPS

Use the diced potatoes that are left over to make soup, hash browns, latkes or something yummy.

Add a few drops of food coloring for a pop of color.

Bouncy Ball

Adult Supervision • Do Not Eat

Everyone loves a good bouncy ball. But did you ever think you could make one at home? How high can you bounce your own bouncy ball?

- - - - - - - - - - -

Ingredients

+ 1 tbsp (15 ml) white school glue
+ 3 drops food coloring
+ 2 tbsp (30 ml) warm water
+ ½ tsp borax
+ ½ tbsp (5 g) cornstarch

Equipment

+ 2 disposable bowls
+ 2 wooden craft sticks

Pour the school glue into a disposable bowl. Using a wooden craft stick, mix the food coloring into the glue until it is an even color. In the second bowl, mix the water and borax together using the second wooden craft stick. Combine the mixture until the borax is completely dissolved. Add the cornstarch and a ½ teaspoon of the borax solution to the glue mixture. Let it stand for 20 seconds.

Now, stir the mixture together with a wooden craft stick until it becomes very hard to stir. Take half of the mixture out. Roll it around in your hands until a ball forms. The longer you roll it around in your hands, the more solid it will become. You want it to become as solid as a bouncy ball. When you are done, try to bounce it. Voila! You have your bouncy ball.

*See photo insert page 14.

TIP

The remaining half of the mixture can be used to make a Fishnet Squish Ball (page 96) or Squishy Fuzz Ball (page 98).

Glowing Magic Mud

As if Magic Mud (page 100) wasn't cool enough, you can make it glow! There are few things as fun as watching, and playing with, a glowy goo. This one is ultracool.

- - - - - - - - - - - - -

Ingredients
+ 1 batch of Magic Mud (page 100)
+ 2 tbsp (30 ml) tonic water

Equipment
+ Bowl
+ Spoon
+ Black light

Get your Magic Mud, and put it in a safe place. Make sure it's uncovered in a bowl. Leave it alone for about 2 days. It will turn into a crumbly, dry, white powder.

Now, take this dry powder and add your tonic water, a little at a time. Stir it up really well with your spoon each time you add the water. It will get really stiff and hard to stir. You will get a workout on your patience here. It might take some time and lots of stirring. Once it resembles the Magic Mud that you made the first time, you are ready. Turn on your black light, and watch the goo glow while you play with it. Look at your hands! They will be glowing too!

TIPS

You have to use tonic water. Do not substitute a different water.

Why does the goo glow? Tonic water contains quinine. Quinine glows under a black light! Look at the bottle of remaining tonic water. There should be a glowing liquid in the bottle. Supercool!

Edible Fairy Dough

Adult Supervision • Edible

Invoke the powers of the bee with this dough. Break out that honey, and make this glittery work of edible goodness. It wouldn't be fairy dough without the glitter! Make sure to hit it with that special sparkle before you're done.

■ ─ ■ ─ ■ ─ ■ ─ ■ ─ ■ ─ ■ ─ ■

Ingredients

+ Cooking spray
+ ¼ cup (60 ml) honey
+ ¾ cup (120 g) cornstarch
+ 1 tbsp (15 ml) liquid coconut oil
+ 4 drops food coloring
+ 2 tbsp (48 g) edible food glitter

Equipment

+ ¼-cup (60-ml) measuring cup
+ Bowl
+ Spoon

Coat the inside of the measuring cup generously with cooking spray. Fill the measuring cup with honey, and dump it into the bowl. Using the spoon, add about 1 tablespoon (10 g) at a time of the cornstarch to the honey and stir the mixture. Keep adding the cornstarch, completely mixing it in before you add more. You will need to add a bit of coconut oil once in a while to make sure the mixture isn't too sticky. When it gets too hard to incorporate the cornstarch with the spoon, coat your hands with the cooking spray and squish the mixture together with your hands.

Add the food coloring and squish together. Add the edible food glitter, and squish together until the dough is completely mixed up. Now you can play with this fairy dough. Stretch it, knead it and roll it into a ball. Don't forget that it is completely edible. If you want to sneak a nibble here and there, go for it!

Floam

Adult Supervision • Do Not Eat

You have certainly held this substance before. Did you ever think, in your most fantastical dreams, that you'd be able to re-create it at home? Yes, you can!

■ ─ ■ ─ ■ ─ ■ ─ ■ ─ ■ ─ ■ ─ ■

Ingredients

+ 2½ tsp (23 g) borax
+ ¾ cup (180 ml) hot (not boiling) water, divided
+ 1 (5-oz [147-ml]) bottle clear school glue
+ ½ cup (24 g) foam balls (bean-bag filler)

Equipment

+ 2 bowls
+ Spoon

Ask an adult to help you mix the borax with ⅓ cup (80 ml) of hot water in a bowl until completely dissolved. Combine the remaining hot water and the glue in a second bowl. Slowly stir in the borax water. If the mixture is too wet, add a little more borax. If it is too dry, add more water. Stir continuously while you add the foam balls. When it gets too hard to stir with a spoon, knead it together with your hands. You should now have Floam! What shapes can you create?

*See photo insert page 14.

TIPS

Add 3 drops of food coloring to the mixture before you add the foam balls. This will give it a pretty hint of color.

Store in an airtight container.

Coconut Oil Shaky Dough

Adult Supervision • Do Not Eat

What a supereasy dough! It makes cleanup a breeze. Just some shakes and rolls of the bag, and it magically appears.

- - - - - - - - - - - - - - - -

Ingredients

+ ⅓ cup (80 g) coconut oil
+ ½ small bottle of food coloring (optional)
+ 1½ cups (186 g) flour

Equipment

+ Microwave-safe container
+ 1 (1-gal [3.75-L]) resealable plastic bag

With an adult's help, warm up your coconut oil in the microwave for about 30 seconds to melt it. If you like, add food coloring to the oil. Put your flour in the resealable plastic bag. Pour the oil into the bag and shake and knead the dough until it's mixed. Now you have light, fluffy, awesomely easy dough!

Air-Dry Clay

Adult Supervision • Do Not Eat

Another fun way to make a hardened sculpture! Let that budding artist inside you out! Let your imagination run wild while squishing and shaping this dough. Top your masterpiece off with a splash of color!

- - - - - - - - - - - - - - - -

Ingredients

+ ½ cup (80 g) cornstarch, plus 1 handful
+ ½ cup (120 ml) white school glue
+ 1 tbsp (15 ml) baby oil
+ 1 tbsp (15 ml) white vinegar
+ Acrylic paints

Equipment

+ Bowl
+ Spoon
+ Paintbrush

Mix the cornstarch, glue, baby oil and vinegar in a bowl with a spoon. You will have a supersticky dough. Sprinkle a handful of cornstarch down on your flat, clean working surface. Take out your dough mixture and place it over the cornstarch. With a little cornstarch covering your hands to prevent sticking, roll and knead your mixture into the cornstarch on the flat surface. You are done when you have a smooth dough. Now you can make it into fun shapes. Let it air dry for about 48 hours. Then get out your acrylic paints and make it your own masterpiece.

*See photo insert page 14.

> ## TIP
> You can store unused dough in a resealable plastic bag with a teaspoon of baby oil.

Sand Clay

Do Not Eat

This clay is great for making memory items. Squish your footprint in the dough, and it will look like you just walked across the sand at the beach. Finish it off with some cool decorations or color!

-- -- -- -- -- -- -- -- -- --

Ingredients

+ 2½ cups (905 g) play sand (you can find this at a craft or hardware store)
+ 2 cups (250 g) flour
+ 1¾ cups (478 g) salt
+ 1½ cups (360 ml) warm water

Equipment

+ Plastic craft tub
+ Spoon

Dump the play sand, flour and salt into the craft tub. Mix the water in with the spoon until combined. Now comes the fun part. Get your hands in there. Knead and squish it until a dough forms. Add more sand if it is too wet. Add more water if it is too dry. The dough can be split into 5 balls. Each one can be made into the creation you desire.

When your creations are done, let them air dry, or you can place them on a cookie sheet in a 250°F (121°C) oven for 3 to 5 hours, depending on the thickness of the creations.

> ### TIPS
> This is a great dough to use for children's hand- and footprints. Just roll each ball to about a ½-inch (1.3-cm) thickness, and have the child place their hand or foot in the dough. Dry as directed.

Play Putty

Adult Supervision • Do Not Eat

Looking for a superquick putty to play with? You found it! Three items squeezed, rolled and mixed in a bag. It can't get much easier than that.

-- -- -- -- -- -- -- -- -- --

Ingredients

+ ¾ cup (180 ml) liquid starch
+ ½ cup (120 ml) white school glue
+ ¼ cup (60 ml) tempera paint

Equipment

+ 1 (1-gal [3.75-L]) resealable plastic bag

Place the starch, glue and paint into the resealable plastic bag. Seal the bag completely. Knead, mix and roll the bag around until all the ingredients are mixed. Presto! You have a fun play putty that is supereasy to make, and even more fun to play with!

> ### TIP
> Store in an airtight container.

Clean Mud

Adult Supervision • Do Not Eat

Let's face it, mud is a mess. Only the coolest of the cool kids can make mud that isn't dirty at all! In fact, it's made with soap. It's squeaky-clean, muddy fun.

- - - - - - - - - - - -

Ingredients

+ 1 roll toilet paper
+ 1 bar soap (any kind will do)
+ 1 tbsp (27 g) borax (this is completely optional but will make your mud last longer)
+ 4 drops food coloring (optional)
+ 2 to 3 cups (480 to 720 ml) water

Equipment

+ Bowl
+ Cheese grater
+ Spoon

Unroll your toilet paper and break it into little pieces. Put the pieces in your bowl. With an adult's help, grate your soap on a cheese grater into the bowl. Mix together the soap and toilet paper (and the borax and food coloring, if you like) with about 2 cups (480 ml) of water. Add more water until your mud is a fun consistency! Boom. Done!

*See photo insert page 15.

TIPS

Let the mixture sit overnight to get it extra goopy like mud.

Store in an airtight container.

Soft Mud

Do Not Eat

It's like jumping in puddles on a rainy day, but much cleaner. Break out your toy pots and pans! I feel some wicked cool mud pies coming on.

- - - - - - - - - - - -

Ingredients

+ 2 cups (442 g) baking soda
+ ½ tsp coconut oil
+ ½ cup (120 ml) water

Equipment

+ Bowl

Mix the baking soda, coconut oil and water together in a bowl until the desired consistency is reached. If it is too wet, add more baking soda. If it is too dry, add more water. Bam! That's it!

TIPS

This can be messy, but it is very easy to clean up. Water will make it melt away.

Store in an airtight container. Limited shelf life.

Cereal Clay

Adult Supervision • Edible

Thick like clay. Edible like candy. You simply cannot go wrong with this recipe. Invite your friends over, and everyone can dig into making this cereal clay. Yum!

- - - - - - - - - - - -

Ingredients

+ ¼ cup (58 g) real butter, plus more for coating
+ 1 large (16-oz [453-g]) bag of mini marshmallows
+ 1 regular-size box of your favorite cereal

Equipment

+ Large saucepan
+ Large spoon
+ Plastic craft bin

Have an adult help you melt the butter in the large saucepan on medium heat. Carefully dump in the bag of marshmallows, and stir continuously until melted. This will be very sticky. With an adult's help, take the saucepan off the burner and turn off the burner. Rub butter all over the spoon, but not on the handle. Mix your cereal in, about a ½ cup (100 g) at a time. This will get harder and harder to stir. Just use those muscles and keep stirring.

Once all the cereal is added, have an adult help you drop the mixture into the craft bin. Put a small amount of butter all over the palms of your hands. If the cereal mixture is cool enough, you can smoosh and mush it around with your hands. The best part . . . you can eat it!!

*See photo insert page 15.

TIP
Use colored marshmallows, or add 3 drops of your favorite food coloring!!

Puffy Paint

Do Not Eat

Puffy paint is a mystical substance that adds a dimension to ordinary art. Suddenly you are painting in 3D. The possibilities are endless.

- - - - - - - - - - - -

Ingredients

+ 1 cup (120 g) shaving cream
+ ⅓ cup (80 ml) white school glue
+ A few drops food coloring, each in a different color (red, orange, yellow, green, blue or purple)

Equipment

+ Large bowl
+ Craft stick
+ 2 to 3 small bowls or plastic containers
+ Paintbrush
+ Paper

Mix the shaving cream and glue together in the large bowl using the craft stick. Once combined, separate that mixture into smaller bowls or plastic containers (you can skip this step if you are making it all one color). Add a few drops of food coloring to each container, and stir until combined. Repeat for as many colors as you want to make.

Use the paintbrush to "paint" them on the paper. You want to make sure you use a good amount of the paint so it's nice and puffy. When you're done, let your picture dry completely. It will have a fun squishy texture once it is dry!

TIP
Layer your paint to see a really cool effect.

Homemade Smiley-Emoji Squishy

Do Not Eat

Squishies. The craze is here to stay! Why spend your hard-earned allowance on a store-bought squishy when they are totally easy to make at home? Once you've mastered this smiley emoji, the sky's the limit! What else can you create?

- - - - - - - - - - - -

Ingredients

+ 1 round cosmetic sponge (makeup sponge you can cut in a circle)
+ Yellow, red, black and white fabric paint or Puffy Paint (page 106)

Equipment

+ Plastic table cover
+ Plastic gloves
+ Small paintbrush

Cover your work surface in the plastic table cover. Set everything you need out on this cover. The only paint you want to use is either fabric paint or Puffy Paint. These paints are a bit stretchy when dry, and work better for squishing. Wearing the plastic gloves, drop a big glob of the yellow paint onto the sponge. Work the color all around the sponge using your fingers. Make sure you cover the entire sponge. Let the sponge dry completely. Using the paintbrush and the paint, paint eyes and a smile on the front of the sponge. Let it dry completely. You now have a squishable friend you can take with you. You can also tell everyone that you made it with your own hands!

*See photo insert page 15.

Magic Glitter Bottles

Adult Supervision • Do Not Eat

This ultracool goopy mixture lives in its very own bottle. It is like your own little miniature world of magical floating sparkly goo. It is mesmerizing!

- - - - - - - - - - - -

Ingredients

+ ½ cup (120 ml) warm-to-hot water (roughly)
+ 1 (6-oz [177-ml]) bottle glitter glue
+ 2½ tbsp (60 g) glitter
+ Clear glue to top off bottle
+ Super glue

Equipment

+ 1 (16- or 20-oz [473- or 591-ml]) clean, empty disposable water bottle

Remove any labels or sticky goo from the outside of the bottle. Fill about ¾ of the water bottle with the warm-to-hot water, leaving room for your glitter glue and glitter. Add the bottle of glitter glue and the glitter to your bottle. Put the lid on the bottle, and shake it well to mix the ingredients together. Your bottle should be filled most of the way up. Add clear glue to top off the bottle.

Have an adult super glue the lid onto the water bottle, and let it dry. Once the lid is completely dry, you will have a magic glitter bottle. You can shake up the bottle so it is a mixture of swirly, twirly glitter. Wait about 5 minutes, and that glitter will all fall to the bottom of the bottle. You can then shake and swirl your bottle, starting the awesome glitter show once again.

*See photo insert page 15.

> **TIP**
> Try using different colors of glue and glitter!

(five)

BOREDOM BUSTERS

Boredom is the garden in which play grows. It is a motivation for action and a blank slate for creativity.

Holly's Chapter Pick: I think the Wooden Block Townhouses (page 128) are delightful. There are a million ways to play with them and when not in use they double as a precious room decoration.

Rachel's Chapter Pick: Building Paper Cup Castles (page 115) is one of our kids' favorite things to do. Whenever I want/need the kids to be engaged, it's time to bring out the stack of cups. Your kids will love this activity!

Baggie Maze

Mazes are an adventure on paper. A single pencil line journeys into the unknown. There is a sense of wonder at each crossroad of the possibility of reaching the goal.

Creating a baggie maze is a fun craft that is also great entertainment on the go. It is something that can be dropped into a purse or bag to be used as a quiet-time game.

- - - - - - - - - - - - - -

Materials
(to make one double-sided maze)

+ Scissors
+ Cardboard—upcycled from a cereal box or other rescued recyclable
+ Resealable plastic sandwich bag
+ 4 or 5 drinking straws
+ Glue dots or tape
+ Small marble or other object

Cut the cardboard into a square that snugly fits into the sandwich bag. Clip one of the corners for a "start" and cut a quarter-size (2.5-cm-diameter) circle on another corner for the goal. Snip the straws into smaller pieces and use the glue dots to glue them on the cardboard, creating a maze path. (We used glue dots so we didn't need to wait for glue to dry.) You can also use tape.

The interior of the bag will create "sides" to the maze so the exterior of the cardboard square does not have to be outlined with straws. Place the marble in the maze, seal the bag and, holding the bag flat, tilt it to guide the marble through the maze.

Modifications for Younger Kids
For younger children, monitor them and either glue or tape the top of the bag closed. Also, creating an easier maze will result in less frustration for your child.

Modifications for Older Kids
Have older kids create a double-sided maze. They can then solve both sides of their baggie maze.

> ### TIP
> Social scientists claim that doing mazes helps build brain connections and develop problem-solving skills.

Bird Zip Line

Riding a zip line feels like you are flying. Spread your arms out wide and feel the wind on your face while you glide to the bottom. This craft builds a bird that will fly just like you can, zip line style! Create a string track and add a little kid power combined with gravity.

- - - - - - - - - - - - - -

Materials
(to make one bird/zip line)

+ Sheet of paper—cardstock is best
+ Pencil
+ Scissors
+ Markers/crayons
+ Tape
+ Drinking straw
+ Ball of yarn

To make the bird: Fold a piece of paper in half lengthwise and trace out the profile of a flying bird on one half with the fold at the top. Cut along the pencil lines. Use markers to decorate the bird. Open the bird and tape a straw along the inside fold.

(continued)

To make the zip line: Stretch the yarn between two secure anchor spots where string can be attached. It should be at a height that kids can easily reach. Thread a bird onto each string before tying both ends of it to the anchor spots.

Kids can "throw" the birds down the yarn to make them fly. Multiple zip lines can be set up next to each other for bird races.

Modifications for Younger Kids
Placing the string at kid-size shoulder level will have younger participants running up and down the yarn, holding the bird.

Modifications for Older Kids
Have older kids design a bird that is bottom-heavy and then split the underside of the straw so that the bird can be unattached and reattached from the string without untying the ends. Then challenge older kids to create a zip line course for their bird to fly.

Dry-Erase Doodles

My favorite thing to draw as a child was a sunrise. After a visit to the mountains, I modified my regular pattern to include pointy snowcapped mountains in the background behind the sun. It was years later when someone mentioned to me that there was no possible way for the sun to rise in front of the mountains! It was my own artistic license.

This activity box is a really easy travel or rainy-day activity. There are suggested templates to place in a CD case and transform into an artistic master-piece with dry-erase markers, but the possibilities are endless.

- - - - - - - - - - - - - -

Materials
+ Empty clear CD case
+ A variety of paper pages, photos, maps, etc.
+ Scissors
+ Dry-erase markers

Create a Doodle Board Background
The inside of a CD case is 5½ x 4¾ inches (14 x 12 cm). Create a background for doodling by cutting different templates to size from your paper collection and inserting them into the case.

Ideas for backgrounds
- **Kid photo**—Doodle to add character and fun!
- **Hangman gallows**—Start a game of Hangman by drawing the gallows template. Kids can play over and over.
- **Kid-created maze**—Give kids properly sized paper to draw a maze and then place the maze in another box for someone else to solve.
- **Open sky**—Add a piece of light blue paper to the box for clouds, planes and birds to be doodled.
- **Black box**—Insert a plain piece of paper with just a black box drawn in the middle. Have kids create whatever they can imagine around the box.

The good news is that a CD case will hold multiple templates and they can be kept and stored in the case.

Modifications for Younger Kids
Create a series of letter and number cards that kids can trace.

Modifications for Older Kids
Have older children design the backgrounds of their box within a theme that they love. Try a fashion series of color swatches, dress forms and blank bodies to accessorize.

TIP
Sneak a few unexpected templates in the box when no one is looking for a fun surprise.

Bouncing Balloons

Yo-yos go down and then defy gravity with an unexpected ascent. The rhythmic drop and return require skill both physically and mentally. Making a yo-yo follow your lead and continue its momentum is a challenge for anyone, regardless of age.

While you can't do all the traditional yo-yo tricks with this homemade version, it is a fun way to practice eye-hand coordination. It is created from balloons, playdough and rubber bands, allowing it to mimic the yo-yo action, which is much easier to control.

– – – – – – – – – – – – – –

Materials

+ Colorful balloons
+ Playdough (see page 72), sand or flour
+ Scissors
+ Large rubber band (or multiple bands if small)
+ Masking tape

Fill a balloon with the playdough. If you don't have playdough you can use sand or flour. Then, tie the balloon shut.

Cut some small holes into a second balloon. Carefully stretch the second balloon over the playdough-filled balloon, allowing the color of the lower balloon to peek through the top layer holes.

Tie the rubber band around the knot in the balloon. If your rubber band is not long enough, make a "string" of bands by tying them to each other.

To play, draw an X on the floor with tape and use it as a target. Try to bounce the yo-yo on the object to see how many times you can bounce it.

Modifications for Younger Kids

Skip the rubber bands and game. Let the kids squish the filled yo-yo ball.

Modifications for Older Kids

Set up a series of numbered X's on the floor in a random pattern and instruct the child to work through the numbers in sequence. Each time an incorrect number is hit, the game starts over at the number one.

TIP

Playdough, sand or flour in a balloon mimics the adult "stress ball" and can be a source of calming sensation to kids.

DIY Straw Building Set

We think of this activity as straw doodling, because an ordinary straw can be transformed by the insertion of a pipe cleaner. This simple alteration can create a building set to be used over and over in different and magnificent ways.

– – – – – – – – – – – – – –

Materials

+ Box of (or 3) flexible drinking straws
+ Scissors
+ Pipe cleaners (optional)
+ Tape

(continued)

To put your straws together, pinch one end of a straw and stuff it into the connecting straw. Using the angles of the flexible straws, repeat until you have the desired shape, cutting the straws, if needed. If it is too difficult for your children to stuff the straws together, thread the pipe cleaners through the straws to use as connectors.

Kids can create all sorts of 3-D shapes, buildings and art sculptures by manipulating the straws. In addition to being stuffed together, straw pieces can be attached to each other by twisting the end of the pipe cleaners run through them. Shapes created by straws can be attached to each other with a simple piece of tape for even more possibilities. Creations can be as large as the amount of materials you might have!

Modifications for Younger Kids

For younger participants, use pipe cleaners and straws to create an endless loop for them to play with so they don't have to attach pipe cleaner ends together. They will enjoy bending and shaping their circle into new shapes.

Modifications for Older Kids

Have older kids test out several sizes of straws before creating the full set. Let them test build and determine what size materials they want for their building project and then create the set within those parameters.

*See photo insert page 16.

Fruit Necklace

Accessories are a big hit at our house and this accessory doubles as a snack! The fun starts with your kids making their snack, wearing it, and then eating it. Girls and boys alike will enjoy getting to create and then eat their snack necklace made from stringing fruit onto dental floss.

— — — — — — — — — — — —

Materials

+ Dental floss
+ Large plastic needle
+ 1 cup (145 g) berries and/or cut-up fruit (all should be bite size)

Watch your kids as they thread the dental floss through the needle and add the fruit to their necklace.

Tie the necklace onto your child and enjoy!

Modifications for Younger Kids

Because eye-hand coordination can be challenging for small fingers, using fruit is a great introduction to sewing. Little ones may need help threading the needle.

Modifications for Older Kids

Encourage your older child to create patterns. Or think of other foods besides fruit that they could add to the necklace, such as bagel pieces, pretzels, cereal and so forth.

TIP

This is a great snack activity if you are traveling. Instead of using berries that might stain your car, have your kids create a pretzel necklace. They can make the necklace and then munch on it while traveling on the road.

Greeting Card Puzzles

A window in our living room displays all the Christmas cards we receive each December, attached with a piece of tape. By Christmas, there are rows and rows of cards almost completely obscuring the view. I never know exactly what to do with them once the holiday is over. They are too pretty to throw away, but too many to keep. The same goes for birthday and special-event cards. That is the inspiration behind this activity to recycle cards into puzzles that kids can play with over and over.

- - - - - - - - - - - - - -

Materials

+ Used greeting cards
+ Scissors
+ Glue (optional)

Choose a greeting card that has a large picture on the front or trim a card down to just the image. Make puzzle-like cuts, starting with straight lines perpendicular to the edge for a simple puzzle.

For a more complex puzzle, glue two greeting card images back-to-back that are the same size and then cut the pieces. This will create a double-sided puzzle.

Modifications for Younger Kids

Laminate the card prior to cutting for more durability. Make the puzzle pieces large.

Modifications for Older Kids

You can have your child make the pieces smaller, or store several cards of puzzles together in the same bag. Half the activity will be sorting the various cards to begin the puzzles. You can also have older kids glue a collage of greeting cards onto a large piece of construction paper and then cut the entire collage into puzzle pieces.

TIP

If the greetings within the card were special, cut down the card fold and glue the two pieces together so the image is on the front and the words are on the back, then cut the puzzle as a two-sided challenge.

Grape Structures

This "building set" combines two common kitchen items—grapes and toothpicks. It is surprisingly versatile. You can make simple shapes or build crazy 3-D sculptures and buildings. Or, if lots of toothpicks in one grape is more your speed, then just call it a porcupine.

Spend the afternoon building together and at the end, it doubles as a snack . . . just don't eat the toothpicks!

- - - - - - - - - - - - - -

Materials

+ Grapes—lots of them!
+ Box of toothpicks

Put the grapes in a pile and create geometric shapes by stuffing the toothpicks into the fruit. You can create circle dome houses, A-frame homes, tall towers and bridges. The sky is the limit!

Modifications for Younger Kids

If your child is having a hard time creating structures, try helping him or her make train tracks.

Modifications for Older Kids

Look up photos of some architectural landmarks. See if you can replicate them with the grapes and sticks.

(continued)

Marshmallow Launcher

The story of David and Goliath is the best advertisement for slingshots. The thought of a child with a homemade weapon, doing what an army could not, is empowering. Our kids find twigs shaped like a Y and string it with a rubber band to shoot rocks across the backyard.

Unfortunately, our homemade weapons don't have the precision of David's and often a rock hurls in the wrong direction, creating play panic. This modification of the ancient slingshot is more reliable for firing and uses marshmallows for ammunition.

- - - - - - - - - - - - - - - - - -

Materials

+ Scissors
+ Small disposable plastic cups
+ Balloons—one per cup
+ Bag of marshmallows (large or small is fine)

Start by cutting off the bottom of a plastic cup. This may be challenging if you are using a sturdy plastic version and should be done by adults.

Cut ½ inch (1.3 cm) off the top of the balloon and tie a knot in the end you use for blowing it up.

Spread the balloon over the now open bottom of the cup.

Place a large marshmallow or several mini marshmallows in the cup; pull back the balloon knot and release. Watch the marshmallows fly.

Modifications for Younger Kids
Younger kids need supervision around both balloons and marshmallows, so please use caution. Let them be your launch assistant.

Modifications for Older Kids
Older kids can chart the distance of a marshmallow launch and figure out which size marshmallows work the best for distance travel. Create a target and see which size can be controlled the best to hit the bull's-eye.

Masking Tape Road and Cityscape

A well-crafted pretend city is the perfect vacation. It doesn't cost any money to visit and you can control where you stay, what you eat and the tourist attractions that you see. If you want your city to have the Eiffel Tower, you can make that happen. If you want your city to have a roller coaster that goes through the Town Hall, you can create it. If you want your city to have ice-cream trucks on every corner, it is your call.

This activity uses painter's tape to create that pretend city. The city can start small in the living room and grow in population and square mileage to the kitchen and hall. Because it is painter's tape, city destruction and removal from REAL life is a breeze.

- - - - - - - - - - - - - - - - - -

Materials

+ Wide painter's tape
+ Marker
+ Toy cars and/or action figures

Use the tape to create roads, the shadowlike outlines of buildings and landmarks. Let kids get creative in city design—the couch may make the perfect mall. Think outside the box: let your cityscape crawl up the wall or across the furniture.

Modifications for Younger Kids

Instead of having your children create a full city, have them just create a track for their cars to drive or their dolls to walk on.

Modifications for Older Kids

Play a game of Treasure. Give them a map—have them re-create the "map" on the floor/wall. When they are finished, mark the map with a treasure location. Have children follow the map to get their car or figure to the destination.

TIP

Making a network of roads that your child can see from a "bird's-eye view" is a great way to practice direction commands like "Go right" or "Turn to your left" or "Make a U-turn and go back." Maybe you can create a diorama of your own neighborhood and practice telling directions with street names to help your child if he/she ever gets lost.

Paper Cup Castle

Growing up, I was sure that I was born into the wrong family or that somewhere in my family tree a royal bloodline was being held a secret. It just didn't seem right that I wasn't a true princess. I was born to be a princess who wore a sparkly crown and was in line to rule the land.

Surprisingly, no secrets were revealed and all my princess crown wearing and rule making were banished to the land of make-believe. Thankfully, the land of make-believe can be visited by any undiscovered prince and princess.

This simple activity starts as a package of plastic cups and a few pieces of paper. With some strategic building, it ends as a castle in the land of make-believe.

- - - - - - - - - - - -

Materials
(to make one castle)

+ 5 to 8 sheets of paper
+ 100+ plastic cups (large cups work best)

To make the castle: Fold sheets of paper like an accordion to create strong paper platforms and bridges. Use cups as the stones of the castle.

Build the castle as large as possible with the available building materials.

Castles, walls, drawbridges, trees, townhouses and so many more things can be built out of paper cups and paper beams. The kingdoms can stand tall or spread out over the entire living room floor.

Modifications for Younger Kids

Replace the paper beams with strips of cardboard cut from leftover boxes. They make a flatter building surface.

(continued)

Modifications for Older Kids

Challenge older kids to a minimum castle height requirement or have them scurry around the house, looking for additional building materials to fortify the castle.

TIP

Before play, have a peace treaty signed by all parties stating that neighboring kingdoms will not be invaded without the blessing of said kingdom. Knocking down castles is only fun if everyone is on board with the action.

Ping-Pong Ball Run

A children's museum in our area has a wall that is made of metal. In buckets at the base of that wall are all sorts of pipes with magnets attached to one side to make tracks on the wall that will transport a ball with a little help from gravity. My kids love to play on the wall. Sometimes when we visit the museum, it is just to visit the wall.

Because my husband said a metal wall in our home was out of the question, I downsized this activity a bit to be recycled toilet paper and paper towel tubes stuck to the fridge.

- - - - - - - - - - - - -

Materials

+ Roll of magnetic tape
+ 6 to 10 empty paper towel and toilet paper tubes
+ Scissors
+ Masking tape
+ Ping-Pong balls

Peel the backing off the magnetic tape and press the sticky side along the side of the tubes so that the tubes can be hung vertically and the magnets make contact with the metal.

Repeat for many different sizes of pieces to give variety to the Ping-Pong ball run.

On one piece, use masking tape to cover one end of a tube, so that you have a storage segment to allow the balls to be put away and stored on the fridge.

Modifications for Younger Kids

Set up a simple run at their level and hand them the Ping-Pong ball. It won't be long until they figure out how to make it go down the tube track.

Modifications for Older Kids

Older kids can find other things around the house to attach to the fridge as ball obstacles and tracks. They can cut the paper towel tubes into segments with windows, flaps and ends.

TIPS

Place a sticker over the flat surface of the attached magnet. This is done to protect the metal surface from scuffs the magnet can cause from sliding on the fridge.

Looking for another version of this activity? Check out the PVC Tube Play Wall activity (page 121) that is guaranteed to entertain your kids for a good hour.

Pipe Cleaner Disguises

This activity is a mature version of peek-a-boo. Everyone is in on the joke that these really aren't disguises, but it is too fun to ruin with the truth. Grab some pipe cleaners and get ready for some laughter because this is going to get silly.

- - - - - - - - - - - - -

Materials

+ LOTS of different colors and sizes of pipe cleaners
+ Glue dots or double-sided tape

Create a unique disguise for yourself. We have some suggestions . . .

Spy Glasses

Take a pipe cleaner and make it into a spiral like a shell—you will need two. When finished, push the center of the spirals out to create a sort of cone. Attach the "cones" to the center of eyeglasses formed from pipe cleaners.

Antennae

Get your bug on! Create antennae and pretend to be an insect . . . or an alien. Use a couple of pipe cleaners to create a headband. Add antennae. Consider making the antennae from spirals or curling the ends of them.

Other pipe cleaner accessories you can make:

- Swords
- Hats
- Mustaches
- Cat whiskers
- Bushy eyebrows
- Flowers

Modifications for Younger Kids

Instead of having your children make or wear the disguises, print out a large picture of their face. Have your children visually "try on" the disguises on their picture.

Modifications for Older Kids

Have one child make the disguise for another child. Pick a character (e.g., a rock star, a small animal, a circus performer, etc.) and try to imagine disguises that they would use or that would define them. Become the character.

*See photo insert page 16.

TIPS

Are you worried about the ends of the pipe cleaners poking one of your kids? Just fold the sharp end in and twist it inside itself. Your pipe cleaner should now be blunted and safer for small tots to enjoy.

This is a great activity for kids to do on a long car trip. Give them a collection of pipe cleaners and a mirror. They will giggle at one another as you drive.

Do you have extra pipe cleaners? Use some to create giant bubble wands to use along with bubble shooters (see page 13).

Playing Card Building Sets

We have drawers full of playing cards. Some were handed down from previous generations, some were picked up on travels, some were gifts and some were purchased at the last minute because, despite the drawers full of playing cards, we just couldn't find a full deck.

Recycle those tattered, incomplete decks into a building block set that is easily transported and endless in its play potential.

- - - - - - - - - - - -

Materials

+ Deck of playing cards (can be incomplete deck)
+ Scissors

Cut four slits in each card—1½ inches (4 cm) from each end of the long sides. The slits don't have to be deeper than ½ inch (1.3 cm), but they do need to be perpendicular to the edge.

Kids can use one or more sets to build large structures and sculptures. We are moving WAY beyond a house of cards!

Modifications for Younger Kids

Create a card-size building piece out of cardboard or heavy cardstock, because many playing cards can be a bit slick and hard for smaller fingers to manipulate.

Modifications for Older Kids

Make several decks of cards for a massive building experience.

TIP

Despite the alteration of the cards, they will still fit back into the box, which makes these sets the perfect take-along toy.

Shadow Play

I remember vividly the day I really sat down and thought about my shadow. Well, it started out sitting, but then I got up and tried to trick it. I jumped and swayed and ducked and ran. No matter what I did, that shadow followed. I decided just to ignore it except for some covert peeks—a peek where only my eyes would move so my shadow wouldn't reflect that I was looking.

This activity gets the entire family involved because everyone has a shadow. Bring some life and jazz to your family's next dance party by playing with shadows as you dance.

- - - - - - - - - - - -

Materials

+ Painter's tape (to hang the sheet on the wall)
+ Large white sheet—or a blank wall
+ Directional light
+ Music

Use painter's tape to hang your sheet on the wall, then turn on the light. Explore with distance to see where you need to dance to get the crispest shadow of yourself. Turn on the music and watch your shadow dance.

Modifications for Younger Kids

Be sure to keep the light away from where the kids are dancing. The directional lights tend to get hot.

Modifications for Older Kids

With your children participating, make a list of some of your family's favorite activities. Throw the ideas into a hat and pick the ideas out. Try to reenact the scenes of your activities together as shadows. For an extra challenge, have them try to choreograph a scene between two people.

Pocket Puzzle Game

Grandma and Grandpa always had a very large and very challenging puzzle going on the dining room table. Grandma had it on a piece of cardboard so it could be moved in the event of a family gathering, but often the family gathering was around the puzzle. Every time someone walked by the table, he/she would pause to try to add another piece to the ever-evolving picture.

I love this next activity for the legacy of it. It is an open-ended puzzle where everyone can play. Using foam pieces, magnets and a metal mint container, you can create a puzzle to work together at home or on the go.

— — — — — — — — — — — —

Materials
(to make one pocket puzzle)

+ A variety of colored sticky foam sheets
+ Magnetic sheet or old magnetic business cards
+ Graph paper
+ Scissors
+ Small tin box

Peel the backing from the foam sheets and stick the magnets to the foam. We worked with small sections so we didn't waste all the magnets or foam. Lay the graph paper over the magnetic foam sheet and cut out a collection of shapes, following the lines in the graph paper. Repeat with the other colors of foam sheets. Try to think of a wide variety of shapes and designs, following the lines of the graph paper—so the puzzle will fit together when done. Tape a piece of graph paper inside the lid on the tin.

Have your kids play with their puzzle solo or as a group, taking turns adding a new piece. The goal is to fill the entire lid so that there aren't any blank spaces without pieces.

Modifications for Younger Kids
Make the pieces bigger and use a lunchbox instead of a small tin to hold the parts.

Modifications for Older Kids
Add the rule that they can't have pieces of the same color touch. Or have them try to create an image, like a house, inside the puzzle. You can also make this a timed event. Give them 3 minutes to completely fill the surface with no gaps. Shorten the time if they need more challenge. To make the game more complicated for older kids, make a rule that they can only place pieces of one color.

*See photo insert page 16.

TIP
Make a set of puzzle pieces for the fridge. Great for both holding to-do notes and to help entertain a child during meal preparation!

Sticky-Note Pom-Pom Maze

This project transforms sticky notes into a maze that can be designed and constructed by a kid. The fun thing is that even though they designed the maze, it will still be a challenge to maneuver a pom-pom through it with a straw and some air power.

— — — — — — — — — — — —

Materials

+ 2+ stacks of sticky notes
+ Tabletop surface (or the floor)
+ Straws—one per child playing
+ A variety of different pom-poms

(continued)

Create a maze track with the thin post-it notes (or masking tape). Line up the notes close together on a smooth surface, creating corners, turns and twists across the table.

Have your children pick out a straw and a pom-pom and start at the beginning of the maze. They need to blow their pom-pom to go through the maze without falling off the track. If they go outside of the lines of the "track" they need to take their pom-pom back to start and begin again.

Modifications for Younger Kids
Have your children work on blowing the straw evenly to get their pom-pom to move. This is a great way to work on breathing control. Our youngest tykes just liked blowing their pom-poms anywhere. They can have a simple start/finish line or a set of bases to get their pom-poms to.

Modifications for Older Kids
Cut the notes in half to make a narrower trail. Add some twists and turns in the maze, making it more difficult for kids to navigate their pom-pom around the barriers.

For a science twist, have your kids experiment. Is the pom-pom easier to control if they have a thinner straw? What happens when the size of the pom-pom changes?

TIPS
Wondering how to create a maze? Try filling in an entire 2 x 3-foot (61 x 91.5-cm) area with the sticky notes. When the entire "box" is filled, remove the notes to reveal the maze route.

Regulating breathing by blowing pom-poms is a great way to learn breath control. This is also a good "calm down." Breathing steadily will help mellow excited little bodies.

PVC Pipe Tent

Wouldn't it be great if Tinker Toys were life-size so you could build a house and then live in it? The giant building possibilities would be endless!

I think that is why I love this project so much. Once you have created a PVC pipe set for play, it can be used and reused both inside and out to make anything you can dream up, including this homemade tent.

— — — — — — — — — — —

Materials
+ Ratcheting PVC cutter
+ 8 (10-foot [3-m]-long, ½-inch [1.3-cm] -diameter) PVC plumbing pipes
+ 10 (½-inch [1.3-cm]-diameter) 90 degree elbow pieces
+ 12 (½-inch [1.3-cm]-diameter) T-shaped pieces
+ Permanent marker
+ Bedsheets

Using the ratcheting PVC cutter, cut twelve 4-foot (122-cm)-long sections of pipe. These pieces will create the tent base.

The four roof segments need to create a right angle when placed together, so you will need to use the remaining long pieces to cut four segments that are 33⅞ inches (86 cm) long. Immediately label these pieces with a marker, making an "R" to remind yourself that they are the roof segments.

Using some of the leftover pieces cut a dozen 2-inch (5-cm)-long segments to use to create corners. Hang the bedsheets over the roof and wrap around the sides.

A recap: The pieces required for this tent:

- 12 (4-foot [122-cm])-long segments
- 4 (33⅞-inch [86-cm])-long segments labeled "R"
- 10 (90 degree) elbows
- 12 T pieces
- 12 (2-inch [5-cm])-long segments

Modifications for Younger Kids

If only smaller kids are included in this project, it would be wise to cut all measurements in half and make a miniature version of this tent. This is the perfect family activity to help build and then the kids can play.

Modifications for Older Kids

Have older kids design a structure and then create directions to make it. The directions outlined above were devised with some help of the Pythagorean theorem and my fifth grader's math skills.

*See photo insert page 16.

TIP

There is a lot of bang for your buck with a PVC pipe play set. The most expensive part was the ratcheting cutter, which cost approximately $10. The rest of the set was under $25.

PVC Tube Play Wall

Chain reactions are not always the easy way to the finish line, but they are great entertainment. Accomplishing something simple through complex actions was the basis of Rube Goldberg's inventions. He created elaborate means to a common task with one step triggering the next.

This activity puts the power of complex actions to accomplish a common result in the hands of kids in the form of interchangeable PVC pipes. They can harness gravity and set and reset the steps toward the goal. They think they know what will happen next, but are often surprised!

- - - - - - - - - - - - -

Materials

+ A variety of 2¼-inch (5.5-cm) PVC connectors
+ Plastic funnel
+ Drill
+ 2-inch (5-cm)-diameter suction cups—one for each connector
+ Container that fits on windowsill
+ Measuring cup(s)
+ Dried beans, small pom-poms, marbles, beads, seeds, cold cereal, etc.

Choose a variety of 2¼-inch (5.5-cm) PVC connectors. We used seven connectors—three straight, two obtuse angles, one T piece and one right angle—and a plastic funnel.

Drill a hole in the plastic funnel and each of the connectors. Fill each hole with a suction cup.

(continued)

On a window at kid level, arrange the first version of a "fall wall"—create a path or two that cascades from the top, emptying into the container sitting on the windowsill. Test the chain reaction with a cupful of beans, small pom-poms, marbles or even breakfast cereal.

Kids can work together to change the path of the falling material and experiment with measuring cups of different ingredients to find out how things fall.

Modifications for Younger Kids

Depending on the age of the child, choose an ingredient that is safe for play. Wash the Play Wall elements in the dishwasher, clean the space around the bottom and allow only cereal as the ingredient for those who are likely to put things in their mouth.

Modifications for Older Kids

Create a smaller "target" inside the windowsill container with a measuring cup for them to fill with a specific amount of a specific ingredient. Have older children design a pathway that divides into a specific number of trails at the bottom. Give older children a challenge to "fix" the path designed by a smaller child in two moves.

TIP

Set up the tubes in the tub for a wet, water run.

Sensory Bag Collection

Sensory bags are curious things. They are a mixture of textures and feeling sensations sealed into a mess-proof play experience. For some kids who shy away from messy hands, it is a way they can be introduced to what a mess feels like. For others, it is another way to play that won't end in a trip to the bathtub for a full body wash-down.

The ingredients usually include a liquid and solids that aren't normally found together, for a unique touch adventure. We have collected several of our favorites that can be created with things you already have at home. Feel free to make substitutions and enhancements customized for what your child loves.

– – – – – – – – – – – – – –

Materials

+ Assorted sensory items (see suggestions)
+ Resealable plastic freezer bags
+ Clear packing tape

Add the sensory elements inside the bag, filling it just enough so when the bag is lying on its side, the contents completely cover the surface in a layer less than 1 inch (2.5 cm) deep. Try to remove all the air from the bag. Seal the bag tightly and reinforce the closure with tape.

Lumpy Ocean

Combine blue hair gel and Styrofoam bits (could be stuffed animal filling or packing peanuts cut into small pieces). This bag is delightfully squishy and cool to the touch with soft bumps to explore.

Mess-Free Paint

Add paint in your child's favorite color inside a bag and then give him/her a cotton swab to draw pictures or practice handwriting. The pressure of the swab will cause the paint to part, leaving a magical writing surface. Use this canvas as a wipe-off board for a game of "What am I drawing?"

Flower Texture

Combine clear hair gel and some leftover silk flowers without stems. This bag is pretty to look at, fun to feel and a great pool or bath toy.

Modifications for Younger Kids

Very young kids need to be supervised around plastic bags. If your child tends to handle things roughly, double the bag and add an extra layer of tape!

Modifications for Older Kids

While this is usually thought of as an activity for younger kids, older kids can create a themed bag with their favorite items. Adding a base of thick liquid or gel can make this a fun desk accessory with stress-relieving properties!

*See photo insert page 17.

Straw Glider

In my mind, a toy airplane resembles the real thing—two wings, a nose and often a tail. If it flies, it looks like that. This paper glider is different. It doesn't look like anything that would fly at all.

So, grab a straw and a piece of paper and build the glider that defies gravity, as I know it. You will be pleasantly surprised as your "UFO-like" creation sails.

Materials
(to make a single glider)

+ 1 sheet of cardstock or another stiff paper
+ Scissors
+ Tape
+ Drinking straw

Cut the paper into two strips. Tape each strip into a paper hoop with one of the hoops being slightly larger than the other. Then tape the hoops onto the straw.

Set up a series of bases throughout the house. Pillows work great as bases. Have each child throw a glider at the first base. If the glider reaches the first base, that kid can advance to it and on their next turn throw toward the next base. The person who completes all the bases first is the winner.

Modifications for Younger Kids

Younger kids can be given a zone of grace around each base appropriate with their ability—so instead of needing to touch the base with the glider, they can be within a 2-foot (61-cm) radius.

Modifications for Older Kids

Older kids can experiment with different glider designs. Does the glider go farther with bigger hoops or smaller ones? What if the hoops were closer together or farther apart? Can the glider fly with three hoops?

TIP

Are your kids bored at the restaurant? Recycle straws and beverage cozies to create these flying masterpieces—just be sure to leave the restaurant before you test them in flight!

Stuffed Animal Marionette

One of my favorite movie scenes is the puppet show in *The Sound of Music*. The elaborate puppet show was performed by the kids for the rest of the family. There was a gold and red stage with curtains and fancy marionettes. The children stood above, manipulating all the action with long and invisible strings. I can still see the lonely goatherd and goat dancing in front of the mountain backdrop. Lay ee odl lay ee odl-oo.

Inspired by the Von Trapps but without the Austrian château budget, this activity breathes life into stuffed animals.

- - - - - - - - - - - - -

Materials
(to transform one stuffed animal into a puppet)

+ 2 rulers
+ Ball of yarn
+ Scissors
+ Stuffed animal
+ Binder clip or stapler

Make an X with the rulers and tie the middle securely with yarn, leaving a length of yarn hanging from the middle. At each end of the four points, attach another strand of yarn, through the hole near the end of each ruler.

Tie the four strings from the points to the arms and legs of the animal. Attach the middle string to the back of the stuffed animal's head by using a binder clip or stapling it securely.

Holding on to the rulers, tip in different directions to make the stuffed animal walk and dance.

Modifications for Younger Kids
Keeping the yarn strands short will keep them less tangled during play.

Modifications for Older Kids
You may need to buy rulers in bulk because creating an entire cast can revive interest in animals that may have been hiding under the bed for years!

Tin Can Drums

There is something about making noise that is simply delightful to kids. Toy manufacturers have caught on to this, resulting in increasingly frantic toys' blasting bells, whistles, talking and singing accompanied by a full band. These toys will end up quickly confiscated just for a moment of peace by normally calm parents.

This activity takes away the bells, whistles, talking and full band to go back to the basics of sound—the drum. When kids can experiment with sounds in a quiet environment, they can start recognizing the different tones. Grab a tin can and some balloons—we are making a drum!

- - - - - - - - - - - - -

Materials
(to make a single drum)

+ Balloons of various colors
+ Scissors
+ Empty cans (or other cylindrical metal containers)
+ Rubber bands
+ Spoons and sticks—wooden spoons and chopsticks work great

Cut off the elongated portion of a balloon (where you blow into) and stretch it over the end of a can. Choose a complementary color of balloon and repeat the process, with the addition of clipping a few holes in the second balloon. Secure both with a rubber band to the tin can.

Make several different drums. Using different-size tin cans or other cylinders can help create different sounds.

Using wooden spoons or chopsticks, play each drum to hear the different sounds each makes. You can even just use your hands and see how the tone changes. Create a family band!

Modifications for Younger Kids
Because balloon parts can be dangerous, substitute waxed paper or cellophane for the balloon. Using an empty oatmeal container makes a larger drum, and it has no sharp edges to be concerned about.

Modifications for Older Kids
Older kids can use different types of materials to create a drum surface and different drum barrels. Adding rice, dried beans, marbles or other items to the drum barrel can also affect sound.

TIP
Are you looking for more fun? Use the finished tin can drum as a small trampoline for vaulting objects, or small action figures, into the air.

Tree Wood Blocks

Building is great for growing brains. The act of stacking items helps kids develop spatial awareness and understand the relationship between cause and effect. Our kids love stacking blocks of all shapes and sizes.

As our children have grown, their building interests have expanded but never waned. They love to create elaborate towers, houses and cityscapes. Some days it feels like there are not enough blocks in the world to entertain their creativity. We were thrilled when a tree in our backyard needed to be cut down: we could create a whole new set of blocks!

- - - - - - - - - - - - - -

Materials
+ 2 or 3 tree limbs, roughly 3 inches (7.5 cm) in diameter
+ Table saw (we used an electric one)
+ Sandpaper (coarse and fine grain)
+ Gloves for your child
+ Butcher block oil (linseed, or food-grade mineral oil or anything marketed as safe for food surfaces—and therefore a child's mouth)

Cut disks from your tree limbs, using the table saw. Older children might be able to help by marking off how long they would like the blocks to be—a wide variety of sizes makes building a fun challenge.

(continued)

After you have cut the disks, use sandpaper to smooth any rough edges. This is the hard part. For the best blocks, you will want to give your wood a chance to dry out and age. Stack your cut blocks in a corner of the garage, away from moisture, and allow them to harden. This is especially important if you used wood from a recently live tree.

Once the wood has aged for a month or two, sand the edges again. Put gloves on your children and give them a clean rag that has been lightly dipped in butcher block oil. Have them rub the oil into the blocks. This will help preserve them.

Modifications for Younger Kids

While the creation of these toy blocks is best suited for older kids, playing with them is something kids of all ages will enjoy.

Modifications for Older Kids

Have your child collect a variety of small sticks at the same time that you are cutting up the tree. They can use these in coordination with the blocks to build their structures. Add some props to their building play: yarn and a bandana, as well as figures and animals, will open the doors to endless hours of pretend play.

TIPS

These blocks make a great gift for holidays! Place a couple dozen disks into a box with some woods animals for the child in your life to enjoy. For an adult gift, make more narrow disks and gift them as coasters.

Tin Can Jump

The satisfaction in mastering something difficult by yourself, as a child, is hard to top. Repeating something over and over again until it can be done may seem like work to the outside world, but in the mind of the persistent child it is worth it when success is achieved. In today's childhood, many of these solo accomplishments are achieved through video games and practicing organized sports' skills.

This activity takes a step back into generations past for a simple gross motor skill developed with a solo jump rope using a tin can.

Materials
(to make one jump rope)

+ Empty medium-size tin can
+ Sandpaper or sturdy tape
+ Hammer
+ Thick nail
+ Rope

Sand down any sharp edges on the tin can with sandpaper or cover them with sturdy tape. Using a hammer and nail, create a hole in the end. Thread both ends of a rope through the hole and secure with a knot.

Step one foot inside the rope circle and swing it around, jumping over the moving can with the other leg.

Modifications for Younger Kids

This can be modified to a two-person game for kids who are too young to coordinate it solo. Adults or older children, who can successfully jump the rope alone, can have younger children stand at their side next to their jump rope leg. They can participate by jumping over the moving can as it flies underneath them.

Modifications for Older Kids

Older kids can be given challenges, such as a number of jumps in a row to achieve or once one side is coordinated, switch legs and master the other side as well.

> **TIP**
> This can be an indoor rainy-day activity—just cover the can first with felt or faux craft fur to decrease the sound and any damage that the can could cause to flooring.

Toe Painting with a Paint Recipe

My first exposure to finger painting was in kindergarten. Parents had been instructed to send an art smock (one of Dad's old shirts) so that we could paint at school. In my mind, that meant paintbrushes and canvases, but when the finger paints were brought out to paint on a large, paper-covered easel, I was hooked.

The paint was so cool to touch and fingers can manipulate paint in a different way than a brush. This activity increases the sensory experience and uses toes to paint. Toe painting is a new way to explore with color!

- - - - - - - - - - - - - -

Materials

+ Shaving cream
+ Tempera paint in a variety of colors
+ Light corn syrup—1 tsp per color (optional)
+ Wet towel (for quick cleanup)

Make a pile of shaving cream that is roughly a cup (about 230 g). Add a squirt of paint and mix until you have the desired color. Add a teaspoon of corn syrup. If you don't care about the finished product as much you can leave out the corn syrup. The corn syrup gives the paint a semigloss finish.

Paint colors can be mixed in plastic cups to create a whole bunch of colored paint batches. Turn the cups upside down to fully appreciate the thick and creamy consistency that is nearly impossible to spill!

Let your children paint a picture with bare feet. Have a bucket of water and a towel ready for when they are finished.

Modifications for Younger Kids

Instead of "toe painting," they can paint with their fingers. If you are working on prewriting skills with your kids, have them use a paintbrush. It will help them develop the hand control needed when it is time for them to begin writing. Do you have a child who puts everything in his/her mouth? Consider using plain yogurt combined with food coloring as the paint, instead of the shaving cream and tempera in this recipe.

Modifications for Older Kids

Add some challenge and ask your kids to paint with their bums in the air—they will have fun trying to figure out how to write without "resting." It is a great way for them to both develop core strength and practice controlled movements (needed for many sports).

This is a fun group activity for an art-themed party. Lay a long piece of butcher paper out and watch the kids paint with their feet.

*See photo insert page 17.

(continued)

Wooden Block Townhouses

Saturday afternoons are family time at our house. We have a set of wooden blocks that always seem to make their way to the middle of the living room and it isn't long before the adults usually take over and make a structure tall enough to touch the ceiling. Kids are welcome to help on the bottom parts, but as the skyscraper grows, the kids know to stand farther and farther away. It is for their protection because after the skyscraper successfully touches the ceiling, a pivotal base piece is pulled out followed by a tremendous crash as wooden blocks fall from the sky.

These wooden block townhouses are the perfect complement to the toys kids already have and love. In our case, this makes a lovely suburban play set while the dangerous city is being constructed and destructed.

- - - - - - - - - - - - - - - -

Materials

+ Small scraps from two-by-fours
+ Sandpaper
+ Painter's tape
+ Paintbrushes
+ White paint
+ Paint markers

First, sand any rough edges on the wooden blocks with sandpaper. Using painter's tape, tape off square and rectangular windows on the wood block surface.

Paint the "windows" white. Peel off the tape and let dry. Once dry, use paint markers to outline the window details and let dry.

Your wooden block townhouses are all ready for play. You can stack them on top of one another to create a high-rise, or line them up along a street and grab the toy cars.

Modifications for Younger Kids
Younger kids can do all the painting where tape is involved. These are great toys for even small kids.

Be sure to use nontoxic paint, in case smaller players put the blocks in their mouth.

Modifications for Older Kids
Let older kids design more elaborate townhouse decor. Access to a saw could result in different roof pitches. More colors could create a townhouse row reminiscent of San Francisco's finest streets.

1

People Sticks (page 23)

Shrinking Cup Flower Sculptures (page 27)

2

Solar Oven Crayon Art (page 28)

Story Layers (page 29)

Paper Bag Puppet People (page 32)

Paper Roll Train (page 32)

Coffee Filter Owls (page 33)

Paper Cup Farm Animals (page 34)

Cupcake Liner Jellyfish (page 34)

Paper Straw Beads (page 35)

4

Craft Stick Caterpillars (page 35)

Paper Bag Town (page 36)

aper Plate Fishbowl (page 36)

Glow-in-the-Dark Galaxy Jar (page 37)

utterfly Suncatcher (page 37)

Paper Plate Snail (page 38)

5

Glow-in-the-Dark Firefly (page 38)

Clothespin Pirates (page 39)

6

Mosaic Paper Plate Rainbow (page 39)

Paper Roll Octopus (page 40)

Cupcake Liner Flowers (page 40)

Craft Stick Birds (page 41)

Paper Plate Marble Maze (page 41)

Water Bottle Flowers (page 42)

START

FINISH

7

Crayon Scratch Art (page 42)

Ping-Pong Ball Monsters (page 43)

Yarn Pumpkins (page 43)

Snowman Paper Cups (page 44)

8

Paper Bag Octopus (page 44)

Chomping Alligator Clothespins (page 45)

Plastic Bottle Whirligigs (page 45)

Paper Plate Watermelon Suncatchers (page 46)

Coffee Filter Watercolor Roses (page 46)

Happy Sunshine Clothespins (page 47)

Melted-Snowman Slime (page 51)

Pillow Slime (page 53)

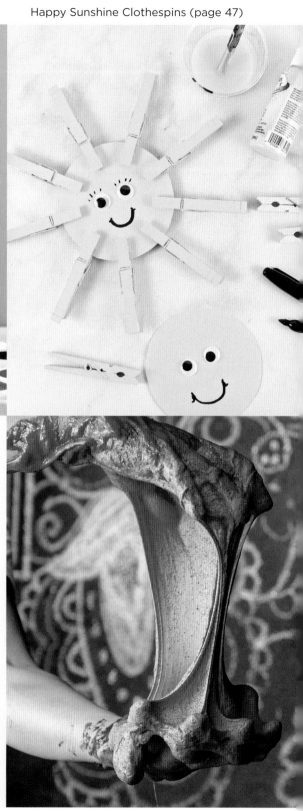

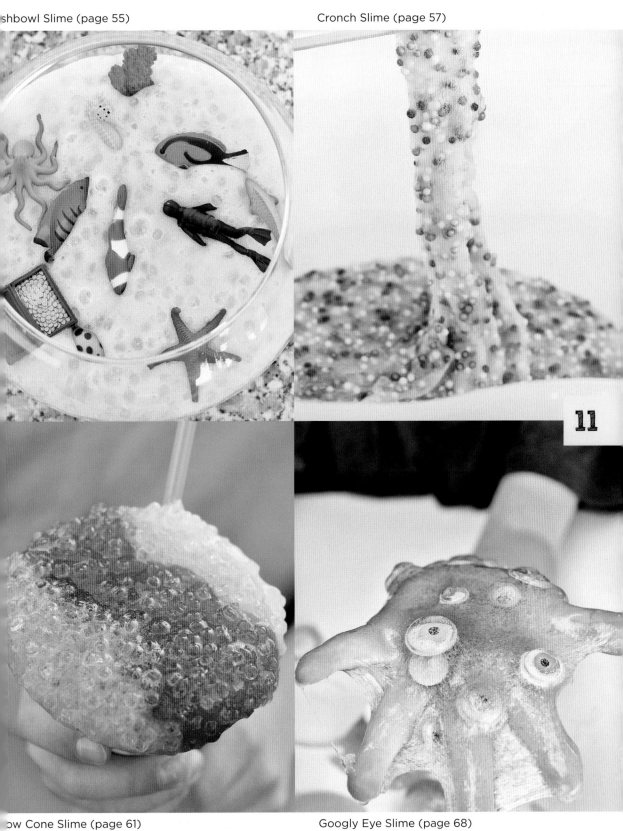

Fishbowl Slime (page 55)

Cronch Slime (page 57)

11

Snow Cone Slime (page 61)

Googly Eye Slime (page 68)

Hot Chocolate Playdough (page 72)

Glitter Playdough (page 78)

12

Galaxy Dough (page 83)

Dino-Dig Playdough (page 87)

13

Forever Bubbles (page 97)

Bouncy Ball (page 100)

14

Floam (page 102)

Air-Dry Clay (page 103)

15

DIY Straw Building Set (page 111)

Pipe Cleaner Disguises (page 117)

16

Pocket Puzzle Game (page 119)

PVC Pipe Tent (page 120)

Part Two

LEARNING GAMES

(six)

TEAMWORK AND STRATEGY

There is a game in nearly everything. It isn't about the rules or who wins. Games are a great way to learn skills like teamwork, strategy, conflict, decision making, cause and effect, problems, solutions and payoffs in a low-stakes situation. Games are just fun!

Holly's Pick: It is hard for me to pick just one game as a favorite. The ones that we play the most at home are Funnel Golf Toss (page 140) and Family Four Square (page 135). Both games are highly competitive, inspire "house rules" and generally end in friendly trash-talking.

Rachel's Pick: Our boys were amazed at how far the Egg Carton Glider sails (page 139)! It is, by far, their favorite "airplane"—easy to make and encourages your kids to eat eggs so they can use the carton to fly.

Over & Under Obstacle Course

Creating an indoor obstacle course is an easy way to get kids moving inside. It works great on a rainy, too cold or too hot day to work out the wiggles. Course design is only limited by the obstacle potential seen in furniture and objects around the house. Starting with something simple like this over and under obstacle course can inspire creative station additions to make the obstacle course uniquely your own.

- - - - - - - - - - - -

Materials

+ 3 x 5-inch (7.5 x 12.5-cm) cards
+ Marker
+ Chairs/stools/ottomans
+ Tape

On each 3 x 5-inch (7.5 x 12.5-cm) card, have a child draw an arrow. You will need an arrow for each of the chair obstacles on your course.

Set up chairs, stools and ottomans, leaving space between them, throughout a room or hallway. Your course can be limited to one room or spread out throughout the house. On each piece of furniture, tape an arrow that indicates whether that obstacle needs to be negotiated by going over or under it. You can also use arrows to mark the course and direct kids around things.

Set start and finish lines.

Kids will love running the course just by following the arrows, but if you want to add a little competition, then time them on a stopwatch and have them try to beat their time on each run through.

Modifications for Younger Kids

Shorten the course for the youngest participants and make an under-only path.

Modifications for Older Kids

Let older kids design the course within the parameters of what furniture is course-worthy. The last time we did this at our house, the kids had a course with 22 stations! Have them chart their times for each trial.

TIP
Create homemade medals and a three-tier award stand for an indoor Olympic ceremony based on the results of the over and under obstacle competition.

Balloon Bean Bags

When I was in sixth grade, I learned to juggle. It wasn't something that would entertain others in a coordinated way. It was something that I spent hours mastering in the large semifinished basement at home.

These bean bags are super easy to make—perfect for little hands and for aspiring jugglers.

- - - - - - - - - - - -

Materials

+ A ⅓-cup (80-ml) measuring cup
+ Rice, wheat berries, sand or flour
+ Balloons
+ Funnel

We measured precisely ⅓ cup (80 ml) of balloon "filler." We wanted every balloon bag to weigh the same amount. Secure the balloon to the bottom of a funnel and pour your measured amount into the funnel and fill up the balloon. Tie the balloons.

Use a bean bag to toss back and forth among all participants. Once one bag is in play, add another. It is fun to watch how intently kids will pay attention trying to predict when the bean bag is headed in their direction.

Add a pattern to the toss—two people throw to each other at the same time or each person tosses to the person on the left. Have someone lead the directions and change the pattern.

This is also a great solo play activity. Starting with one bag, toss it into the air and catch it, eventually working toward juggling with three bags . . . or more!

Modifications for Younger Kids

Instead of making bags that weigh the same amounts, consider making each bag different. Have younger children explore the different textures of the various fillers, and organize them by weight or "feeling."

Modifications for Older Kids

When creating the bean bags, have older kids try to make three bags exactly the same weight. Weigh them on a scale when you are finished. See whether they are the same and make adjustments to the filling as needed. Use the three matched bags to learn to juggle.

TIP

Help your kids develop hand strength. Use flour as the balloon filler and it becomes a "stress ball." These also make great "hot potatoes" for an impromptu game.

Bathtime Memory Game

The game of Memory is a staple of childhood because it is one of the few games where adults and kids are competitive equals. It was one of the first games that I beat my dad in. As a parent now, I can see that he likely didn't throw the game. Children are good at remembering and they delight in victory!

This Memory game is a solo bath version. It is created with sponge tiles that can be decorated in the theme of the child's choice.

- - - - - - - - - - - - - - -

Materials

+ 6 or more sponges
+ Scissors
+ Permanent marker

Cut the sponges into uniform rectangles. The size and shape doesn't matter as long as they are all the same. Pair the pieces and with a permanent marker create the exact same pattern on one side of each paired piece.

When the sponge tiles are moist, they will stick to the wall of most bathtub surfaces. Place the tiles pattern side down in randomly selected rows. Kids play by turning over two tiles each turn, trying to find the matching pair.

Modifications for Younger Kids

Larger and fewer sponge tiles work best and make fabulous bath toys even if the child isn't in the mood for playing a game.

Modifications for Older Kids

Use the pairs to match upper- and lowercase letters, or numbers and the number words. Place sight words on the tiles for a fun reading practice.

*See photo insert page 17.

Beach Ball Carry

Group problem solving happens within a family daily. It is something that we might not think about, but figuring out how to juggle food preferences, sleeping schedules, sporting schedules, laundry, homework and family fun within the family's available time is a big task. Creating games around working as a group can help even the family's smallest members start creatively finding ways to work together for a common goal.

This activity is a simple way to team build among a group of children or a family unit. A sheet and a ball can be the catalyst for a group solution.

- - - - - - - - - - - - - - -

Materials
(for two or more children)

+ Bedsheet
+ Large beach ball

Use the sheet to carry the ball to a specified destination. This can be a simple start and finish line or obstacles can be placed in the way to negotiate around, under and over, depending on the age of your participants. If the group drops the ball on the ground during the process, they start back at the beginning.

Modifications for Younger Kids
- Make the ball smaller. Tennis balls also work. You can have your children do an obstacle course where they have to drop multiple balls into different pockets.
- Allow the kids to use two hands to hold the sheet.
- If they are too young to enjoy following directions, maybe just make the only rule that the ball cannot touch the ground and watch them bounce the ball in the air, trying to catch it together.

Modifications for Older Kids
- Use a small sheet and a big ball. Tell them they are not allowed to touch the ball once placed on the sheet.
- Make them only use one hand and try to figure out ways to hold the sheet and keep the ball on it.
- Add speed. Have your children see how fast they can complete their mission.
- Change the height. Make the place where they have to deposit the ball up high, like on top of an outdoor toy or bush. They have to problem solve to find a way to get the ball up there.
- Help your kids become effective communicators. Blindfold a child and ask a partner to help him/her complete the task by relying on communication.

Garden Game Boards

We are happiest when we get a daily dose of the outdoors. It is not unusual for us to be outside for the majority of a day. While the younger kids enjoy just digging in the dirt and collecting leaves, the older kids prefer something more structured.

If your kids love being outside, but are also social and want to be "doing" something, this might be the perfect project for you. Your kids can scheme up and re-create their favorite games and you can use them over and over!

- - - - - - - - - - - - - - -

Materials

+ Small pizza box
+ Waxed paper
+ Quick-set cement
+ Powdered chalk or acrylic paint to dye the cement
+ Disposable plastic knife

Suggested items or ways to create your game boards. Use all or just some of the ideas.

+ Coins, shells, marbles, rocks and beads
+ Paint
+ Nails

Line your pizza box with waxed paper. Mix the cement according to the instructions provided by the manufacturer. Add crushed chalk or acrylic paint to the cement to dye it if you want a colorful board. Carefully fill the box with the cement. After the cement has started to "gel," smooth the top of the cement with the plastic knife to help even out the lumps. Add embellishment items from the above list to create your game board! You will want to put your embellished board somewhere dry to set for 24 hours before removing the box and the paper backing.

Game Board Ideas

+ **GeoBoard**: Add nails in increments staggered around the board. To play, grab a handful of rubber bands and stretch them around the nails to create different shapes.
+ **Tic-Tac-Toe Board**: Use old pencils or pens to create the "grid" for the tic-tac-toe board. Use two different types of leaves from your yard as the game pieces for this classic!
+ **Connect the Dots**: Evenly place marbles along the top of your board, in a grid pattern. To play, use chalk or blades of grass to connect the dots. You can play multiple games with this board. You can create mazes, you can try to see who can close the most "boxes," you can draw a design going from "dot to dot," and so forth.

Modifications for Younger Kids

Just make a smooth surface and use it as a chalkboard. This is especially great to have if you don't like having your kids decorate all over the patio—give them a "creative space."

Modifications for Older Kids

Ask your kids to create a new game: maybe mix two of their favorite games together and have them create a set of rules to follow so as to play their new game.

Family Four Square

The simple game of Four Square was a staple of my childhood. It was a game that I played with classmates before school on stretches of bumpy asphalt with stick and stone boundary markers.

I hadn't thought about the game until nearly a year ago, when my oldest son took me outside to teach me a game they play at school all the time. It was fun to see the look on his face when I showed him that Four Square isn't a skill you lose with time.

This is a team adaptation of the traditional game where the team competes against itself in pattern play to set a new family record.

Materials

+ Sidewalk chalk (page 21) or painter's tape
+ Driveway
+ Rubber ball

Use chalk or tape to measure out a square with a width of approximately 20 feet (about 6 m). Divide the large square into four equal squares of 10 feet (about 3 m) each.

Number the squares 1 through 4, with special marks in the fourth square.

(continued)

Each player stands in one of the squares. Extra players form a line at the outside boundary of square 1.

The player in square 4 serves the ball by bouncing it and hitting it gently in an underhand, open palm motion to another square. The receiving player allows the ball to bounce one time and then hits it underhand and open palm to the next player's square in the sequence.

The object of the game is for each player to hit the ball to the next player in a way that they can complete the action, trying to keep their streak of no double bounces or out of bounds hits, going through as many rounds as possible. Once a streak is broken, all players rotate (1 goes to 2; 2 to 3; and so on, with the 4 starting at square 1 or the end of the square 1 line) and start another streak.

Each of the patterns is played for one round and it is up to the 4 square server to change the pattern when the ball arrives back to him. If the sequence is broken, then the next server starts at the first pattern again.

- Clockwise
- Counterclockwise
- Crisscross

The sequence repeats until broken, with the team keeping track of how many rounds they successfully complete.

Modifications for Younger Kids

Younger kids will do better with a lighter, larger ball. Depending on their age/skill, implementing special rules like two bounces or rolls only to their square can make them an important part of the team.

Modifications for Older Kids

Older kids can take turns calling the plays— reminding everyone of the direction of play or which pattern is next in line. Give them the ability to choose a fourth pattern to the sequence, such as:

- Crisscross rolls only
- Big bounces left
- Double bounces right

TIP
This is a great game to play with grandparents as long as they are given special rules according to their skill level, just like the younger players! At our house, Grandma is always given two bounces.

Catapult Competition

Weapons are a big deal at our house. It wasn't my kids' environment that created this obsession; it is just how they are! Early on we didn't have any toy weapons for play, which led to my children constructing them.

I thought it might be best to harness this weapon creativity for good vs. evil, and this catapult competition is the result of this maternal guidance.

Kids can use things around the house to construct a catapult and then compete for catapult dominance bragging rights.

- - - - - - - - - - - - - - -

Materials
(to make one catapult)

+ Scissors
+ 14 wide craft sticks
+ 7 rubber bands
+ Plastic spoon
+ Painter's tape
+ Tape measure
+ Ping-Pong balls or other projectiles like pom-poms, cotton balls, etc.

Start by snipping 2 inches (5 cm) off each end of one craft stick, using scissors. Stack nine craft sticks, then center the shorter craft stick on top and then add two more craft sticks. Secure that bundle with two rubber bands placed about one-third of the way in from each end. The shortened stick will be the third stick from the top.

Center a plastic spoon upright against the sides of the craft stick stack. Use a rubber band on each side to wrap it crisscross to keep it in place. Take a third rubber band and loop it so that the top and bottom are around the front of the spoon above and below the craft stick bundle, and the back transverses the back of the bundle.

Add two more craft sticks perpendicular to the stack by inserting them into the space created by the shortened craft stick on each side. Add two more rubber bands—one on each end—to keep the perpendicular sticks in place.

Make a starting line at one end of the play area out of painter's tape. This is where the catapults will be positioned. Stretch the tape measure out at a perpendicular angle from the starting line.

Take turns shooting the projectiles from the catapult. With a small piece of painter's tape that has been labeled with the shooter's initials, mark the landing places. Measure the flight distance and record on a scoreboard.

The player with the highest distance average is declared the winner.

Modification for Younger Kids

One of the frustrating things about a homemade catapult is that it might take a little more coordination to keep the projectile in the spoon while pulling it back than the child can handle. Add a small loop of painter's tape to lightly hold the projectile in the spoon. The catapult action will overcome this slight resistance and allow a younger child to play along.

Modifications for Older Kids

Older kids can create multiple models based on trial and error to design the ultimate catapult for battle. They can test the craft stick catapults against ones that they make with other building toys you may have, like LEGO blocks, Tinker Toys and Erector sets.

TIP

This activity is great for a group. Precut the one shortened stick and make up a bag for each child that has all the catapult pieces. Build them together and then have a catapult distance battle.

Chalk Tangle

Recess was the highlight of my day. There were all the favorite games like Four Square, Dodgeball, Red Rover and Tetherball. And then there were the rainy days when my teacher would reach for the spinner card and pull out the Twister mat, making rainy-day recess as fun as any other day.

There is no reason to wait for rain. This outdoor Twister-inspired activity uses sidewalk chalk and homemade dice to take the fun outside.

- - - - - - - - - - - - - -

Materials

+ At least 6 colors of sidewalk chalk (page 21)
+ Dice

(continued)

With sidewalk chalk create a grid six squares across and six squares down. Randomly color in the squares with six different chalk colors, making six squares of each color.

With one of the dice, color each side of the die a different color with chalk. Participants all start standing in the color of their choice. The die roller will call out a body part and then roll the die to determine which color will receive that body part. Participants scramble to comply with the instructions without falling over.

Modifications for Younger Kids

Make the shapes smaller and closer together. Instead of reaching and staying still during the game, smaller participants can try to jump to the color called.

This is a great activity for those kids learning right and left! It will also help your children develop stronger core muscles as they balance on all fours. If you don't have six colors of sidewalk chalk, try using differently shaped flat objects from around the house (a book, a lid, etc.). Have your children land on a square, triangle, circle, diamond, rectangle or hexagon.

Modifications for Older Kids

Create a second die that has body parts listed: right arm, left arm, right leg, left leg, head and so on. Roll both dice to play the game. The kids have to match both the color and the body part.

*See photo insert page 17.

TIP

Dip your chalk into water before drawing with it on the sidewalk; the colors will be brighter this way.

Craft Stick Domino Game

My family is filled with game players. Saturday night is the designated game night. We have hours of competition over Monopoly, Rook, Clue and other games. One game that all of the members of our family love, from preschooler to grandparent, is Dominoes. This activity creates domino tiles out of craft sticks for a simplified game that doesn't need to be saved for game night.

– – – – – – – – – – –

Materials

+ 20 to 30 mini craft sticks (we used ice cream sticks)
+ Markers or paint pens

Break out the markers! This is a fun activity for your kids. Your child gets to decorate two ends of two sticks. Throw them back into the pile and grab another two sticks to decorate. Continue until every stick has had artwork added to both ends of the sticks.

For young children, it can be hard to create two identical images. If your children are too young to understand the concept of "copying" their artworks, maybe they can make the original and you can copy the pattern that they created on one stick—making the "match."

Patterns can be anything under the sun (including the sun) and don't have to be limited to pictures or symbols. Use letters, numbers and words, too.

The number of sticks you use is up to you. The more you have, the bigger the game. We suggest starting with at least twenty.

Modifications for Younger Kids

Play a game of I Spy collaboratively with your younger preschoolers. With all the patterns facing upright, pick up one stick and ask the kids to find the partner. Match them together and model how to play dominoes as you pick new patterns.

Modifications for Older Kids

Older kids might appreciate more structure. As you create patterns, line them up in a train of matching ends to ensure that you have just one set of matching ends and that they are arranged in a way that the train is continuous and the caboose matches the engine to complete a circle.

*See photo insert page 18.

Egg Carton Glider Target Throw

Many airplane kits that we have purchased through the years don't last too long. An inevitable crash takes them out of commission within a few minutes of assembly. Thankfully, this DIY kit uses things found around the house and is sturdier for play, so it doesn't have to be banished to a high shelf to keep it intact. In fact, make a few gliders to use in this target throwing game.

- - - - - - - - - - - - - -

Materials
(to make one glider)

+ Pencil/marker
+ Styrofoam egg carton—an 18-count carton works best, but a dozen also functions
+ Scissors
+ Colorful tape (optional)
+ Heavy-duty binder clip
+ Hula hoop

Using a pencil or marker, sketch your glider design on the Styrofoam egg carton, creating the largest wing span possible. Cut along the lines you created.

Decorate the glider with colorful tape and markers. Affix a binder clip to the front to add weight and stability to the glider.

One player is in charge of moving the target (vertically held hula hoop) and the others throw the planes toward the target. The object is to work together to get the planes to fly smoothly through the hula hoop.

Modifications for Younger Kids

Younger kids will need help with the sketching and cutting of the glider. They can direct the tape placement and decorate with markers. If there are babies in the family, give them the leftover (clean) egg carton pieces to explore and destroy under supervision.

Modifications for Older Kids

Older kids can create a fleet of airplanes, experimenting with different shapes, styles and balances, honing a design that works the best for reaching a target. For older kids who have a younger sibling, increase their challenge by placing the youngest child in charge of the goal. You may end up throwing to a very moving target!

Funnel Golf Toss

Funnel Golf Toss is a modified version of a game my brother and I used to play on the golf course when we accompanied my dad for eighteen (very long) holes of golf. This version doesn't require clubs or acres of grass. It can be set up in the space that you have outdoors or taken to the park to mimic the acres available at the golf course.

- - - - - - - - - - - - - - -

Materials

+ Construction paper
+ Scissors
+ Markers
+ 5 to 18 plastic funnels (one for each hole)
+ Skewer sticks
+ Tape
+ Small ball like a Ping-Pong ball, golf ball or even a small bouncy ball

Cut the construction paper into triangular flags. Number your flags starting with 1. Make one for each funnel that you have. Attach the flags to skewer sticks with tape.

Push the small end of the plastic funnel into the ground to create a golf "hole." The top of the funnel doesn't need to be flush with the ground because this game doesn't include putting. Place a numbered flag next to each hole. Designate a starting place a distance from flag 1.

We use rules similar to those for the game of golf. Players have to pick up their ball where it lays and not take any steps before throwing. Once a hole is completed, a radius of 3 feet (92 cm) around that hole is the "tee box" for the next hole.

Each throw counts as a stroke and the player with the lowest score at the end of the game wins.

Modifications for Younger Kids

A heavier ball like a golf ball is easier to control and throw. Very small children can be spotted the advantage of taking steps between throws.

Modifications for Older Kids

A lighter ball like a Ping-Pong ball can help level the playing field when playing with younger children. It can't be thrown as far and is harder to land in the funnel hole without bouncing out.

TIP
A discount store can be a treasure trove of inexpensive funnels. Look for nested sets. The smaller funnels can be used alongside the larger ones, for older, more experienced opponents.

Great Airplane Race

Making paper airplanes is one of our go-to boredom busters because we always have the materials on hand. This activity uses cereal boxes to make larger aircraft, creating mega-size folded airplanes that are perfect for a race as large as their size.

- - - - - - - - - - - - - - -

Materials

+ Clean, empty cereal box
+ Scissors
+ Tape
+ Piece of rope (optional)

Open up the empty cereal box, creating one large piece of cardboard. Cut off the glued tabs as well as any flaps so you are left with a large rectangle.

Fold the box into a traditional paper airplane. Tape the airplane together across the wings to secure it.

Create a finish line out of tape or rope placed on the ground. Each player throws his plane toward the goal. If the plane does not cross the finish line in the first throw, then he walks to where the plane landed and without taking an additional step, throws again, keeping track of how many throws it takes to get to the end.

Modifications for Younger Kids
Younger kids will need some help creating the plane. The stiff cardboard is challenging for little hands. They could use stickers to create a unique design. Use the counting of the throws to reinforce number skills.

Modifications for Older Kids
Older kids can get creative with plane design. They can experiment with new folds and weights and check the results until they find a way to fly farther in one throw.

TIP
If you are using this primarily for outside play, consider weatherizing it by spray painting the plane and adding a traditional paper clip to the nose for flight durability.

Homemade Building Block Puzzle

This homemade puzzle project uses the toys your kids already have and love in a new way. A handful of favorite blocks and a printer can start a new learning process that your kids will embrace. Depending on their age, you can modify it to be simple or have them create a complex set of building instructions.

- - - - - - - - - -

Materials
+ Building blocks
+ Paper or cardstock
+ Copier
+ Lamination (optional)

Lay the blocks on the copier bed and cover with a white piece of paper or cardstock. The blocks can create a picture or pattern or just be arranged randomly.

Make a color copy of the blocks.

Mix up the pieces used for the original creation with some additional pieces. Have the child use the copy as a template to position the piece on top to re-create the structure.

Modifications for Younger Kids
Use large blocks and less assembly for the template picture as a simple shape-sorter activity.

Modifications for Older Kids
Older kids can make color copies of various steps required to make a more complicated structure. Instead of simple blocks, they could use building sets to create their own assembly guide.

*See photo insert page 18.

Paper Plate Reversion

One of our favorite family vacation locations has life-size board games situated throughout the village. You can stop and play a very large set of Chess, Scrabble, Jenga and Connect Four, among some others. The games are the biggest attractions despite other (and more expensive) things to do.

We didn't just want that experience on vacation, so we came home and made our own large version of Othello, which we call Reversi. It can be played indoors and packed up to play another day.

Materials

+ Glue (or double-sided tape)
+ 36 paper or plastic plates in two different colors
+ Masking tape

Glue two plates together so that each side is a different color, creating eighteen game pieces. Use tape to create a 6 x 6 square grid on the floor.

Start with four game pieces in the middle four spaces—two of one color and two of the other color. Then the players take turns placing their color piece on the other side of an opponent's piece. Once a color piece is surrounded on two sides by another color, it can be flipped. The object of the game is to flip as many of your opponent's pieces as possible. The game ends when all the spaces are filled. The person with the most color showing wins.

Modifications for Younger Kids

A big grid on the floor and colorful pieces don't have to have real rules! Let kids create stacks of color or make simple art in the grid. Practicing colors and counting while playing can enforce basic skills.

Modifications for Older Kids

This is a fun game for kids of all ages and something that kids can be competitive with adults. Add more rows to make the game more complicated for older kids. Let your space be your guide and create a massive board with additional pieces for a really, really big game. You can also play the game with a stopwatch and anyone taking more than 5 seconds forfeits that turn.

Human Knot

Some kids are drawn to knots. They have an uncanny way of being able to tie and untie them. My relative Jeannette is like that. She has always been the go-to person for untangling just about anything. She is the one you would want to take with you on a kite flying expedition.

This activity was inspired in part by her love of knots. Use group participants' limbs wrapped together to create a life-size puzzle that requires giggles to solve.

Five or more kiddos works well; fewer than ten is best. Have the kids group together (not orderly, it works best if this "hand grab" is chaotic). Have the children raise their left hands, and have them grab one of the raised hands (not their own). Then repeat with their right hands. Everyone should now be bunched up together, holding hands with two other people. They are one giant human knot!

Without letting go of each other's hands, the kids need to figure out how to unknot the human pretzel that they formed. They will need to climb under and over each other in order to detangle the knot. In the end, the hands should make a giant circle.

Modifications for Younger Kids

Creating a human knot with fewer participants can make it easier to solve. Have one of the kids not in the knot give the participants directions to help them solve the problem.

Modifications for Older Kids

Watch them struggle. This can be a fun group activity with several groups of the same number of kids competing against each other to unknot the quickest.

Recycled Bottle Cup Catch

So many products these days have really fun bottles that can be upcycled into really cool toys. This activity was inspired by my morning coffee habit. I always have refrigerated creamer and the bottles have a unique shape. The product labels are shrink-wrapped, which means that they are easily removed to find a blank canvas for all sorts of crafty goodness.

A string, a bottle and a Ping-Pong ball make a fun cup catch game that you can play by yourself or with a partner.

- - - - - - - - - - - - - - -

Materials
(to make one cup catch)

+ Empty plastic bottle
+ Serrated knife
+ Paint (optional)
+ Small ball—I used a Ping-Pong ball
+ Screw eye hook
+ Glue (optional)
+ String

Remove any labels from the empty plastic bottle and then cut off the bottom of the bottle with a serrated knife. Many plastic bottles have indented rings that work great as a cutting guide.

I spray painted the bottles at this point, but leaving it plain works great, too.

For the Solo Game

Poke a small hole in the Ping-Pong ball and then screw in the hook. If it seems loose, then unscrew the hook and add a little glue to the screw threads before reinserting.

Tie a string to the screw hook and loop the other end through the bottle cap so both ends are secure. You want the string length to be short enough that the ball is not hitting the ground when the child is playing with the toy.

For the Play-Together Game

Remove the stringed Ping-Pong ball from the plastic bottle, make a second cup catcher and use an untethered Ping-Pong ball to fling back and forth.

Modifications for Younger Kids

Have younger kids play on the floor and try to capture the rolling Ping-Pong ball under the cup.

Modifications for Older Kids

This is a great activity for older kids that really challenges them. Have them come up with rules for both games so they can keep score.

Topsy Turvy Game

My grandpa had a desktop toy that I loved to play with when I visited. It was a set of metal rods that were on a slight decline with a metal ball. By placing the ball at the bottom of the hill and carefully moving the rods in and out, I could cautiously propel the ball upward.

This two-person game is inspired by that desktop game featuring gravity. Using two pool noodles and a discount store ball, the object is to move the rods to propel the ball into a bucket.

- - - - - - - - - -

Materials

+ 2 pool noodles
+ 2 buckets
+ Lightweight ball

The two players face each other and hold the ends of the pool noodles in each hand. A bucket is placed at the feet of each participant. The ball is positioned on top of the pool noodles.

Players work together to move the ball to one end and drop the ball into the bucket and then back again to the other bucket. This teamwork game is more about the process than the score.

Modifications for Younger Kids

Pair younger kids with an older partner to assist their movements and coordinate ball movement.

Modifications for Older Kids

Older kids can assign one partner to be stationary and not change the position of their end of the pool noodles, creating a challenge for the other player to move the ball toward the stationary partner's bucket. Score can be kept from the results.

TIP

Working together on ball movement strategies can help kids develop the skills to manage a task without fighting.

Human Jousting

This was the way my brother and I solved conflict as older kids. If one was really frustrated with the other, he or she would call for a joust to settle it. I think it works for two reasons: There are times when you really want to hit your brother. There are times when a little humor will put in perspective the issue at hand.

This activity is just plain silly fun with or without conflict. It also will have any spectators in stitches as they watch two people armed with hand face shields and waving, uncoordinated arm spears joust until it is broken by laughter.

- - - - - - - - - -

The participants stretch their right arm out in front of them, with their right hand about eye level. The left arm wraps underneath the outstretched right arm and the left hand comes up to cover the face entirely.

The right arm is now the spear. The left hand is the face shield.

Participants face each other and take three steps back. Maintaining spear and shield form, they move toward each other to fight until laughter breaks out.

Modifications for Younger Kids

Younger kids may need help wrapping themselves up into the proper form and should be paired with an opponent who fights gently.

Modifications for Older Kids

Set up a tournament where the winner of each bout is the person who didn't smile the longest. A silly bracket of events can be a fun party activity.

Red Light Run

Red Light, Green Light is the first organized game that I remember playing as a child. The excitement of sneaking forward to the goal when the caller's back was turned felt like getting away with something dangerous.

One step. Two steps. I will try three . . . oh no!

Each game was unconsciously a study in predictions and reading people.

We love this traditional game and have a modern twist that starts with a craft to create a contemporary signal light.

-- -- -- -- -- -- -- -- -- -- -- --

Materials
(to make one red light)

+ Tissue box
+ 2 or 3 sheets of white construction paper
+ Tape or glue
+ Lid for tracing
+ 1 sheet each red, yellow and green construction paper
+ Scissors
+ Dark marker

Cover the tissue box with the white paper and tape or glue in place. Using a small lid, trace circles onto the red, yellow and green paper. Cut out four circles in each of the colors. To make it obvious which "light" was lit, we drew dark lines over half of the "lights."

Secure the circles to the box as the lights. We made sure three of the sides only had one light "visible" or without lines on it. On the fourth side we added a "one-way" arrow to tell the kids to turn around.

Have one child roll the "light." The rest of the kids should be at a line across the room/field. Whatever the light says the kids get to do. For example, if it is green they run very fast. If it is yellow they walk slowly. Red they freeze. The race changes as fast as the roller can turn the light. The coveted position in our family was being the light post.

Modifications for Younger Kids

Younger kids don't have to abide by the freeze rule between rolls. They can run free until the next light is chosen.

Younger participants can also be given a head start of time or number of rolls before the older kids join the game.

This game is a great way for young kids to practice listening to simple instructions. It's a great game to help prepare your kids for walking in parking lots or other potentially dangerous areas by using the same instructions as the game commands: "red light—stop" or "yellow—be careful and walk slowly" or "green—you are good to go play."

Modifications for Older Kids

For older participants, add more structure to the game. Try creating roads or paths that they need to drive on. Add some street rules, like they can only pass on the right, or that they have to come to a complete stop before they turn, and so forth.

> ### TIP
> If you don't have the ability to run, consider using Red Light, Green Light as an indoor/outdoor singing game. Red means be quiet, yellow means to sing normally, green means to holler at the top of your lungs.

Shoe Box Pinball

The flashing lights, the music and that elusive ring, ring, ring when the goal is hit makes even watching pinball fun. But deep down in every pinball player is the desire to conquer the coordination it requires and the timing that it demands.

This DIY pinball game starts as a shoe box craft and transforms into a game of coordination. When the game is over, it can be easily stored back in its shoe box shell.

- - - - - - - - - - - - - - - - -

Materials
(to make one game)

+ Scissors
+ 2 foam sheets with sticker backs, or plain foam
+ Cardboard or cardstock—may be needed to stiffen the foam sheets
+ Glue (if the foam lacks a sticky back)
+ 6 unsharpened pencils
+ 1 sharpened pencil
+ Shoe box lid
+ Tape
+ Marble or small bouncy ball

Cut a foam strip approximately 1 inch (2.5 cm) wide and 5 inches (12.5 cm) long. If the foam doesn't keep its shape well, then cut a cardboard strip that is 1 inch (2.5 cm) wide and 2 inches (5 cm) long. Peel the backing off the foam (or cover the foam with a light layer of glue) and place an unsharpened pencil halfway down the length of the foam strip just under the eraser. Fold the foam together over the pencil, sandwiching the cardboard strip. Repeat until you have 6 paddles.

Using the sharpened pencil, push through the bottom of the shoe box, creating holes to put the paddles in that can be controlled from below. Insert the unsharpened pencil "paddles" into the holes.

At each end make a hole for a goal and outline with tape.

Each player uses the paddles to advance the ball toward the goal at the opposite end of the shoe box.

The player that makes five goals first wins.

Modifications for Younger Kids

This is a fun solo game when made with only one goal. Kids can figure out which pencils they need to move to hit the ball above.

This is a simple way for kids to see cause and reaction. A movement below the box can change the course of the ball in the box. Use differently color pencils to help identify which pencil is causing which action.

Modifications for Older Kids

Designing the box ahead of time to give each player a certain number of pencils to control like a foosball game can make it more competitive and fair. Using a larger box and setting it up on the backs of two chairs can stabilize the game for play.

*See photo insert page 18.

Team Banded Together

In high school I attended a leadership camp for three glorious days of team-building exercises. As a team we scaled walls, went through obstacles and caught one another as we fell backward off a platform. I was in team-loving heaven.

The family is the ultimate team. A group of people born to work together! This series of activities using a stretchy T-shirt band can help build team family!

- - - - - - - - - - - - - - - - -

Materials

+ Stretchy material like old T-shirts or sportlike material
+ Sewing machine (optional)

Using strips from old T-shirts or purchased material with a good stretch, create a band that is 12 to 18 inches (30.5 to 45.5 cm) wide and 12 feet (3.7 m) long. Sew the ends of the 12-foot (3.7-m)-long strip together to create a complete circle. Using knots to bind the ends together will work as well. It needs to be strong . . . *it is about to get tested!*

Gather the participants together on a soft playing surface. Three or four players works well, and a backyard lawn is the perfect surface.

One person is designated as the coach and will give the directions. The other players get inside the band, placing the band at waist level.

The kids' first impulse is to run in opposite directions inside the band. This in itself will take a minute to sort out.

Stretchy Band Games

- **Taxi Game:** Have the driver be the smallest child in a multi-age situation. The driver is to go in one direction as fast as possible while the other kids move to the "back" of the band and try to slow down the driver—without making the driver fall.
- **Shape Creation:** Shout out a shape for the kids to make and watch as the kids try to shift to fashion that shape with the band. Depending on the number in the band, this can take some balance and thought.
- **Obstacle Course:** Set up a few obstacles that the team must successfully negotiate to cross the "finish line"—together.

- **Big Boss:** Have a coach call out directions such as "Turn right," "Rotate to the left," "Switch leaders," "Walk backward," and so on. The participants follow the commands while maintaining the band around their waists.
- **Impossi-pull:** Everyone in the loop pulls away from the center, but only at the resistance of the smallest member. It takes adjusting to keep the pressure at a strength that accommodates all.

Modifications for Younger Kids

The stretchier the fabric, the more unexpected force can happen from the band. Make sure that if there is a large gap in participant size, an older child or parent is working from the inside to make sure the smaller participant is not being run over. One easy way to do that is to place that younger child in charge of leading the group or giving instructions.

Modifications for Older Kids

Older kids can be the "coach" or buddy of smaller participants in multi-age/size scenarios. When older kids play together, the instructions and obstacles can be more complicated, emphasizing the need to communicate as a team to finish the task.

Want to make this game more complicated for older kids? Mix this activity with the Red Light Run (page 145).

TIP

Do you have two kids who are constantly at war? Use an activity like this to team them up against a parent and watch how a common goal can overcome differences.

Tin Can Target

My kids are simply noisy. It doesn't seem to matter how many times I hush them; at some point in the day they will be sent ouside to expend all that sound energy. The other thing that goes along with all that noise is the innate need to throw things. "No throwing inside the house" is a reminder that is given daily. This game incorporates both childish tendencies, along with items from our recycle bin, to create a fun musical game.

We use recycled tin cans as targets for throwing spoons, rewarding those who hit the cans with a delightful ring.

- - - - - - - - - - - - - - - - -

Materials

+ Empty, clean tin cans, in a variety of shapes and sizes
+ Sandpaper or wide, sturdy tape
+ Nail
+ Hammer
+ Rope
+ Bolt
+ Lots of ice cream spoons
+ Paint and embellishments (optional)

Make sure the inside of the can is free of sharp edges by smoothing with sandpaper or covering them with sturdy tape. Use a nail and hammer to make a hole in the closed end of the can. Thread one end of the rope through the hole and tie the bolt on the end inside the can. Use an ice cream spoon to fix the bolt in a ringer position by adding it several inches above the bolt to stop rope slippage through the hole. Your child has now created a can "bell." Repeat the process until you have a collection of different size "bells" for your children to hit.

We made our cans easier to spot and more fun to bang with decorations. With the help of paint, stickers and bands of tape we decorated our cans.

Modifications for Younger Kids

For younger kids, enjoy watching them run around banging on the tin can bells. You can also make it easier for them by placing the bells close together. You can encourage your children to create a pattern or a rhythm with their banging, or ask them to work with a partner to create a "song" together.

Modifications for Older Kids

Find a place to hang the bells. We used the trees in our backyard, but a ladder or even a fence can work well if there are no trees or hanging hooks available. Each player is given an equal stack of spoons. They stand on a designated spot away from the target and throw the spoon, trying to hit the can. A ring of the bell counts as a point, which is signified by moving one of their remaining spoons into a "point pile." The player who runs out of spoons first wins.

The Great Toy Toss

Did all the toy bins at your house explode?

Never fear, The Great Toy Toss is coming to the rescue. This game will get kids working together toward a clean up cause with nary a complaint. Kids can be paired together or work in teams to launch stuffed animals toward a laundry basket goal.

- - - - - - - - - - - - - - - - -

Materials

+ 2 pillowcases
+ Collection of stuffed animals
+ Laundry basket or toy bin

Two kids each hold the end of a pillowcase. It is positioned like a stretcher with a toy placed in the middle.

Kids work together to bounce a toy into the air with the aim of landing it in the desired laundry basket goal.

The Great Toy Toss with 4+ Kids

Have two or more teams. Have team A call for a toy from team B. Team A tosses the toy without touching it, with the help of the pillowcase. Team B tries to catch the toy on their pillowcase, then drops it into the toy bin.

To increase the difficulty, set two laundry baskets on opposite sides of the room, with each team trying to get animals in their respective goals. Animals from the opposite team need to be bounced into the goal while animals from their pile need to be bounced to the opposite team's pillowcase trampoline.

Modifications for Younger Kids

Use the pillowcase to create a toy trampoline. No need for a goal; this is just plain fun!

For the youngest participants, hide the toy underneath the pillowcase. Watch your child play peek-a-boo with the toy.

Modifications for Older Kids

Teams can create an elaborate bounce obstacle course or pattern that the toy needs to go through to get to the goal. For instance, they may require the first trampoline to bounce the toy three times and then launch to the other player or team that has to take the toy in three rotations before launching back. Let kids get creative with instructions, which will become surprisingly complicated!

TIP

When you make cleanup into a game it helps reenergize kiddos and brings a smile to what otherwise might be a disappointing time of the day. We also sing "cleanup" songs to cue our preschoolers that it is "time to work."

Watch It Fall

There is a part inside each of us that wants to get away with something. To make a mess. To cause a disaster. To just "see what would happen if . . . ." We would love to cause a chain reaction, defy nature or stop the inevitable. It is an intense willing against the unavoidable.

This is a simple game created from kitchen utensils and recyclables that will have family members holding their breath as they test their ability to stop what is certain to happen.

- - - - - - - - - -

Materials

+ Pom-poms or packing peanuts
+ Large spaghetti strainer
+ Package of pipe cleaners or wooden skewers
+ Something to balance the strainer on (e.g., books or blocks)

Place a layer of pom-poms or packing peanuts in the bottom of the strainer to approximately 4 inches (10 cm) deep. Push pipe cleaners through one side of the strainer and out the other. Continue to add pipe cleaners at random angles until the strainer can be turned over without the pom-poms falling out. Turn the strainer upside down and place on several books or blocks so that the underside of the strainer can be seen.

Each player takes a turn pulling out the pipe cleaner of his/her choice. If the removal causes pom-poms to fall, then those fallen pom-poms are placed in front of that player. At the end of the game, the person who has the smallest pile of fallen pom-poms wins.

(continued)

Modifications for Younger Kids

Don't worry about trying to stop the pom-poms from falling; let the kids watch as their actions cause reactions. Tots will enjoy playing with them even without the "rules" of the game. If your tot still puts small items in his mouth, play "threading" and watch your child gain fine motor skills as he threads pipe cleaners in the colander.

Modifications for Older Kids

Let older kids set up the game with the goal of finding a strategy for pulling the most pipe cleaners out without any pom-poms falling.

*See photo insert page 18.

Water Bomb Games

Sponges, with just a couple of adaptations, make a great toy to use in a variety of water games. We have enjoyed our sponge water "bombs" in the bathtub, tried to avoid getting wet in a game of Sponge Dodgeball and played Duck, Duck, Goose . . . only "Goose" was "You're wet! Bet you can't catch me!"

This activity creates a sponge bomb and adds a few suggestions for games to play.

- - - - - - - - - - - - - - - - -

Materials
(makes two water bombs)

+ Scissors
+ 5 different-colored sponges
+ Sturdy string

Cut the sponges lengthwise. You can get three or four strips from most sponges. Stack half of the sponge strips together, mixing the colored strips for variety. Very tightly, tie the string around the center of the stacked sponges. As you cinch the string and knot it, the sponge strips should bunch out—like a giant pom-pom.

Grab a bucket of water, some kids and have fun!

Sponge Dodgeball

Have your children try to get you or their friends "out" by hitting them with the wet sponge balls.

Duck, Duck, Goose

Have your children sit in a circle as they play this classic game. As the child walks around the circumference of the circle, saying, "Duck, Duck," have them lightly touch the kids as they walk . . . but when it comes to "Goose," have the child who is "It" squeeze the water sponge onto the "Goose." "Jail" can be a kiddie pool in the center filled with water.

Paint Pollock Style

Fill a couple of buckets with a variety of colors of sidewalk paint (page 219). Put the sponge balls into the buckets. When the kids want to paint with that color, have them throw the paint-soaked ball at the sidewalk, or sling paint along the way. Hose off your children and the walkway when you are finished.

Modifications for Younger Kids

Different-size sponge strips will create different textures of sponge bombs—play around with the design. You can even use dish rags or cut-up pieces of felt or fleece and add these to your balls. These make great sensory toys when dry to let tots explore what each feels like.

Throw a couple of these into the tub for a fun bathtime game. When dry, these are great quiet toys to have in the diaper bag for a young tot.

Modifications for Older Kids

Leave a bucket of these at the door and welcome your children home to a game of sponge ball "War." They will love you for it!

(seven)

FANTASTIC READING

Oftentimes, we think of beginning reading only as learning the alphabet. Although learning to read does include the knowledge of letters, it encompasses so much more. These games include everything from letter names and sounds to learning sight words and extending sentences. The following games touch upon just a few components of early literacy and are a great way to reinforce and teach early-reading concepts.

It is recommended that in addition to playing a learning game with your child each day, you also read to your children for 10 to 15 minutes. Discuss the story with your child. Talk about the characters, setting and storyline. Talking about the story strengthens reading comprehension and vocabulary. We have found that the best times for reading stories are:

- First thing in the morning
- Right after lunchtime
- After dinner
- Before bedtime

Make sure to read a variety of fiction and nonfiction books, allowing your child to self-select the books they are interested in. Trips to the local public library or bookstore will help increase the number of books in your home library and encourage more reading.

Stack a Word

*Focus Skill: blending letter sounds in spoken words •
Great For: moving while you learn*

Learning to read can be exciting for children. Learning how to blend letter sounds is one of the foundations to success. Players use movement and visual clues as they stack the cans to form words.

Materials

+ Construction paper
+ Scissors
+ 10 cans of similar size
+ Black marker
+ Tape

Directions to Make

Cut 10 pieces of paper to wrap around the cans.

Write two vowels and two consonants on each paper. Vary letter combinations to include all letters.

Attach a letter paper to each can with tape.

Write down on a separate paper select consonant-vowel-consonant (CVC) words in focused word families.

Directions to Play

One player calls out words from the focused word family sheet.

The other player uses the cans to sound out the words and stack on one another to form each word.

Continue to create words until all the cans are used.

Game Variations

Use cans to create letters in family members' names.

Create word family sets by adding an additional vowel-only can.

Create nonsense words and sound out them while stacking on top of each other.

*See photo insert page 19.

Roll the Alphabet

Focus Skill: saying the alphabet in order

Children often can sing the alphabet, but have trouble saying it. The letters l, m, n, o, p are separate letters. These letters are the building blocks for literacy; naming the letters is one component. So, grab a ball and get rolling. See if you can get from A to Z without letting the ball roll away!

Materials

+ ABC chart or poster
+ Playground ball

Directions to Make

Prior to playing, sing the ABC song with your child.

Show your child the alphabet poster. Sing the song again and point to each letter as you sing it.

Directions to Play

Have the child sit on the floor with their feet touching yours. Explain that you are going to say a letter and roll the ball to them. Roll the ball to them and say "A."

They will say the next letter in the alphabet and roll the ball to you.

Continue the game in this manner until you reach the end, Z. Try to roll the entire alphabet without having the ball roll away.

Move farther apart from each other and repeat the game.

Game Variations

As children become more confident with rolling the ball, try to bounce the alphabet.

For an extra challenge, say a word that begins with that letter. Apple, bear, coin, dog . . .

Roll the letters in the child's name.

Mystery Alphabet

Focus Skill: identifying lowercase letters •
Great For: on-the-go learning

Everyone loves a good mystery. In this game children will close their eyes and take turns being a letter detective by feeling the shape of the hidden letter. This game teaches children to be more aware of the shape of each letter. Knowing the shape of the letters will help children transition to reading as they see these same shape formations within books.

- - - - - - - - - - - - - -

Materials

+ ABC puzzle
+ Small paper or canvas lunch bag

Directions to Play

The first person will place a letter in the bag while the other will close his or her eyes.

Put your hand in the bag to feel the letter. NO PEEKING!

Try to guess the letter name and say the sound the letter makes.

Take the letter out to check if your guess was right.

If you guess right, then it is your turn to select the next letter. If your guess was wrong, close your eyes and let the first person select another letter.

Continue the game until all the letters have been identified.

Game Variations

Instead of saying the letter name and sound, have the child say a word that begins with that sound. If the letter is M, they may say, "Monkey starts with m."

As the letters are pulled out of the bag, arrange them in alphabetical order.

Use a shape puzzle in lieu of letters for a shape math game.

NOTE

All children learn differently. Activating the sense of touch is different from relying on eyes. When you are playing learning games with your child, make sure to include a variety of senses. Take note of which activities your child tends to enjoy more. Do those often!

Zip-Line Letters

*Focus Skill: letter identification, letter sounds •
Great For: moving while you learn*

Zoom the alphabet across the room in this high-flying zip-line adventure. Uppercase letter names and sounds are traditionally taught first. If your child has mastered the uppercase letters, then consider writing all lowercase or even making a set of both and matching the letters before zooming.

- - - - - - - - - - - -

Materials

+ 2-inch (5-cm) tag board squares (one piece of paper will make 20)
+ Black permanent marker
+ Paper clips
+ Tape
+ 15 feet (14.5 m) of yarn

Directions to Make

Write one uppercase letter on each tag board square until all the letters have been used.

Bend the paper clip to create a hook.

Tape the paper clip hook to the back of each letter square, making sure that one half is sticking out of the top of the square.

Directions to Play

Tie one end of the yarn to a solid stationary object, such as the handle of a closed door. Hold the other in your hand.

Slide a letter card and hook onto the yarn near your hand. Pull the yarn tight.

Raise your arm and watch the letter soar.

As the letter zips across the room, make its sound. Example: BBBBB, MMMMM or ZZZZZZZZZZZZZZZZZZ!

Build another zip line parallel to the first.

Invite a friend or family member to race letters.

Game Variations

String the letters on in order or zoom your name.

Put three or more letters together on the zip line to spell a word.

Pictures with beginning word sounds can zip after the letters.

Squirt the Letter Fish

Focus Skill: identifying the most common sound for the letters • Great For: moving while you learn

Learning letter sounds is a splash with this outside water game. Young children need to interact with letters in a variety of ways. This will help them gain familiarity with the way each letter looks and sounds. The goal is for children to see a letter and be able to name the sound instantaneously. If they can name the sound after thinking about it for a while, that is fantastic. Keep playing with the letters to speed up the recognition!

- - - - - - - - - - - -

Materials

+ Chalk
+ Spray bottle or water bottle with water

Directions to Make

Chalk the outline for 26 fish on the driveway or fence.

Write a letter inside each fish.

Directions to Play

Call out a letter sound, such as B, that is heard at the beginning of the word big.

Have your child spray the letter fish that makes the sound.

Continue to call out letter sounds until all have been identified.

Game Variations

Call out the letter name instead of the letter sound to work on letter identification.

Use letter cards and have the child first draw a letter from a bucket and find its match to squirt.

Call out a word and have your child spray the letter fish that makes the first sound in that word.

Stringing Letters

Focus Skill: identifying alphabetical order

Memorizing the shapes of letters will quickly help your child learn to identify the alphabet. Players create fun, hands-on letters using glue and string. Once ready, they make the perfect material to hang in alphabetical order for even more letter practice.

- - - - - - - - - - - - - -

Materials

+ Yarn
+ Scissors
+ Wax paper
+ Glue
+ Container
+ Sturdy rope
+ 26 clothespins

Directions to Make

Cut yarn into pieces of various lengths.

Lay out wax paper on a smooth surface for letters to dry on.

Have children dip yarn pieces into a glue container and then shape the wet yarn into letter formations on the wax paper.

Allow yarn to dry before playing the game.

String a long and sturdy rope up in the room and attach clothespins onto it.

Directions to Play

Players work together to place letters in alphabetic order by attaching them to the rope with the clothespins.

As they place the letters, encourage them to name the letters they are attaching to the rope.

Game Variations

Use letters to create a child's name on the rope.

Use letters to create sight words.

Create a timed challenge to see how fast they can put letters up in alphabetical order.

*See photo insert page 19.

> ### NOTE
> This game needs to be created over the course of a few days to allow for drying. Consider starting with the letters in a child's name or a specific grouping of letter formations, like E, L, T, I, H.

Caterpillar Cover

Focus Skill: matching uppercase and lowercase letters

Children of all ages are fascinated with both caterpillars and colorful lids. Gather your recyclables to make and play this eco-friendly game. Your kids will have a blast practicing letter matching with a little fine motor strengthening too.

- - - - - - - - - - - - - - - - - -

Materials

+ 10 or more plastic lids
+ Printer paper
+ Pencil
+ Crayons
+ Permanent marker

Directions to Make

Trace the lids onto the paper to make circles for the caterpillar's body. Make one caterpillar for each player.

Draw a face and antennae on an end circle. Color and add legs to the caterpillar.

Write one lowercase letter inside each remaining circle.

Write one uppercase letter on each plastic lid.

Directions to Play

Turn the lids upside down.

Flip one lid. Read the letter, then place it on the caterpillar, covering its lowercase pair.

Repeat until the caterpillar's body is filled.

Game Variations

Make the caterpillar the same length as your child's name. Write the letters in the circles and on the lids.

Make several caterpillars for focus on sight words or spelling words.

Use number words in the circles and dots to represent the numerical amount on the lids.

1, 2, 3, Let's Find the A, B, C's

Focus Skill: knowing the letter names in order • Great For: moving while you learn

In this spin-off of the classic hide-and-seek game, children search for letters and place them in alphabetical order as quickly as possible. It's a great game for rainy days, to get kids moving and learning the letters.

- - - - - - - - - - - - - - - - - -

Materials

+ 14 (3 x 5-inch [7.5 x 13-cm]) notecards
+ Scissors
+ Black marker
+ String

Directions to Make

Cut each of the notecards in half.

Write one letter of the alphabet on each card. Make sure to use all capital letters or all lowercase letters.

Lay the string straight on the ground.

Directions to Play

One player hides the alphabet cards in the selected area while the other players close their eyes.

When all the cards are hidden, the players open their eyes and say, "1, 2, 3, Let's find the A, B, C's."

As they find each letter, they bring it back to the string on the floor. They say the name of the letter and place it in alphabetical order. Use the string alphabet from Stringing Letters (page 155) as a guide.

Game Variations

For advanced learners, have the children say the name of the letter and name a word that begins with that sound.

Swap words in a sentence for letters and have the children search for and build a sentence.

Instead of hiding the letters around the room, place the letters in a sensory bin to find.

Letter Toss Race

Focus Skill: recognizing uppercase and lowercase letters and sounds • Great For: moving while you learn

Who can find and name the letters of the alphabet the fastest? Challenge your child to name and toss the letters of the alphabet with this playful alphabet movement game. This game is a fun, hands-on way to focus on learning letters and letter sounds with your child.

- - - - - - - - - - - - - - - -

Materials

+ Index cards
+ Black marker
+ Alphabet stickers (optional)
+ Foam, wooden or plastic letters
+ Bucket

Directions to Make

Create letter cards for the game by writing each alphabet letter on a card. Optionally, use alphabet stickers to add color. Complete with your child.

Directions to Play

Lay out the plastic letters of the alphabet for players to select from.

Set up the letter cards and bucket within tossing distance of the letters.

One player holds up the letter card.

The second player identifies the letter and finds it in the plastic letter pile.

The second player then tosses it into the letter bucket by the other player.

Game Variations

Create cards with images that represent each letter sound and ask players to locate and identify the letter to be tossed.

Create cards with lowercase letters and allow players to only choose from uppercase letters in the pile to play.

Use two buckets and two sets of letters for players to race to find the letters the quickest, with one person holding the cards for players.

Build a Letter

Focus Skill: identifying uppercase and lowercase letters

What are letters made of? Sticks, circles and curves of course! This game is perfect for your little engineer who likes to build things. Make a set of shapes and then have your child pick three and see which letters they can make. Our favorite letter is Q because it uses two curves and a short stick. Which letter is your favorite?

- - - - - - - - - - - - - - - -

(continued)

Materials

+ Cardstock or cereal boxes
+ Ruler
+ Scissors
+ Paper
+ Marker

Directions to Make

Using the cardstock, cut two each of:

+ Rectangles ½ inch x 3 inches (1.3 x 7.5 cm)
+ Rectangles ½ inch x 6 inches (1.3 x 15 cm)
+ 6-inch (15-cm) circles
+ 3-inch (7.5-cm) circles with middles removed
+ 6-inch (15-cm) ovals cut in half with middles removed

Write the alphabet (uppercase or lowercase letters) in order on the piece of paper to use as a reference and a game recording sheet.

Directions to Play

Pick three shapes from the pile.

Build a letter.

Put an X over the letter on the alphabet.

Put the pieces back into the pile.

Repeat steps 1 through 4.

See if you can build all the letters in the alphabet.

Game Variations

Build a shape.

Make a pattern with the pieces.

Use all of the pieces to build simple consonant-vowel-consonant words.

*See photo insert page 19.

Slide and Say

*Focus Skill: blending single-syllable words •
Great For: moving while you learn*

Next time you are at the park, bring along some alphabet letters to play this word-blending game with your child. The kids LOVE sliding letters down the slide and making new words. Learning at the park just feels inherently more playful! This game is a great way to combine gross motor movement, outside play and reading.

Materials

+ Letters from a puzzle

Directions to Play

Set the alphabet pieces out at the top of the slide.

Call out a single-syllable word. Sample words: red, hit, hot, cut, cup, mat, rug.

Have the child select the letters needed to make the word.

Encourage them to say the letter sounds as they slide each down the slide.

The child then slides down and says the word as they slide.

The letters are collected and brought back to the top.

Game Variations

Slide a single letter, saying the sound as you slide.

Write entire sight words on note cards, slide and say the words.

Use numbers instead of letters. Slide the number. Then you slide. When you get to the bottom, hop that many times.

Star Hop

Focus Skill: isolating and pronouncing middle sounds in simple three-letter words • Great For: moving while you learn

Much of traditional learning seems to take place in a desk. Although important, it's also vital to get kids moving and shaking. This sound game will encourage children to pay extra attention to the middle sounds in words. Driveway reading is always a favorite at our house!

- - - - - - - - -

Materials

+ Sidewalk chalk
+ List of consonant-vowel-consonant (CVC) words (sample words: cat, dig, bag, rig, bet, fig, red, man, bug, ten, run, can, let, fit, mat)

Directions to Make

Clean an area on a sidewalk or driveway.

Draw a straight line that is 6 feet (1.8 m) long.

Draw a 6-inch (15-cm) circle, star and another circle 2 feet (60 cm) apart on the line.

Write the word "start" 1 foot (30 cm) before a circle.

Directions to Play

The child stands on the word "start."

The parent or teacher calls out a CVC word.

The child then hops on the circle and calls out the first sound. They then hop on the star and call out the middle sound. They hop on the second circle and say the last sound.

The parent or teacher points to the star and asks, "What sound did you hear in the middle of the word?" The child then calls out the star sound. If needed, encourage the player to re-hop the word.

Game Variations

Write the CVC words on 3 x 5-inch (7.5 x 13-cm) notecards. Have one child call out the words for the others to hop.

Leave a bucket of chalk at the end of the line. Encourage the players to hop the sounds then write the word on the sidewalk.

For extra support, work with one or two word families at a time. Slowly add in words as each sound is mastered.

> ### NOTE
> Being able to identify the middle sound in words is often harder than finding the initial or end sounds. Use a suggested game variation or switch the star to the beginning or end of the line for a while before focusing on the middle sounds.

Fill the Bucket

Focus Skill: initial letter sounds • Great For: moving while you learn

Toys and learning tools are all around you. Use them in a new way in this early-literacy game that focuses on isolating initial, or beginning, sounds in words. The kids always look forward to a friendly race to fill the letter buckets. Set out a few small restaurant toys and your kids are sure to find a few items for each letter . . . Okay, who are we kidding? You have our permission to skip the hard ones! Unless, of course, you have a zebra in your house.

- - - - - - - - -

Materials

+ Plastic letters or homemade letter cards
+ Bag or container for letters
+ 3 plastic buckets or containers
+ Small toys or objects

(continued)

Directions to Make

Place the plastic letters or letter cards in the bag or container. Mix.

Directions to Play

Select three letters from the bag. Read the letters selected. Say the name and the sound the letter makes.

Set one letter in front of each bucket.

Race around the room to find small toys and objects that begin with that letter. If B was selected, you may add a ball, bear, bat, bag or banana to the bucket.

When the game is over, dump the buckets out and name the objects. Remove any that do not start with the selected letter. Then count the number of objects in each bucket. The letter with the most WINS!

Game Variations

Use colors instead of letter sounds.

Pre-select the objects for the three letters and have the child race to sort them into the buckets.

Vary the number of buckets from 1 to 5, using fewer for younger learners and more for an added challenge.

*See photo insert page 19.

ABC Water Challenge

Focus Skill: identifying most frequent letter sounds

How fast can you find a letter sound? With this sound challenge players quickly search for the letter sounds that are being called out. Knowing the sound each letter makes is phonics, and vital to being able to sound out words. Letter sounds are the foundation of early reading for kids.

Materials

+ Water-friendly vertical surface
+ Foam letters
+ Container big enough to fit the foam letters
+ Water
+ Alphabet chart

Directions to Make

Create a setup for letters to be placed on a vertical surface. Create or purchase foam letters, then set up the container with water for letters.

Directions to Play

One player or adult calls out the letter sound from the alphabet chart.

The second player locates the letter in the water and places it on the vertical surface.

The game continues until all the letter sounds have been called and placed on the surface.

Game Variations

Set a time and see how fast each player can find the letter sounds.

For younger children, start with a smaller amount of letters and letter sounds.

Create images for each letter sound for players to use to find a match.

Label the Room

Focus Skill: reading simple words • Great For: moving while you learn

In this reading game, children race to label the objects in the room with words. Not only is this a great way to learn new words, it is a fast way to add more environmental print to your learning area. Environmental print words are those your child sees in their world. These words must be taught and used on a day-to-day basis for them to be most effective.

Materials

+ 3 x 5-inch (7.5 x 13-cm) notecards
+ Marker
+ Painter's tape
+ Timer

Directions to Make

Select 10 objects in your learning area. Write the word or phrase of each object on a notecard.

Roll up tape and stick to the back of each word card.

Directions to Play

Put five cards on the fingers of one hand. Read the words on the cards.

Have the child place all five cards next to the object they represent. Don't give any hints!

Walk around and read the cards out loud. Celebrate if the word is in the correct place. Allow the child to re-place the card if it is not labeled correctly.

Game Variations

Include a picture sketch next to each word.

Write a full sentence on each card.

Make a chart with all of the words used. Match the word card to the chart prior to placing it next to the object it represents.

Family Photo Word Puzzles

Focus Skill: word recognition •
Great For: on-the-go learning

Family names are often the first words our children learn to say, read and write. Use your digital images in a new way by creating fun, hands-on family photo puzzles your child will love. As they piece together the pictures of family members, they will begin to practice word recognition of their names, too.

Materials

+ Camera
+ 6 to 10 printed 4 x 6-inch (10 x 15-cm) photographs of family members
+ 6 to 10 squares of 6 x 6-inch (15 x 15-cm) construction paper
+ Scissors
+ Ziplock bag

Directions to Make

Encourage your child to take photos of family members.

Select photos of each family member to print.

Glue each photo onto a piece of construction paper, leaving a 2-inch (5-cm) space below the photo.

Write family members' names or key words below the photos, making sure to leave space between each letter.

Cut each image into vertical puzzle pieces, with one letter on each piece.

Directions to Play

Place the photo pieces with letters into the bag.

Take turns drawing puzzle pieces from the bag. As your child removes the piece they will arrange pieces into the proper letter order to create the word.

Once assembled, encourage your child to practice naming the words and letters in the family members' names.

Game Variations

Create additional photo word cards for household objects or favorite animals.

Create letter puzzles by taking photos to represent each letter of the alphabet.

Write a sentence under each picture.

*See photo insert page 20.

Word Family Toss

Focus Skill: reading words from the same word family endings, rhyming words • Great For: moving while you learn

Word families are words that share a common set of letters that make a similar sound. The "_at" family words are often taught first: cat, hat, bat, mat, rat and sat are all in the "_at" word family. Learning these words helps children gain familiarity with common spelling patterns. Repeated readings of a word help build familiarity and confidence with reading. Using beach balls brings a playful element to reading words and gets kids moving and working together!

- - - - - - - - - - - - -

Materials

+ 3 rainbow-colored beach balls
+ Permanent marker

Directions to Make

Select three word families to focus on, such as "_at," "_en" and "_ig."

Write the words from the selected word families on each beach ball color section.

cat, rat, mat, hat, pat, sat

pig, wig, dig, fig, big, zig

pen, men, hen, ten, when, den

Directions to Play

In this game, children will gently toss the word family ball to each other. As they catch the ball, they will read the first word they see.

If the ball drops, then the child reads all the words on the ball.

Play continues for several rounds.

Swap out balls as children gain familiarity with reading the words.

Game Variations

If children are in a long line, start the ball at the beginning of the line and play pass the word. Players call out the first word they see on the ball as they receive it.

For an extra challenge, try throwing and catching two word family balls at a time.

Use this game to practice assigned spelling or vocabulary words

*See photo insert page 20.

Fluttering Butterflies

Focus Skill: isolating and pronouncing final sounds • Great For: moving while you learn

Let your word butterflies fly, then catch them as the word ends. Say the last sound you hear, then let them fly again! Playing with words is extremely beneficial for helping children to develop a better ear for sounds. This game is all about listening for those sounds.

- - - - - - - - - - - - -

Materials

+ Tissue paper rectangles, 2 x 4 inches (5 x 10 cm)

Directions to Make

Select two tissue paper rectangles. Set them on top of each other and pinch the middles together.

Twist at the middle so the two rectangles stay together in a butterfly shape.

Directions to Play

Throw a butterfly up in the air.

Say a word slowly as the butterfly flutters downward.

Catch the butterfly as the word ends.

Say the last sound heard in the word.

Repeat with another word.

Game Variations

Try to find the ending sounds in longer words.

Encourage your child to think of and say words that end with the same sound.

Catch the butterfly on the beginning or middle sound to emphasize different sounds in the word.

NOTE
We used our same twisted butterflies for two weeks of word-catching fun and they did not come untwisted! If you wanted to tie a bow in the middle, you could.

Preposition Charades

Focus Skill: using and reading the most frequently occurring prepositions • Great For: on-the-go learning

Use your creativity to act out the chosen preposition. Children must know what prepositions are, so that when they come across them in a story they will be able to comprehend what is happening. Pick up any storybook and read for the prepositions. They are there! Then get silly with this pre-reading game that requires a wee bit of acting skills. See if you can get your teammates to correctly guess the word.

Materials
+ 3 x 5-inch (7.5 x 13-cm) notecards
+ Scissors
+ Pencil
+ Box
+ Toys

Directions to Make
Cut each of the notecards in half.

Write one preposition word on each card: in, on, near, under, over, below, above, around, between, behind, in front of, up, down, out, over.

Directions to Play
Turn the cards word side down.

Have the child read the word and act out the word using the box and toy props.

The other players try to guess the preposition using a sentence to describe the preposition.

The player who guesses the preposition correctly then draws a new card from the pile.

Play continues until all cards have been read and performed.

Game Variations
Play this game using a dollhouse and accessories to act out the prepositions.

For extra support, have the adult read the word out loud and children work in pairs to act out the preposition.

Draw a card, act it out and have the players write their sentence guesses on a piece of paper.

Muffin Tin Syllable Counting

Focus Skill: counting syllables in spoken words

Say and count syllables in this self-checking muffin tin game. Sneak in a little fine motor practice and boost early literacy skills while picking up buttons. Let the kids help draw the game pieces and you tie in art and creativity too.

- - - - - - - - - - - - - -

Materials

+ 2-inch (5-cm) circle
+ Cardstock
+ Pencil
+ Crayons or markers
+ Scissors
+ 12 cup muffin tin
+ Buttons

Directions to Make

Trace around the 2-inch (5-cm) circle 12 times on the cardstock.

Draw a picture of a person, place or thing inside each circle. Cutting pictures from magazines works too! Some examples are dog, caterpillar, fish, bicycle, shoe, car, banana, apple, book, table, circus and library.

Color and cut out each picture.

Turn the circles over and make a dot for each syllable in the word. The back of the circle with the dog picture would have one dot; caterpillar would have four.

Directions to Play

Place the pictures, image side up, in the muffin tin. The player names the picture out loud and counts the number of syllables in the word.

The player drops the same number of buttons as syllables in the tin.

Play continues until all compartments have been filled with buttons. When this happens, the player self-checks and corrects the number of syllables by turning the picture over and comparing the number of buttons in each compartment with the number of circles on the back of the image.

Game Variations

Focus the pictures on a specific learning theme such as natural life, ocean or transportation.

Select and read a story. Use vocabulary words and characters from the story to make the picture cards.

Focus on number sense by changing the pictures to numbers. Have the player count out the buttons to match the written number.

*See photo insert page 20.

Make It Longer

Focus Skill: expanding complete sentences •
Great For: on-the-go learning

My kids get in the car and start playing this game automatically—it is one of their favorite on-the-go literacy games and is really good for strengthening vocabulary skills. Even the 2-year-old joins in. He likes to be the one who starts the sentences.

For this game, take a simple sentence and add just one describing word to make it longer. Vocabulary is one of the five components to literacy instruction. This game encourages children to really understand the words they are using. A young child may not be able to read the words catch and furry, but they understand what they mean. This game is done orally to really focus on this vocabulary development.

Reviewing describing words prior to playing the game may make it easier for children to come up with ways to make their sentences longer!

- - - - - - - - - - - - - -

Materials

+ None

Directions to Play

One child begins by saying a simple sentence out loud. For example, I see a dog.

The next player uses the same words and adds one word or phrase to the sentence. I see a black dog.

The players continue to repeat the sentence on their turn and add a word or phrase more on each turn.

I see a black dog run fast.

I see a furry black dog run fast.

I see a furry black dog run fast to catch a mouse.

I see a furry black dog run fast to catch a gray mouse.

I see a furry black dog run fast to catch a little gray mouse.

The game stops when the sentence becomes too long to remember!

Game Variations

Have advanced learners write their last sentence down on paper.

Provide props such as stuffed animals for children to act out the sentence, which aids in memory.

Encourage the use of specific spelling or vocabulary words in the sentences.

Storytelling Puzzles

Focus Skill: comparing characters in a story •
Great For: on-the-go learning

Characters in stories draw our children's attention. Using handmade puzzles that you create together, players learn to discuss and compare the various types of characters. Story time discussions about characters enhance reading comprehension and vocabulary development.

- - - - - - - - - - - -

Materials

+ Favorite storybook
+ Images from selected story
+ Paper
+ Scanner/printer
+ Scissors
+ Plastic bag

Directions to Make

Create images from favorite parts of a story by drawing or using a scanner to copy and print.

Cut each image into 4 to 6 puzzle pieces.

Directions to Play

Player selects pieces from the bag in correct order to form images from the story.

Encourage players to identify the characters and setting in the story with each image formed.

Game Variations

Players can place images in sequence from the story.

Players sort completed puzzles into groups of similarities based on characters and setting.

Create a magnetic game by placing magnetic stripes on the back of puzzle pieces.

Real or Nonsense?

Focus Skill: blending together sounds to make simple words

Make up silly words (and real ones too) by rolling homemade letter dice. Grab a cubed tissue box, cover with paper and add a few letters. Then let your kids roll, read and call out the new word—is it real or nonsense? My kids have added their own "spin" to the game and make a silly face when the word rolled doesn't make sense. Bat, get, fan and men are all real words, but gip is a nonsense word!

- - - - - - - - - - - - - - - - -

Materials

+ Paper
+ Scissors
+ 3 square tissue boxes
+ Tape or glue
+ Black marker

Directions to Make

Cut 18 squares of paper to cover each side of the tissue boxes. Tape or glue the paper to the boxes.

Write consonants on the sides of two boxes and vowels on the third box.

Dice 1: b, c, f, p, r, m

Dice 2: t, d, g, h, l, n

Dice 3: a, e, i, o, u, a

Directions to Play

Roll the three dice.

Arrange them in order so the vowel is in the middle.

Say the sounds for each letter. Blend the sounds together to say the word.

Shout the word out. Is it real or nonsense?

Game Variations

For long vowel words, add in an extra vowel dice.

To practice the long vowel with silent e words, add in an extra die with all e's.

To work on words with just one vowel sound, use only one letter for the vowel die.

Sight Word Sensory Bottle

Focus Skill: sight word recognition, fluency

Add a little sparkle and bedazzle to your literacy learning with some shiny beads and sequins. Make a few of these sight word sensory bottles to use throughout the year. Set them out on a small table near your bookshelves for an interactive sight word experience. Look for different colors, textures and words. Listen to the sounds the fillers make as you shake the bottle to find all the sight words in this sensory bottle game. Rotate the bottles as your child has demonstrated mastery of the selected words.

- - - - - - - - - - - - - - - - -

Materials

+ Empty, clean 2-liter soda bottle
+ Tiny filler items such as rice, beads, sequins or bells
+ Small foam rectangles
+ Black permanent marker
+ One-minute sand timer

Directions to Make

Fill the bottle halfway with tiny fillers of your choosing.

Write five chosen sight words on the foam rectangles. Sample sight words: I, the, and, see, it.

Add the words to the bottle.

Close the lid tightly and shake until the words and fillers mix.

Directions to Play

Set the timer for 1 minute.

Roll the bottle and read.

See if you can find all five words before the time ends.

Game Variations

Dump the contents of the bottle into a plastic bin to create a sensory play experience.

Fill the bottle with words from a specific word family for decoding practice.

Use letter beads instead of words. Have the child search for the letters in alphabetical order!

*See photo insert page 20.

NOTE

Sight words are common words in the English language that your child will encounter throughout his or her life. Learning to recognize and read these words quickly will help with reading fluency. Some of these words cannot be sounded out and must be memorized through games and repeated exposure.

Sight Word Gems

*Focus Skill: identfying sight words with fluency •
Great For: on-the-go learning*

Learning to read becomes quite magical with these sight word gems. Players quickly search to find the match, which helps them build fluency with sight word recognition. A child's ability to quickly recognize sight words helps them to become successful readers. You can put your sight word gems in a plastic bag for on-the-go fun at restaurants.

- - - - - - - - - - - - - -

Materials

+ Glass gems
+ Permanent black marker
+ Scrapbook or construction paper
+ List of basic sight words
+ Small container for storage

Directions to Make

Write the selected sight words onto the glass gems with the permanent marker and allow to dry. Use words (like one, my, the, to, you) that cannot be traditionally sounded out like consonant-vowel-consonant (CVC) words.

Write the same words onto a colorful sheet of paper, ensuring that they are easily read.

Directions to Play

Place the sight word sheet on a flat surface.

Read the sight words out loud with the players.

Ask each player to select a sight word gem and find the match.

When the player places the sight word gem onto the match, encourage them to identify the word.

Continue until all of the words have been used.

Game Variations

Create sight word matches for players to find the match in a memory game.

Play sight word scavenger hunt using gems around the room.

Write the letters on the glass gems and have each player create the sight word listed on the paper.

(eight)

AMAZING WRITING ADVENTURES

Playing writing games with children is an easy way to make writing fun and promote reading. Children develop reading skills such as decoding new words alongside their writing skills. Often, a child's writing skills will clue adults in on the writer's understanding of letters and words.

Younger writers begin with scribbles on a page and move toward the formation of objects and eventually letters, words, sentences and stories. Adults can help support this growth and development by providing opportunities for children to write.

Use big blank white sheets of paper to start with and a variety of writing materials. Pens, markers and crayons are all great instruments for young learners. Encourage creative exploration with writing strokes. As the child shows an interest in letters, encourage them to listen for and write the sounds in words. Correct spelling comes with an increased understanding in patterns of words.

Words in the Sand

Focus Skill: identifying and writing sight words

Find hidden words on seashells in the sand to encourage your child to learn to read. Players quickly memorize each word by writing it into the sand in a texture-rich experience. This multi-sensory game helps to engage children's senses as they learn their sight words.

Materials

+ Permanent black marker
+ Seashells
+ 2 plastic containers or trays
+ Sand

Directions to Make

Write sight words onto seashells.

Place the seashells in one container.

Place sand in the second container or tray.

Directions to Play

Players take turns pulling seashells from the container.

Once they've selected them, players identify the word and write it in the sand container.

Continue to play until all the word seashells are discovered and written in the sand.

Game Variations

Create letters in the sand for younger players to discover and write.

Form words from letter shells in the sand and write them in the sand container.

Write numbers on the shells for players to discover and write.

*See photo insert page 21.

Make a Word

Focus Skill: spelling three-letter words with two consonants and one vowel in the middle

Phonics is a big part of early literacy. This make-a-word game provides opportunities for children to apply their knowledge of letters and sounds to build words in a fun way, then connect them to the written word.

Materials

+ 5 (3 x 5-inch [7.5 x 13-cm]) notecards
+ Scissors
+ Black and red markers
+ Die
+ Pencil
+ Paper

Directions to Make

Cut each of the notecards in half.

Write one letter on each card. Make sure to use two vowels and eight consonants total. It is optional to write the vowels in red. Sample set of letters: a, e, c, m, t, p, r, b, h, n.

Directions to Play

Turn the cards letter side down.

Roll the die. Say the number rolled out loud.

Count out that many letter cards.

Make a word with the selected letters.

Write that word on a piece of paper.

Continue making new words with the selected cards. When no more words can be made, count the total number of words made. There is a three-minute time limit to each turn.

Turn the cards upside down and pass the dice to the next player.

(continued)

After three rounds, total the number of words written. The player with the most wins the game!

Game Variations

For beginning readers, use only one vowel card. Keep that card face up and roll for the consonants.

Encourage the players to select three words to write sentences with at the end of each game.

Turn all the cards over and work together to make a list of all the possible words that could be made with the selected letters.

Guess My Favorite

Focus Skill: composing an opinion

Writing about favorite books and toys is a great way to make writing meaningful to your child. The added guessing creates anticipation and excitement for literacy! This writing game is adaptable to all skill levels. Children can draw, write words or use sentences depending on their writing ability. With early writers, an adult can write the words the child wants to say next to the picture.

- - - - - - - - - - - - - -

Materials

+ Half sheets of cardstock
+ Writing materials

Directions to Play

Select a favorite book or toy from the shelves. Do NOT tell the other players what it is.

Write down information about the toy or book and why it is your favorite.

Sample:

It's a book.

It has a cute caterpillar on it.

It is a fun book with holes on each page.

I like to count the fruit.

What book is it?

Read the clues out loud. Let the other players guess what book it is.

Repeat steps 1 through 3 with another favorite book or toy.

Game Variations

Set out a group of five fruits and play the game with only these items.

Have two children choose the same object and write their opinions about it. Compare.

Encourage advanced learners to create a set of clue cards and staple them together to make a Guess My Favorites homemade book.

You Draw, I Draw, Let's Make a Sentence

Focus Skill: producing a complete sentence

Unleash your inner artist with this partner drawing and writing game. Use your imagination and creativity to turn a rock into an ice cream cone. Each silly little doodle will inspire a sentence. This game also challenges children to expand their vocabulary skills. What to write about will not be a problem for children since they have drawn pictures throughout the game, activating the words in their mind. Having an adult write the sentence helps young children make the connection between oral and written language.

- - - - - - - - - - - - - -

Materials

+ Printer paper
+ Pencil
+ Crayons (optional)

Directions to Make

Talk about what makes a sentence. Each sentence must have a subject. A subject is who or what the sentence is about. A sentence also has a verb, or action word that tells what the subject is doing. "The train chugs along the tracks." In this sentence, the train is the subject and chugs is the verb.

Directions to Play

One player doodles a quick simple object on the piece of paper. They pass the picture to the next player.

The second player adds on to the object or draws another one next to the first.

The two players then create a sentence orally to describe their picture. An adult writes the sentence on the paper.

Repeat steps 1 through 3 until the paper is filled with pictures and sentences.

Game Variations

Encourage advanced learners to write the sentences on their own.

Play the game in a large group. Each person begins with a piece of paper. They draw an object and pass the paper to the player on the right. They then draw on the paper in front of them. Play continues until each player has drawn something on each paper. When the paper returns to the original owner, the player makes up a sentence for their picture.

Focus on writing words by having the players label the objects with words instead of making a sentence.

Shop the Alphabet

Focus Skill: writing a list

Going to the grocery store with your child can be a great learning experience. When you're armed with a clipboard, paper and pencil, your next shopping trip will be a breeze. Can you find a food for every letter of the alphabet?

Materials

+ Clipboard
+ Paper
+ Pencil

Directions to Make

Clip a piece of paper on the clipboard. Write the letters of the alphabet on the left-hand side of the page.

Directions to Play

Take the clipboard to the grocery store. Each player may have his or her own game board or work together to complete one. Name a food item that you see. Say the beginning sound, and then write the word next to that letter on the page. For example, A: apple. B: banana. C: carrots. Inventive and phonetic spelling is encouraged for young learners.

Each letter may be used only one time. Find one food item that begins with each letter before you reach the checkout counter.

Game Variations

For younger learners, the child may identify the food and beginning sound and the adult writes the word for the child to trace.

Select only four letters and make a list of everything found beginning with those sounds.

For advanced learners, challenge them to take the grocery list and alphabetize it.

*See photo insert page 21.

Sneak-a-Peek Letters

Focus Skill: writing beginning sounds in words

What begins with B? Let's sneak-a-peek for a clue in this super cute kid-made writing game. Young children gravitate toward being able to cut pictures out of magazines. Turn this fun craft activity into a writing game that focuses on the beginning letters of words.

- - - - - - - - - - - - -

Materials

+ Paper
+ Scissors
+ Kid-friendly magazines
+ Glue

Directions to Make

Fold the paper in half the long way.

Cut three slits evenly spaced apart on one half of the sheet.

Directions to Play

Find a picture in the magazine. Cut it out and glue it under a flap.

Say the name of the picture. Figure out the beginning sound. Write the letter for that sound on the top of the flap.

Repeat until the top three flaps are filled with letters and the spaces below are filled with pictures.

Hand the game board to another child. They will say the sound the letter makes and try to guess the word that begins with that sound. If they need a clue, they can sneak a-peek.

Repeat for all three letters.

Game Variations

Write the word on the top. Lift the flap for a self-checking reading game.

Encourage children to write a full sentence clue on the top flap.

Write a story with a beginning, middle and end on each flap. Use pictures from a magazine to illustrate each section under the words.

Build a Word

Focus Skill: learning how to write words from left to right

Words come to life for players as they build their first words using handmade alphabet blocks. Players use items from their play area or familiar places and items to begin to learn how to spell them out. This game gives players the chance to practice in a bigger way as they start to form words from left to right with the blocks and then again on paper.

- - - - - - - - - - - - -

Materials

+ Cardboard or tagboard
+ Scissors
+ Tape
+ Black marker
+ Alphabet stickers (optional)
+ Packaging tape (optional)
+ Construction paper or scrapbook paper

Directions to Make

Use the cardboard to create a box for dice by cutting it into a lowercase "t" shape. Repeat to make 6 in all.

Fold the sides for a box and tape together.

Write letters of the alphabet onto the blocks. Alphabet stickers or store-bought alphabet blocks can be used as an alternative.

Cover the blocks with packaging tape for durability if you'd like.

Select everyday items from around the house, pets and family members for words to use with game.

Write the words for the items onto the paper with your child to make the word sheet.

On a separate sheet of paper, copy or draw images and make a blank line for the word.

Directions to Play

Select a word from the word sheet.

Using the ABC blocks, build the word.

Use the word sheet to check your spelling.

Once correct, write down the word that you created next to the picture on the paper.

Game Variations

Create word families with the ABC blocks.

Write down letters on a sheet of poster board and encourage players to place blocks onto matching letters.

Stack ABC letters with similarities, such as curves, slants and straight lines.

*See photo insert page 21.

Mystery Words

Focus Skill: writing words

Grab some glue and paper and head to the sandbox for this crafty writing game that even sneaks in some fine motor strengthening. Make sure to have a few extra pieces of paper available for children to keep sand writing.

Materials

+ Glue
+ Half sheets of paper or cardstock
+ Sand
+ Stapler (optional)

Directions to Play

Choose a word in your mind, but don't say it out loud. Glue the shape of the beginning letter on the piece of paper. Sprinkle sand over the glue and gently shake off. Ask the player to your right to guess your word based on that first letter. They will have three guesses. If they have guessed correctly, it is their turn to start glue writing a different word.

If the first three guesses are not correct, then player one adds another glue letter to the word, sprinkles sand over the glue and gently shakes the sand off. The player to the right has three more guesses.

Play continues until the word has been identified.

Repeat steps 1 through 3 so each child playing the game has the opportunity to build at least two words.

Let the words dry.

Staple the paper together to make a sandy word book!

Game Variations

Write the child's name with the sand.

Write your school spelling words.

Make five sets of rhyming words and play a matching game.

All in My House

Focus Skill: creating a sentence with words

Kids easily create their own sentences inspired by their home environment. Using word sticks, kids will form sentences from left to right with confidence. Selecting from predetermined words gives them more chances to create several sentences at writing time.

– – – – – – – – – – – –

Materials

+ 30 to 50 wooden craft sticks
+ Black marker
+ Paper
+ Container for storage

Directions to Make

Create a list of words with your child about parts of their home.

+ Create a list of things in their home.
+ Create a list of people in their home.
+ Create a list of actions at home.

Write the selected words onto wooden craft sticks.

Sort the words into four piles with person, place, action and thing.

Write on sticks basic sight words—such as too, like, my, is, the, on, at, can, I, see—for each player to keep with them at all times by their house.

Create a house outline using extra wooden craft sticks to place word sticks into.

Directions to Play

Ask players to choose wooden craft sticks from all four categories: person, place, action and thing.

Then encourage them to create a sentence using those sticks (example: The cat is sleeping in the bedroom, Mom is cooking in the kitchen) and any of the sight word sticks.

Place the completed sentence into the wooden craft stick house.

Game Variations

Players can sort wooden craft stick words by nouns and verbs.

Players can write completed sentences onto a sheet of paper.

Players can form houses with the word sticks in proper sentence order.

Write On

Focus Skill: participating in shared writing projects

This writing game works well in small groups of kids who have mastered writing sentences. It provides children with a way to practice their creative writing skills in a fun game that results in a shared story.

Just one adult and child? No problem. This game can be played with just two players as well! What are you waiting for? Grab a pencil and start writing!

– – – – – – – – – – – –

Materials

+ Lined paper for each player
+ Pencil
+ Timer

Directions to Play

Every child begins the game with one piece of paper. The time starts and each child begins to write a story.

The parent or teacher keeps time. After 4 minutes, everyone stops and passes their story to the right. The timekeeper waits for everyone to receive their new papers and says, "Write on."

Children read what has been written on the page and continue writing the story.

Repeat steps 2 and 3 for a minimum of three more rounds. Return the story to its original writer.

Allow the children time to write the story ending if it has not already been done.

Read the stories out loud.

Game Variations

For younger children, play this writing game with pictures. Use three boxes. Each player will tell the beginning, middle or ending of the story with their drawings.

Have an adult write down the child's story and let them trace or fill in some key words.

Use a large piece of paper. Have children alternate telling the story while the adult writes down the words.

Storytelling Seashells

Focus Skill: writing a story

Spin a tale with these cute kid-made storytelling seashells. Collect some shells while you are on a beach vacation or purchase them at your local craft store. Paint characters and places from their favorite stories inside each shell. Turn them over and select a few to weave your own tale and write your story!

- - - - - - - - - - - - -

Materials

+ Clean shells
+ Newspaper
+ Acrylic paints
+ Plastic lid
+ Paintbrush
+ Paper
+ Pencil

Directions to Make

Set the clean shells inside up on the newspaper.

Pour a small amount of paint onto a plastic lid. Set near the shells.

Encourage your child to paint small pictures of characters and places/settings from the fairy tales they know inside the shells. Examples: mermaid—ocean, king—castle, boy in blue—haystack, mouse—clock.

Allow the shells to dry.

Directions to Play

Place the character shells face down in one pile and the setting shells face down in another pile.

Select one character and one setting shell.

Use the selected shells as the beginning of the story. Add a preposition word (inside, behind, on, next to) to make the title.

Write the story down on paper.

Game Variations

Play this game as an oral storytelling activity.

Short on time? Encourage children to write one sentence rather than the whole story.

Perform the story for an audience.

(nine)

MAKE MATH FUN!

Developing a solid foundation in mathematics is vital to a child's future success in school. It is important for children to know how to count and recognize numbers, but also to grasp what those numbers represent and be able to manipulate them to solve problems. The best way to strengthen these academic concepts is through repetition of hands-on, playful learning.

Math manipulatives can be made out of store-bought supplies, household materials and natural found objects. A traditional early childhood classroom will most likely have blocks, colored counters, a scale and analog clocks. Recyclables such as bottle lids, paper tubes, corks and containers are also useful. Sticks, stones, leaves and flowers from the natural environment can all be counted, sorted and used in math games as well.

There are many ways you can help get and keep your child excited about math. Point out the many times when you use math throughout your day. Play store-bought board games and homemade games, too. Smile when you talk about numbers. Celebrate when your child masters a mathematics skill.

Number Hoops

Focus Skill: solving number sentences • Great For: moving while you learn

Players have fun shouting out their answer and throwing it through the hula hoop to help learn their math facts. Using balls with the answers, players solve given number sentences like 4 + 2 = _ and quickly grab the answer and throw the number 6 through the target. Making this a math game with movement will help them use more senses as they learn.

━ ━ ━ ━ ━ ━ ━ ━ ━ ━ ━ ━ ━ ━

Materials

+ Paper
+ Black marker
+ Scissors
+ Hula hoop
+ Tape
+ 11 balls

Directions to Make

Write number sentences on paper. Select ones that equal no more than 10. For example: 4 + 1 = __ or 2 + 2 = __.

Cut them into cards for players to choose from.

Hang up a hula hoop so that players can toss balls through it.

Write numbers 0 to 10 on paper and cut into cards for answers.

With tape, attach the number answers to the balls from 0 to 10.

Directions to Play

Player selects a number sentence to solve.

Player solves the problem by finding the ball with the correct answer and throwing the numbered ball through the hanging hula hoop.

Each player continues until all the number sentences have been selected.

Game Variations

Hang up multiple hula hoops and have players select which number to throw the ball through based on the answer to the number sentence.

Have players throw number balls through the hula hoop in numerical order.

Have players toss numbered balls in skip counting order through the hula hoop.

Build a Number Puzzle

Focus Skill: recognizing numbers • Great For: on-the-go learning

Discover how quickly you can put together a number! Challenge your friend to see who is the fastest in building numbers. Learning the shapes of numbers can help children learn to write and recognize them more easily.

━ ━ ━ ━ ━ ━ ━ ━ ━ ━ ━ ━ ━ ━

Materials

+ Black marker
+ Construction paper
+ Scissors
+ Contact paper or packing tape (optional)

Directions to Make

Draw a large outline of numbers 0 to 10 onto various colors of paper.

Cut out the numbers.

Cover the numbers with contact paper for durability, if you'd like.

Cut each number into three pieces to create puzzle pieces.

(continued)

Directions to Play

Arrange the number puzzle pieces on a flat surface.

Each player selects a piece when it is their turn and begins to form a number.

Players take turns drawing number pieces strategically to form the most numbers.

The game ends when all of the pieces have been drawn.

The winner is the one with the most completed number puzzles!

Game Variations

For added difficulty, keep the number puzzle pieces in a bag or have players close their eyes when selecting, so they cannot see the pieces they are drawing.

Cut the number shapes into more or fewer pieces or race to see who builds the quickest.

Use the child's own recycled artwork to form the paper pieces.

Bead It!

Focus Skill: representing numbers 1 to 9 •
Great For: on-the-go learning

Beads come in all sorts of shapes and colors. Children love to thread them onto strings and craft wires. Not only is this great for fine motor practice, but it's also a springboard into early mathematics. In this game, children will race the clock to bead numbers 1 to 9. Store this game in a zip-top bag and tuck it into your purse for on-the-go learning.

- - - - - - - - - - - -

Materials

+ 5 craft wires
+ Scissors
+ Small paper rectangles, 1 x 2 inches (2.5 x 5 cm)
+ Tape
+ Permanent marker
+ Sand timer
+ Pony beads

Directions to Make

Cut each craft wire in half.

Tape one side of the paper rectangle to the bottom of the craft wire and fold over to form a square. Repeat for nine craft wires total.

Write the numbers 1 to 9 on the squares.

Directions to Play

Turn the sand timer over.

Bead the same number of beads on each wire as written on the paper square.

Shape the wire into the shape of the number.

Try to build as many numbers as possible before the timer runs out.

Game Variations

Build and put the numbers in order from the least to the greatest.

Use a specific pattern when beading the numbers.

Call out a number and have the child build the beads for the numbers that equal that sum. If "10" is called, the child could build the 4 and 6 craft wires.

25 Squish

Focus Skill: addition to 25

Connect fine motor strengthening and mathematics with this hands-on playdough squishing game! Children will roll spheres to match the numbers they roll, then count and add the sum. The next player adds more spheres to the pile until the total reaches 25 or more. Then they get to SQUISH them! This game provides children with much needed concrete math practice with numbers up to 25.

– – – – – – – – – – – – –

Materials

+ Yarn
+ Pencil
+ Paper
+ Die
+ Playdough

Directions to Make

Use the yarn to make a large circle on the table. This will signify the workspace for the child. All playdough spheres will be placed inside this circle.

Write the words 25 SQUISH on the top of the paper.

Directly under the words, make six rows for addition number sentences under the title. Each line will look like this ___ + ____ = _____.

Directions to Play

For the first round: Roll the die. Count and write the number rolled on the recording sheet in the first space. Roll the same number of playdough spheres and put them in the yarn circle. Roll the die again. Count and write the number in the second space on the recording sheet. Make the same number of playdough spheres and add them to the yarn circle. Count the total and write the total on the recording sheet in the last blank.

Pass the die, paper and pencil to the next player.

The next player will count the number of spheres in the circle. They will write this number in the first blank of the next number sentence. They will then roll the die one time and write that number in the second blank. The child will make that many more spheres and add them to the yarn circle. When the playdough spheres have been added to the yarn circle, the child must count and find out how many spheres are in the circle. This is finding the sum or total amount. This total number is written on the third blank space in the number sentence.

Pass the die and repeat step 3 until there are 25 or more spheres in the yarn circle.

The player who makes 25 or more gets to squish each sphere.

Game Variations

Start with 25 spheres. Smash on each turn for a simple subtraction game.

For an added challenge—bump the final number up to 50 or 100!

No playdough? Use dot markers and have players add a dot for the numbers rolled onto a large sheet of paper.

*See photo insert page 21.

3, 2, 1, Blast Off!

Focus Skill: recognizing numbers and number order

Challenge your child to install the rocket ship windows in the correct number order before blasting off into space. Players attach windows onto the spaceship to practice their number skills in a playful way.

- - - - - - - - - - - - - -

Materials

+ Rocket ship outline
+ Black marker
+ Poster board
+ 10 small white circles
+ Clothespins
+ Tape

Directions to Make

Draw and color a rocket ship with your child on the poster board.

On the rocket, write numbers 1 to 10 for each window, to be clipped on in order from top to bottom.

Write the numbers 1 to 10 on the white circles for windows.

Attach the numbered white circles for the windows onto each clothespin with tape.

Directions to Play

Players take turns selecting numbered window clothespins from the pile and attaching to the correct number on the rocket ship.

Game continues until all of the rocket ship windows are installed.

Once filled, countdown to BLAST OFF!

Game Variations

For advanced children use numbers 1 to 20.

Write number sentences on the windows and have them solve them by placing the correct number on the rocket ship.

Focus on skip counting by counting by tens, fives or twos with the numbers on the rocket ship and windows.

*See photo insert page 22.

Sunshine Numbers

Focus Skill: representing a given number of dots with the numeral

Shine a little math into your day with this crafty clothespin number-matching game. Children will delight in adding the rays to the paper plate sun over and over again. They will have repeated exposure to how many dots each number represents. This will help them develop a deeper understanding of what each number is. Repetition helps strengthen a child's understanding of any given academic concept.

- - - - - - - - - - - - - -

Materials

+ Paper plate
+ Markers
+ Yellow paper
+ Scissors
+ Glue
+ 16 clothespins

Directions to Make

Have your child decorate the paper plate with the markers.

Cut out thin rectangles from the yellow paper. These will be the sun's rays.

Glue one rectangle to each clothespin.

Write the numbers 0 to 15 on the outside edge of the paper plate.

Make small dots on each yellow rectangle equal to the numbers 0 to 15.

Directions to Play

Count the number of dots on the sun ray.

Match the ray to the written number on the paper plate. Clip on top.

Repeat with the remaining clothespins until you have a full shining sun!

Game Variations

For younger children, match the number with the number.

For advanced learners, write number sentences on the sun rays. Put the answers on the edge of the paper plate.

Use two color rays, yellow and orange. Have children make and extend a pattern.

*See photo insert page 22.

How Many Bricks

Focus Skill: sorting and grouping items into specific number grouping

Finding math in everyday moments encourages your child to learn to group items by specific numbers. This is the perfect game for playtime, snack time or on-the-go. Children begin to build confidence in their ability to count as they explore numbers.

– – – – – – – – – – – – –

Materials

+ Black marker
+ Paper
+ Scissors
+ Plastic bricks or any small item
+ Container
+ 11 muffin tin liners, plastic or paper

Directions to Make

Write the numbers 0 to 10 on paper and cut them out into number cards.

Collect a pile of plastic bricks or any small toy, or even snack items, to count.

Place the small items into a container.

Place the number cards next to the container with items.

Each player lines up the muffin liners to start playing.

Directions to Play

Player selects a number card and orally counts the plastic bricks, then places them into a muffin liner.

Players take turns until they have filled all of their muffin liners, matching the numbers with the correct number of items.

Game Variations

Players can connect each plastic brick on top of one another to add up to the chosen number.

Play game with snack items such as small crackers, popcorn or fruit pieces.

For advanced players, have them create number sentences to solve before selecting the number they collect from the container.

*See photo insert page 22.

Monster Playdough Math

Focus Skill: recognizing numbers

Make math memorable with a monster bash! Using googly eyes and your child's imagination, learning to recognize numbers can be a hands-on experience. Learning to group items into set number groups is an important beginning math skill.

– – – – – – – – – – – – – –

Materials

+ Black marker
+ Paper
+ Scissors
+ Plastic numbers (optional)
+ Googly eyes
+ Small container
+ Playdough

Directions to Make

Use the marker and paper to make number cards from 0 to 10. Cut them into cards or use plastic numbers instead.

Directions to Play

Give each player googly eyes in a small container and playdough.

As players take their turn, they select a number from the pile and create a monster with eyes to match the number drawn.

Encourage each player to create monsters with eyes from 0 to 10.

Game Variations

Each player can create monsters with a specific number of arms instead of eyes.

For advanced players, challenge them with math facts and use eyes to show the answer.

Create multiple monsters to match the number drawn.

*See photo insert page 22.

STAMP Your Way to the Finish!

Focus Skill: counting forward, beginning from a given number within the known sequence

Have you ever made your own board game before? If you have a paper and pencil and can draw circles, then it's super easy to make. Make one for yourself or a friend to play. Better yet—make a bunch and trade them with friends. Then count and stamp your way to the finish!

– – – – – – – – – – – – – –

Materials

+ Paper
+ Pencil
+ Self-inking stamps
+ Dice

Directions to Make

Take a piece of paper and draw a ton of small circles in a line. The line of circles can curve around the paper. The more circles the better.

Write the word START at the beginning of your line of circles. Write END after the last circle.

Directions to Play

Put your self-inking stamper on the start. For more than one player, use different color stamps.

Roll the dice and stamp that number of circles. Say the numbers as they are stamped.

Pass the dice to the next player. Roll and stamp.

The stamp that reaches the end first wins the game!

Game Variations

Write in bonus circles: Land on this circle and roll again.

Use a 100 chart as a game board.

Switch stamps for coins so that your game board can be reused.

Rock Number Hunt

Focus Skill: recognizing numbers •
Great For: moving while you learn

Kids discover that numbers rock by being challenged to discover them in their own environment and create their own number groups. Players go on a treasure hunt to discover where the numbers are hiding.

- - - - - - - - - - - -

Materials

+ 22 rocks
+ Paint
+ Paintbrush
+ Container for each player

Directions to Make

Paint numbers onto the rocks with your child and allow to dry.

On the other side of the rocks paint shapes to total 10 circles, 6 squares and 6 triangles.

Allow time for the paint on the rocks to dry.

Hide the rocks.

Directions to Play

Players go on a scavenger hunt to collect the number rocks.

As players discover the rocks, encourage them to identify the number they find.

Players collect number rocks in their container.

Once all the number rocks are found, players will practice counting using the other side of the rocks for counters.

Players will form a group of rocks to match the selected number.

Game Variations

Use rocks to play a shape hunt game.

Use rocks to create a shape pattern.

Place rocks in numerical order from 0 to 10.

Butterfly Symmetry

Focus Skill: using listening skills to re-create images using shapes

The mystery of symmetry becomes more interesting when one of your senses is challenged with symmetrical wing design. Players use shapes to create butterfly wings that match by following oral directions. Focusing on symmetry helps a child to develop basic skills of geometry at an early age.

- - - - - - - - - - - -

Materials

+ Poster board
+ Markers or paint
+ Scissors
+ Blindfold

Directions to Make

Create a large butterfly outline from the poster board.

Design matching shapes for decorating the wings using the same poster board.

(continued)

Directions to Play

Place the butterfly down on a flat surface to start the game.

Set out the shapes to decorate each wing.

One player puts on a blindfold while the other describes where to place the pieces to design the butterfly wings.

Then the player describes to the blindfolded player where to place which shape to create the same design on the other wing to create symmetry.

Switch turns and try again.

Game Variations

Create two butterflies and race to see who can create a symmetrical butterfly first.

Create puzzle wings that only work in a specific way.

Hang the butterfly on the wall and have players attempt to design symmetrical wings blindfolded.

Scoop 10

Focus Skill: counting and recognizing numbers 0 to 20

Have you ever grabbed a handful of something and "known" how many there were just by glancing at the objects in your hand? This math skill involves special reasoning and number sense. It is also a great way to strengthen your child's understanding of math vocabulary terms: more than, less than and equal to. Join in the game too. See if you can scoop 10!

- - - - - - - - - - - - - -

Materials

+ Plastic bowl
+ Pennies (or buttons of the same size)
+ 2 pieces of paper
+ Pencil

Directions to Make

Fill the bowl with pennies.

Count and set 10 pennies on a piece of paper next to the game as a visual reference of what 10 pennies look like.

On the second sheet of paper, write the names of the players across the top.

Directions to Play

Player one reaches into the bowl and grabs a handful of pennies.

They open their hand and make an immediate guess out loud: less than, more than or equal to 10 pennies.

The same player then counts the coins. If their guess was correct, they write a point down.

The next player scoops, guesses and counts. Play continues until a player reaches five total points.

Game Variations

Scoop for five.

Use small objects of varying sizes, such as small building bricks, for an extra challenge.

Let each child keep the coins they scooped for three turns. Then have them add the total number of coins.

Superhero Zoom

Focus Skill: counting by 10s to 100 •
Great For: moving while you learn

Zip and zap your way to 100 in this active backyard game that connects math, movement and outside play in a meaningful way. Run from one hero shield to the next as you count by 10s. Don't forget your invisible wands. Superhero capes are optional!

- - - - - - - - - - - - - - - - - -

Materials

+ 11 sheets of cardstock
+ Pencil
+ Scissors
+ Dot markers
+ Hole punch
+ Yarn

Directions to Make

Draw and cut out one hero shield from each sheet of cardstock.

Stamp 10 dots on each shield with the dot markers.

Hole punch one circle on the top of each shield.

Thread a 10-inch (25-cm) piece of yarn through the hole and tie it in a loop to hang.

Directions to Play

Hang the hero shields across the backyard.

Select one hero shield to start. Tap your invisible hero wand at it and say 10.

Fly to the next hero shield. Tap it and say 20.

Keep flying, tapping and counting by 10s until each player reaches 100.

Game Variations

Place the hero shields on the ground in a circle. Walk and count.

Write the numbers in the shields instead of dots: 10, 20, 30, 40, 50, 60, 70, 80, 90, 100.

Focus on counting by 5s by putting 5 dots on each shield and making a total of 20 shields.

Bees in the Hive

Focus Skill: counting groups of numbers 0 to 10

Shiny gem bees come to life as they buzz into their number hives with this hands-on math game to help children learn to recognize and group numbers. Players even have the chance to create beehives using recycled materials.

- - - - - - - - - - - - - - - - - -

Materials

+ 11 recycled plastic containers like milk cartons, juice containers or water bottles
+ ADULTS ONLY: Sharp knife to make opening in containers
+ Yellow and brown paint
+ Paintbrush
+ Bubble wrap
+ Permanent black marker and yellow marker
+ Glass gems
+ Paper and marker (optional)

Directions to Make

Make beehives with recycled containers by having an adult cut out a hole in each container.

Paint the recycled containers yellow.

Create a beehive look by using bubble wrap dipped in brown paint and then stamping onto the recycled containers.

Create bees by using yellow and black markers on glass gems to make stripes and eyes.

Write a number on each hive from 0 to 10 or write on pieces of paper.

(continued)

Directions to Play

Players take the bees and place the correct number into each beehive.

Players win when all the hives are filled with the correct number of bees.

Game Variations

Make beehives into word family hives and create word bees.

Create math fact bees to place into the correct beehives.

Add magnets to bees to create bees that can fly into their hives on a magnetic surface.

Pattern Snake in a Sack

Focus Skill: creating and extending patterns

Patterns can be found all around us. This backyard scavenger hunt for rocks can be a fun way to start exploring patterns and build critical-thinking skills. Players use painted rocks to create their own snake patterns.

- - - - - - - - - - - - -

Materials

+ 27 smooth rocks of similar sizes
+ 3 bigger-sized rocks for snake heads
+ 3 colors of paint
+ Paintbrushes
+ 6 googly eyes
+ 3 felt strips
+ Craft glue
+ Paper lunch sack or fabric bag

Directions to Make

Gather 27 rocks of similar sizes and three bigger-sized rocks.

Paint the three larger rocks to represent snake heads.

Attach googly eyes and a felt tongue to the snake head with craft glue and allow to dry.

Using the three selected colors, paint the remaining rocks in sets of nine and allow to dry. When complete there will be nine of each color.

While the paint is drying, encourage your child to decorate the outside of the sack with the words "Snake in a Sack."

When the rock paint is dry, place the rocks in the bag.

Directions to Play

Each player selects a large snake head and places it on the floor in front of them.

Each player takes a turn selecting a rock from the bag to create a pattern snake.

They can choose to keep the color if it will help them create and extend a pattern.

If the color drawn from the bag doesn't match their pattern, they put it back and the next player draws.

The game ends when the first player is able to make a pattern snake with nine rocks.

Game Variations

Make a vertical pattern using rocks to create pattern towers.

Younger players can use rocks to focus on number groupings.

Use rocks to outline a designated shape.

> ### NOTE
> Rocks can be reused from the Rock Number Hunt activity on page 183 for this activity.

Move It!

Focus Skill: recognizing and representing the numbers 0 to 20 • Great For: moving while you learn

Get your wiggles out with this high-action counting game. Children draw an action card from one pile and a movement card from another, then perform that action. Use this math game in between sit-down lessons to give young children a chance to move and learn. When their bodies do math, they can develop a deeper connection to numbers. It is also a great game to informally assess children's understanding of numbers. If they draw the number 6 card, say 6 and jump 6 times, then you know that they understand what the number 6 is and how many it represents.

- - - - - - - - - - - - -

Materials

+ 31 (3 x 5-inch [7.5 x 13-cm]) notecards
+ Pencil

Directions to Make

Write 10 movement actions on 10 of the notecards.

+ Hop on one foot
+ Run in place
+ Skip
+ Bend your knees
+ Jump
+ Reach up high
+ Gallop
+ Clap
+ Twirl
+ Touch the ground

Write the numbers 0 to 20 on the remaining notecards.

Directions to Play

Place the cards upside down in two separate piles.

Player one turns a number card over and says the number out loud.

Player two turns an action card over and reads the action out loud.

Both players stand up and do the action for the selected number of times.

Play continues for five or more rounds.

Game Variations

Use the numbers 0 to 5 for beginning learners.

Have players draw two number cards and perform the action for the difference.

When playing in a large group, have two children draw the cards and the entire group perform the action.

Make 10

Focus Skill: making 10 when added to the given number

Card games are a great way to bring more math into your everyday world in a fun way. Children can sort them by colors or numbers. You can put the cards in numerical order. You can even practice addition with cards. This activity has you adding the cards in many different ways to make 10. When you do find a way to make 10, discard your cards and flip more cards over from your pile. Be the first to turn over your pile of cards.

- - - - - - - - - - - - -

Materials

+ Deck of cards

Directions to Make

Remove the jacks, queens, kings and jokers from the deck of cards.

(continued)

Directions to Play

Deal the cards facedown evenly to all players.

Each player turns over four cards and sets them to the right of their pile.

The youngest player goes first. They look over their cards for a way to make 10. Aces are equal to 1. If they can make the sum of 10, they pick the cards up and place them in a discard pile, then turn the cards from their pile over to fill in the spaces. If they cannot make 10, they choose one card to place at the bottom of the pile and turn one card over from their pile to fill the space. There will always be only four cards faceup in front of each child at all times.

The next player takes their turn, repeating the last step.

Play continues until one player has turned over all of his or her card pile.

Game Variations

Keep the cards totaling 10 separate. Write down the different ways to make 10 after each game.

Select a different number for players to make, such as 6. Allow them to use addition or subtraction to make the selected number.

Try the game with three or five cards turned faceup. Discuss the effect on the game. Does it make it easier or harder to make 10?

Filling Fishbowls

Focus Skill: grouping items into groups of 10 and skip counting

There's a sale at the pet store for 10 goldfish and a bowl. Players count out 10 fish to fill each bowl for their customers, to practice counting in groups of 10. Using water beads, players practice counting from 1 to 10. Plus, as they count they set up groups to start developing skills of skip counting.

- - - - - - - - - -

Materials

+ 100-plus water beads
+ Large container filled with water
+ Paper
+ Markers
+ Scissors
+ 10 clear small cups
+ Plastic scooper

Directions to Make

Soak the water beads in water to enlarge.

Use the paper, markers and scissors to make a pet store sign in the shape of a fish (i.e., $1.00 for 10 Fish)

Directions to Play

Players work to fill each cup "fishbowl" with 10 waterbead "fish" by scooping out of the large container filled with water beads.

Once all 10 cups are filled, encourage players to count by 10s to 100 to complete the sale.

Game Variations

Fill cups based on assigned numbers from 1 to 10.

Create number sentences to solve. Players respond with the answer using water bead fish.

Create a sorting game for younger children by sorting water beads by color.

Fly Ball

Focus Skill: counting and writing, "How many?" •
Great For: moving while you learn

Ding-dong! It's a special delivery. Luckily your box comes complete with packing paper! Don't just toss it in the recycle bin; rip the paper up into pieces and try your hand at Paperball. Let your kids toss the balled up paper high in the air and listen to their squeals of delight when their paper balls land in the box. This math game provides children with the opportunity to practice counting and answering the question, "How many?"

- - - - - - - - - - - - - - - -

Materials

+ Paper (newspaper, tissue paper or packing paper)
+ Small box
+ Measuring tape
+ Tape (optional)
+ String
+ Pencil
+ 1 piece of lined paper

Directions to Make

Rip the paper into 10 larger pieces. Make paper balls with each piece.

Set a box out.

Measure 8 feet (2.4 m) from the box and tape or set a string at that distance for the throwing line.

Directions to Play

Stand facing the box with your toes behind the line.

Throw each paper ball toward the box.

How many balls landed in the box? Count the number of balls that land inside.

Write the number of balls that land in the box on the recording sheet.

Repeat steps 1 to 4 for another five rounds. As the game continues, mix things up by varying the distance from the box. Throw from various positions, such as standing, sitting or even lying down!

Game Variations

Write a number on each ball. Throw them into the box in numerical order.

Turn the box on its side and try to kick the paper balls in.

Use only four paper balls and call out the fraction of balls that landed in the box.

Tap and Toss

Focus Skill: counting by 2s to 100 •
Great For: moving while you learn

Watch out, this math game creates giggles galore, while providing your little ones with an opportunity to skip count by 2s to 100. Let your balloon fly to the sky as the children count on by 2s until the balloon drops.

- - - - - - - - - - - - - - - -

Materials

+ Inflated balloon

Directions to Play

Toss the balloon in the air to start the game. Tap the balloon back in the air one time and whisper the odd number. 1—tap. On the second tap, say the number out loud and toss it in the air toward a team member. 2—toss.

They tap the balloon in the air, whispering the number. 3—tap. Then they toss it high in the air toward another team member and say the even number out loud. 4—toss.

Try to make it to 100. If the balloon drops, start over at the nearest multiple of 10.

(continued)

Game Variations

Challenge the players to play the game without saying the odd numbers.

Have children play on their own.

For younger learners, have them toss the balloon and say the numbers in sequential order.

Practice counting by 5s. Tap four times quietly and toss on the fifth.

Luck of the Draw

Focus Skill: counting objects by matching each number with a specific object • Great For: moving while you learn

In this game, your child will pick a number card from the pile and read it. Then, they will have to do that number of items for their chores. Admittedly, one may argue this may not be the "funnest" game for your child, but it's sure fun for the adults! This game works well when folding clothes and tidying up toys. As much "fun" as it is, it really is a great way to teach counting by ones to a higher number.

- - - - - - - - - - - - - - -

Materials

+ Deck of cards with the face cards removed

Directions to Play

Select a specific chore.

Hold the cards facedown.

Let the child select a card.

Read the number out loud. Pick up and count that specific amount of objects.

The next player repeats steps 2 to 4 until the chore has been completed.

Game Variations

If you have a lot of objects that need picking up, consider having the child draw two cards and pick up the same number of objects as the sum.

Have them select two cards and pick up the difference.

Add in the face cards and assign them a special task. Draw a jack and you get to sweep the floor! The queen means you must pick up 10 items left-handed, the king right-handed.

Shape Memory

Focus Skill: building and identifying three-dimensional shapes

The great thing about this game is that you do not need any fancy supplies or game cards; just grab a pack of playdough from your craft supply closet and play! My kids usually last about five rounds of the game, or 20 minutes. It is a great game for siblings to play at the dinner table while you are preparing dinner.

- - - - - - - - - - - - - - -

Materials

+ Playdough
+ Paper cups

Directions to Make

Build two sets of three-dimensional shapes out of playdough: cube, pyramid, sphere, cone, cylinder. There will be 10 total shapes made.

Directions to Play

Count out 10 cups.

Hide one three-dimensional shape under each cup. Mix the cups.

The youngest player starts first and turns over two cups. If the shapes match, they keep the pair. If they do not, they say the name of the shape out loud and turn the cups over.

The play continues to the right until all pairs have been found.

Game Variations

Start with only six cups and three pairs of shapes.

Turn the cups right side up and play the game with the shapes visible.

For an additional challenge, make two-dimensional shapes as well and increase the amount of shape pairs used.

Shape Tiles

Focus Skill: creating a shape out of smaller shapes

Is it a rocket, a cat or a tree? Players use magnetic shape tiles to create their own new shapes with this hands-on magnetic game. This playful game teaches a child to create objects from a variety of shapes.

Materials

+ 24 square pieces of cardstock
+ Markers or paint and paintbrush
+ Magnetic tape
+ Magnetic surface

Directions to Make

Draw portions of shapes on the paper tiles with the markers or paint. Make six half circles, six right triangles, six squares and six rectangles.

Attach magnetic tape to the back of each paper tile.

Directions to Play

Each player takes a turn creating a shape out of the magnetic paper tiles to form a bigger shape on a fridge or other magnetic surface.

Challenge players to create another shape using two, three or even four tiles together.

The player who can create the most shapes wins.

Game Variations

Have each player create a pattern using the shape tiles.

Create a "tell a story" game using the tiles and have children describe the story.

Copycat shapes. Each player re-creates the image created on paper using magnetic shapes.

Mystery Math

Focus Skill: solving addition equations

This math game requires no preparation and is great for groups of three or more children. Try this while waiting in line for an event or sneak in one round in-between lessons.

Materials

+ None

Directions to Play

Two children stand back to back and hold up any number of fingers.

A third child, the Math Master, looks at both numbers and calls out the sum.

The children then race to figure out which number the other is holding up. The first player to guess the correct number wins. The winner becomes the Math Master.

The children return to the group and two different children stand back to back and repeat steps 1 to 3.

Game Variations

Play with the numbers 0 to 5 by limiting the game to the use of just one hand.

Have a fourth player write the number sentence on a large chart after the answer has been called.

As an extra challenge, the Math Master can call out the difference of the numbers.

Cupcake Shapes

Focus Skill: recognizing shapes

Decorating cupcakes can be such fun! Add some shapes to create a playful learning game that can extend to various skills needed to prepare for school. Players create cupcakes by attaching matching shape pieces onto hanging contact paper to help learn their shapes.

- - - - - - - - - - - - - - -

Materials

+ Construction paper
+ Scissors
+ Contact paper
+ Tape
+ Sequins, glitter or confetti

Directions to Make

Create six large cupcake shapes using a half circle of colored construction paper for the top to represent cupcake frosting.

Cut out six pyramid shapes for the cupcake liner. Fold paper accordion style to give it the cupcake-liner look if you'd like.

Cut out and place a shape in the middle of each liner (circle, triangle, square, rectangle, diamond or star).

Cut out multiples of each shape for game pieces and cover them with contact paper.

Attach the cupcakes to a wall or window with tape.

Cover the cupcakes with contact paper with the sticky side up.

Directions to Play

Players select shapes from the pile and match to the correct shape by placing onto the cupcake frosting area.

Continue to match shapes to each cupcake until all the shapes are attached correctly.

Players can also add cupcake decorations with confetti, glitter or sequins.

Continue playing by removing and mixing up shapes and then re-sorting.

Game Variations

Create cupcakes for number recognition.

Create cupcakes for uppercase and lowercase recognition.

*See photo insert page 23.

Parachute Subtraction

Focus Skill: simple subtraction • Great For: moving while you learn

Set aside one day every week to bring out your parachute. There are so many fun gross motor and math games to play, and the kids LOVE parachute time. It is a much anticipated activity in our homes and classrooms. This math game focuses on learning and practicing simple subtraction. Throw in a few soft foam balls and start shaking!

- - - - - - - - - - - - - - -

Materials

+ Parachute or circular vinyl table cloth
+ 10 soft foam balls

Directions to Play

Spread the parachute out and space children out evenly around it.

Shake, move and play for five minutes prior to starting the game.

When ready, count and throw 10 balls into the middle of the parachute.

Shake the parachute to the count of 10, trying to keep the balls in the middle.

Stop.

Count the number of balls that fell off. Say the number sentence to represent what happened. If 3 balls fell off, you would say: 10 − 3 =__?

Have the children call out the answer.

Throw all 10 balls back into the middle of the parachute and repeat.

Game Variations

Add more or fewer balls to change the level of difficulty.

Shake foam letters instead of balls. See which letters remain on the parachute.

Use balloons and write the numbers on each with a permanent marker.

Grocery Store

Focus Skill: identifying coins and their monetary value

Learning coin names and values can be empowering for young children. In this game, shoppers use their grocery cart and money to purchase items at the store. This activity allows players to pretend and get creative with math.

- - - - - - - - - - - - - - -

Materials

+ Grocery store flyers, magazines or newspaper ads
+ Scissors
+ Black marker
+ 3 x 5-inch (7.5 x 13-cm) notecards
+ Crayons or markers
+ Paper for store banner
+ 4 lids per player
+ 1 small box per player
+ 7 pipe cleaners per player
+ Coins (penny, nickel, dime, quarter)

Directions to Make

Players cut out pieces from each food group from the flyers.

Write on each notecard a price for each food item and display in the pretend store.

Using crayons or markers, create a banner for the store and hang up.

Each player creates their own grocery cart by attaching lids to a box with pipe cleaners for the wheels. Attach pipe cleaners onto the box to make the handle. Decorate your cart (box) with crayons or markers. (Kids will need adult help to create.)

Directions to Play

Each player takes a turn selecting an item from display and adds it to their cart.

Player gives the storekeeper player the money for the item from their money pile.

Players continue to take turns shopping until all the items and/or money are gone.

Game Variations

Have players add up the values of their items and then make a payment.

Have players write a list of items and then purchase them from the store to encourage writing.

Challenge players to find specific food groups on their turn.

Memory Photo Shapes

Focus Skill: identifing name of shapes

Children love to see images of themselves. This memory shape game uses photos to give them a whole new way to learn about shapes. Players discover matches by using visual discrimination.

- - - - - - - - - - - - - -

Materials

+ Photos
+ Construction paper
+ Scissors
+ Glue stick
+ Craft knife (optional)

Directions to Make

Take images of your child and print the photos. Cut out outlines on 4 x 6-inch (10 x 15-cm) paper in the shapes of a circle, triangle, square, rectangle, diamond and star. Make two sets of each shape. Overlay the shape outlines onto the child's photos and glue together.

Directions to Play

Lay out the photo shapes onto a flat surface with the image side down.

Players take turns selecting two photos at a time to find a shape match.

Players continue to draw pieces to match each shape.

Game Variations

Create patterns with the photo shapes.

Use a craft knife to cut out shapes from the photos and keep the 4 x 6-inch (10 x 15-cm) shape whole to use as the game piece. Use the removed shape as a puzzle piece for the child to solve the missing piece by shapes.

Create a number photo memory game.

Fact Family City

Focus Skill: identifying that various number combinations can equal the same number

Which street do you live on? Explore fact families in this playful skyscraper city game that helps children problem solve to discover which street the building is on by solving number sentences. Players are asked to sort buildings into groups based on the answers they solve on them while playing this game.

- - - - - - - - - - - - - -

Materials

+ Various colors of construction paper
+ Crayons
+ Scissors
+ Black marker
+ 6 pieces of black paper, 2 x 11.5 inches (5 x 29 cm)
+ 30 strips of yellow construction paper, ¼ x 1 inch (6 mm x 2.5 cm)
+ Glue stick

Directions to Make

Create several buildings with your child using the construction paper and crayons (approximately 2 x 4 inches [5 x 10 cm] in size).

Once complete, write number sentences equaling 6 or less on a section of the building, leaving a blank space for the answer (3 + 1, 5 − 1, 4 + 0, etc.).

Create five number streets using the black paper strips.

Write one number on each block from 1 to 6.

Cut out 30 small yellow strips and glue them to the black number streets. Use six strips on each street to indicate lane dividers.

Directions to Play

Place the number streets onto a flat surface in numerical order.

Place assorted buildings for players to choose from.

Players take their turn by drawing a math fact building and placing it on the correct number street.

Each player takes a turn until all of the buildings have been used.

Game Variations

For younger children, create number buildings and place in numerical order.

Create buildings of different heights and line them on street by size.

For advanced players, increase the total sum of each street to make it more challenging.

*See photo insert page 23.

Rock Clock Mystery

Hint: You can paint the numbers on the back of the rocks from Pattern Snake in a Sack (page 186)! • Focus Skill: solving time story problems

Telling analog time takes a lot of practice for young learners. This activity gets children building and interacting with the placement of numbers on a clock as well as moving the hands (sticks) around to set the time. Try your hand at building this rock clock and creating short time stories to solve.

- - - - - - - - - - - - - - -

Materials

+ 12 rocks
+ Paint
+ Painbrush
+ 2 sticks

Directions to Make

Paint the rocks.

Paint a number 1 to 12 on each rock. Allow to dry overnight. (The rocks from Rock Number Hunt on page 183 can also be used for this game.)

Directions to Play

Use the rocks to build a clock in the shape of a circle on a flat surface.

Set the sticks in the middle as the hour and minute hands.

One child tells a story with a time problem.

Sample

Sam went to the park at 8:00.

He stayed for 1 hour and then went home.

What time did he go home?

The player to the right uses the hands of the rock clock to show the answer.

If correct, then he gets to make up a time story. If incorrect, he must change the hands on the clock to show the correct time before telling the next story.

Game Variations

Set the hour and minute hands on the clock. Act out something you would typically do at that time of day.

Have one player call out a time and another player shows that time on the rock clock.

Mix the rocks and race to rebuild the rock clock.

Estimation Station

Focus Skill: estimation

Knowing how much space an object takes up is called special reasoning. This math skill is used when playing this estimation game along with an understanding of numbers. How close to the actual number can you guess? Set up this math learning center on a child-size table as an invitation to estimate.

- - - - - - - - - - - - -

Materials

+ 5 empty containers of varying sizes
+ Bricks or building blocks
+ Paper and pencil or number tiles

Directions to Make

Fill each container with bricks. Do not count.

Set the filled containers side-by-side on a table.

Place a paper and pencil or number tiles in front of each container.

Directions to Play

The first player stands in front of the first container. They make an educated guess, or estimate, of how many bricks they think are in the container. They write this number down on the paper or place their number tiles next to that container.

They move to the next container and repeat: estimate and write. The next player makes a number estimation at the first container. They write or place the number below the first player's guess.

The game continues until all players have written or placed their estimations for each container.

At the end, remove the bricks from each container. Count the number of bricks. The estimated number that is closest to the actual number of bricks wins. Draw a big star next to the winning number.

Game Variations

Play this game over a period of several days, allowing for one number entry per day.

Limit the number of containers.

Use a different filler, such as buttons, pom-poms or shape erasers.

*See photo insert page 23.

(ten)

MAGICAL MUSIC, ART AND GOING GLOBAL

Exploring the arts with your child can be magical. A trip to an art museum or to a musical performance can be the highlight of their week. Look in your community for opportunities to be engaged in the arts. As you explore, help your child discover the patterns in a piece of art or the music you're listening to. Ask them how an art piece makes them feel. Challenge them to re-create what they see and hear when they return home. Help increase their language and observation skills by encouraging a child to describe the details of their work. Celebrate their efforts as you become a child's No. 1 fan. Most importantly, give children the opportunity and tools to be expressive and creative!

Young children start becoming globally aware by taking a closer look at the immediate world around them. They start to learn more about themselves, their family and their neighborhood. As this knowledge develops and grows, they are more able to grasp bigger concepts, such as what the world is and how to use a globe, and learn about other people's cultures and celebrations.

We make a point to allow our children to experience other cultures with food, art, crafts, music, geography, presentations and games.

Sing and Shake

Hint: Use this activity along with Parachute Subtraction (page 192)! • Focus Skill: responding to music through singing and motion • Great For: moving while you learn

Stomp to the beat as you float the parachute up high! This music and movement game is a great activity for children to work together as a team to respond to a variety of different motions. It provides children with an interactive way to respond to music through singing and motion.

— — — — — — — — — — —

Materials

+ Parachute

Directions to Play

Children stand evenly spaced around the parachute. One child picks a movement to add to the song, such as stomp your feet.

The group sings and performs the selected movement. The next child then has a turn to call out the movement.

The game continues until all children have had the opportunity to call out a movement to add into the song.

To the tune of "If You're Happy and You Know It"

When the parachute shakes high,
stomp your feet.

When the parachute shakes high,
stomp your feet.

When the parachute is high,
floating up into the sky,

When the parachute shakes high,
stomp your feet.

Alternate Ideas

- Tiptoe
- Wiggle your hips
- Shake your head
- Yell "Hooray"

Game Variations

Switch a balloon for a parachute and sing, "When the balloon goes up high . . ."

Write the action words on paper to tie in reading.

Change the words of the song to focus on counting. "When the parachute shakes high, stomp 3 times."

*See photo insert page 23.

Follow the Leader

Focus Skill: experimenting with ways to make music • Great For: moving while you learn

Let your child lead this game by making music in their own special way: high, low, fast or slow. Experiment with a variety of tempos and patterns in music. Take a turn being the leader too and demonstrate new ways to play. Show them how to tap hard and soft to create different sounds. Tap on different places on the oatmeal container. Does it sound the same if you tap on the sides as if you tap the top?

— — — — — — — — — — —

Materials

+ Scissors
+ Construction paper
+ Oatmeal container
+ Markers
+ Glue

Directions to Make

Cut the paper to fit around the oatmeal container. Encourage your child to decorate the paper with markers.

Glue the paper to the outside of the oatmeal container.

Directions to Play

Select one player to go first. They will tap or play their oatmeal drum and the rest of the players will copy their movements.

After a minute, change leaders. Encourage children to vary how fast or slow they play their oatmeal drum.

Game Variations

For advanced learners, teach them about notes and rests. Encourage them to make patterns such as tap-tap-rest with their drum.

Stand up and march around the room while playing. Let the leader go first.

Experiment with a variety of instruments such as shakers, rain sticks and bells.

Fast and Slow Art

Focus Skill: identifying changes in a pattern of music from fast to slow

Use your listening and creative skills to create your own art based on exploring the music beat. Players discover just how slow and fast music can be in a visual way.

- - - - - - - - - - - - -

Materials

+ Paint
+ Paper plates or container
+ Paper
+ Paintbrush
+ Sponge
+ Music player

Directions to Make

Place paint onto a plate and lay out one sheet of paper per player.

Directions to Play

Players listen to the music and are challenged to paint with slow brush strokes with slow music and fast taps when music is fast.

Use a sponge to print up and down with the beat of the music.

Allow the paper to dry and hang the game up to enjoy their artwork.

Game Variations

Using pre-painted pieces, encourage players to dance based on the painting style they are shown.

Create a music masterpiece by rolling out a long sheet of paper and allow players to paint with their feet as the music changes from fast to slow, altering their steps.

Play music and encourage players to make movements that match the speed of the music.

Keep a Steady Beat

Focus Skill: playing instruments and moving to demonstrate awareness of beat • Great For: moving while you learn

Bring out the oatmeal drum that your child created in Follow the Leader (page 198) for this music and movement game. The leader will tap out a steady beat and the children will respond by moving their feet to the music.

- - - - - - - - - - - - -

Materials

+ Oatmeal drum

(continued)

Directions to Play

One child starts as the leader. They select a steady beat and consistently tap that beat. Tap, tap, tap, tap.

The other children respond to the beat by moving their feet and walking, hopping, running, jumping or tiptoeing around the room. Tap the drum slowly for a walk, fast for a run and tap on the rim for a tiptoe.

When the music stops, the children freeze.

Repeat with another child as the leader.

Game Variations

Play this game with a variety of musical instruments such as maracas and bells.

Play music on the radio and have children move to the beat.

Provide each child with an instrument. Have all the players move and shake to the same beat.

Where in the World

Focus Skill: identifying various styles of music from around the world

Discover that instruments and rhythms from various parts of the world have different sounds. Players explore different regions and celebrate the diversity in music.

- - - - - - - - - - - - - - -

Materials

+ 10 music samples featuring instrumental and vocal music from around the world
+ Black paper
+ Scissors
+ World map

Directions to Make

Using online resources, find music samples from around the world.

Cut out 10 music notes per player, using black paper.

Directions to Play

Before the game begins, play music with the children and share with them what continent each style of music belongs to by placing a note on the specific continent.

Each player gets 10 music notes to place on the continent when they listen to the 10 selections of music.

Game Variations

Match images of people dancing around the world with the music when played.

Cut out outlines of the continents to place on the region where various music styles are played.

For advanced players, provide countries for them to select when they hear the selected pieces of music.

Outdoor Sound Garden

Focus Skill: identifying patterns in sounds

Children explore the way items sound when you use a variety of materials to bang together. Go outdoors and create a sound garden and challenge players to grow their own sound patterns.

- - - - - - - - - - - - - - -

Materials

+ Variety of recycled kitchen items (colander, muffin tin, ice cube tray, spatula, whisk, etc.)
+ Optional: wood wall to attach items to
+ Paper
+ Black marker

Directions to Make

Gather materials and arrange outdoors on soft grass or a blanket or attach to a wood wall.

Create sound pattern cards by drawing images of recycled kitchen items in various patterns (muffin tin, ice cube tray, muffin tin, ice cube tray, etc.).

Directions to Play

Allow players to experiment with the sounds of the variety of recycled kitchen items.

Have players create repetitive patterns using their kitchen utensils on the kitchen items.

The next player tries to replicate the sound pattern of the first player.

Using sound pattern cards, each player takes turns copying the images on the cards to create sound patterns.

Game Variations

Players work to find the sound garden items with the lower sounds.

Players work to find the sound garden items with the higher sounds.

Players create their own sound patterns and write on paper for other players to duplicate.

*See photo insert page 24.

Print Mysteries

Focus Skill: identifying objects used to create art prints

Did you ever wonder how an artist did that? Children analyze pieces of art to discover what tools they used to create the impressions on the canvas. Players use their own artwork to create a memory game.

Materials

+ Variety of random objects for printing (sponge, scrubber, toothbrush, potato masher, bolt, lids, marbles, pipe cleaner, cookie cutter, ball of paper, paper clip, cup, magnetic letter, etc.)
+ Tray
+ Paint
+ Paper
+ Pencil

Directions to Make

Each player selects one object from the tray to dip into paint and stamp on their paper to create a piece of art. Write on the back of the paper what object they used to make the print with. (The game works best with 15 to 20 pieces of completed art.)

Directions to Play

Play a guessing game with players by having them pick up a painting and find which object on the tray created the prints with paint. Return the object to the tray.

The game continues until a match has been made for all of the pieces of art.

Game Variations

Increase the difficulty of the game by covering the items used for players to guess from.

Add a few random items to the tray to try to trick the players.

Cut the paper in half once the painting is dry to create a matching game or cut in a few pieces to create a puzzle for players.

Roll a Shape

Focus Skill: using geometric forms in a work of art

Explore geometry through art with this playful art game. Not only will the children have a blast playing the game, they will also have a cute project to take home and hang on the refrigerator. It is a great game for playdates with large groups of children since it can be made ahead of time and is relatively low mess as far as art projects go!

— — — — — — — — — — — —

Materials

+ White multipurpose paper
+ Scissors
+ Square tissue box
+ Glue
+ Marker
+ Scrapbook paper
+ Die
+ Large white paper

Directions to Make

Cut six white squares the same size as the tissue box. Glue one on each side. Draw a different shape on each side: square, rectangle, oval, circle, triangle, diamond.

Cut a variety of those shapes from scrapbook paper. Vary the sizes.

Directions to Play

One player shakes the die. The shape that is rolled may be selected from the pile of scrapbook paper shapes.

They pass the die to the next player and finish gluing the shape onto their large white paper.

Play continues for a minimum of six rounds.

Game Variations

Make the die with a focus on colors instead of shapes.

Use a variety of art mediums (crayons, stickers, markers, paint). Write the different choices on each side of the die.

Write a sentence that tells what to add to the picture such as: "Draw a zigzag."

Art Dominoes

Focus Skill: using a variety of materials to create images • Great For: moving while you learn

Children love to paint and create art. Create your own floor-sized art domino game with your child using their own marble paintings and focus on learning how to identify dot patterns.

— — — — — — — — — —

Materials

+ Paper
+ 20 sheets of 8½ x 11-inch (21.5 x 28-cm) box or tray
+ Marble
+ Paint
+ Scissors
+ 20 sheets of 8 x 11½-inch (20 x 29-cm) cardstock
+ Glue

Directions to Make

Place a sheet of paper in the box or tray and then dip the marble into paint and roll around. Repeat with additional paint or various colors to create a design. Duplicate five times to have multiple pieces of painted paper and allow to dry.

Cut out 168 circles approximately 1 inch (2.5 cm) in diameter from the six painted sheets of paper to use for dots on the dominoes.

Cut 14 sheets of 8 x 11.5-inch (20 x 29-cm) paper in half to create art dominoes.

Glue circles onto cardstock in traditional domino pattern. Use dot patterns from 0 to 6. (Search online for sample layouts if needed.)

Directions to Play

Place art dominoes in a pile and have each player select seven dominoes. Place the remainder of art dominoes in a pile to draw from. One player turns over the top card for beginning game piece.

Players hold art dominoes like cards and take turns laying down their cards to match the art domino piece on the floor. If unable to match a domino, player selects a new domino from the pile.

Play continues until a player has played all of their art dominoes.

Game Variations

Use recycled cereal boxes to create art dominoes that can stand up and make chain reactions just like the smaller version.

Join together two art dominoes to create number problems to solve.

Players race to place their selected pieces in numerical order based on the total amount of art on the dominoes.

Night at the Museum

Focus Skill: learning to identify different styles of art • Great For: moving while you learn

Experience your own night at the museum by discovering famous pieces of art with your special artist flashlight. This activity exposes children to art masterpieces at an early age to help to develop knowledge and appreciation.

- - - - - - - - - - - - - - - -

Materials

+ Printed images of famous pieces of art
+ Printed images of artist with image next to them
+ Flashlight

Directions to Make

Select and print 10 pieces of famous art from online images with your child.

Create a piece of paper for a scavenger hunt by placing an image of the famous artist and the piece of work beside them.

Add the text of the artist and artwork name to the scavenger hunt and discuss names with players.

Directions to Play

Hang the pieces of art around the room in a dim light setting.

Using the flashlight, encourage players to search around the room for the pieces of art in the museum.

Once a player finds a piece of art they check it off the list until they have found each piece of artwork.

Game Variations

Give each player an artist image and ask them to find the piece of art they created.

Create a memory game with the famous pieces of art selected.

Create a puzzle with each image for players to solve.

Dragon Castle

Focus Skill: creating three-dimensional art

Explore a time from long ago with a castle and one special dragon who likes to explore in all sorts of directions through the castle. Players learn to create a three-dimensional piece of art that becomes an inspiration for imaginary play. Plus adults can sneak in a little vocabulary as you encourage players to explore positional words.

- - - - - - - - - - - - - -

Materials

+ Cardboard box
+ Scissors
+ Markers
+ Paper
+ Egg carton
+ Googly eyes
+ Glue
+ Paint
+ Paintbrush
+ 3 x 5-inch (7.5 x 13-cm) index cards

Directions to Make

Remove the top pieces of the box and then cut out the edges to make the box look like the edges of a castle (adult task).

Add a doorway on top and two sides but keep the bottom so it can lift up and down for entrance.

Cut out windows on each side of the castle (or color with markers).

Decorate the castle with markers and paper to create stonework and plants surrounding the castle.

Create a dragon using an egg carton, googly eyes and paint.

Write on index cards directional words including beside, in front of, behind, on top of, above, between, inside and under.

Directions to Play

After players have created their three-dimensional piece of art, it's time to explore the castle.

Each player takes a turn by picking a positional word from the word pile and placing the dragon in the castle using the positional word chosen.

Players continue to take turns selecting positional word cards and placing the dragon accordingly.

Game Variations

Play a hide-and-seek game by having one player hide a gold coin while the other one discovers it in the castle with the dragon and labels it with the correct positional word.

Hang famous pieces of art in the castle and have players draw cards with art and find the match.

Create a positional word book illustrating the dragon's position within the castle for a fun sight word book.

*See photo insert page 24.

Pattern Wheel

Focus Skill: using lines, shapes and forms to make patterns

There is something magical about a group of five to seven children all working together to complete a collaborative art project. I just love the hum of busy, happy kids expressing their creativity. This game is great for helping to develop a caring community of learners, creative expression and a little math too!

Try making a few wheels in varying sizes. Hang them from a clothesline or bulletin board for a festive display.

- - - - - - - - - - - - - -

Materials

+ Scissors
+ Large paper
+ Markers

Directions to Make

Cut a large circle from the paper.

Draw lines to divide the circle into six equal pieces.

Directions to Play

The first player closes their eyes and reaches into the marker container for a color.

The player to their right calls out a style of line or shape: zigzag, dots, squiggles, etc.

The first player then must use that style of line or shape in a pattern to decorate their part of the circle.

Play continues until all children have received one color marker and a style of line or shape to draw. They complete their section.

When the entire pattern wheel is complete, display!

Game Variations

Draw for two colors and let the player to the right call out two different styles of lines or shapes.

Switch a circle for another shape: pentagon, octagon or diamond.

Use stamps or paint instead of markers to explore a variety of art materials.

Where Is the Duck?

Focus Skill: identifying north, south, east and west on a map

Track your duck around the map using directional words to make it come back home. Children practice using the words north, east, south and west as their duck takes a journey through the oceans of the world.

Materials

+ 20 (1 x 3-inch [2.5 x 7.5-cm]) pieces of paper, plus more for creating ducks and home star
+ Scissors
+ Printed map of the Earth
+ Marker

Directions to Make

Create small ducks for each player with the paper. Create a paper star.

Print out or create a large map of the Earth.

Divide the map into 12 squares by folding.

Place the star on the map where you live to use as the duck's home.

Write the words north, south, east and west on 20 cards.

Directions to Play

Each player gets a duck and selects a side to start from.

Players draw a direction from the pile and move their duck in that direction one square over.

The players try to work their way to the star to end the game.

Game Variations

Challenge players to land on specific countries or continents.

Create multiple stopping points for the duck to collect on its journey around the world.

Have players choose from positional words around the map of the Earth.

Treasure Hunt

Focus Skill: drawing and using a map; using relative location of people, places and things; using positional words • Great For: moving while you learn

Get kids excited about making and using a map with this fun treasure hunt game. This is a great activity for playdates and birthday parties. Stuff your treasure box with party goody bags for the kids to take home. Small erasers, spinning tops and stickers make great non-candy prizes.

– – – – – – – – – – – – – –

Materials

+ 2 empty boxes
+ Markers and stickers
+ Small treasure items
+ 2 pieces of paper
+ Pencil

Directions to Make

Divide the children into two groups.

Let each group decorate a box with markers and stickers. Have them fill the box with the treasures when they are done.

Select an area for each group to make their map.

Let them choose a starting point based on the relative location to an object. Example: Start at the big oak tree. Draw a picture of a tree and write the word start.

Have them draw a picture and/or write sentences to describe the steps taken to reach the treasure. Use prepositional words such as over, under, next to, above.

The directions should end at a place where the box can hide. Hide the box there.

Directions to Play

Select one team to go first. Give them the child-made map to follow.

Let them read and follow the directions to find the treasure. Cheer them on.

Once they have found the treasure, let the other team repeat steps 1 and 2.

Game Variations

Use word clues or picture clues only.

For younger learners, the adults may make the map and hide the treasure ahead of time.

For advanced learners, use a tape measure. Have them record the exact measurements between places.

Land vs. Water

Focus Skill: distinguishing between land and water on maps and globes

Explore the differences between land and water on a globe with this game. Many party stores and some online stores will carry inflatable globes. If you can't find one, you can always make your own with a permanent marker and plain ball.

– – – – – – – – – – – – – –

Materials

+ Paper
+ Pencil
+ Inflatable globe

Directions to Make

Write a large "T" on the paper.

Add the words water and land to each side to make the game board.

Directions to Play

Assign one player to be the record keeper.

Toss the ball to another player. The child will catch the ball with two hands.

They will look to see where their right pointer finger lands and call out: "land" or "water."

The recorder will make a tally mark on that side of the paper.

Repeat steps 2 to 4 for a total of 20 tosses.

Add up each side tallies. Who won—land or water?

Game Variations

Write the specific name of the land or ocean each player points to.

For more advanced players, discuss how the Earth is made up of more than 75 percent water and other world facts.

Play this game using a map. Close your eyes and point.

Celebration Jar

Focus Skill: recognizing and comparing celebrations and holidays of others

Children delight in talking about themselves and their families. This game gives them the chance to share more about their own celebrations while learning about others.

– – – – – – – – – – – – –

Materials

+ Scrapbook paper
+ Scissors
+ Pencil
+ Mason jar

Directions to Make

Cut colorful strips of paper.

Write a celebration question on each strip of paper. Sample questions include: What is your favorite holiday? How does your family celebrate birthdays? What winter holidays does your family celebrate? What is your favorite food to eat for Thanksgiving? What kind of gifts do you give to others on their birthday? What kind of gifts do you give others for holidays? How does your family decorate for the holidays?

Fold and place in the jar.

Directions to Play

The youngest player selects a question from the jar. With the help of an adult, they read the question and answer it.

Each player in the game then has a chance to answer it as well.

When everyone has answered the question, the next player draws a strip from the celebration jar and repeats steps 1 and 2.

Game Variations

For a speed game of celebrations, allow one-word answers.

Switch celebration questions for other themes: science topics, state facts, inspirational quotes or religious sayings.

Create a homemade board game with the questions instead of placing them in the jar.

*See photo insert page 24.

State Toss

Focus Skill: identifying the states in the United States of America • Great For: moving while you learn

Encourage children to explore the United States by tossing a rock onto various state outlines. Using a secret trick that artists use, create your own outline of the United States with chalk and focus on learning all 50 states.

- - - - - - - - - - -

Materials

+ Map of the United States
+ Chalk
+ Rocks
+ Paint
+ Paintbrush
+ Paper
+ Pencils

Directions to Make

Print out a map of the United States and fold into 16 squares.

Have an adult create a grid of 16 squares with chalk on the ground or place dots at the intersections.

Adults and players work together to re-create the map with chalk. Draw the lines represented in each grid on the printed paper onto the ground in the corresponding grid box or dot intersections depending on the method you select.

Paint a self-portrait with paint on the rocks for game pieces.

Create a traveling tracking sheet for each player with text and image outlines of the states.

Directions to Play

Players take turns tossing their own rock onto the map of the United States.

Once a rock lands the player identifies the state they have landed on by marking it on their travel tracking sheet. Encourage players to name the specific state (Florida, Colorado, Minnesota, etc.). They can color it in with chalk (optional).

Game ends when all players have landed on each state, completing their journey around the United States of America.

Game Variations

Play game using a map of the continents.

Play game using a map of a country.

Play game using a map of a state or city.

*See photo insert page 24.

I Need It

Focus Skill: distinguishing between needs and wants • Great For: on-the-go learning

Needs and wants can be tough for young children to differentiate between. This can be evident in a trip to a toy store. Although it is okay to have wants, part of early childhood learning is to be able to separate the two. See if your child can identify the difference between something they need to survive and items that they want. Talk about how needs and wants may be similar or different in families all around the world.

- - - - - - - - - - -

Materials

+ Large sheet of paper
+ Red and blue markers
+ Pencil

Directions to Make

Write the word WANT in red and NEED in blue at the top of the paper.

Brainstorm a list of items children may need and want.

Need: food, shoes, clothing, shelter, backpack, school supplies.

Want: movie tickets, candy, new toys, coloring books.

Write these items in a list on the large sheet of paper.

Directions to Play

Hand two children the different-colored markers.

Read an item from the list. If the item is a want, the child holding the red marker gets to circle it. If it is a need, the child with the blue marker circles it.

If the child has circled a word or phrase, they pass their marker on to another player.

Play continues until all words and phrases have been circled.

Game Variations

Make a statement of want or need and encourage children to agree or disagree with it by showing a thumbs-up signal. I need toy cars = thumbs down.

Draw a picture of something you want on a piece of paper, a need on another piece. Assemble all the pictures into two separate kid-made books: I want . . . I need . . .

Read the item on the list. Have the children state whether they need or want it.

How Many of You?

Focus Skill: identifying famous landmarks around the world

Have you ever wondered how many of you it would take to reach the top of your house or even the Statue of Liberty? Players explore nonstandard measurement using their own height to compare to famous landmarks.

- - - - - - - - - - - - - - -

Materials

+ Photo image of child
+ 5 sheets of paper for game pieces
+ 2 sheets of paper for landmarks and height measurements

Directions to Make

Place multiple images of your child onto a Word document and print out. The image size should be 2 inches (5 cm) tall. Twenty-one images on five sheets of paper will provide enough game pieces.

Together search online to find images of famous landmarks to use for the game.

Write down how tall each chosen landmark is.

Print out images of landmarks with height and use as game pieces. Select four different structures per printed page.

Directions to Play

Each player chooses a famous landmark from the pile.

One player says "go" and each player works to re-create the size of the landmark using the game pieces.

The player that finishes first correctly wins that round.

Game Variations

Work together as a team to see how quickly you can measure the height of a famous landmark.

Sort the various landmarks by height.

Compare items around your house like your home, trees or car for players to learn on a smaller scale.

Technology Timeline

Focus Skill: making a timeline of important events

Technology plays a significant role in many young children's lives. Test your knowledge of the history of technology with this collaborative game to get kids thinking. Encourage children to talk about the significance of these technologies on their lives. Research using books and kid-friendly websites if help is needed!

- - - - - - - - - - - - - - -

Materials

+ 3 x 5-inch (7.5 x 13-cm) notecards
+ Pencil

Directions to Make

Write a form of technology on each card: television, Hubble telescope, video game, telephone, camera, personal computer, etc.

Directions to Play

Hand the cards to the children. Read the words out loud.

Allow the group to arrange the cards in the order in which they think each was invented.

Check. Provide hints to help them change any technology items on their timeline.

Game Variations

Focus on specific inventors, scientific discoveries or forms of travel.

Let each player choose one item to learn more about prior to the game beginning. Allow them to be the expert and teach others about their technology invention.

Make a card for the dates and have children order the numbers and use dates on the inventions on the timeline as well.

NOTE

Don't show them these dates until after the game: 1876 telephone, 1888 camera, 1927 television, 1972 video game, 1983 personal computer, 1990 Hubble telescope.

Roll a Landform

Focus Skill: identifying various types of landforms around the world

What is that called? Players roll the dice to see what types of landforms they can match on the Earth. Many children live in an area with limited types of landforms. Children can use this game to discover others as they explore their world.

- - - - - - - - - - - - - - -

Materials

+ Square tissue box or homemade cardboard box
+ Construction paper
+ Markers or crayons
+ Scissors
+ Glue
+ 2 pieces of paper
+ Pencil

Directions to Make

Create six images for the various types of landforms. Include mountain, lake, river, ocean, island, plateau, glacier, coast, canyon, plains, hill, valley or desert.

Attach images onto the side of the box.

Create a tally sheet with landform images.

Directions to Play

Players roll the box to identify a landform.

Once it lands, a player marks a tally mark on the recording form that corresponds to the matching landform.

The player who reaches six landforms first wins!

Game Variations

Focus images on types of bodies of water.

Focus images on types of mountains.

Create with images that feature different types of environments.

Continent Fortune-Teller

Focus Skill: identifying the seven continents

Grab a partner and go global with this paper-folding fortune-teller game. Make your game board, then count and move for your challenge. Locate the continents on the map, refold the game board back together and count again! We know you will soon be able to identify all seven continents.

— — — — — — — — — — —

Materials

+ Square piece of paper
+ Pencil
+ Map or globe

Directions to Make

Fold the square paper in half at both diagonals. Crease and unfold. Fold the square again at each middle. Unfold.

Bring each corner evenly to the middle of the square.

Flip the square over and fold the corners evenly into the middle of the square again.

Fold in half and flip over.

Place your fingers into the slits and open.

Open each triangle and write one of the following on each half: Find North America, Find South America, Point to Australia, Point to Europe, Find Asia, Find Africa, Point to Antarctica, Point and Name an Ocean.

To complete the fortune-teller, write numbers 1 to 8 on the inside triangles.

Directions to Play

Player one places their fingers in the fortune-teller and opens to show four numbers.

Player two picks one of the four numbers and player one moves the fortune-teller back and forth that many times.

Player two picks another number. Player one then opens the fortune-teller to read their task.

Player two completes the task using the map or globe.

The game repeats with player two holding the fortune-teller.

Game Variations

Write famous landforms, major cities or important landmarks on the inside triangles.

Use this game to practice math facts. Write a number sentence on each triangle for kids to solve before moving back and forth.

Write sight words on each triangle. Move the fortune-teller the number of letters in the word. Write a sentence using that word on the inside for them to read out loud.

Part Three

SCIENCE

(eleven)

SUPER FUN EXPERIMENTS

Science is play at its most curious. It looks at something ordinary and explores the whys and hows behind it. Children's natural examination of the world can be emboldened when their questions are a catalyst for playing with science.

Holly's Picks: I am always amazed by the magic of vinegar plus baking soda, which is why my favorite science activities are Sandbox Volcano (page 225), Fizzy Color Drop (page 220) and Fizzing Sidewalk Paint (page 219).

Rachel's Pick: Of all the science experiments we have done over the years, Naked Eggs (page 223) stick out in my kids' memories. They got to touch, see, feel and experience a cell—physically. I love how science encourages curiosity and respect for the world around them!

Archaeology Dig with Supersoft Dough

Searching for treasures is a basic human desire. The delight of discovery is real whether it be prehistoric bones on an archaeological dig or a plastic toy buried in playdough. This homemade dough is one of my favorites. It is sweet smelling and soft to the touch, which makes it the perfect medium for an archaeological toy dig.

Materials
(to make one dig site)

+ Medium-size bowl
+ About ½ cup (120 ml) leftover hair conditioner (see Tip)
+ About 1 cup (160 g) cornstarch
+ Glitter and food dye (optional)
+ Airtight bag
+ Baking dish
+ Little toys (e.g., dinosaurs)
+ Archaeology tools (e.g., coffee stirrers, toothpicks and/or spoons)

In a medium-size bowl, mix the conditioner and cornstarch together until it is the consistency of playdough. The amounts vary depending on the type of conditioner. Typically, you need about ½ cup (120 ml) of conditioner to 1 cup (160 g) of cornstarch. If it is too sticky, add more cornstarch; if it is crumbly or hard, add more conditioner.

Half the fun is mixing the ingredients. Add glitter for an extra sparkle. Food dye to color the dough is optional. Store in an airtight bag. Add small amounts of conditioner or oil to the dough after it has been stored to rehydrate the dough before playing with it.

In preparation for the dig, layer the bottom of a baking dish with your dinos. Press the soft dough over the tops of your toys. Try to extricate the toys, leaving as little remaining dough on the items, using "tools" found in your kitchen.

Modifications for Younger Kids

Add a tablespoon (15 ml) of oil to the dough. It will help the objects be removed more easily.

Modifications for Older Kids

Have them try multiple batches, and see whether it is easier or harder to perform an archaeology dig in a moist dough or a crumbly one. Experience the problems that archaeologists face due to soil conditions.

TIP

Do you have leftover sunscreen from last summer? You can replace the hair conditioner in this recipe with any lotion.

Book Bridge Building

Anyone who has built with wooden blocks has been intrigued by the mystery of the bridge architecture. *How does it span that distance without falling in the middle?* It is a question that can spur hours of building, in hopes of discovering the answer.

This is a favorite activity because we always have what we need on hand. We use the books we already own and two dining room chairs as the building materials for our architectural bridge design. Kids will play with the concept of span and innately problem solve complex mathematical questions while placing books through trial and error. They can build various types of bridges (beam, truss, cantilever) and see which works best.

(continued)

Materials

+ 25 or more hardcover books
+ 2 chairs

Examine a bridge next time you are out driving with your child. Discuss how the base starts before the actual bridge does. When home, re-create a bridge by beginning with a base with the books and then moving each subsequent book closer and closer to the center while not dropping any books.

Modifications for Younger Kids

Younger kids can build a shorter bridge on the floor and experiment with how to create a span that is slightly wider than a book length.

Put your treasured books on a high shelf during this activity and start with the kids' books. Younger kids will drop and dent books during play—so prepare by giving them the books that won't be harmed or worried about.

Modifications for Older Kids

Add variety, use chairs of different sizes and watch your child problem solve and adapt the bridge to span different gaps.

Test the strength of your bridge by building a tower over the top of your bridge. The extra books are weight. How does it hold up?

If you have a large personal library, then give the kids a challenge to get across the kitchen floor with the use of only three chairs and a stack of books. Give them a problem to solve that seems just a little bit impossible.

CD Spinning Top

There is a reason why spinning top toys have been popular as long as there have been children. They are easy to make with just about any type of material, and they have a coolness factor that is ageless.

This modern version spins around a marble axis with a little pickup from gyroscopic action. It stays upright as long as the inertia can keep up the speed needed to avoid toppling. This activity is simple to assemble and can teach your kids about color theory and the way our brains automatically mix colors—fascinating.

Materials

+ Small marble
+ Modeling clay—roughly the amount of two sticks of gum
+ Old CD
+ Permanent markers (optional)

Stick the marble into a quarter-size (roughly 2.5 cm-diameter) piece of clay and then stuff that into the CD hole. The marble should be mostly exposed. You do not want to cover the whole marble with clay. Place your creation on a smooth surface; balance the CD on the marble and spin! Watch it swirl!

Color Mash

Using markers, color one half of the CD with one primary color and the other half with a different primary color. Watch the colors combine into a secondary color when spinning as your brain mixes the colors together.

Spin Marathon

See who can keep the top spinning for the longest time. Explain to your child how centrifugal force helps your spinning CD resist the laws of gravity; as long as the force of the turn is greater than the force of gravity, the CD will not "topple."

Modifications for Younger Kids

Younger kids can practice the movement required to set the top in motion. If they are too young to successfully get the top spinning, then having them try to stop a spinning top can be lots of fun.

Modifications for Older Kids

Have older kids make several tops and try to keep at least one of them in motion for a set amount of time. It will test their ability to predict which top is slowing down and try to judge which top requires immediate attention.

TIP

Play with the CDs as reflectors. Have kids shine a flashlight on the CD as it spins. Watch the light dance on the ceiling. Give the kids a point on a wall to try to illuminate and see what it takes to make that happen. Talk to your kids about angles and try to predict where the light will bounce if you change the position of the flashlight.

Compost Soup

One of my favorite childhood stories is Stone Soup. It shows how ingredients that aren't much on their own can be combined into something that blesses an entire community. That story is in the back of my head when we create compost soup. Any one of the composting ingredients on its own is considered trash, but when they are combined they make a wonderful "soup" for garden worms.

This activity is a way for kids to really get involved in the composting process in mixing and creating a final product that will be a blessing to any garden. Four things are needed for composting organisms to be able to work their magic: carbon (brown and dry matter), nitrogen (wet green and colorful matter), oxygen (mixing it so the air can get in) and water (grab a watering can).

Materials

+ Giant bowl or big tub
+ A collection of spoons and scoops
+ Dirt
+ Grass clippings
+ Sawdust
+ Eggshells
+ Vegetable scraps
+ Dryer lint
+ Coffee grounds
+ Stale bread crumbs
+ Other compostable items

Head outside and grab a giant bowl or big tub and a variety of spoons and scoops, along with your bucket of scraps.

Think outside the box with biodegradable items to include in your compost bin. We have included shredded 100 percent cotton clothes, toilet paper tubes, stale candy and *tons* of other items. It is great to feed the plants and worms while lessening our trash.

Mash, mix and stir all the compost ingredients into a gloriously messy compost soup.

We like to use pretend dishes for a pretend worm tea party. When the kids are done mixing their soup, they can pour cupfuls of the compost around the plants in your garden, giving them a nutritious snack.

(continued)

Modifications for Younger Kids

Younger kids can help remind the family of compostable materials to save in the kitchen. They are really good at a mission!

Modifications for Older Kids

Older kids can create their own unique composting mix to put on their part of the garden to see whether they can improve plant growth.

Cork Boats & a Tinfoil River

With this activity, kids will innately learn about water displacement and how to weight and shape a boat in different ways for different results. They can test their hypothesis about which ship will sail the best and which will flip and sink. Because these cork boats are so simple, you can make a fleet!

- - - - - - - - - -

Materials

+ Knife
+ Corks—each cork makes 2 boats
+ 1 or 2 toothpicks per boat
+ Sturdy tape
+ Rubber bands
+ Tinfoil (optional)
+ Drinking straws (optional)

To make a simple sailboat: Cut the cork in half lengthwise. Stick a toothpick into the center of the cork and use the tape to fashion a sail.

To make a weight-bearing raft: Use tape or rubber bands to secure a line of corks to one another. Add toothpicks and tape for sails. You will want to try a number of variations. See how many corks you can unite to create the most stable ship, or which arrangement will sail the fastest.

Optional: To make a river: Cut a long length of tinfoil for your kids to play with. Roll the edges so the foil will hold water. Place the river outside and add some water. This doesn't have to be running water; you can create more of a lakelike river. Place the cork boats in the water.

Figure out a way to sail the boats "down" the river. It could be by adding cups of water to one end of the river or having the kids use a straw to sail the ships toward a goal.

Get out a stopwatch and see how long it will take for your boats to make it to the finish line.

Modifications for Younger Kids

Give them a cup of water to pour and keep each boat floating downriver. Let them use their hands as the boat's motor.

This activity works well as a solo (or small people pair) activity in the bathtub.

Modifications for Older Kids

Older kids can work on not only an offensive race with a straw, but a defensive race as well. Allow them to attempt to blow their competition out of the water. Literally.

DIY Bouncy Ball

As you collect the ingredients for your balls, look at the textures—glue is sticky and cornstarch is powdery. Neither one can bounce on its own. The molecules of the ingredients are small and generally incomplete. But when you add a catalyst to the glue, starch and water, it transforms the characteristic properties of these ingredients— creating a rubbery-textured polymer. To make this ball, your kids just linked and mixed molecules together.

A quick word of caution: this recipe includes borax, which is not edible. Please don't let children chew on the finished product or taste it during any steps along the way.

- - - - - - - - - -

Materials

(to make two bouncy balls)

+ 4 tbsp (60 ml) warm water
+ 1 tsp borax (find it in the laundry detergent section of your local store)
+ 2 disposable cups
+ Disposable spoon, for stirring
+ 2 tbsp (30 ml) glue
+ 2 tbsp (16 g) cornstarch
+ Food coloring (optional)
+ Measuring spoons

Pour the water and borax into the first cup and stir the mixture until it is dissolved.

Next, pour the glue, cornstarch, food coloring and ½ teaspoon of the mixture from the first cup into the second cup. After the cornstarch and glue are mixed together pour contents of cup #2 into cup #1. Our ball recipe seems to work best if you mix the glue, cornstarch and food coloring first, and *then* pour it into the borax mixture.

Let the ingredients in the second cup interact on their own for about 15 seconds, then stir. We found that a folding method was the most effective way to stir the ingredients. Once the mixture becomes difficult to stir, scoop it out of the cup, divide in half and roll into two balls. There will be a watery borax mixture left in the container. You will want to dispose of that liquid and throw away the container.

We stored the ball in a resealable plastic bag for several days and it stayed fresh until it simply picked up too much dirt and we had to throw it out!

Modifications for Younger Kids
Younger children can have fun bouncing the balls—see which one of them can bounce their ball the highest.

Modifications for Older Kids
Older kids can test different sizes to make modifications to elicit more bounce action. Encourage your kids to tweak the ingredients—how does the ball change if you add more or less of just one ingredient? They can also test out different shapes and how that affects how the ball bounces. We found that this is a forgiving recipe—almost all of our versions bounced to some degree.

*See photo insert page 25.

> ### TIP
> The ingredients and instructions to make a homemade bouncy ball make a great gift when packaged together in a small plastic bucket.

Fizzing Sidewalk Paint

This activity trumps ordinary sidewalk chalk with a little science magic by creating a chalk-based paint and then spritzing on a little fizz. It all starts with pH. When solutions that are pH base mix with an acid, action happens!

Materials

+ Large mixing bowl
+ 1 (1-lb [454-g]) box baking soda
+ ½ cup (80 g) cornstarch
+ Warm water
+ Several containers to hold the paint
+ Food coloring
+ Paintbrush(es)
+ Spray bottle filled with vinegar—1 per child
+ Buckets for cleanup

(continued)

In a large mixing bowl, mix the baking soda and the cornstarch together. Add the warm (almost hot) water, stirring until it is the consistency of pancake batter. Split the recipe into several containers, adding the food coloring color of your choice to each.

Use the homemade paint to create a scene or flick it with a paintbrush into a modern masterpiece. It is best to work fast because the paint dries quickly (but can always be diluted with the addition of more warm water).

Once the painting is in place, it is time for something a little extra. Spray the artwork with the vinegar-filled bottle and watch what happens. Your artwork will sizzle and pop!

About Cleanup
A bucketful of water splashed across the art can make it disappear. Because that is fun, too, you might not want to wait for rain.

Modifications for Younger Kids
If a paintbrush is hard to negotiate in the paint, give your children a spoon and let them drip or drop spoonfuls of paint onto the pavement. For the little ones, be sure to fully supervise when they spray vinegar. It can sting little eyes.

Modifications for Older Kids
This activity is an easy way to work in a lesson on reactions between acids and base chemicals and talk about why this works. Maybe you can have your budding scientists adapt the recipe to see whether they can get bigger bubbles and more fizz in their next batch of paint.

*See photo insert page 25.

TIP
Do you have a prewriting preschooler? Use a turkey baster to squirt vinegar at the paint. The grasping and squeezing helps strengthen finger muscles they will use when they are writing.

Fizzy Color Drop

Baking soda and vinegar go together like peas and carrots . . . well, in my house they are more popular than peas and carrots, but that is a whole other issue.

The amazing play experience that happens when you use baking soda as a canvas for colorful vinegar drops equals a good hour of intense and exploratory fun. When baking soda (base) and vinegar (acid) combine, they become carbonic acid. The carbonic acid is so unstable that it quickly falls apart, resulting in bubbles of carbon dioxide. These are the same type of bubbles that cause quick breads to rise.

This is a really good rainy-day activity. If the sun is shining, move outside to enjoy it.

- - - - - - - - - - - - -

Materials
+ Baking sheet or flat plastic container
+ 1 (1-lb [454-g]) box baking soda
+ Plastic cups
+ 1 to 2 cups (235 to 475 ml) vinegar
+ Food coloring
+ Medicine droppers, plastic syringes or turkey baster

Cover the bottom of a baking sheet or flat plastic container with a ½-inch (1.3-cm)-deep layer of baking soda.

In plastic cups, fill each partially with vinegar and a different food coloring color.

Using a medicine dropper or plastic syringe, fill it with the colored vinegar mixture and drop it onto the baking soda canvas. Watch as the colorful fizzing reaction happens. Play with the colors to make new colors as they bubble.

Modifications for Younger Kids
If the medicine dropper or plastic syringe is a challenge to control, consider using an ear bulb, which is more easily grasped by little hands.

Alternatively, put the drops of food coloring onto the baking sheet, then cover lightly with the baking soda. Let your child use a spoon to drop teaspoonfuls of vinegar onto the white canvas and see a surprise burst of color emerge.

Modifications for Older Kids

Creating a temporary masterpiece, such as a rainbow or another scene, by dropping the colors can be a playful challenge. Take a picture of the final product.

Slimy Copy Machine with Goop Recipe

The Sunday paper was the absolute best way to test the duplicating powers of Silly Putty. If you did it just right, you could create a color copy of a favorite comic. The ink used in newspapers has changed over time, resulting in less than perfect copies, but you can revive the experience in your own home with pencil drawings.

We are channeling those early Sunday experiences with this fun recipe to make homemade putty and then use it to copy images, text or textures. All sorts of fun!

- - - - - - - - - - - - -

Materials

+ Small bowl
+ ½ tsp borax
+ ¼ cup (60 ml) warm water
+ Spoon, for mixing
+ ¼ cup (32 g) cornstarch
+ 2 to 3 oz (60 to 90 ml) white glue (roughly ½ of a 4-oz [120-ml] container)
+ Food coloring (liquid kind)
+ Durable, resealable plastic freezer bag
+ A variety of printed papers and writing mediums

In a small bowl, dissolve the borax in the water; set aside.

Combine the borax mixture with the remaining ingredients in a durable resealable plastic freezer bag.

The mix will seem clumpy and stringy, but mix for several minutes, until all the ingredients are combined.

Let it sit for 30 minutes or longer. Give the cornstarch time to absorb the moisture before kneading the bag again. We found it takes about 20 to 30 minutes of kneading to gain a putty consistency.

Roll your homemade putty out until it is flat. Find different pages with writing on them. Press the pages into the goop and see the mirrored image retained by the goop.

Try a variety of different texts, papers and writing mediums. Which sticks better? Pencil? Pen? Marker? Experiment by writing on the goop and transferring it back to the paper.

Modifications for Younger Kids

Leave the borax out of the recipe. The goop will have a different consistency, but this adaptation will make the recipe nontoxic if ingested. Borax is laundry detergent booster and is not edible.

Modifications for Older Kids

Change the amount of cornstarch that you add . . . using all of the ingredients, you can create slime (use more glue and water, less cornstarch) and bouncy balls (page 219).

TIP

Want a fun way to store your goop? Fill balloons with your slimy mixture. It will keep longer in the balloon and be a fun, mess-less way to squish the goop until you are ready to play with it again.

Hydrofoils

The simple concepts behind how things float are fun to explore. They turn a sink or bathtub into a science laboratory. It all starts with boat design. Then testing of that design. Then making informed alterations and starting all over again.

Water holds together in such a way that it creates a pressure that pushes things up. Gravity wants to pull the boat down. The result is a cosmic fight we call buoyancy. Overcome gravity or harness the power of density to avoid sinking.

This activity uses water (hydro) and tinfoil (foil) to test your little boat designers' skills.

- - - - - - - - - - - - - -

Materials

+ Tinfoil
+ Jar of coins
+ Sink, bucket or bathtub

Give each participant a similarly sized piece of tinfoil and have them fashion it into a structure that will float. Each prototype can be tested in the water and modifications made by folding and smushing (totally a scientific word) the moldable foil. Once the design is satisfactory, then it is time for testing.

Next, the participants start adding coins to their design to see how many they can add before the design fails and sinks. If everyone is using pennies, then you can easily keep track of which design held up the best by counting the money that it holds.

Modifications for Younger Kids

This is the perfect bathtub experiment. Younger kids can create a fleet of boats with several pieces of tinfoil and then attempt to let their other bath toys float on their boats.

Modifications for Older Kids

Have older kids hypothesize as to which design will hold up the best and then compete in the testing. Let them research buoyancy and then test their findings.

Introduce waves to the test by carefully adding water (rain—mimicking a storm) to show how a little water over a short boat side can have disastrous effects.

Milk Explosions

This activity uses milk and food coloring to create art. The milk fat holds the color until dish soap breaks the tension of the fat, releasing the dye throughout the milk in a burst of color. Because of this unique property, milk can be used to create fascinating artworks.

- - - - - - - - - - - - - -

Materials

+ Whole milk (cream is even better!)
+ Dish
+ Multiple colors of food coloring
+ Cotton swab or toothpick
+ Liquid dish soap
+ Several pieces of cardstock

Pour the milk into a dish. You don't want a whole lot, just enough to cover the bottom of your dish. Add drops of food dye, then dip a cotton swab into the soap and lightly touch the surface of the milk. Watch the milk explode in color. As the colors are swirling, dip a piece of cardstock into the milk. You should have a very lightly patterned swirl on your paper. Your child captured the milk explosion!

For a more evident keepsake of this experiment, dip a second piece of cardstock into the milk; make sure the page is good and wet. It's okay for it to have puddles even. This is a messy project.

Drop a drip of food coloring onto the milky page. The dye should stay pretty stationary where you put it. Dab the center of the "drip" with soap and watch the ink run away from your swab. Repeat across the sheet with a variety of colors.

We were pleased with the shiny card that was the result of our morning with science.

Modifications for Younger Kids

Have an adult do the food dye drips. You only want one or two, as those bottles are hard to control. Have them work with one color at a time.

Modifications for Older Kids

Do a science experiment: use 2% milk, whole milk and cream. Which one isolates the dye the most? Which one spreads the dye most easily? Why?

Have your older children personalize the finished work with embellishments—transform the paper into postcards to mail to a friend.

This technique can be used to create a colorful canvas for more art. Let the first layer dry and then further illustrate the design with markers or more paint.

Naked Egg Experiment

This activity puts a cell in the hands of kids. They can see, touch, even pop the membrane with their fingers, and explore how the cell's permeable membrane diffuses molecules (i.e., stays hydrated) in a way they understand.

The acetic acid in the vinegar breaks up the calcium carbonate crystals in the eggshell. At the end of this experiment, you will have a naked egg! (We advise that you start with at least three or four eggs because your child will break one or more; eggs without their shells are very fragile.)

Materials
(to make one naked egg [see headnote])

+ 3 or 4 eggs
+ Large glass bowl
+ 1 cup (235 ml) vinegar

This experiment takes several days to complete. To begin, place your eggs in a large glass bowl. You will want to leave about an inch (2.5 cm) of space between each egg because they are going to swell as their shell dissolves. Cover the eggs with roughly an inch (2.5 cm) of vinegar. The eggs will float. Watch. Almost immediately you will see the eggs begin to spin and bubbles rise to the surface. The bubbles are the release of gas. The shells are a base and the vinegar is an acid—combined base and acid elements create gas (or bubbles). If you put a piece of plastic wrap over your bowl, you will see it balloon up as it fills with gas. You will want to keep your eggs in the vinegar for three days, to fully dissolve the shell. As the shell disintegrates in the vinegar you can see the membrane and witness the egg expand. The egg is expanding as the vinegar (water) is diffused by osmosis into the egg, causing it to swell.

Modifications for Younger Kids

Let them enjoy gently holding the naked egg. Don't be surprised if the egg bursts. They are fragile in their shell-free state.

Modifications for Older Kids

Take one of the naked eggs and put it into a sugar solution (corn syrup, flat soda, even juice). Watch what happens to the egg after it sits in the sugar all day. Your egg will no longer be pretty and round, but should shrivel and turn brown. This is a great experiment to do with your kids, to explain to them what happens to our cells when we consume sugar.

*See photo insert page 25.

(continued)

Ocean in a Bottle

Every year we make a trek to the Outer Banks of North Carolina. We love to watch the waves crash against the sandy beaches. This simple science experiment is inspired by our weeks at the sea.

A wave transfers energy, not water. The water stays in the same place and passes kinetic energy. This wave in a bottle is fun to make and has the bonus that the finished product is mesmerizing to watch. In addition to being a great way to learn about waves and tides, the ocean bottle is a nice calm-down bedtime or naptime activity.

– – – – – – – – – – – – – – –

Materials

+ Nonmetallic glitter (optional)
+ Empty, clean plastic bottle, with a secure top
+ Handful of small shells
+ Blue food coloring
+ Water
+ Enough baby oil to fill the plastic bottle halfway
+ Glue

Pour ½ inch (1.3 cm) or so of plastic glitter crystals into the bottom of your bottle. It is best to use glitter that is not metallic. The metal-based glitters tend to corrode in water after a while. Add a couple of shells. Fill your bottle halfway with blue water. Top off the bottle with the baby oil. Be sure to leave about an inch (2.5 cm) of "air space" at the top.

Glue the bottle top securely to the bottle to avoid spills.

Shake the bottle to explore how waves are formed.

How does the Earth's tilt affect the waves of the ocean?

Tilt the bottle onto its side and slightly shift the bottle to simulate the Earth's rotation on its axis. Watch what happens to the waves. This shift of the water is similar to the tidal waves that our oceans experience as the Earth rotates and tilts around the Moon and the Sun, as the gravitational pull moves the waters of the ocean.

What happens when the bottom of the ocean floor shifts? Bang the bottle. Can you see the water fluctuate?

Modifications for Younger Kids

Use the bottle as a vacation reminder. Let younger kids help decide what to put in the bottle. Start with sand and some shells collected at the beach. Add a little silver glitter, but keep it quietly ocean like. It is a sweet thing to keep out to trigger vacation memories.

Modifications for Older Kids

In addition to using glitter and creating an ocean bottle—grab another water bottle and do an experiment, testing the dirt in your backyard. Grab a couple of cups of soil from your backyard. Fill your bottle with the soil, leaving an inch (2.5 cm) or two of space. Fill the bottle with water. Shake. Watch the sediment layers of the different components of your soil form.

> ### TIP
> This is a great time-out activity. Ask your child to sit calmly and watch the waves settle after the bottle has been shaken. Your child can get up once the sand glitter is back on the bottom of the bottle.

Sandbox Volcano

My boys have been obsessed with volcanoes. On family road trips we often drive by an extinct volcano that sits close to the highway. It towers above the otherwise flat land and is the only landmark for miles and miles. Each time we pass it there is a heated discussion about what would happen if it erupted as we passed and suspicion that it really isn't extinct.

This harmless volcano can be made in the kids' sandbox next to toy car highways to experiment with the "what if" of kids' minds. You may not have magma handy, but since you hold the vinegar and baking soda, you determine when the volcano erupts!

Materials

+ Funnel
+ Empty plastic water bottle with a secure top
+ Baking soda
+ Squirt of whipping cream
+ Red food coloring
+ Sandbox (backyard dirt works great, too)
+ Vinegar

Using a funnel, fill the water bottle halfway with baking soda. Then add a little bit of whipping cream. On top of that, add the food coloring.

Put the top on the water bottle. Take the bottle filled with goo out to the sandbox and bury it so just the neck of the bottle is exposed.

Once the volcano has been fully constructed, take the cap off the water bottle and pour in the vinegar.

Watch the lava flow down the mountain and redirect any toy traffic that may be headed for doom.

Modifications for Younger Kids

Adults or older kids can create what is inside the water bottle and younger kids can construct what is outside.

Modifications for Older Kids

The addition of whipping cream makes the eruption less violent and thicker. Older kids can experiment with various degrees of lava thickness for the perfect natural disaster.

> ### TIP
> This could be done in the kitchen sink or bathtub, with a volcano mountain made out of tinfoil.

Snack Map

I was pretty sure someday I would happen across a treasure map. It would be on faded, crinkled parchment with old ink faded due to age. In one corner would be a big X that marked the spot of the treasure I would dig up. Likely, pirates would have abandoned the search, but I am very persistent and would find the chest of gold. It hasn't happened . . . yet.

This activity uses snack time as an excuse to have a fun treasure hunt around the house. It helps kids learn map reading skills and is sure to become a family favorite.

— — — — — — — — — — — — —

Materials

+ Paper—one page per map
+ Sticker dots (optional)
+ Markers
+ Snacks in plastic cups or wrappers to be hidden

Create a basic floor plan sketch of your home, adding in a few details here and there to define the space, such as the stove, fireplace, couch, door and bookshelves.

Use sticker dots to mark where the snacks are located if you want to be able to reuse the map, or mark with an X for onetime use.

Leave the snack map in a place where the kids will find it, then stand back and watch the fun.

Modifications for Younger Kids

Draw a picture of just one room and help them identify the landmarks on the map.

Laminate the map so kids can hide toys for one another and then reuse the map, marking the toy's hidden location.

Modifications for Older Kids

Make the map more complicated or just give them directions based on landmarks, left/right or compass directions.

Bath Sparkling Stones

Kids tend to have a good connection with rocks because they are easy to collect. We took the rock inspiration a bit further and created bathtub "sparkly stones."

The basis of this recipe is Epsom salt, which isn't really a salt. It is a naturally occurring mineral called magnesium sulfate. Not only can it help you get clean, but it also has relaxation properties. This recipe can be modified to customize the scent, which just may encourage longer baths and cleaner results!

— — — — — — — — — — — — —

Materials
(to make about eight sparkling stones)

+ 1 cup (240 g) Epsom salt
+ Food coloring
+ 1 tbsp (14 g) baking soda
+ 1½ tbsp (22 ml) lemon juice (use plain water if you do not want the rocks to fizz)
+ Plastic cups/bowls
+ Essential oils for scent (optional)
+ About 8 small disposable cups
+ Plastic spoon or stirring stick

Mix the Epsom salt, 4 drops of food coloring, baking soda and lemon juice together in an oversize plastic cup or bowl. Add a drop or two of essential oil to create the desired scent.

Repeat for additional colors and scents.

To make salt rocks, press the mixture into the bottom of a disposable cup about 2 inches (5 cm) deep. If you want a variety of colors, layer the colors in a plastic display container using the back of a spoon or a stirring stick to push each layer down. Set aside overnight to dry. Gently press out from the bottom of the cup to retrieve the final bath salt stone. Add the rock to your next bath.

Seal and store next to the tub for decoration or bath use.

Modifications for Younger Kids

Create the recipe, leaving out the essential oils. Also, be sure to watch that your children don't eat the salt—Epsom salt is inedible. You can replace the salt with baking soda alone. The rocks won't be as pretty but will be harmless if ingested.

Modifications for Older Kids

Add another layer of complication to your science experiment. Try to create fizzling stones. It took my elementary-school-age kids a couple of tries, but they had a blast mixing ingredients until they discovered a mixture that fizzled. They doubled the baking soda in the rock (as the chemical base) and added vitamin C powder (for the acid).

And then this is the tricky part . . . you will want to put in just enough liquid to be able to press the minerals together and form a stone, but be careful. If you put in too much, the stone will start fizzing before it is finished. Using very little water, press the ingredients into your mold and let it dry. To activate the "fizz," drop the stone into water. Your sparkly stone will now bubble.

*See photo insert page 25.

Germs, Germs, Germs

While germs may be perceived as bugs, the truth is that we can't see them without a microscope. There are many types of germs, including bacteria, viruses, fungi and protozoa. They are miniature invaders that can be warded off by a serious hand-washing attack!

It can be challenging for kids to get the concept of fully washing their hands when they *look clean*. It is easier to quickly wash by running hands under water with little or no soap.

This activity can tangibly show the importance of hand washing and how germs can be places even when you can't see them.

— — — — — — — — — — — —

Materials

+ Spray bottle
+ 3 slices of bread
+ 3 resealable plastic sandwich bags
+ Marker to label the bags

Lightly spray the three slices of bread with water.

Have an older child or adult wash his/her hands thoroughly and then place one piece of bread into a bag, seal it and label it #1.

For bag #2, let kids handle the bread without washing their hands and then seal it.

With the third piece of bread, let the kids rub it between their hands, along the kitchen counter, and even drop it on the floor. Seal it into the remaining bag and label it #3.

(continued)

Leave the baggies in a dark space for a couple of days.

Make a simple table with predictions from each child as to what each piece of bread will look like in a few days.

In our most recent experiment, bag #1 hadn't changed much. Bag #2 had some interesting white and crusty yellow growth on it. But the one that was the most colorful was the third piece of bread. It had significant growth of some funky green fuzzy stuff.

Modifications for Younger Kids
Use pictures to label the bags and table so they can remember which bag contains the bread that went through each process.

Modifications for Older Kids
Older kids can create a larger experiment by exposing bread slices to specific household surfaces and then charting the results.

TIP
Cover kids' hands with fine glitter and then use a flashlight to watch how it transfers when things are touched. Then have them try to wash the glitter off their hands completely.

Number Detective

Kids love a good mystery. In a book, the clues unravel page by page until the case is solved. In a movie, each scene intertwines information necessary to figure out the solution.

You won't need a magnifying glass or a tweed cap for this mystery, but you will need to raid your recycling bin and get ready for some number fun.

– – – – – – – – – – – –

Materials
+ 10 empty water bottles
+ Paint—a leftover gallon (4-L can) of paint works best
+ Cardboard
+ 10 sharpened pencils
+ 55 marbles

Create a series of ten identical containers out of empty water bottles. Dip each water bottle into old paint and then turn upside down to dry. I used a homemade drying rack made of a piece of folded cardboard punctured by ten sharpened pencils, allowing the bottles to stay secure on the pencil base.

Once dried, distribute the marbles into the ten containers. Put one marble in the first bottle, two marbles in the second bottle, three marbles in the third bottle and so on. Fill all the bottles, ending with the tenth bottle having ten marbles.

You could use any containers you have around the house, or if you don't feel like painting, covering the bottles with construction paper could work well, too.

The object is to let kids put the bottles in order from one marble inside to ten marbles inside by using their detective skills: How heavy is the bottle? How many marbles does it sound as if there are inside when you shake the bottle? How does that compare to the bottle you just evaluated?

Modifications for Younger Kids

Pick out two or three of the bottles that have a wide difference in the number of marbles inside, like one, five and ten.

If they identified the order correctly, then hand them another bottle to see whether they can figure out where it might fit.

Modifications for Older Kids

Remove two of the bottles and mix them up again. Have the player try to guess which numbers were removed.

> ### TIP
> When you are done with your bottles, prop them open and play a game of bowling. Roll a ball at the bottle pins and see how many you can knock down.

Pneumatic Motor

Air is a funny thing. It is everywhere, but we can't really see it. We know it is there when it moves, smells funny or changes temperature.

Air pressure is the push air places on everything. Since air molecules are far apart, they can be compressed to fit into a smaller space. A pneumatic device uses the expansion of the air to work.

This pneumatic motor uses a homemade version of bellows. With a push, it can create a flow of air behind a object. Even though you can't see the air, you will see the results.

Materials

+ 2 kitchen sponges
+ Resealable plastic bag
+ Drinking straw
+ Tape
+ Small light toys (e.g., pom-pom, small ball, toy car, hair bow, etc.)

Place two kitchen sponges, one on top of the other, inside the plastic bag.

Insert a drinking straw between the two sponges so that one end of the straw is inside the bag and the other end is sitting outside the bag.

Seal the bag and then secure it with tape.

Place a pom-pom on a flat surface and place the bag behind it so that the straw is positioned to blow the pom-pom. Press down hard on the sponges and watch the pom-pom roll away!

To get a stronger pump of air, blow into the straw, filling up the bag, and then repeat the process.

Modifications for Younger Kids

Instead of adding sponges and a straw to push items, simplify the experiment. Just fill a resealable plastic bag with air, seal it shut, then "pop" it open by pushing on the top of the bag (or even jumping on it). Your kids will be surprised with a bang! When air pressure changes quickly it creates a bang—much like the thunder in a storm.

Modifications for Older Kids

Have older kids hold the bag at different angles and propel objects of different sizes and weights.

> ### TIP
> Make two of these and play a game of table-top air soccer with makeshift goals at each end of the playing field.

Spiderweb Door

Spiderwebs are fascinating and beautiful. My mom and I used to hunt for the biggest and most complicated spiderwebs. The best time to find them is early in the morning while the dew is still fresh, making the webs glisten in the light.

This spiderweb-inspired activity is perfect for a rainy day stuck indoors. Getting kids active in limited space is one of the challenges of parenthood. Time to spin our own web!

Negotiating passage through the spiderweb will stress kids' balance and challenge their kinesthetic awareness. Repeated practice will help them become more coordinated and improve proprioception (a sense of where your body is in space/relation to itself).

- - - - - - - - - - - - - - - -

Materials

+ Painters' tape
+ Ball of yarn
+ Balloon or lightweight ball

Tape the yarn to a doorway in varying intervals to make a "web." You can experiment with which shapes and angles work best for the space and participants.

Kids can take turns climbing through the web. A balloon or light ball to toss back and forth will get kids problem solving in a coordinated effort.

Modifications for Younger Kids

Create a floor option for movement through the web for younger participants. It can still appear small and difficult, but taking out the necessity to move over an obstacle will make it easier.

Modifications for Older Kids

Have them try to get through the web without the yarn falling down. If that is not enough of a challenge, have them attempt to get through without even touching the yarn. They can work on setting up a new web with a completely different experience.

> ### TIP
> Want to re-create a spiderweb that mimics the silk's stickiness? Substitute tape for the yarn in this activity. It can be used for climbing or for catching thrown paper-wad "bugs."

Tin Can Birdhouse and Feeder

Grandmother was a bird-watcher and would take her binoculars everywhere we walked. It was rare that she came across a bird that she didn't recognize and had to look up in her giant bird book.

This craft transforms a coffee can into a birdhouse and feeder. Situate this outside a window to bring bird life closer and observe the fun.

- - - - - - - - - - - - - - - -

Materials
(to make one bird feeder)

+ Can opener
+ Large coffee can with a lid
+ Heavy-duty tape
+ Thick cardboard
+ Scissors
+ Birdseed
+ Hole punch
+ Pencil
+ Bits of yarn (optional)
+ Screw
+ Rope

Use a can opener to cut half of the bottom of the can. Have an adult carefully fold the half of the bottom in, forming a crescent. Be careful; the edges are sharp. Cover any remaining edges with heavy tape. Cut a circle from the cardboard to fit into the center of the can. Use tape to secure the circle in the can. That circle becomes a divider for the two rooms in the can. On the side with the half-circle, fill the bottom with birdseed.

Cut a circle opening in the lid of the coffee can. With a hole punch, make a hole below the large circle. Stuff a pencil into that hole. Secure the lid to the can with heavy-duty tape. The pencil is the perch. You can fill the house section with some bits of yarn to make it appealing for nest building.

We collected twigs from around our yard, which were secured to the sides with a glue gun.

Screw a hole in the side of the can and use yarn to hang it. Try to hang the can away from tree limbs and the house to help maintain it as a bird vs. squirrel house.

Modifications for Younger Kids
Younger kids can decorate the can lid for a special bird "front door."

Modifications for Older Kids
Older kids can design birdhouse/feeder decor. The decoration options are limitless and could coordinate with whatever they dream up.

Musical Science Pool

While banging merrily away, and without realizing it, your children are learning about sound waves and how beats "feel" in addition to the sound they hear. They are exploring the different reactions that applied force cause on the pan.

The vibrations created through banging can be manipulated with various water levels, resulting in a different pitch. This activity may sound like complete chaos, but a kiddie pool is the perfect laboratory for discovery!

Materials
+ Kiddie pool or shallow area of a larger pool
+ A collection of metal pots and pans
+ Metal spoons
+ Tin cans in a variety of sizes and shapes (with any sharp edges filed down)

Situate the kids in the water where they can be seated comfortably.

Turn a pot upside down just above water level. Bang on the pot with a spoon while you lower it into the water. Notice that the pitch of the drum changes as the water level rises in the pot.

Explore the strength of water's surface tension. As you fill a pot, turn it upside down in the pool (trying to keep the water inside), and pull the pot up. If you are careful, you can see the water lift as you pull the pot up.

You can also fill the cans with water. Tap the sides of the cans. Explore the sounds coming from the cans. How does the sound change as you pour more water into the can?

Put a small water puddle on the top of a pot or can. Bang the sides gently. What happens to the water on the top? Can you see the sound waves in the water puddle?

Modifications for Younger Kids
After making noise with the pots and pans, your child will probably enjoy simply pouring the water from container to container. This makes a good bath activity as long as the noise/mess isn't going to be an issue!

Modifications for Older Kids
Use various levels of water in a collection of cups to create a scale. Try to play a tune.

(twelve)

SCIENCE GAMES

Young children are natural-born scientists. They observe and discover new things each day as they explore their surrounding environment. Making time for these moments is one of the best gifts you can give a child. Encourage them to share their observations and ask questions often about their discoveries. Science is all around us, from the insects in our backyard, plants in a garden, cooking in the kitchen, moon in the sky and even water play in the bathtub.

We can set up moments for observation by creating environments that foster opportunities for science. Provide science tools for discovery, like a magnifying glass, magnets and measuring cups, to help children learn to explore and test their science theories. A nature tray can be a fun place to start, with items you collect while taking a walk.

Here are a few games to play with your child to help them discover that science is all around them and to help build a solid foundation of science knowledge. The games are created to reinforce science standards that children are expected to learn as they enter school.

Magnetic Construction Site

Focus Skill: identifying that magnets can attract

Create a moving construction site by placing select objects into this manipulative game. Players learn items can be magnetic and nonmagnetic as they discover the various selected items on the construction site. A basic skill of a scientist is how to classify and sort items.

- - - - - - - - - - - - - - -

Materials

+ Sand
+ Large plastic bin
+ Several magnetic items (bolts, nuts, metal containers, magnets, etc.)
+ Several nonmagnetic items (plastic figurines, Legos, coins, etc.)
+ Paper
+ Marker
+ Large magnet
+ Pretend construction vehicles

Directions to Make

Pour the sand into the large plastic bin for the base where objects will be hiding. Place magnetic and nonmagnetic objects on the dirt (sand), hiding some within the sand if you like.

With the paper, create a game board with the words "magnetic" and "not magnetic" on it to sort items onto.

Directions to Play

Players take turns using the large magnet and construction vehicles to search for magnetic items.

As players remove items from the sand they will place them on the game board under the proper section of magnetic or not magnetic.

Continue to play until all of the items are classified.

Game Variations

Race the clock to find all of the magnetic items at the construction site.

Dig for letters on the construction site and put them in alphabetical order.

Dig for words on the construction site and sort into word families with like endings.

Saftey Tip

Discuss safety rules about magnets with your child first. Store magnets out of reach. Monitor use at all times.

*See photo insert page 26.

Senses Scavenger Hunt

Focus Skill: identifying and using the five senses •
Great For: moving while you learn

The rocks in the playground are bumpy. The leaves crinkle in the wind. Snacks of oranges smell sweet. In this science game, children use their keen observation skills to take note of the objects that demonstrate characteristics that can be noticed using the five senses.

- - - - - - - - - - - - - - -

Materials

+ Paper
+ Pencil
+ Clipboard
+ Copier

Directions to Make

Write a list of object characteristics based on the five senses—touch, taste, smell, see and hear: bumpy, smooth, sweet, sour, red, green, purple, crinkles, dings.

(continued)

Next to each characteristic, draw a small box.

Make a copy of this list for each player or small group of players.

Directions to Play

Walk around searching for items to match each characteristic.

When an item matching the description is found, check the box near the characteristic.

Continue playing the game until an object for each listed item has been found.

Game Variations

Gather the items ahead of time and place them in a basket.

Have children write the object next to the describing word.

Focus on just one sense and the vocabulary words to describe those items.

Growing a Vegetable Garden

Focus Skill: identifying major parts of plants (e.g., roots, stem, leaf, flower)

Use colorful playdough to grow vegetables in your own pretend garden. Do you know where to find the vegetables that are ready to be picked? Players create vegetables and the plants they come from on the mat to re-create where and how they grow. This game helps a child learn to discover that vegetables are not from a store but from the earth, grown in a particular way.

Materials

+ Marker
+ 1 large piece of paper
+ Plastic cover sheet or laminate paper
+ 12 squares of paper, 1.5 x 1.5 inch (4 x 4 cm)
+ Playdough in vegetable colors

Directions to Make

Discuss the parts of a plant and how they grow with your child.

Draw a line on the paper to indicate the ground for the playdough garden to grow. Place paper inside of cover sheet.

Write the numbers 0 to 11 on the square cards.

Directions to Play

Say a type of vegetable out loud. Pick a number card.

Make that many vegetables of that kind in your garden. Be sure to include the roots, stem, leaf and flower, if applicable.

Repeat until you have a vegetable garden filled with playdough vegetables.

Game Variations

Create the vegetables in numerical order.

Make groups of different vegetables. Compare using "like" or "as."

Change the theme to fruit and create number trees.

Rocket Ship Adventure

Focus Skill: identifying elements of night, day and space • Great For: moving while you learn

Launch your rocket ship into space to discover the Sun, Moon, stars and even the planets as you race to make it back to Earth in time. Players learn to identify and recognize items that are found in space.

- - - - - - - - - - - - -

Materials

+ Recycled cardboard box and recycled items
+ Markers
+ Paper
+ Scissors
+ 3 x 5-inch (7.5 x 13-cm) index cards
+ Tape
+ Sand timer

Directions to Make

Players build and decorate a rocket ship out of a recycled cardboard box.

Create or print images of elements in space including the Sun, stars, planets and phases of the Moon. Feel free to add a few images of rockets, astronauts, comets, etc., to add more space fun.

Create smaller images and write the words to make game cards on the index cards and place into a pile.

Arrange or hang up the images from space around the room with tape.

Directions to Play

Player selects an index card from the pile and tells the other player to race the rocket to collect that space element and bring it back to mission control on Earth. Set the timer for each time the player leaves Earth.

Each player continues to take turns selecting objects from space from the cards and racing to bring them back to Earth.

The game continues until all the elements of space have been selected and returned to Earth.

Game Variations

Using many players, have two rockets that race to each space element by having one player sit inside the rocket and the other player push it.

From your rocket, collect images of the Moon phases in order.

From your rocket, collect images of the planets in order from the Sun.

Animal Sounds Bowling

Focus Skill: classifying and identifying animals and their young • Great For: moving while you learn

Each animal has a unique name for children to discover and learn about. Use baby animal names and sounds to identify the grown-up animal in a unique twist on the game of bowling. Moo and meow along as you explore the science of animals.

- - - - - - - - - - - - -

Materials

+ Paper
+ Markers
+ 10 recycled plastic water bottles
+ Tape
+ Ball

(continued)

Directions to Make

Draw or print out images of baby animals and adult animals (cow, calf, pig, piglet, duck, duckling, etc.).

Write the name of the animal under each picture.

Attach adult animal images onto the front of the bottles with tape.

Place the baby animals in a pile to draw from.

Directions to Play

Players set up the adult animal bottles at the end of the area.

One player draws a baby animal image and calls out the animal sound.

The other player uses the ball to try to knock down the bottle with the adult animal on it.

Players take turns trying to knock down the animals based on animal sounds.

Game Variations

Write the word on the card to select and then attach the image onto the bottles.

Attach animal pictures onto balls and as a player picks up the ball have them find the matching bottle to try to knock down.

Players select card from animal images and then they try to find the word written with chalk on the sidewalk.

Make It Sink

Focus Skill: identifying objects that sink or float

Children are intrigued by water and how items interact with it. Encourage science exploration by seeing who can make their container sink the fastest. A skill we ask young scientists to focus on is to compare and contrast their observations, and water creates the perfect environment to do that.

Materials

+ Large plastic container
+ Water
+ Large tray
+ Bolts
+ Nuts
+ Coins
+ Plastic beads
+ Pom-poms
+ Sand
+ Rocks
+ Any other small objects that can get wet
+ Small plastic containers with lids or plastic eggs

Directions to Make

Fill the large container with water.

Set objects on the large tray for players to select from.

Directions to Play

Players take turns using the items from the tray to fill their small plastic container.

Players attach the lids and place into the water. Each player tries to see how quickly they can get their container to sink.

Game Variations

Players select a specific number of items to fill their container with to see who can make it sink first.

Players select the most amount of items to make their container float.

Players select the least amount of items to make their container sink.

Fizzing Fact Families

Focus Skill: observing the changes in the properties of matter

Add a little fizz to numbers to play this learning game focused on creating fact families with your child. Bonus is for players to discover that properties can change when you mix two ingredients.

- - - - - - - - - - - - - - -

Materials

+ 3 x 5-inch (7.5 x 13-cm) index cards
+ Black marker
+ 2 small squirt bottles
+ Baking soda
+ Kool-Aid packet
+ Water
+ Large rectangular container

Directions to Make

Write math facts on the index cards, leaving the answer off. For example, write 1 + 1 = __.

Fill one squirt bottle with baking soda and the other with Kool-Aid powder and water. Set up a large container to squirt contents into.

Directions to Play

The player selects a math fact card from the pile. To solve the equation the player writes the answer with the squirt bottle filled with baking soda into the large container.

If the answer is correct the player uses the liquid squirt bottle filled with Kool-Aid to make a special scientific reaction. The reaction of the two ingredients combined produces a gas called carbon dioxide (CO_2), which creates bubbles. This process is called carbonation.

Players continue to solve math equations and form fizzing number solutions until all of the cards have been solved.

Game Variations

Younger players can find number matches and then create a fizzing number.

Players can find number matches and then make number dots to match the number for counting.

Advanced players can create multiplication number sentences and create a number fizz with the answer.

*See photo insert page 26.

> ### NOTE
> Consider playing this bubbling science game in an area that's safe for potential colorful spills.

Ice Castle Challenge

Focus Skill: understanding that properties change with heat

Who can create the tallest ice castle? Using strategic thinking, players can create their own ice structure that will last the test of gravity and heat.

- - - - - - - - - - - - - - -

Materials

+ Water
+ 2 to 4 ice trays
+ Various small-size containers
+ Food coloring (optional)
+ 2 large trays or cookie sheets
+ Timer
+ Paper
+ Pencil

(continued)

Directions to Make

Pour water into ice cube trays and various shaped containers (food coloring optional).

Place in freezer overnight.

Directions to Play

Challenge players to build the tallest ice castle onto large trays or cookie sheets with the provided ice blocks.

Encourage players to design structures that will withstand the challenge of heat in a sunny location.

Create the castles, set a timer and observe the changes that occur over time.

Keep a record of how long each ice castle stands to determine the winner.

Game Variations

Create a castle as a group building together.

Create an ice castle with additional materials such as bricks, gems, counters, etc.

Drip warm water on top to challenge the design and see how long it can stand.

*See photo insert page 26.

NOTE
Food coloring may stain.

Life Cycle Blocks

*Focus Skill: identifying patterns in life cycles •
Great For: moving while you learn*

Children are fascinated by nature's life cycles. Race the clock to see who is the fastest at creating a life cycle tower. The game helps a child learn to recognize and verbalize the patterns all around us in nature.

Materials

+ 5 to 10 sheets of white paper
+ Crayons or markers
+ Scissors
+ 4 recycled square tissue boxes or recycled cardboard to make boxes
+ Tape
+ Sand timer

Directions to Make

Draw images or print from a computer the life cycles of frogs, butterflies, chickens, flowers, people or apple trees onto paper the size of your box.

Cut the life cycle stages apart. Gather the tissue boxes.

Attach each image onto the sides of the boxes with tape so that both boxes match. Each box only gets one portion of the life cycle.

Directions to Play

Each player takes turns racing the sand timer to stack up the selected life cycle in order. For example, a completed life cycle for the butterfly would have an egg, caterpillar, chrysalis and butterfly with all four boxes stacked on top of each other in order.

Encourage players to name the stages of their chosen life cycle once their stack is complete.

Knock over and repeat.

Game Variations

Use varied-size boxes to match sizes during life cycles to create a tiered tower.

Stack up similar stages in the life cycles.

Sort images on the rug and place in chronological order.

Monster Food Groups

Focus Skill: learning to identify food groups

Use grocery store flyers and magazines to help your child learn about food groups with these adorable food group monsters. Players quickly learn which food groups fuel their body with energy and help them grow.

— — — — — — — — — — —

Materials

+ Construction paper
+ Paper bags
+ Glue
+ Googly eyes
+ Scissors
+ Grocery flyers or magazines

Directions to Make

Use construction paper to create five monsters on paper bags. Attach paper with glue.

Add googly eyes to increase the monster effect.

Cut out an opening in the bag for a mouth to feed.

Label each bag with a food group: fruits, vegetables, dairy, grains and proteins.

Encourage players to cut out pictures of food groups from the flyers.

Directions to Play

During each player's turn they select a food item and feed the correct food group monster.

Players continue until all the food has been fed to the food group monsters.

Game Variations

Create a book about what your monster can eat featuring healthy options from the monster food groups.

For advanced players, add a point value to food groups to help build a foundation in nutrition.

Sort images of foods by feeding number monsters.

Water Bead Race

Focus Skill: understanding that the movement of objects requires force

Race your water beads to see which surface is the fastest using ramps and force to challenge your competitor. Begin to explore basic science concepts by using forces and inclined planes as a type of simple machine.

— — — — — — — — — — —

Materials

+ Water beads
+ Water
+ Plastic container
+ Pool noodles or variety of flat materials for ramps
+ ADULTS ONLY: knife

Directions to Make

Soak water beads in water in a container to expand.

Have an adult cut pool noodles in half in various sizes.

Directions to Play

Players close their eyes to select materials to create a water bead ramp.

Using the selected item, each player designs their own ramp.

Players race each round to see whose design has the fastest incline by placing their water bead onto the design ramp.

Provide additional challenge rounds by removing ramps and using air as the force.

(continued)

Game Variations

Challenge players to see who can make their water bead travel the farthest.

Challenge players to have their water bead stop on a chosen target.

Add additional difficulty by increasing the number of ramps required to build for a race.

Superhero Water

Focus Skill: identifying and using standard units of measurement

Can you measure superpowers? In this activity, kids create their own superheroes by carefully measuring water into their superhero cups. They practice using standard measurement units as they build a superhero from the bottom up, adding a new feature at every ¼-cup (60-ml) mark. See how fast you can build your superhero!

Materials

+ Foam
+ Scissors
+ 2 clear cups for each player
+ Black permanent marker
+ Bucket
+ Water

Directions to Make

Prepare a water-friendly area for the game.

Using the foam, cut out a set of superhero capes, masks, belts and belt buckles for each player. Vary the superhero designs if desired.

For each player, take one clear cup and use the black permanent marker to make small lines indicating ¼ cup (60 ml), ½ cup (120 ml), ¾ cup (180 ml) and 1 cup (240 ml). This will be the player's superhero cup.

Set another clear cup next to the superhero cup for each player. This cup will be used to pour the water.

Fill the bucket with water and place it where all the kids can access it easily.

Directions to Play

Players will dip their clear cup into the bucket of water then carefully pour "superpower water" into their superhero cup. When they reach a specific marking, they have to stop and add a superhero accessory. ¼ cup (60 ml) = belt, ½ cup (120 ml) = buckle, ¾ cup (180 ml) = cape, 1 cup (240 ml) = mask. The foam will stick to the measuring cup when you add water to the surface.

Players continue to pour the superpower water and build their superheroes. Race to see who is the fastest to make a complete superhero!

Game Variations

Create nonstandard units of measurement by using water bottles instead and pour to specific lined levels to create a superhero.

See which superhero bottle can fly the farthest when filled up with various levels of water.

Add different colors to the water to mix and create colorful superheroes.

*See photo insert page 26.

(thirteen)

ROCKET SCIENCE

Have you ever wondered why you don't shoot off into space when you jump; how a rocket gets off the ground; or why a toy car rolling down a ramp moves faster than on flat surface? It takes a massive amount of power to launch a spacecraft into space. It has to overcome gravity, cope with the many hazards of space and then survive a bumpy return back through the Earth's atmosphere without falling apart from the huge amount of heat and friction generated.

From a Rocket Blaster (page 242) to a Mobile Launch Pad (page 257), you'll experience all of the fun of space camp in your own backyard!

Gravity Splat

Scientific Concept—Gravity

Have you ever wondered why things fall to the ground when you drop them; why we don't all float around above the ground; or why astronauts can jump much higher on the Moon than on Earth? It's all because of a pulling force called gravity.

Bigger objects have a greater gravitational force. The Moon is much smaller than the Earth and so has much weaker gravity. The Moon's gravity is about one-sixth of that on Earth, which is why you can jump higher there.

▬ ▬ ▬ ▬ ▬ ▬ ▬ ▬ ▬ ▬ ▬

Materials

+ Large piece of white paper/white sheet/ cardboard
+ Small water balloons
+ Funnel
+ Water-based, non-toxic paint
+ Water

Pick an area outside that can be paint splattered (ask an adult first!), and lay down the paper or sheet.

To make the paint balloons, blow up the balloon, let the air out and then place a small funnel into the top of the balloon. Pour in a good amount of paint before filling with water from the tap and tying the balloon end securely. Give your balloon a good shake to mix the water and paint. The water helps stretch the balloon so it will break more easily.

Once you've made a few balloons, think about how to test them. What do you think will happen when you drop the balloons? You know they will drop to the ground (remember this is because of the pulling force of gravity), but what else might happen?

Hold a balloon as high up as you can and drop it onto the paper—does it break? If not, what do you think you could do to make it splat and why?

Try dropping paint-filled balloons from different heights and observe how the splatter pattern changes. What do you think might be different about a splat from a low height and one from higher up? Why do you think this is?

Don't forget to clear up the balloon pieces afterward as these can be harmful to animals.

More Fun

Try dropping an air-filled balloon and a paint/ water-filled balloon at the same time. Do you think they will hit the ground simultaneously or at different times? Why do you think this is?

Learning Points

This activity uses paint-filled water balloons to demonstrate the force of gravity pulling an object down to Earth. The paint gives a great visual of the impact of the balloon hitting the ground, allowing you to compare how the speed of the balloon at impact changes the size of the paint splat. Remember, the greater the height an object falls from, the more speed it has when it hits the ground.

*See photo insert page 27.

Rocket Blaster

Scientific Concepts—Trajectory, gravity

This Rocket Blaster is a great fun way to learn about gravity and trajectory. When you pull back and release the mechanism, you should notice that the pom-poms inside don't fall straight to the ground. This is because there are two forces acting on them. Gravity tries to pull the pom-poms down while the forward force from the inner tube propels them forward. These two forces create a curved path to the ground.

▬ ▬ ▬ ▬ ▬ ▬ ▬ ▬ ▬ ▬ ▬

Materials

+ Rubber band
+ Scisssors
+ 2 cardboard tubes about 12 inches (30 cm) long (one should fit inside the other)
+ Screwdriver, or something else to make a hole with
+ Cardstock or plastic lid, for the inner cardboard tube
+ Tape
+ Paper, for decoration
+ Paint, for decoration
+ Small round pom-poms

Cut the rubber band so that it forms a single length, then take the wider tube and make a hole using a screwdriver through both sides about 1 inch (2.5 cm) from one end.

For the smaller tube, make two more holes close to the middle, making sure there is enough of the narrower tube sticking out of the bottom of the larger tube when you put them inside each other for you to hold.

Seal one end of the narrow tube with a piece of cardstock and tape. You can decorate the outside with paper or paint, if desired.

Align the holes by placing the smaller tube inside the larger one (the sealed end of the narrow tube should be inside the wider tube) and thread the rubber band through all the holes. Attach each end of the rubber band to the outside of the wider tube with tape. To test if the mechanism works, pull the inner tube down and let go.

Drop some pom-poms inside the mechanism, pull back the inner tube and let go. The pom-poms should fly through the air.

More Fun

What happens if you use bigger pom-poms? Do they fly as far?

Can you measure how far different-sized pom-poms travel?

Learning Points

A real rocket needs to overcome the force of gravity pulling it downward, which it does by creating an upward thrust force from its engines. The thrust force upward must be greater than the downward gravitational force for a rocket to lift off.

*See photo insert page 27.

Space Marble Run

Scientific Concepts—Friction, gravity

A great marble run is constructed so the marbles keep rolling all the way to the end, which might be more difficult that it sounds. To keep your marble rolling, you need to understand the forces acting on it.

Gravity pulls down on the marble forcing it to roll down any slopes on the track. While gravity is forcing a marble down a track, frictional forces are slowing the marble down as the marble and marble run rub against each other. The marble will stop if the force of friction is greater than the force of gravity.

- - - - - - - - -

Materials

+ Long cardboard tubes, cut in half
+ Large sheet of thick cardboard
+ Tape or glue
+ Marbles
+ Aluminum foil, colored cardstock and paint to decorate
+ Bubble wrap, optional
+ Paper towels or kitchen roll, optional

(continued)

Cut the cardboard tubes into different lengths. These should all be shorter than the width of the large sheet of cardboard. Try placing them down on the large cardboard sheet and start to plan the marble run. Would you like a long, slow marble run, or a quick, fast run? Think about how to position the tubes to make the marble run fast and how you would change them to make it slower. Attach the tubes using tape or glue.

Think about how the marble will roll. It will roll downward because of gravity and slow down because of friction, but how could you get the marble to roll upward? You'll need it to be traveling fast enough to overcome gravity. Try a tube with a steep drop followed by a smaller slope upwards. You might have to experiment with different slopes to allow the marble to reach the top of the upward slope.

Use aluminum foil, colored cardstock and paint to decorate your marble run.

Test your marble run using a marble. Does it work as you expected?

More Fun

Split into two teams with a group of friends and see who can make the best track to keep a marble rolling for the longest amount of time. Each team should start with the same length of tubing.

Can you change the surface of your tubes so the marble moves more slowly? Try bubble wrap or paper towels on the inside. These surfaces are rougher than the inside of a cardboard tube so the frictional force will be greater, meaning the marble moves more slowly.

Learning Points

How do you think you could make a very long marble run?

Hint—you'll need to create a very slightly sloping track which is just steep enough to overcome friction and keep the marble rolling.

Gravity Pinball Machine

Scientific Concept—Gravity

If you tried the Space Marble Run (page 243), you'll know that two of the forces acting on a moving object are gravity and friction. A pinball machine is a bit different, as it needs to overcome gravity to shoot a marble or small ball uphill, which can then make its own way down due to gravity.

There are lots of things to think about when making a pinball machine. You need a mechanism to shoot the ball upwards so it falls down quickly; objects down the center to slow the fall of the marble; and if you're feeling very adventurous, you could even make a flipper to flip the marble upwards again.

■ ■ ■ ■ ■ ■ ■ ■ ■ ■ ■ ■ ■

Materials

+ Cardboard box
+ Small cardboard tubes
+ Straws
+ Tape
+ Craft knife
+ Strips of cardboard
+ Marble or small ball

You'll need a shallow box to make a good pinball machine. Make sure you've removed the top so you have a base with four edges before starting.

You'll need a mechanism to shoot the marble up the ramp. Either use two cardboard tubes, one of which fits inside the other, or a bundle of straws taped together to make the inner tube. You can also make this in a similar way to the Rocket Blaster on page 242.

Once you've made the mechanism and attached it to one side of the pinball machine box, you'll need to make a hole in the box using a craft knife where you want the mechanism to sit. Add a strip of cardboard to the corner of the box above the launch mechanism so the marble curves around the top of the box rather than dropping straight back down.

Think about how to set up obstacles on the inside. If you want the marble to drop down the pinball machine quickly, make the ramps steep. If you want the marble to roll more slowly, make the ramps more gradual.

More Fun

Try adding some holes that the marble will drop through if it rolls over them. What else could you add to the pinball machine to slow the descent of the marble or speed it up?

Change the incline of your pinball machine by leaning it on a stack of books. You should find the marble drops down the pinball machine faster with a steeper slope.

Learning Points

Several factors will affect how fast your marble drops. First is the slope of the pinball machine. A steep slope will mean the ball falls faster. You can slow the fall by adding ramps on the inside. A long gradual ramp will reduce the speed the ball is traveling at more than a short steep ramp, so think about how you'd like the marble to travel before making your plan.

*See photo insert page 27.

Drop the Astronaut

Scientific Concept—Gravity

Have you ever accidentally dropped an egg on the floor and watched it smash? When you drop an object, it is pulled to the ground by gravity, picking up speed as it falls. Remember gravity is a force that pulls an object to the ground.

One way to stop an egg from smashing when it hits the floor is to create an outer casing that reduces the impact of the hard landing on the egg. If you want to make this activity a little less messy, you could boil your astronaut eggs!

Materials

+ Cardboard tubes
+ Colored cardstock for decoration
+ Eggs (boiled for less mess)
+ Cotton wool, bubble wrap, paper towels, pasta
+ Tape
+ Tape measure or ruler

Your challenge is to create a safe rocket to allow your eggy astronaut to reach the ground without a single crack.

First, decorate the cardboard tubes so they look like rockets. Think about how you can protect the eggs so they don't break when they hit the ground.

Wrap an egg in cotton wool inside a tube. Remember to make sure there's enough cotton wool to stop the egg from moving. You could also try bubble wrap, paper towels, pasta or anything else you think might protect the egg. When you're ready, seal the bottom with tape.

Once the rockets are prepared, think about the type of surface you want to drop them on. You want a hard surface to really put your protection methods to the test. When you're ready, drop the protected astronaut from as far up as you can reach.

When experimenting, it's important to make the tests fair, so use a ruler or tape measure to make sure you drop each egg rocket from the same height. Or, you could ask the same person to drop them from as far up as they can reach.

More Fun

Blow the contents out of an egg so you have just the shell. Draw on the shell so it looks like an astronaut and package it up to send to a friend. Can you package it so well that the eggshell arrives at its destination completely intact?

*See photo insert page 27.

Fly with Magnets

Scientific Concepts—Magnetism, gravity

Rockets overcome the force of gravity trying to pull them back down to Earth by generating a massive amount of thrust, which pushes the rocket upwards.

This simple trick shows how to overcome gravity not by generating thrust, but by using a little magnet trickery.

Magnets have two poles: a north pole and south pole. If you place two magnets together end to end, opposite poles will attract and be drawn to each other, while like poles repel each other.

Magnets also attract some metals (like iron and steel), a feature which this activity takes advantage of.

- - - - - - - - - - - - -

Materials

+ Scissors
+ Black and white cardstock
+ Cardboard box
+ Chalk
+ Double-sided tape
+ Thin thread
+ Steel paper clip
+ Magnet

Magnets should always be used with adult supervision to avoid swallowing.

Think about the space scene you'd like to create. Would you like the astronaut to be on the Moon, or floating in space? Will they be exploring Mars or traveling farther afield?

Cut out a piece of the black cardstock to fit tightly inside the box and draw a space-themed scene on the cardstock using chalk. This will form the background for the magnetic box. Attach the card to the back of the cardboard box using the double-sided tape.

Tie the thin thread to the paper clip and place the magnet on top of the box. Check that the paper clip is attracted to the magnet through the box. If it's not, you'll need a stronger magnet.

Attach the non-paper clip end of the thread to the bottom of the box using tape, remembering to leave just enough length so the paper clip seems to float in the air. Once you've mastered suspending the paper clip, draw a small astronaut or rocket on white card or paper and attach it to the paper clip. You should now have a rocket or astronaut flying in space!

More Fun

Try moving the magnet around. Can you make your astronaut or rocket spin or fly around?

What's the biggest gap between the box lid and paper clip you can create without the paper clip falling down?

Learning Points

The magnetic force between the paper clip and magnet on the top of the box is stronger than gravity's pull. This means the paper clip remains suspended in the air rather than falling to the ground. If you move the paper clip farther from the magnet, the pull of the magnet becomes less. This makes gravity the stronger force acting on the paper clip, which drops to the ground.

*See photo insert page 28.

Lift It!

Scientific Concept—Friction

This activity is a great demonstration of friction and a fun trick to show your friends, too! Tell them you can lift a bottle with a pencil without the pencil touching the sides and see if they think you can do it. Remember friction is one of the forces acting on a rocket as it flies through the air.

- - - - - - - - - - - - -

Materials

+ Funnel
+ Small plastic water bottle
+ Rice, uncooked
+ Pencil

Use the funnel to fill the bottle up with rice, leaving just a bit of space at the top. Tap the bottle's base on a flat surface to let the rice settle.

Carefully push a pencil into the bottle of rice and then pull up again gently. Repeat this motion until the pencil becomes harder and harder to pull out of the bottle as the amount of friction between the pencil and rice increases.

Once the pencil is stuck, try to lift up the bottle of rice with the pencil.

More Fun
What happens if you use less rice?

Learning Points
As you push the pencil into the bottle the grains of rice are being pushed together, rubbing up against each other, creating friction. Eventually the rice grains push against the pencil with enough friction to keep the pencil stuck in place.

*See photo insert page 28.

Friction Ramp

Scientific Concept—Friction

Have you ever tried sliding on a wooden floor? It's much easier to slide when you wear socks because there is less friction between the smooth surface of the socks and the floor than your feet and the floor. A rocket trying to reach space must overcome the slowing effect of friction.

This Friction Ramp is a great way to demonstrate how the amount of friction changes depending on the material used.

You should find the cars move more slowly down the rougher materials, as there is more friction between them.

- - - - - - - - - - - - -

Materials

+ Large cardboard sheet
+ Scissors
+ Bubble wrap
+ Corrugated paper
+ Carpet
+ Cellophane or plastic wrap
+ Double-sided tape
+ Building blocks or books
+ Toy cars
+ Timer

Your friction ramp can have as many lanes with as many different surfaces as you want. The only limit is the amount of space you have.

Divide the cardboard sheet into lanes of the same size and then cut the materials you want to test to the correct size so they cover each of the lanes completely. Try bubble wrap, corrugated paper, carpet or cellophane. Once you're happy with the layout, use double-sided tape to attach each material to the ramp.

You'll need the ramp to slope downwards, so lean it up against a tower of blocks or books. Using the cars and the timer, record how long it takes for the same car to travel down each lane of the ramp. You'll need to hold the car at the top of the ramp and let it go without pushing it, or the force you push the car with will impact how long it takes to roll down the ramp.

More Fun
Can you add a ramp going upwards to the bottom of your friction ramp and record how far each car travels up the second ramp?

(continued)

Learning Points

Remember friction is the resistance of motion when one object rubs against another. The rougher the surface, the more friction is created. Have you ever hurt your knee when sliding on carpet? This is because lots of friction is created between your skin and the carpet.

Friction between tires and the road stop cars from skidding. When the road surface is icy, there is less friction, which makes it more likely cars will skid. In wintery conditions, sand is added to roads to make the road surface rougher, increasing friction and reducing the risk of cars sliding around.

Rocket Zip Line

Scientific Concept—Friction

Friction can be used to slow an object down or speed it up. If we increase the frictional force, the object will move more slowly, and if we reduce friction, it will move faster and more easily.

This activity uses a rocket made from a plastic bottle attached to a zip wire. You can make your rocket move quickly down the zip wire by using a smooth string where there will not be much friction between the straw of the rocket and the string. Or, you can use a rough string where increased frictional forces will slow the descent of your rocket.

– – – – – – – – – – – – – – –

Materials

+ Straws
+ Small plastic bottle
+ Glue
+ Rough and smooth string
+ Timer
+ Pipe cleaners

Attach a straw to the side of a plastic bottle with glue. When this is dry, thread the string through the straw before setting up your zip line wire.

Find a suitable area to set up the zip line wire. You'll need to attach the string to the ground and something higher up so you have a slope. A tree works well if you're outside.

If you want to decorate your plastic bottle, you can, but this isn't necessary. Hold the bottle at the top of the zip wire and release at the same time as starting the timer. Stop the timer when the bottle reaches the bottom.

You can increase the frictional force further by placing a pipe cleaner inside the straw stuck to the bottle. This should make the bottle slide down the zip wire more slowly.

More Fun

Try this activity using different types of string to see if increasing friction slows the descent of the bottle. You could set up several zip wires at once and race the bottles with friends, but remember to keep the length and slope of the zip wire the same to make it a fair comparison.

*See photo insert page 28.

Milk Jug Rocket Cone

Scientific Concept—Newton's First Law

A rocket cone is another simple demonstration of Newton's laws. The rocket cone is at rest on top of the milk jug, but as soon as a force is applied, which in this case is air being forced out of the jug as you squeeze it, the force of the air against the cone sends it shooting upwards.

– – – – – – – – – – – – – – –

Materials

+ Paper
+ Tape
+ Felt tip pens, optional
+ Empty plastic milk container

Create a cone shape using the paper. This should have a diameter of about 6 inches (15 cm), but can be slightly bigger or smaller. Use the tape to hold the cone in place. If you want to decorate the cone with the felt tip pens so it looks more like a rocket, go ahead, but you don't have to.

Next, examine the empty milk container. Try squeezing it gently and then much harder: You should be able to feel the air leaving the bottle with more force when you squeeze hard than when you squeeze gently. It's the air leaving the bottle that is going to propel the cone rocket up into the air.

When you're ready to launch the rocket, place the cone on top of the milk container and squeeze hard. The paper cone should shoot up into the air! Can you measure how high it flies?

More Fun

Try adding fins to your rocket. Does it fly as high? By adding fins, you've increased the mass of the rocket. According to Newton's Second Law (page 252), the acceleration of an object is affected by the mass, so you should find a rocket cone with more mass doesn't accelerate upwards as fast.

What happens if you make the cone bigger?

Learning Point

You should find that the harder you push the sides of the bottle together the greater the force of the air leaving the bottle and the higher the rocket cone will go.

Save the Rocket

Scientific Concepts—Newton's First Law, friction, inertia

This simple trick demonstrates Newton's First Law. Your rocket blocks will remain still until another force acts on them. The idea is to remove the cloth under the blocks so quickly and smoothly that no force acts on them and they stay in place.

-- -- -- -- -- -- -- -- --

Materials

+ Small piece of smooth cloth
+ Wooden blocks

Place the cloth on a table so about half is on the table and half is off. The cloth needs to be big enough so you can easily pull the half hanging off the table. The cloth should be smooth to keep the amount of friction between the cloth and the blocks as low as possible. In the center, create a rocket from the wooden blocks. The block rocket is stable and in a state of inertia until a force moves it. If you wobble the table hard enough, the rocket will topple over as a force has acted on it.

Try slowly moving the cloth around at a constant speed—you should find the rocket tower stays in place, moving with the cloth. But if you change direction or jerk the cloth, the rocket should fall over, as the force acting on it is unbalancing.

The next bit is tricky and might require some practice.

Pull the cloth as fast as possible. If you're fast and smooth enough with the motion, you should find your block rocket stays in place.

More Fun

Try making your rocket taller; does it make the trick harder?

(continued)

What do you think would happen if you used a piece of rough material like a thick towel? Remember you need the amount of friction between the cloth and blocks to be very small and a rough surface means more friction.

Learning Point

If you pull the cloth slowly and jerkily, the blocks will topple as there is too much friction, but if you make the movement fast and smooth they should stay in place.

Rocket Race

Scientific Concept—Newton's Second Law

When designing rockets, careful thought has to be put into how much the rocket weighs, as the heavier the rocket, the greater the thrust needed to lift it.

This activity requires an empty box. If you add extra mass to the box, it should be harder to push or pull. This is because the force needed to move the box is greater when the mass of the box is increased.

- - - - - - - - - - - - - - - -

Materials

+ Cardboard boxes
+ Chalk
+ Wooden blocks, books or willing volunteer

You'll need a flat area of floor or ground for this activity. It can be done inside or outside, but a wooden floor or smooth outdoor surface works best to start. Make sure the box is strong and sturdy.

Draw a start and finish line with chalk about 10 feet (3 m) apart. Place the box at the start line and carefully push it to the finish line.

Next, fill the box with wooden blocks or books, or if the box is big enough, you could ask a friend to sit inside. Carefully try to push the box from the start to the finish line again. You should find it's much harder to push the box when it's heavier.

Is it easier to pull or push?

More Fun

Can you design a handle for the box? Does this make pushing or pulling the box easier?

Ball Collision Ramp

Scientific Concepts—Newton's Second Law, momentum

In this activity, you roll a marble down a ramp so it collides with another marble at the bottom. You should find that momentum is conserved during the collision, which means the motion from the marble rolling is transferred to the stationary marble at the bottom of the ramp.

Only moving objects have momentum, but momentum doesn't always stay the same: It changes if the object changes direction, speeds up or slows down.

- - - - - - - - - - - - - - - -

Materials

+ Thick cardboard
+ Box or blocks
+ Marbles or other small balls
+ Ruler

Create a ramp by placing a sheet of thick cardboard on top of a box or stack of blocks. Place one marble or small ball at the bottom of the ramp and one at the top.

If you let the first marble roll down the ramp, its momentum will increase as it picks up speed. The marble at the bottom of the ramp is stationary until the moving marble hits it. When the two marbles collide, momentum is transferred from the rolling marble to the stationary marble, which then starts to move.

Using the ruler, can you measure how far the stationary marble rolls?

Remember, the total momentum doesn't change. It is conserved.

More Fun

Try replacing the marble at the top with a smaller ball. A smaller ball has a smaller mass, therefore a smaller momentum, so you should find the stationary marble doesn't move as far.

Learning Point

You could also think of momentum as how hard it is to stop something from moving. We know it's harder to stop something moving fast than something moving more slowly, as the fast moving object has more momentum.

Moon Buggy Race

Scientific Concept—Newton's Second Law

For a rocket to lift off from its launch pad, the thrust from the engine must be greater than the weight of the rocket. The heavier the rocket, the greater the force needed to move it.

We can demonstrate this very simply using moon buggies. If we make the moon buggies heavier, the force needed to move them is greater.

- - - - - - - - - - -

Materials

+ Large sheet of cardboard
+ Felt tip pens
+ Ruler
+ Axles and wheels
+ Small cardboard box
+ Pen and paper, to record the results
+ Marbles

Draw a road on the large sheet of cardboard using felt tip pens and use a ruler to help you add a scale to the side so you can record how far the moon buggy travels. You then need to draw a start line at the beginning of the scale.

To create a simple moon buggy, carefully make holes in the center of each wheel. These could be lids or circles cut from thick cardboard. Attach a wheel to one end of each axle. Make holes at each end of the cardboard box (this is the body of the moon buggy) for the axles to pass through. Push the axles through the holes and attach the second wheel to each side.

Place one moon buggy at the start line and gently push it. Use the scale to record how far the moon buggy travels. Do this three times and find the average distance moved by adding up each distance and dividing by three (or however many results you have).

After your first test, make the moon buggy heavier. Fill it with marbles and push it using the same force you used for the buggy with no extra load. Do this three times and find the average distance traveled in the same way.

More Fun

Investigate what happens if you add even more weight to the moon buggy. Can you predict how far a moon buggy twice as heavy as the first will travel?

Can you think of another way to propel the moon buggy? Could you try blowing it as hard as you can?

Learning Points

You should find that the heavier moon buggy doesn't move as far; this is because Newton's Second Law states that force equals mass times acceleration, so if you increase the mass, but use the same force, the acceleration will be less.

*See photo insert page 28.

Film Canister Rocket

Scientific Concept—Newton's laws of motion

A film canister rocket is a great demonstration of all three of Newton's laws of motion.

Newton's First Law
Newton's First Law states that an object will stay still unless a force acts on it. The film canister remains motionless until we add materials to create a force.

Newton's Second Law
Newton's Second Law states that the acceleration of an object is affected by the mass of an object.

If you make the film canister heavier, you should find it accelerates more slowly than a lighter canister and doesn't fly as high.

Newton's Third Law
Newton's Third Law states that for every action there is an equal and opposite reaction. In the case of the film canister, the downward force of the gas on the canister lid creates an opposite upwards force on the body of the canister, which shoots up into the air.

To reach space, a rocket must escape past the Earth's gravitational force, which wants to pull it down. Rockets do this by generating a massive amount of thrust. The engine needs to create the greatest thrust possible in the shortest time in order to overcome gravity. Thrust is created using Newton's Third Law. The combustion of rocket fuel creates hot exhaust gas, which escapes from the rocket producing a downward force, and the reaction force then creates an upward thrust force.

- - - - - - - - - - - - - -

Materials
+ Chalk
+ Goggles
+ Film canister
+ Water
+ Effervescent heartburn or vitamin tablets
+ Baking soda
+ Tissue
+ Vinegar

Find a safe spot outside to launch the rocket. The launch area needs to be a flat, hard surface, with a safe distance from other people. Use chalk to draw safety lines at least 9 feet (3 m) from the rocket. Observers should stay behind the lines.

Decide which rocket fuel (effervescent vitamin/heartburn tablets or baking soda and vinegar) you want to test first and think how you're going to decide which is the best fuel. Will it be the one that makes the rocket fly the highest and fastest? Or the one that uses the least fuel, makes the least mess and is the easiest to use?

Remember that the film canister rockets fly upwards very quickly, so be sure to wear safety goggles and stand back.

Effervescent Heartburn or Vitamin Tablets
Fill the film canister halfway with water and place one tablet inside. Carefully replace the lid and put the canister in the launch area with the lid on the floor. Remember the film canisters fly upwards very quickly, so stand back immediately and ask an adult to help.

Baking Soda and Vinegar
Wrap a couple of teaspoons of baking soda inside a tissue, and then fill the film canister halfway with vinegar. Drop the tissue-wrapped baking soda inside and replace the lid. Put the canister lid down in the launch area and stand back. Ask an adult to help.

More Fun

Can you decorate your film canister to look more like a rocket? Do you think the extra weight will affect how the rocket flies?

Learning Points

When water is added to the heartburn or vitamin tablets, they start to break down, releasing carbon dioxide gas. The buildup of carbon dioxide inside the canister creates pressure, which builds up until eventually it becomes strong enough to force the cap down, which in turn forces the canister part upwards. Newton's Third Law is at work again.

The baking soda and vinegar rocket needs to have the baking soda wrapped in tissue to stop the baking soda from reacting with the vinegar too quickly. If most of the gas is released before you can replace the lid, the pressure inside the canister won't be enough for it to launch.

Water-Powered Bottle Rocket

Scientific Concept—Newton's laws of motion

A bottle rocket is another great demonstration of all of Newton's three laws of motion. The rocket remains motionless unless a force acts on it (Newton's First Law). The amount of force is affected by the amount of air pumped into the rocket and the force can be increased by adding water (Newton's Second Law). Air and water being forced from the nozzle creates an equal and opposite reaction force which propels the rocket upwards (Newton's Third Law).

Pressure builds up inside the bottle when air is pumped into it. When the pressure is enough to force out the cork, water shoots from the bottle downwards, making the bottle push back upward, forcing it into the air.

— — — — — — — — — — — — — —

Materials

+ Empty plastic bottle
+ Paint, optional
+ Duct tape, optional
+ Cardstock and transparent tape, optional
+ Foot pump with a needle adaptor
+ Cork that fits the bottle opening
+ Water
+ Goggles

Please make sure an adult is around as the rocket takes off very suddenly and forcefully. Do not approach the rocket once you have started pumping!

If you want to decorate the bottle to look more like a space rocket, you can paint it, cover it with duct tape and/or use cardstock attached with tape to make a nose cone and fins. Just remember adding extra weight will affect how the bottle rocket flies. If you do add fins, try to make them strong enough so the rocket can stand up on them. If the fins aren't strong enough, you'll need to build something to hold the rocket upright.

Push the needle adaptor of the pump through the cork: it needs to go all the way through to allow air into the bottle.

Add water to the bottle so it's about one quarter full. Once you've added water, push the cork in. This should be a very tight fit so no air can escape.

Always wear safety goggles when launching a bottle rocket.

When you're happy with the rocket, take it outside and connect the pump to the needle adaptor. Ask an adult to slowly pump air into the bottle. Remember to ask any spectators to stand well back as the rocket will fly upwards quickly.

More Fun

Try adding extra weight to your rocket. What do you think will happen?

(continued)

Learning Point

Instead of using water, a real rocket burns fuel to create a hot gas. The hot gas escaping downward from the rocket pushes the rocket upward and it is this creation of thrust that allows a rocket to overcome gravity and blast off into space.

Streamline a Bottle Rocket

Scientific Concepts—Drag, air resistance

Drag, or air resistance, doesn't affect rockets once they have reached space as there is no air there, but it does affect a rocket trying to get to space. There are four forces that act on a rocket. These are lift, drag, weight and thrust. Drag is similar to friction and is affected by the size and shape of the rocket. Some shapes create less drag as air passes over them more easily. Imagine a ball falling to the ground, pushing air particles out of the way as it falls.

The more streamlined an object is, the more easily air can flow over the surface, causing less air resistance.

Challenge—reduce drag so your rocket flies for longer!

- - - - - - - - - - - - - -

Materials

+ Water-Powered Bottle Rocket (page 253)
+ Foot pump with needle adapter
+ Cork that fits the bottle opening
+ Water
+ Cardstock
+ Tape
+ Goggles
+ Timer

The nose cone of a rocket is the pointy bit at the end. This is the first part of the rocket to meet the air and its shape and size affect the amount of air resistance created as a rocket flies through the air. You can test different nose cone shapes to investigate how each affects how the rocket flies.

Think about what shapes of nose cone you'd like to test. You could try a cone, hemisphere, pyramid or a flat end. Can you think of any other shapes that would work?

Set up the bottle rocket with the foot pump, cork and water as on page 253.

Construct various nose cones from cardstock in different shapes and sizes. Add each test cone one by one, using tape to attach them.

Always wear safety goggles when launching bottle rockets.

Launch each rocket and record how long it stays in the air using the timer. Remember everything must be the same apart from the cone for each launch.

More Fun

What else could you change to make the rocket more or less streamlined?

Learning Points

The shape of a rocket's nose cone, its diameter and the speed it's traveling all affect the amount of air resistance slowing it down. Narrow rockets (small diameter) and an aerodynamic nose cone both help to reduce the amount of air resistance created.

A more streamlined nose cone should mean that the bottle rocket flies for longer as there is less air resistance to slow it down.

Coffee Filter Parachute

Scientific Concepts—Air resistance, drag, surface area

When rockets return to Earth, parachutes can be used to slow their descent. These parachutes are a fun way to learn about air resistance. We know that air resistance slows the fall of an object and it increases with surface area. This means a bigger parachute should slow the fall of an object the most.

Can you test this?

- - - - - - - - - - - - - - -

Materials

+ Coffee filters, different sizes
+ Hole punch
+ String
+ Small containers
+ Small toy figure or paper clips
+ Timer

Make four small holes evenly spaced around the edges of each coffee filter using a hole punch. These will act as the parachute sheets.

Cut out enough pieces of string for all the parachutes you want to make. You'll need four for each parachute and they should all be the same length, it doesn't matter too much how long the string is, but about as long as your arm will work well.

Carefully tie a piece of string to each parachute hole, and attach the other ends evenly around a small container.

Try adding small objects such as a small toy figure, paper clips or anything that will add weight to the parachute to the small container.

Drop each parachute and time how long they take to reach the ground.

Remember that to test each parachute fairly, you need to use the same objects in the container and drop each from the same height.

More Fun

What do you think will happen if you add more weight to the parachute?

Learning Point

You should find that a bigger parachute catches the air better than a small parachute to slow the fall. This is because a bigger parachute has a larger surface area and creates more air resistance, slowing the fall.

Feel the Force

Scientific Concept—Air resistance

Rockets are made smooth and pointy to reduce the amount of air resistance acting on them when they take off. Reducing air resistance in this way is called making something streamlined.

- - - - - - - - - - - - - - -

Materials

+ Large sheet of paper or cardstock
+ Stick
+ Tape
+ Empty water bottle
+ Scissors

Attach a large piece of cardstock to the end of the stick with tape. Make sure you have lots of space and wave the stick around. Put an empty water bottle on the floor and try to blow it over by moving the air close to the bottle with your stick.

(continued)

Use the scissors to make the cardstock stuck to the stick smaller by about ¾ inch (2 cm) from each edge. Wave the stick around and try to blow the bottle over again. Keep reducing the size of the cardstock by ¾ inch (2 cm) and note how it feels when you wave it and how easy it is to blow the bottle over.

You should find that it feels harder to move the stick when the cardstock is bigger as there is more air resistance acting on it. The bottle should be easier to knock over the bigger the cardstock is as more air is being pushed out of the way.

More Fun

Try the investigation again using different sizes of cardstock.

Drop a folded piece of cardstock and an open piece of cardstock of the same size to the ground from the same height. What happens?

Learning Points

If you run faster, you should find that you feel even more air resistance. This is because when you run faster you push more air out of the way, which then pushes back more.

Let's Glide

Scientific Concept—Drag

Everything flying through the air has four forces acting on it: thrust, drag, lift and gravity. Rockets are straight and thin to reduce drag, helping them reach the incredible speeds needed to escape the Earth's gravitational force.

This glider is the opposite of a rocket in that it has big wings to increase drag, so it can stay in the air longer.

- - - - - - - - - - - - - -

Materials

+ Straws or pipe cleaners
+ Tissue paper, paper, contact paper or cardstock
+ Tape

Think about what shape you'd like the glider to be. You could try a square, triangle, cube or hexagon: the choice is yours.

Create the shape using straws or pipe cleaners and cover with your choice of paper. A good glider to practice with is a triangle covered in tissue paper. The tissue paper is light and the triangle shape makes it strong.

Try throwing the glider from a height and measure how far it flies. Investigate using lots of different shapes and materials to find the best combination.

More Fun

Can you time how long the glider flies in the air?

Learning Point

A glider with a bigger surface area should fly for longer as it creates more air resistance, which slows its fall.

17

18

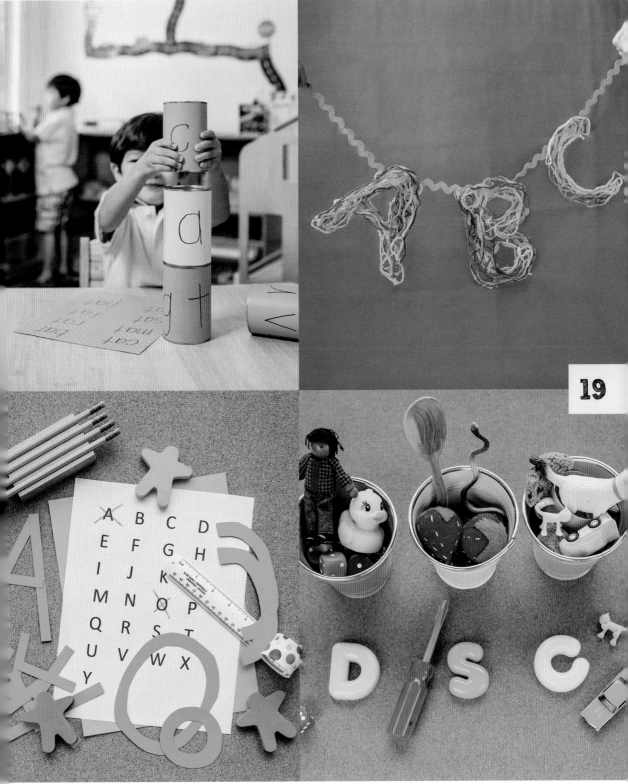

19

Family Photo Word Puzzles (page 161)

Word Family Toss (page 162)

20

Muffin Tin Syllable Counting (page 164)

Sight Word Sensory Bottle (page 166)

Words in the Sand (page 169)

Shop the Alphabet (page 171)

21

Build a Word (page 172)

25 Squish (page 179)

22

23

Outdoor Sound Garden (page 200)

Dragon Castle (page 204)

24

Celebration Jar (page 207)

State Toss (page 208)

25

Magnetic Constrution Site (page 233)

Fizzing Fact Families (page 237)

Ice Castle Challenge (page 237)

Superhero Water (page 240)

ravity Splat (page 242)

Rocket Blaster (page 242)

27

ravity Pinball Machine (page 244)

Drop the Astronaut (page 245)

Fly with Magnets (page 246)

Lift It! (page 246)

28

Rocket Zip Line (page 248)

Moon Buggy Race (page 251)

Rocket Launch Station for a Bottle Rocket (page 258)

Baking Soda–Powered Cork Rocket (page 260)

29

Steam Rocket (page 263)

Strong Suit (page 267)

Filter Paper Chromatography Planets (page 280)

Spin Art Galaxies (page 282)

30

Popping Planets (page 283)

Playdough Earth Layers (page 286)

Adorable Life Cycle Craft (page 326)

Become a Beautiful Butterfly (page 327)

ADULT
Butterfly

Egg

PUPA

CATERPILLAR

32

Magnificent Milk Carton Bird Feeder (page 352)

Happy Hummingbird Feeder (page 356)

Mobile Launch Pad

Scientific Concepts—Strong shapes, weak shapes

Mobile launch platforms were used to transport the Saturn V rockets and space shuttles to the launch pad. A mobile launch pad has to be able to hold a huge amount of weight and be capable of moving.

For this activity, you're going to think about how to construct a strong, stable structure by considering what makes a strong shape.

A triangle is stronger than a square as it has only three points of connection and any load applied is equally spread through the shape. Engineers often add a diagonal section to a square (making it into two triangles and therefore stronger).

- - - - - - - - - - - - - - - -

Materials

+ Pen and paper
+ Medium piece of cardboard
+ Scissors
+ 2 axles
+ Straws
+ Wheels
+ Tape
+ Small piece of cardboard
+ Wooden blocks

Think about the properties your mobile launch pad should have. It needs to be light enough to move, yet strong enough to hold something heavy. Draw a design for your launch pad using pen and paper, thinking about strong shapes.

The medium piece of cardboard will be the base of the vehicle. Cut the axles so they are ⅓ inch (1 cm) longer than the width of the base, then cut two straws so they are about ½ inch (1.3 cm) shorter than the axles and thread each axle through a straw. Attach the wheels to the end of each axle. The straw should be able to move freely around the axle. Jar lids or CDs make good wheels.

Attach the axles and wheels to the underside of the base with tape. Check that the wheels turn easily.

Once you have a base, create a platform using straws and a small piece of cardboard. Remember to think about the shapes you use, as triangles are stronger than squares.

Test your platform by adding something heavy like wooden blocks to the top. Remember, rockets are very, very heavy!

More Fun
Try to build a bridge using half eggshells. The shell itself is very brittle, but the dome shape makes it strong.

Learning Points
A dome is very good at spreading weight evenly in all directions so that no part of the dome has to support more weight than another part. If you have four half eggshells, you can balance a stack of books on top of them without causing damage because of the dome shape.

Rocket Launch Station for a Bottle Rocket

Scientific Concept—Gravity

The challenge with this investigation is to build a stand to hold a bottle rocket. The stand should allow the rocket to stand upright before launch, but not restrict it from taking off.

– – – – – – – – – – – – – –

Materials

+ Bottle Rocket and foot pump (page 253)
+ Straws
+ Cardboard box
+ Scissors
+ Cardboard tubes
+ Tape
+ Goggles

First make a bottle rocket. See page 253 for instructions.

Construct the stand, remembering it must support the weight of your bottle rocket and remain on the ground when the rocket takes off.

You can use any materials you want for this activity: It can be as simple or complex as you like. You could start with a very simple design using four straws taped to the side of the bottle rocket to help it stand up. Make a stand with the cardboard box by cutting a hole in the top using scissors so the bottle rocket sits with just the bottleneck in the hole. Cut a hole in the side of the box to allow the tubing from the foot pump to fit through.

To use cardboard tubes, make these into a square shape and attach together with tape. The square should be just big enough so the bottom of the rocket sits nicely inside with the rest of the bottle rocket on top.

For an extra challenge, you could build clamps to hold the rocket in place until it's time for take off.

Be careful to leave space for the pump to attach to the cork in the rocket.

Once you're happy with your design, can you test it? Remember a bottle rocket should be vertical at liftoff.

Always wear safety goggles and ask an adult to help.

More Fun

Can you build a launch station using just one material? Or how about a launch station that will stay upright on a windy day?

*See photo insert page 29.

Balloon Rocket

Scientific Concept—Chemical reactions

Vinegar is an acid and baking soda is a base. When an acid and a base are mixed together, they react to neutralize each other, releasing carbon dioxide gas. This is an example of a chemical reaction. The baking soda and vinegar have to come into contact with each other to react, like the fuel and oxidizer in a rocket.

The carbon dioxide fills the bottle and then the balloon. If enough gas enters the balloon, the balloon will blow up.

– – – – – – – – – – – – – –

Materials

+ Balloon
+ Felt tip pens
+ 2 tsp (9 g) baking soda
+ Small bottle
+ 10 tsp (50 ml) vinegar

Blow up the balloon a little and let the air out. This allows the balloon to expand more easily when the gas from the chemical reaction enters it.

Draw a rocket on the balloon using a felt tip pen. This is easiest to do when the balloon is blown up, but don't tie it off.

Place the baking soda into the bottle followed by the vinegar, and then quickly place the balloon over the bottle opening. You should be able to see the baking soda and vinegar react as lots of bubbles appear. The bubbles are carbon dioxide, which is released in the neutralization reaction between the baking soda and vinegar.

The carbon dioxide produced in the reaction will first fill the bottle and then the balloon, making it increase in size.

More Fun

Experiment using different amounts of baking soda and vinegar. Which combination gives you the biggest balloon?

Speed It Up

Scientific Concept—Chemical reactions

Reactants are substances you combine to get a reaction. Some react slowly and some much faster, depending on the bonds that need to be broken. For example, gold is very nonreactive, while sodium and potassium are so reactive that they tarnish instantly when exposed to the air. Rocket scientists need to be able to control the speed of the combustion reactions. This is usually done by controlling the speed at which fuel is pumped into the combustion chamber.

Increasing the concentration of reactants and the temperature at which the reaction takes place can speed up chemical reactions.

Materials

+ 2 balloons
+ Felt tip pens
+ Warm and cold water
+ Small bottles
+ Effervescent heartburn or vitamin tablets

Blow up the balloons a little and let the air out. Draw a rocket on each balloon using a felt tip pen. Remember not to seal the balloon end.

Carefully pour the warm water into one bottle and the cold into another bottle so each is about one third full. The same amount of water should be used in each so this is a fair test.

Place one tablet into each bottle then quickly place the balloons over the bottle openings. If you watch carefully, you should see that the tablet in the warm water reacts faster than the tablet in cold water and is used up first. The balloon on the warm water bottle should blow up first as carbon dioxide is released faster in that reaction.

More Fun

Try the investigation again but this time use two tablets and cold water. What do you think will happen?

Learning Points

The higher the concentration, the faster the reaction; this is because there is more of the reactive substance available to react.

The higher the temperature, the faster the reaction; heating up a substance causes the particles to have more energy and move around faster, meaning they have more contact with the other reactive substance.

Which Nozzle Size?

Scientific Concepts—Thrust, lift, chemical reactions

Earlier activities have shown that thrust to lift the rocket is created when the fuel burns. The nozzle is the part of a rocket through which the hot gases from the burning of the fuel escape. This reduces the opening through which gases can escape and so increases the acceleration of the gases as they leave the rocket, maximizing thrust.

Materials

+ Garden hose with a spray attachment
+ Chalk, optional
+ Syringes with different width openings
+ Paint, optional
+ White sheet, optional

To test how a nozzle works, set up a garden hose with a spray attachment and turn it on. First try opening the nozzle as wide as it will go and measure how far the water squirts out. If you do this outside on a dry patio, you could use chalk to mark the farthest distance the spray reaches.

Set the nozzle as small as it will go and mark how far the water squirts. You should find that a smaller hole for the water to be squirted from means it leaves the hose with more force and travels farther. Can you feel the extra thrust when the nozzle opening is smaller?

More Fun

Try squirting water through syringes with different size openings. You should find water travels farther the smaller the opening, and it should feel harder to push the water out of a small syringe. Why do you think this is?

If you're feeling creative, try filling the syringes with paint, then squirt them onto an old white sheet. Are narrower or wider syringes better for reaching the sheet if you take a few steps backward?

Baking Soda-Powered Cork Rocket

Scientific Concept—Chemical reactions

Baking soda and vinegar react to neutralize each other, releasing carbon dioxide. We can use this reaction to make a mini cork rocket.

Materials

+ Goggles
+ Cork
+ Small plastic carbonated beverage bottle
+ 1 tbsp (13 g) baking soda
+ Paper towels or kitchen roll
+ ⅓ cup (70 ml) vinegar

This must be done outside as the cork will shoot up into the air very quickly and with force. Remember to wear eye protection.

Make sure the cork fits inside the top of the empty bottle. It should be a snug fit because you don't want any of the gas to escape. When you're happy with the fit, remove the cork and set it aside.

If you put the baking soda in the bottle on its own, when you add the vinegar, the reaction will happen so fast that most of the gas released by the reaction will be lost in the time it takes to get the cork on. To solve this problem, wrap the baking soda in a paper towel and push it into the bottle. Add the vinegar and push the cork in tightly while keeping the bottle facing away from you in case the cork flies off quickly.

Once the cork is in place, put the bottle down and stand back as soon as you can. The cork will fly through the air with a bang when the pressure inside is strong enough.

More Fun

Try adding a cone and ribbons to your cork. Do these affect how it flies?

*See photo insert page 29.

Pump It Out

Scientific Concept—Chemical reactions

Rocket engines use pumps to mix their fuel and oxidizer in a combustion chamber. The amount of fuel and oxidizer pumped into the combustion chambers controls the amount of thrust generated.

This activity uses very simple pumps found in hand soap containers to mix paint, which is much less explosive but lots of fun.

- - - - - - - - - - - - - -

Materials

+ 2 empty hand soap containers with a pump
+ Paint
+ Large, flat container
+ Baking soda
+ Water
+ Vinegar
+ Dish soap
+ Food coloring

The empty soap dispensers are the pumps and the container is the combustion chamber. We can't burn fuel but we can try some color mixing!

Half fill your hand soap containers with different color paints and pump out some paint from each into the large container. You could have black paint in one pump and white in another, and then vary the amount of white paint you pump compared to black to get different shades of gray. Or you could mix blue and yellow to make green, red and yellow to make orange, or red and blue to make purple.

Can you pump both colors into the container at the same time?

More Fun

Mix a couple of tablespoons (14 to 28 g) of baking soda with water to put in one dispenser and fill the other with vinegar. If you pump both into your container, you should see a neutralization reaction take place with bubbles of gas given off. Try adding dish soap and food coloring to get a lovely thick, colorful foam.

Learning Point

The baking soda and vinegar react only when they are mixed. In a rocket engine, combustion occurs only when the fuel and oxidizer are released into the combustion chamber.

Squeezy Bottle Rocket

Scientific Concept—Trajectory

This easy-to-construct rocket is great for investigating how the angle a rocket is launched from affects its flight. The rockets work because as you squeeze the bottle, air is forced out of the straw in the bottle and pushes against the rocket straw. This force causes the rocket straw to fly through the air.

- - - - - - - - - - - - - - - -

Materials

+ Empty water bottles with a sports cap
+ Scissors
+ 2 straws, 1 wide enough to fit over the other
+ Modeling clay
+ Tape
+ Felt tip pens
+ Cardstock or paper

To make the bottle part of the rocket, it's really important to make sure the sports cap is completely airtight. If air can escape, your rocket won't fly very far.

Cut the thinner straw into quarters and put one segment into the center of the sports cap. Seal the straw around the cap using modeling clay. You can check the seal is complete by squeezing the bottle: If the seal is secure, all of the air from the bottle should come out of the straw, not the bottle neck. This is your rocket launcher!

To make the rocket part, first cut the wider straw into quarters and seal one end with tape; this is to stop air from escaping. Draw a rocket shape with felt tip pens on the cardstock or paper. Remember, the lighter the rocket, the farther it will fly.

Attach the paper rocket onto one side of the rocket straw using tape and place it onto the straw in the rocket launcher.

Squeeze the rocket launcher hard, and you should find that the rocket shoots up into the air. Try launching at different angles to see how you can make the rocket fly farther.

More Fun

Try adding extra weight to your straw rocket by placing a small ball of modeling clay on the end. Does this change how far and for how long it flies?

Learning Points

You should find that your straw rocket flies farther if you launch at an angle forwards rather than straight up. This is because gravity and the forward force created by the rocket launcher act together to create a curved flight path.

Flight Path Angles

Scientific Concept—Angles

If you tried the Squeezy Bottle Rocket (left) or Foam Rocket (page 263), you should have found that changing the angle at which you released the rocket altered its flight path.

Angles are very important when navigating spacecraft. For example, for a successful reentry into the Earth's atmosphere, the entry angle has to be within set limits or the spacecraft can break up or bounce back into space.

A protractor is an instrument used to measure angles. This giant version makes it easy to visualize angles and set your rockets to launch at an angle.

- - - - - - - - - - - - - - - -

Materials

+ Large sheet of cardboard
+ Scissors
+ Felt tip pens
+ Plates or hula hoop
+ Ruler
+ Protractor
+ Squeezy Bottle Rocket (page 262) or Foam Rocket (right)
+ Chalk

To make this giant protractor, you need to cut out a big semicircle from the cardboard. You could do this by drawing around half of a plate or hula hoop.

Once you're happy with your semicircle, start by measuring and drawing a 90 degree line with the ruler, drawn up from the center of the cardboard. Then mark 0 and 180 on the bottom line at each end. Carefully fill in the other angles using the small protractor as a guide.

Use the giant protractor to test the rockets at different angles. What do you think will happen if you shoot the rockets straight up?

More Fun

Try using the protractor to release the rockets at different angles and record how far they travel on the ground using chalk.

Learning Point

Protractors are usually small and made from plastic. This supersize protractor makes it easy to check and measure the angle you want to launch your rockets from.

Foam Rocket

Scientific Concept—Trajectory

Foam rockets work the same way as the Squeezy Bottle Rocket (page 262); you're just using a different material to make the rocket part. If you don't want to make a launcher this time, you can try using just a straw as a launcher and blowing into the straw.

- - - - - - - - - - - - -

Materials

+ Thin foam pipe insulation
+ Scissors
+ Duct tape
+ Cardstock for decoration, optional
+ Tape
+ Straw
+ Squeezy Bottle Rocket launcher (page 262)

Cut a small piece of the foam pipe insulation and seal the end with duct tape. This is your foam rocket. You can make a nose cone and fins using colored cardstock and attach them to the foam rocket with tape if you want.

You can launch your foam rocket with a straw if you don't want to use a bottle launcher like on page 262. First check that the foam rocket fits on top of the straw. If the fit is too tight, either use a thinner straw or try to widen the foam tube by pushing the straw in and out a few times.

When you're happy with the fit, choose a launch angle and blow hard into the straw or use a Squeezy Bottle Rocket launcher. You should find your foam rocket shoots through the air.

More Fun

Launch your foam rocket at different angles to investigate which angle allows the rocket to cover the most ground distance.

*See photo insert page 29.

Static Electricity Rockets

Scientific Concept—Static electricity

Have you ever rubbed a balloon on your hair and watched your hair stand up on end?

When you rub a balloon on your hair or a woolly sweater, the balloon becomes charged with static electricity. This is an electric charge created when some materials are rubbed together.

You can use static electricity to make tissue paper jump up to a balloon.

Do you think it matters how big your tissue paper rockets are? Do you think bigger or smaller rockets will jump the highest?

– – – – – – – – – – – – – – – –

Materials

+ Tissue paper
+ Scissors
+ Balloon

First you need to make your rockets. Cut several different size rocket shapes from the tissue paper. You're going to investigate which jump up to your balloon most easily.

Blow up a balloon and give it a good rub on your hair or a wooly sweater. If you use your hair, you should find it starts to stick up on end as the balloon becomes charged with static electricity and starts to attract your hair.

Hold the balloon over your tissue paper rockets and watch them jump up towards the balloon. If you hold the balloon close to the rockets, they should stick to the surface of the balloon. Tissue paper is so light that it jumps up to the balloon easily. Do you think other types of paper would do the same? Can you design an investigation to find out?

More Fun

How many balloons can you get to stick to a wall (or yourself) at the same time?

Try rubbing a balloon on different types of fabrics. You should find that wool and synthetic fabrics create static electricity most easily.

Learning Points

Atoms are made up of a positively charged nucleus with negatively charged electrons in orbit around it. When objects touch, electrons sometimes jump between them, leaving the object that has lost electrons with a positive charge and the object that has gained electrons with a negative charge. In this case, the balloon gains extra electrons causing a buildup of negative charges, or static electricity. It is the static electricity that pulls on the tissue paper rockets, lifting them into the air and onto the balloon.

Rockets on Ice

Scientific Concept—Friction

Pluto was once thought to be the ninth planet in our solar system, but has since been reclassified as a dwarf planet. Dwarf planets still orbit the Sun but are too small to be planets.

Pluto is a rocky ice planet about 50 times farther from the Sun than Earth, meaning it's incredibly cold. Sunlight takes around 5 hours to reach Pluto, compared to about 8 minutes to reach Earth.

If humans were ever to travel to Pluto, we'd need a form of transport that could move over vast amounts of ice. For a vehicle to move quickly and easily over ice, there needs to not be friction.

— — — — — — — — — —

Materials

+ Water
+ Baking tray
+ Scissors
+ Felt, bubble wrap, paper and cellophane
+ Double-sided tape
+ Milk bottle tops
+ Straws

You can make a sheet of ice by putting about ⅜ inch (1 cm) of water into the baking tray and placing it in a freezer. Once it's frozen, you need to make your rockets to test.

Cut rocket shapes out of the felt, bubble wrap, paper and cellophane. Use double-sided tape to attach a milk bottle top to one side of each rocket. Place the rockets with the milk bottle top facing upward on the sheet of ice in a row. Try blowing through a straw toward the milk bottle top on each rocket; you should find that the rockets with rougher surfaces are harder to move as there is more friction between the rocket and the ice.

If you wanted a vehicle to grip ice better and not slip, you'd want it to have wheels with a rough surface to increase the amount of friction. If you want it to slide, you'd want a smooth surface.

More Fun

Another way to increase friction between vehicles and ice is to add stone, sand and salt to the surface of the ice. Try spreading a thin layer of sand and salt over your ice sheet; you should find it becomes harder to move the rockets. The salt will also make the ice melt.

Salt makes ice melt by lowering the freezing point of water.

Learning Points

Friction is the force that slows objects down when they rub against each other. Remember friction is stronger on rough surfaces than smooth surfaces.

(fourteen)

SPACE EXPLORATION

The human body is adapted to live on Earth. We're used to being grounded thanks to gravity, pleasant temperatures, lots of contact with other humans and readily available food. Unlike Earth, space is a highly dangerous, hostile environment. Spacecraft must provide everything an astronaut needs to survive: light, heat, food, water, air to breathe and protection from the hazards of space.

Astronauts experience space sickness, weightlessness, high radiation levels and loss of bone mass, and that's just inside the spacecraft!

Strong Suit

Scientific Concept—Properties of materials

A space suit is a vital piece of equipment for astronauts and must protect them from the hazards of space. The suit needs to protect an astronaut from extreme cold, radiation, sunlight and fast moving dust and rocks while providing oxygen, removing carbon dioxide and giving clear vision. It basically has to be a complete life-support system for the wearer.

The materials used to make space suits must be carefully chosen to provide astronauts with all the protection they need from the extreme conditions of space.

In this activity, you're going to freeze different materials to investigate how their properties change when exposed to the cold.

- - - - - - - - - - - - - - -

Materials

+ Scissors
+ Cotton wool
+ Felt
+ Cotton
+ Bubble wrap
+ Aluminum foil
+ Muffin tray, optional
+ Paper and pencil

Cut out a small segment of each material you want to test. These should all be roughly the same size. Make a note of how each material feels and how flexible it is.

The muffin tray isn't essential, but will keep each sample separate and stop them from sticking to each other. You need to carefully put a different material in each segment of the tray making sure they aren't touching and place in the freezer for about 2 hours.

Check each material one by one. How have they changed since being in the freezer? Create a table and record your observations before and after freezing. Did any of the materials surprise you? Can you think of anything else to test?

While it's chilly inside your freezer (about 0°F [-17°C]), outer space is much colder, about -455°F (-270°C)!

More Fun

Can you design a helmet for an astronaut? Think about what would be useful. How about a camera, light or emergency food supply?

*See photo insert page 29.

Keeping Warm

Scientific Concepts—Changes of state, insulation

Spacecraft must be able to keep astronauts at a safe and comfortable temperature, protecting them from the extreme temperatures of space. Spacecraft are constructed of special materials to protect astronauts not only from heat and cold, but also radiation.

This activity explores the effect of heat and light from the Sun on objects on Earth.

- - - - - - - - - - - - - - -

Materials

+ Ice cubes (should be the same shape and size)
+ Aluminum foil
+ Black paper
+ White paper
+ Paper towels
+ Bubble wrap
+ Timer or stopwatch

(continued)

Carefully make ice cubes using the same amount of water for each. The aim of this activity is to slow down the rate at which the ice cubes melt.

Wrap each ice cube in a different material, and leave one unwrapped. The unwrapped ice cube is your control: it means you can see what would happen to the other cubes if they were not wrapped up.

Leave all of the ice cubes in a sunny spot and use a stopwatch to check every 5 minutes to see how much they have melted. Is it easy to tell which have melted the most? If you can't tell easily, you could weigh each cube after 15 minutes.

Which material do you think will protect the cube from melting most efficiently?

More Fun

Instead of covering the ice cubes with a material, try leaving them in different places. Good places to leave them are in the Sun, in the shade, in the fridge and on a windowsill. Which do you think will melt first?

Solar Power

Scientific Concepts—Absorption, reflection

The best and most available source of energy for spacecraft is energy from the Sun. Solar rays can be used to convert solar energy to electricity, which can then be used for power. We can harness the energy of the Sun on Earth to make a solar oven.

A solar oven isn't just the Sun heating up the food inside: it's specially designed to utilize the Sun's thermal energy efficiently. Aluminum foil reflects heat and light. This is used to line the lid of the solar oven, which should be positioned to reflect heat onto the food inside the box.

The bottom of the solar oven should be lined with black paper. Black paper absorbs the heat and light reflected onto it by the foil. Plastic food wrap is placed over the top of the oven to stop the warm air heated by the Sun from escaping.

- - - - - - - - - - - - -

Materials

+ Cardboard box (like a pizza box)
+ Aluminum foil
+ Matte black cardstock or paper
+ Tape
+ Marshmallows, chocolate, cheese or ice cube
+ Plate
+ Stick
+ Plastic wrap

To prepare the oven, you need to cover the inside lid of the cardboard box with aluminum foil and place matte black cardstock on the bottom. Use the tape to hold them in place.

If you don't like marshmallows, you could use chocolate or cheese, or even compare how long it takes an ice cube to melt inside a solar oven and outside. Put the food you chose to melt on a plate and place it on the black cardstock.

Position the box so it faces the Sun, adjusting the lid so the light is reflected onto the food by the aluminum foil. Fix the lid at this position with tape or a stick. You might have to move the oven a little as the position of the Sun changes.

You'll need to cover the oven with plastic food wrap to stop the warm air from escaping. It may take over an hour for your food to melt, depending on the temperature and time of day, so be patient!

Only heat up food that doesn't require heating to eat as the solar oven might not get the food to a safe enough temperature for consumption.

More Fun

Try insulating the inside of your solar oven with a material that traps heat. Bubble wrap or newspaper would work well.

Learning Points

There are three processes at work in a solar oven. The matte black paper absorbs the heat while solar radiation from the Sun is reflected from the aluminum foil onto the food. The food wrap traps the warm air inside as hot air rises! These three processes together heat up the food, making it melt.

Sun Safe

Scientific Concept—Effects of ultraviolet light

Ultraviolet (UV) light is invisible radiation, which can cause sunburn and damage to your eyes if you don't protect yourself properly. The Earth's atmosphere blocks out a lot of radiation, so the levels in space are much higher than on Earth. Luckily, UV light is fairly easy to block. Astronauts' visors reflect UV light to protect the eyes and face, and the rest of the suit protects the body.

UV beads are perfect for learning about UV radiation. They change color faster and have a deeper color with stronger levels of UV light. UV beads turn back to their original color when the UV light source is removed.

- - - - - - - -

Materials

+ UV beads
+ String
+ Sunscreen with different protection factors
+ Paper or cardstock

Thread a bead on string for each type of sunscreen you want to test, plus one extra for the control, and tie a knot at each end to stop the beads from falling off. This activity is best done on a sunny day, but you could try it on a cloudy day too and compare what happens.

Take the bead string outside and watch what happens. The beads should change color almost instantly.

Lay the string on the paper and assign each bead to a type of sunscreen.

Next, completely cover each bead with the assigned sunscreen and label them on the sheet of paper.

Place the string and paper in the sunshine outdoors and record the color each bead changes. Would you be able to tell which sunscreen was on which bead without knowing? Maybe you could ask a friend if they can guess.

More Fun

It might be tricky, but can you half-cover each bead in sunscreen, leaving the other half uncovered so you can see the difference?

Learning Point

Our bodies need UV light to produce vitamin D, which strengthens bones and the immune system, but overexposure also causes sunburn and can damage eyes and skin.

Can You Balance?

Scientific Concept—Effects of living in space on the body

It takes a bit of time for astronauts to adjust to living in space. Here on Earth, gravity helps us balance, and we have a sense of standing the right way up because the weight of our body is on our feet as we stand on the ground. In space, weightlessness means the brain doesn't have these indicators, leading to astronauts feeling a little nauseated when they first go into space.

- - - - - - - - - - - - - - - -

Materials

+ Ball

Try to stand on one leg with your arms in the air. Can you balance easily?

Next, try to stand on one leg and throw a small soft ball to a friend also standing on one leg. Can they catch the ball? Is it easier to stand on your right leg or left leg? See if your game of catch is shorter on one leg than two!

More Fun

Can you hop and play catch at the same time? How do you think a game of catch would be different on the Moon where there is less gravity?

Clean It Up!

Scientific Concept—Properties of materials

Humans need water for survival, but there isn't enough space or weight allowance to take all the water a human would need for a long period in space in a rocket from Earth. The water astronauts drink is cleverly recycled and cleaned, so they can drink the same water over and over again.

One way to clean water is to filter it. Filtering systems in space are very complex, but this easy activity gives you a small insight into the process.

- - - - - - - - - - - - - - - -

Materials

+ Water
+ Glitter, dirt or sand
+ Coffee filter
+ Paper towels
+ Small stones or pebbles
+ Funnel
+ Plastic bottle

Make some dirty water to clean. You can do this by putting a handful of glitter, dirt or sand into the water.

Take a look at the coffee filter, paper towels and stones and think about which will make the best filter.

Once you've decided which to test first, put the material inside a funnel, then put the funnel into an empty plastic bottle before pouring some of your dirty water mixture gently onto the filter. You should find clearer liquid flows through the filter into the bottle below as solid material is trapped on the filter.

Run the same dirty water through the other filters, noting which gives the cleanest water. Is it the one you expected?

Do not drink your filtered water as our drinking water is specially cleaned (not just filtered) to make it safe.

More Fun

Try filtering with stones of different sizes. You should find these also trap some of the solid particles in the dirty water, making it look clearer.

Learning Points

A filter is a material that allows liquid through but traps solid particles, separating solids from liquids.

Growing Taller

Scientific Concept—Measurement

Spending time in space can have serious effects on the human body, as our bodies have adapted to living with gravity on Earth. Living in microgravity for a period of time leads to muscle wastage, changes in blood pressure and bone loss. Imagine spending several months floating instead of walking. The lack of load-bearing exercise can lead to bones becoming weaker, which is why astronauts must exercise for several hours a day in space.

On Earth, the discs that make up our spine are slightly compressed thanks to gravity. In the microgravity of space, that compression no longer happens meaning the discs expand and astronauts become up to 2 inches (5 cm) taller!

Materials

+ Meter ruler or tape measure

Use a ruler to determine how tall you are on Earth.

Calculate how much taller you could be in space. To do this you'll need to add 2 inches (5 cm) on to your height.

Would being 2 inches (5 cm) taller mean you could do anything more than you can now? Does it make you tall enough to ride a new rollercoaster in a theme park or reach a higher shelf in your kitchen?

More Fun

To reduce the effects of microgravity, astronauts in space exercise daily. Can you devise a fun exercise regime for an astronaut to follow? Weight bearing exercises are best, things like jogging, weight training and dancing, but remember astronauts don't have much space to exercise.

Stop the Floating Food!

Scientific Concepts—Gravity, living in space

One of the problems astronauts face in space is that the lack of gravity means food floats away. Imagine sprinkling salt or pepper on your food and then watching it float off!

Water or food crumbs floating around a spacecraft could cause serious damage, so it's very important to keep it contained.

Can you design packaging that allows an astronaut to access their food but also stops it from escaping and flying around the spacecraft?

Materials

+ Straws
+ Food-safe resealable bags
+ Tape, masking tape, duct tape
+ Milk or other liquid

One way to create packaging is to use a straw and resealable bag so food can be sucked up. You'll need to make sure you seal the gap around the straw and bag well enough to stop any liquid from escaping.

Carefully make a hole in the side of a resealable bag and push a straw through the hole. Seal around the hole with tape. To test the seal, pour some water in the bag so it's about one-third full, seal the top and tip the bag upside down, covering the end of the straw with your finger. Does any water escape from the bag? If it doesn't, you've got a good seal.

Try adding milk to your food bag to check if you can drink it without any spills.

(continued)

Can you think of another design to perform the same function? Do any of the different tapes work better than others?

More Fun

Imagine an astronaut wants to have a fancy meal while in space. Can you design a way to stop a knife and fork floating around, but still be usable? What other problem might you have?

Hint—how about using a tray and magnets? Would the food still float around?

Space Circuits

Scientific Concept—Electricity

The International Space Station is powered by electricity from solar power. Solar arrays convert sunlight into electricity for the Space Station to use. Electricity flows through a circuit, but this only works if the circuit is complete. You can make your own circuits and learn how electricity flows using playdough.

– – – – – – – – – – – – –

Materials

+ Playdough
+ AA battery holder with wire leads and batteries
+ Light emitting diodes (LEDs)
+ Star cookie cutter

To make a simple circuit, roll two pieces of the playdough into balls, and check that the batteries are in the battery holder. Place the red lead into one piece of dough and the black into another. Make sure the two balls of dough are not touching.

Look at the LED: one end is longer than the other. It's important to remember that electricity can flow only one way through an LED. The long leg is the positive leg and should be pushed into the playdough ball with the red wire, while the shorter lead should be in the playdough ball with the black wire.

If the LED is in the playdough the right way, you should find it lights up! Electricity always takes the easiest path, so if you push the two playdough balls together it will flow through the playdough and not the LED . . . meaning the LED won't light up!

Once you've got the hang of how a circuit works, use a cookie cutter to make the playdough star or planet shaped. Can you make a space circuit?

More Fun

Can you make a circuit to represent a constellation? Remember, for electricity to flow the circuit must be complete with no breaks.

Learning Points

Playdough conducts electricity because it contains salt. Salt ions allow electricity to flow through the playdough. If you wanted to make an insulating (nonconducting) playdough, you wouldn't add the salt.

Playdough Recipe

+ ¼ cup (60 g) salt
+ 1 cup (125 g) flour
+ Food coloring
+ ½ cup (120 ml) warm water

Mix the salt with the flour. Mix 4 to 6 drops of food coloring with the water. Add the water to the flour mix and knead by hand until well mixed. Store in a tightly sealed container.

Dehydrate It!

Scientific Concept—Food preservation

A big problem for astronauts in space is food. There isn't the room or weight allowance on a spacecraft to transport months worth of food, so what is taken must be light and last for a long time.

Some of the first space foods were packaged up like toothpaste in tubes, which astronauts would squeeze into their mouths. They probably didn't taste very nice, so as time spent in space started to increase, scientists wanted to improve food quality.

One way to provide good food, but keep the weight down, is to cook it, freeze it and then remove the water.

You can try dehydrating your own food in an oven, or use the Sun if you live somewhere with strong sunlight.

- - - - - - - - - - - - -

Materials

+ Food to dehydrate (apples or tomatoes work well)
+ Baking sheet

Ask a grown-up to help with this activity. To make dried apples, have an adult carefully slice the apple into thin slices and spread them out on a baking sheet. Place the apples in an oven on the lowest setting for 6 to 8 hours. If you want them more crisp like apple chips, use a higher setting, around 350°F (177°C) for about an hour or until they look crisp and slightly brown. Try weighing a couple of apple slices before and after drying to see how much weight you save by drying them.

If it's a sunny day, you can try to dehydrate foods in the Sun. This is especially good for tomatoes. You'll need to thinly slice the tomatoes and place them on a baking sheet in the sunshine. It'll take a few days for the tomatoes to dry out so remember to cover them and bring them in at night.

More Fun

Try drying herbs. Give them a good wash, and then bundle them together before hanging them up in the Sun to dry.

Learning Point

Dehydrating food allows it to last a long time at normal temperatures and retain its nutritional value, making it great for astronauts spending a period of time in space.

Rehydrate It!

Scientific Concept—Food preservation

All living things need water to survive—without water, your body would stop working properly. If your body doesn't have enough water, you are dehydrated. Severe dehydration can make you feel very poorly.

We've tried dehydrating foods; now it's time to rehydrate them. To rehydrate a food, you need to restore the water. Astronauts use water to rehydrate their food in space.

- - - - - - - - - - - - -

Materials

+ Cold water
+ Bowl
+ Foods to rehydrate (raisins, dried apples; small jelly sweets also work)

Pour the cold water into the bowl and put the dehydrated food in the water. It takes a bit of time for water to be reabsorbed by the food, so be patient and top up with water if the bowl starts to run dry.

You should find the dehydrated food plumps up over a few hours!

Only use clean, cold water to rehydrate your food, unless you're going to boil it before eating.

(continued)

More Fun

In the future, astronauts might be able to grow their own food in space. Try growing cress (greens) or herbs that you can eat at home. Remember plants need to be kept in a cool, light place and watered regularly.

Learning Point

Did you know about 20 percent of our water intake comes from food? Foods like watermelon, celery and cucumber all have a high water content, so are great for helping you stay hydrated.

Parachute

Scientific Concepts—Gravity, air resistance

When objects fall, two forces act on them: gravity pulls the object down, while air resistance slows the fall.

If you drop a piece of paper and a stone at the same time, the stone hits the ground first. This is because there is more air resistance acting on the paper as it has a larger surface area. The paper seems to "catch" the air, which slows it down. The force of gravity acting on both the paper and the stone is the same.

Parachutes are used to slow the fall of an object by increasing air resistance, which reduces the effect of gravity. Rocket capsules use parachutes when they land to use air resistance to slow them down as much as possible.

This activity investigates the relationship between the shape of a parachute and how fast it falls.

Materials

+ Cotton or plastic sheet
+ Scissors
+ String
+ Plastic or paper cup
+ Tape
+ Astronaut or toy figure
+ Timer
+ Scales

Cut out the parachute from the cotton sheet. Think carefully about how big you think the parachute should be. The bigger the parachute, the more it will increase air resistance and slow the fall of the astronaut. The parachute could be a square or a circle shape; do you think this will make a difference?

Ask an adult to carefully make four holes in the parachute, one in each corner. If using a circle shape, space out the holes evenly.

Cut four lengths of string to the same length and tie one to each hole in the parachute. Attach the other ends evenly to the inside of the paper or plastic cup and secure with tape. Add an astronaut or toy figure.

Hold the parachute above your head and ask a friend to time how long it takes to reach the ground. If you make the parachute bigger, you should find it falls to the ground more slowly.

More Fun

Try adding figures of different weights to the parachute and record the time it takes for each to reach the ground.

Can you make a double parachute?

Learning Points

Have you ever watched a feather or other similarly shaped object, like a leaf or piece of paper, drop to the ground? These fall much more slowly than a small heavy object like a stone. This is because air resistance, or drag, slows the feather down more than the stone.

Imagine swimming through the air with your arms pushing the atmosphere out of your way. Then imagine having a big sheet of cardboard attached to each hand. The cards make the surface area of your hands bigger, and increase the air resistance. It's the same with parachutes. The bigger the parachute, the larger the surface area, the greater the air resistance and the slower the object falls.

Drop It!

Scientific Concepts—Gravity, air resistance

If there were no air resistance, a feather and a stone dropped from the same height would hit the ground at the same time. This is because the only force acting on them would be gravity, and the strength of the gravitational force acting on both would be the same.

This activity investigates the relationship between the shape of a parachute and how fast it falls.

- - - - - - - - - - - - -

Materials

+ 2 small empty water bottles
+ Sand, water or rice
+ Weighing scales
+ Paper

Make sure the water bottles are empty, dry and both the same size.

Fill one bottle about half full with sand. Hold both bottles up as high as you can reach and drop them at the same time. They should both hit the ground at the same time because the force of gravity acting on both is the same. Can you weigh your bottles and see how much heavier one is than the other? Does the weight matter?

Next, try dropping a piece of paper rolled into a ball and one held out flat. The ball of paper will hit the ground first as there is more air pushing up onto the sheet of paper slowing it down. Parachutes use air resistance to slow the fall of the object attached.

More Fun

If you make an identical parachute for both your bottles, do you think they will still hit the ground at the same time?

Learning Points

If a stone and a feather were dropped at the same time on the Moon, they would both hit the ground at the same time. This is because, unlike on Earth, there is no air resistance on the Moon, so both the stone and feather would have only the force of gravity acting on them.

Lift with Balloons

Scientific Concept—Gravity

Have you ever wondered why a helium balloon floats, but a normal balloon filled with air drops to the ground?

Objects float if they are lighter than the air around them. A balloon filled with air will drop to the ground, as it is heavier than air thanks to the weight of the balloon. A balloon filled with helium gas will float, as helium gas is less dense than air.

In order to reach space, a rocket must overcome the downward force of gravity. Of course, this cannot be done with helium balloons, but imagine if it was that easy!

– – – – – – – – – – – –

Materials

+ String
+ Helium-filled balloons
+ Small toy (a LEGO figure is a good size)
+ Reusable adhesive putty

Tie the string to the helium balloon, making sure it's long enough for you to reach when you let go of the balloon and it hits the ceiling.

Attach a small toy figure to the string. If the figure stays on the ground when you drop the balloon, add more balloons until the figure lifts into the air.

If the toy figure rises up with just one balloon, try adding adhesive putty to the figure to increase its weight until it drops to the ground again.

More Fun

Can you find a point where your toy figure is floating in the air, not being pulled down by gravity or up by the helium balloon?

Learning Points

Helium is a colorless, tasteless and odorless gas and the second most common element in the universe.

Because helium is lighter than air and chemically unreactive (this means it doesn't react with other chemicals and so is very safe), it's often used to fill balloons and airships.

Feeling the Burn

Scientific Concepts—Gravity, friction, resistance

Reentry into the Earth's atmosphere is a dangerous part of space travel. As a spacecraft falls, it heats up because of friction and air resistance created by air particles hitting the surface of the spacecraft at high speed. The part of a spacecraft that returns to Earth must be protected by heat shields to protect it from the intense heat.

This activity uses black and white paper wrapped around a jar of water to demonstrate the different properties of the two materials.

– – – – – – – – – – – –

Materials

+ 3 jars
+ Cold water
+ 1 sheet of black paper
+ 1 sheet of white paper
+ 1 sheet of foil paper or aluminum foil
+ Thermometer

Put the same amount of cold water in each jar. Cover one jar with black paper, one with white and one with foil. Use a thermometer to record the initial temperature.

Leave the jars outside in the sunshine and check their temperature every 5 minutes. You should find that the black paper absorbs heat and transmits this heat to the jar, heating the water. The heat from the black paper should increase the water temperature more than the white and shiny paper-covered jars, which reflect heat so it doesn't reach the water.

More Fun

Next time you go out, think about what color clothes to wear. Do you want to stay cool or keep warm?

Learning Points

Did you know that some colors absorb more light than others? Dark objects look dark because they absorb light. The light absorbed is transformed into heat energy so dark colors not only absorb light but they emit heat. Have you ever worn a black T-shirt on a warm day and found it made you very hot? It's better to wear a white T-shirt than a black T-shirt on a sunny day because a white T-shirt reflects light, absorbing less heat. Dark-colored materials absorb the most light and heat up more than other colors.

In the Shadows

Scientific Concept—Light traveling in straight lines

Space is very, very cold: around −455°F (−270°C). This is because space doesn't have an atmosphere, so there's nothing to trap the heat. However, the opposite can be said for the Sun, whose surface burns at 10,000°F (5,600°C). If you were on the side of the Moon with the Sun shining on you, it would feel very hot, as the Moon has no atmosphere to absorb sunlight.

Light travels in straight lines, but can be reflected, absorbed or scattered depending on the material it comes into contact with. Shadows form when something blocks the path of the light. You can make a shadow puppet to demonstrate this.

Materials

+ Scissors
+ Black paper
+ White paper
+ Tracing paper
+ Craft sticks
+ Double-sided tape
+ A sunny day or flashlight

Cut out a rocket shape from each of the paper types and attach them to sticks using double-sided tape to make rocket-shaped shadow puppets.

If it's a sunny day, take the puppets outside and use them to make shadows on the ground. You should find the darkest shadows form from the black rockets as these don't let any light pass through them. The tracing paper will let some light through, but not all, so the shadow won't be as dark. If it's a cloudy day, use the flashlight to act as the Sun making a shadow against the puppets.

More Fun

Can you create a shadow theater and make up a story using the shadow puppets?

Learning Point

Try moving the shadow rockets closer to the ground. This should make the shadows smaller. Shadows will also be smallest at midday when the Sun is highest in the sky.

Space Camp Stargazing

Scientific Concept—Astronomy

You don't need a fancy telescope to see the wonders of the night sky. On a clear night you should be able to see planets, star clusters and if you're very lucky, a shooting star.

- - - - - - - - - - - - - - -

Materials

+ Weather appropriate clothing
+ Blanket
+ Insect repellent, optional
+ Binoculars, optional

You'll need a clear night to try stargazing and preferably a place without much light pollution from other sources.

Make sure you're dressed for the weather, grab a blanket and an adult, and see what you can spot.

Don't forget to give your eyes time to get used to the darkness. Can you draw a map of the night sky and keep a diary of what you can see over a period of a few weeks or months?

More Fun

How many constellations can you spot? Orion is a good one to start with: Look for the three stars of his belt in a row. Online resources can show you the constellations visible to you based on your location and the time of year.

How about setting up a space camp in your backyard with some friends? You could start the day with a solar oven and finish with some stargazing.

Learning Points

Astronomy is the study of space, including stars, planets and galaxies.

Walk the Solar System

Scientific Concept—Measurement

Space is mind-blowingly massive. Did you know that more than 1,300 Earths would fit inside Jupiter, and 1.3 million Earths would fit inside the Sun? To walk the solar system requires a huge scale-down of the distances involved, and even then probably needs to be done outside.

Calculating how far each planet is from the Sun is not an easy task, as the distance changes depending where the planet is in its orbit and the numbers involved are so big. Astronomers sometimes use Astronomical Units (AU) as a measurement. An AU is the distance from the Earth to the Sun.

- - - - - - - - - - - - - - -

Materials

+ Chalk

To begin, scale down the distances involved to a manageable figure. An easy way to do this is to use a scaling factor.

If we multiply each planet's distance from the Sun in AU by 40 inches (100 cm), you get a distance you can walk, although you might want to stop at Saturn unless you have a large space.

Draw the Sun on the ground using chalk and then use your scaled-down measurements (see page 279) to walk to each planet, making a mark for each one.

More Fun

Try using a different scaling factor. How do the numbers change? Can you still walk the solar system easily?

Learning Points

Distances in space are so vast that the measurements we use on Earth don't really work. One AU is about 93 million miles (150 million km)! The Earth is only 24,000 miles (40,000 km) around.

Solar System Distances

- Mercury: 0.4 AU
- Venus: 0.7 AU
- Earth: 1.0 AU
- Mars: 1.5 AU
- Asteroid Belt: 2.8 AU
- Jupiter: 5.2 AU
- Saturn: 9.6 AU
- Uranus: 19.2 AU
- Neptune: 30.0 AU
- Pluto: 39.5 AU

Newton's Cradle

Scientific Concept—Conservation of energy

A Newton's Cradle is a great way to demonstrate the laws of conservation of energy. We're going to use marbles for the balls, but you could also use wooden beads and paint them to match each planet.

When the first ball of the cradle collides with the second, the first ball stops, but its momentum is transferred to the second ball. The same thing happens with each ball until the last one is reached. You should find that the last ball swings up with the same momentum as the first.

- - - - - - - - - - - - -

Materials

+ Craft sticks, wooden frame or cardboard box
+ Hot glue gun and glue
+ String or thread
+ Scissors
+ 5 marbles of the same size
+ Tape

First, create a frame for the cradle. You could use craft sticks, a wooden frame or even a cardboard box. A length of about 6 inches (15 cm) and height of 4 inches (10 cm) works well.

Use a hot glue gun to stick your frame together securely if using a wooden frame. If you use a cardboard box, cut out the sides, top and bottom, leaving just a frame behind.

Cut 10 pieces of string or thread (2 for each marble). These should all be the same length and the same length as the height of your frame.

Attach two pieces of string or thread to opposite sides of the marble using glue, and leave to dry. Using a hot glue gun is a good way to do this (ask an adult to help).

Hang the marbles one by one from the top edges of the frame with one string taped to the top of the right side and one to the left giving you a triangle shape. Each marble needs to touch the marble/s next to it and be at exactly the same height.

Once the marbles are in place, gently pull up the first marble and let go. This should make the marble at the opposite end move, leaving the center three marbles stationary.

More Fun

Can you create a bigger version of your cradle?

Learning Points

While the momentum is transferred between the balls, they won't swing forever as other effects (such as friction) means that the arc of the balls lessens with time and they eventually come to a stop.

Filter Paper Chromatography Planets

Scientific Concept—Chromatography

Chromatography is a technique used to separate mixtures. Did you know the ink in felt tip pens is usually made up of more than one color? We can pass the ink through filter paper to separate the colors out.

As well as being a handy scientific technique, chromatography is great for making colorful pictures, and the way the colors spread and mix is perfect for making planets.

- - - - - - - - - - - - - - - - -

Materials

+ Felt tip pens, selection of washable and permanent
+ Filter paper discs
+ Flat tray
+ Droppers
+ Water

Think about the colors you need to make for each planet. Mars mostly looks red, while Jupiter is a mixture of yellow, red, brown and white.

Decide which planet to try first and draw lots of different colored dots on a piece of filter paper. Put the filter paper on a waterproof tray and carefully drip a few drops of water onto each colored dot and watch as the colors spread.

You'll need to hang your filter paper up to dry because if you leave it in a wet tray all the color will eventually leach out.

More Fun

Can you use the same technique to make moons for the planets? Which color felt tips could you use for this?

Learning Points

Mars was named after the Roman god of war because of its red color. Jupiter's Great Red Spot is a huge storm that has been raging away for hundreds of years.

*See photo insert page 30.

Revolving Solar System

Scientific Concepts—Solar system, orbits

Our solar system is just a small part of the vast expanse of space. All of the planets in our solar system move around the Sun in a path called an orbit. They are held in orbit by gravity. The time taken for each planet to spin once is called a day and the time taken for each to complete one orbit of the Sun is a year. Days and years are different lengths for each planet as they spin at different rates and have different length orbits.

To build a model of the solar system, you'll need colored cardstock cut into planet shapes, strips of black cardstock cut into different lengths, split pins and tape.

- - - - - - - - - - - - - - - - -

Materials

+ Scissors
+ Colored cardstock
+ Black strips of cardstock
+ Split paper fasteners or cotter pins
+ Double-sided tape

Decide which planets you're going to include in your model. Are you feeling brave enough to try all of them? Cut out a circle to represent each planet. Think about their size relative to each other. For example, the inner planets are much smaller than the outer planets. Remember we said that 1.3 million Earths would fit inside the Sun and 764 Earths would fit inside Saturn?

You'll also need a cutout of the Sun to go in the center.

Take a small black strip of cardstock and attach one end to the center of your Sun with a split pin. Use double-sided tape to attach Mercury to the opposite end. You should be able to move Mercury in orbit around the Sun. Do the same for each planet in order of how far they are from the Sun to build up the model.

More Fun

Can you add a Moon to orbit the Earth? It might be hard to add Jupiter's many moons, but you could add two to Mars. Phobos is larger than Deimos and closer to the surface.

Learning Point

It is the powerful pull of gravity from the Sun that keeps planets and other objects in the solar system in orbit around it.

Constellation Dot-to-Dots

Scientific Concept—Constellations

A constellation is a group of stars that form a shape and have a name. For example, Ursa Major is in the shape of a bear and the seven brightest stars in the northern sky look a bit like a saucepan. This saucepan is sometimes called the Big Dipper.

We can make constellations using glitter glue or star stickers on black cardstock and then join the dots to see the shape.

Materials

+ Glitter glue pen or star stickers
+ Black cardstock
+ Silver pen

Decide which constellation you'd like to create. The Big Dipper, Cepheus and Canis Major are all nice easy shapes.

Use a glitter glue pen or star stickers to mark out each constellation on black cardstock and then connect the stars together using a silver pen.

Create several constellation pictures and ask a friend to try to join the dots and guess what the constellation looks like.

More Fun

Can you make a matching card game, where one card is the star shape and one a picture representing the constellation? You could mix up the cards, turn them all over and take turns to find the matching star shape and constellation.

Learning Points

Constellations are arrangements of stars representing objects, animals and mythical creatures. Different constellations can be seen in the sky throughout the year, and depend on which hemisphere you live in. This is because of the movement of the Earth as it orbits the Sun.

Space Probe

Scientific Concept—Survival in space

A space probe is a craft that travels through space gathering information and sending it back to Earth. Space probes can be sent into space to orbit or even land on a planet. Space probes don't have people on them and are not usually designed to return to Earth.

Depending on where it is traveling, a space probe must be able to cope with extreme hot or cold temperatures. Can you design a space probe with features to protect it from the heat or cold?

- - - - - - - - - - - - - - -

Materials

+ Insulating materials (cotton wool, bubble wrap)
+ Materials to reflect heat (aluminum foil)
+ Cardboard boxes
+ Cardboard tubes

For this activity, think about the type of materials that absorb or reflect heat. Remember dark materials absorb light, which is transformed into heat energy, while white materials reflect light and absorb less heat. Can you design a model of a space probe using both insulating and heat-reflecting materials?

Space probes often have solar panels to convert energy from the Sun into electricity as well as a propulsion module and antenna for communication. Can you add these into your design?

If you could choose anywhere in our solar system, where would you send your probe? If you're sending your probe to a hot planet, think about how you would protect it from the extreme cold of space and high temperatures on the surface of the planet.

More Fun

Think about what a picture of Mars would look like taken from a space probe. Can you draw how you think it would look?

Spin Art Galaxies

Scientific Concept—Gravity, galaxies

A galaxy is a gigantic group of stars, gas and dust held together by gravity. Our solar system is part of a spiral-shaped galaxy called the Milky Way. The next nearest galaxy to us is the Andromeda galaxy, which is also a spiral. Lenticular galaxies are flat with a central bulge, elliptical galaxies are round and galaxies with no particular shape are called irregular.

Did you know you can use a salad spinner to create a fun galaxy picture? You'll need some black paper or cardstock, paint and glitter.

- - - - - - - - - - - - - - -

Materials

+ Black cardstock or paper
+ Salad spinner that you no longer need to use for food
+ Paint
+ Glitter

Cut the black cardstock to a size that fits neatly inside the salad spinner bowl.

Think about what color you'd like your galaxy picture to be. Squirt paint of those colors onto the card inside the salad spinner. Add a bit of glitter for extra sparkle.

When you're ready to make the spin art, put the lid on the salad spinner and spin for about 30 seconds. Open up the spinner and check the picture. If you think it needs more of a spin, do it again. Try making one picture by spinning the spinner slowly and another by spinning it quickly. What do you notice?

Do your pictures look like any particular type of galaxy?

More Fun

Can you mark some constellations on your spin art pictures?

*See photo insert page 30.

Popping Planets

Scientific Concepts—Forces, gravity, trajectory

This fun activity is another demonstration of forces causing motion. If you pull back on the balloon part of the popper and let go, the force of the balloon makes the ping pong balls fly through the air. You can try pulling the balloon farther and farther back to investigate how increasing the force affects the flight of the balls.

- - - - - - - - - - - - - -

Materials

+ Table tennis balls or pom-poms
+ Permanent pens, felt tip pens or paint
+ Scissors
+ Plastic or paper cup
+ Balloon
+ Double-sided tape

Decorate the balls to look like planets using the pens. Once you've finished the planets, you need to make the popping device.

Cut the bottom off the cup and then cut the end (not the part you blow into) of a balloon. Tie the end of the balloon you would blow into and push the open end over the bottom of your cup. You might need to use some tape to attach the balloon.

Pop a ball planet or pom-pom inside the shooter, pull back the balloon and watch the planet fly.

Try changing the angle, adding more than one ball and using different amounts of force to see how the flights change.

More Fun

What do you think will happen if you use smaller, lighter balls? Will they travel farther?

Learning Points

If you pull back the balloon end farther, the pom-poms or balls should travel farther as a greater force acts to push them forward.

*See photo insert page 30.

Where Is Space?

Scientific Concept—Earth's atmosphere

An atmosphere is a mixture of gases surrounding a planet. The atmosphere of the Earth consists mostly of nitrogen and oxygen. It helps protect the Earth from radiation as well as to absorb heat from the Sun, allowing the Earth to maintain a stable temperature. We couldn't survive on Earth without the protection from radiation and sunlight we get from the atmosphere.

There are five layers within the Earth's atmosphere. The Troposphere contains most of the air and oxygen we need to survive, and weather is formed in this layer.

The Exosphere is the final layer of the atmosphere, which extends into space.

- - - - - - - - - - - - - -

Materials

+ Honey
+ Corn syrup
+ Dish soap
+ Water
+ Vegetable oil
+ Large, narrow jar
+ Sticky labels
+ Pen

(continued)

Pour the substances in the jar one by one in the order they are listed—honey, corn syrup, dish soap, water and vegetable oil. Remember to pour slowly and carefully. The liquids stack on top of each other because they have different densities.

Try not to let the thicker liquids touch the sides of the jar as they will stick, and it will look messy, but sometimes it helps to pour the thinner liquids down the side so they don't damage the lower layers.

Can you fill the first three layers to scale and label them using the sticky labels? You'll have to adjust this depending on the size of your jar, but 1/16 inch (1 mm) to 1 mile (1 km) are good starting points.

More Fun
Can you find an object to float on each layer?

Learning Points
Each of the liquids has a different mass of molecules or different numbers of parts squashed into the same volume of liquid. This gives them different densities allowing one to sit on top of the other—the more dense a liquid is the heavier it is.

Earth's Atmosphere
- Troposphere: 5 to 9 miles (8 to 14.5 km)
- Stratosphere: 9 to 31 miles (14.5 to 50 km)
- Mesosphere: 31 to 53 miles (50 to 85 km)
- Thermosphere: 53 to 372 miles (85 to 600 km)
- Exosphere: 372 to 6,200 miles (600 to 10,000 km)

Balloon-Powered Moon Buggy
Scientific Concept—Newton's Third Law

The surface of the Moon varies considerably. Some areas are flat, some sloped; there are also rocky areas and lots of craters.

A moon buggy must to be able to cope with tricky terrain to survive on the Moon.

This balloon-powered moon buggy is another example of Newton's Third Law (page 252), as air rushes out of the balloon backward but the reaction force pushes the balloon forward.

- - - - - - - - - - - - -

Materials
+ Scissors
+ Straws
+ Axles
+ Wheels (jar lids, CDs)
+ Something for the body of your car (sheet of cardstock, cardboard box, bottle)
+ Tape
+ Small rubber band
+ Balloon

This balloon can be used to power a small vehicle.

Think how you're going to construct your moon buggy. You'll need a chassis, wheels and axles to start with. Cut two straws so they are about 5/8 inch (15 mm) shorter than the axles and push the axles inside the straws. Attach wheels to the end of each axle. The straw must be able to move freely around the axle.

Cut a piece of cardstock or a cardboard box so it is narrower than the axles and attach them together by taping over the straws.

Once you've built the frame, use a small rubber band to attach a balloon to the end of a straw. You then need to tape the straw to the top of the moon buggy. Blow the balloon up by blowing into the straw, place the buggy on the floor, let go and watch it move. If it doesn't work, it might be too heavy, so try to make it lighter.

Of course a balloon-powered moon buggy wouldn't work on the Moon, but can you think of another way to power a moon buggy? How about using the power of the Sun?

More Fun

Think about what else a moon buggy needs: maybe a scoop to collect samples, seats for the astronauts and strong, tough wheels?

What could you add to the wheels to allow them to move over ice without slipping?

Learning Points

If you blow up a balloon and let it go, air escapes from the balloon so quickly the balloon flies around until it runs out of air. When you blow into the balloon, you increase the air pressure inside which makes the balloon material stretch outward. If you let go of the balloon without sealing the end, the energy in the stretched balloon (potential energy) forces air out backward but a reaction force pushes the balloon forward.

How Dense?

Scientific Concept—Density

Stars start their life in a giant cloud of dust, called a nebula. Once a star is formed, it usually burns energy for billions of years. At the end of its life, a star collapses to become a white dwarf star. Larger stars create a huge nuclear explosion called a supernova and then become either a black hole or a neutron star. Neutron stars are tiny, but extremely dense.

This activity shows how different liquids and objects can have different densities.

Materials

+ Plastic jar or bottle with a lid
+ Oil
+ Water
+ Food coloring
+ Glitter
+ Pipette

We can learn about several concepts with a density jar. First, think about what will happen when you add oil and water to the jar. Will the two substances mix? Add them both and find out. Try shaking the jar, what happens?

Oil and water don't ever mix, because water is a polar molecule. It has a positive charge on one end and a negative charge on the other. Water molecules are attracted to each other as the positive end of one water molecule is attracted to the negative end of another water molecule. Oil is nonpolar and so not attracted to the water, meaning the two never mix.

The oil rests on top of the water because it is less dense. Can you think of a denser liquid that would sit under the water? How about molasses or honey?

Try adding some food coloring and glitter to the water layer. Using the pipette, can you make a sparkly star in the jar?

More Fun

What do you think will happen if you add an effervescent heartburn or vitamin tablet to your density jar?

Learning Points

Density refers to how much mass there is in a space. Imagine an empty drawer. If you add five T-shirts the drawer has a certain density, if you add another five T-shirts the density of the drawer increases because the mass has increased but the size of the space in the drawer (volume) has stayed the same.

Playdough Earth Layers

Scientific Concept—Layers of the Earth

Did you know that at the center of the Earth (inner core) is a huge, incredibly hot metal ball? It's made up mostly of iron and is solid only because of the massive amount of pressure the outer layers place on it.

The outer core is liquid and also made of metals. It's this layer that creates the Earth's magnetic field.

The lower mantle is made of rock. It's so hot that the rock should be molten, but like the inner core, the immense amount of pressure makes it solid.

The upper mantle is made of both solid and liquid rock. It becomes less liquid closer to the surface of the Earth where the temperature is cooler.

The crust of the Earth is the top and thinnest layer. Continental crust refers to land and oceanic crust is below the ocean.

Materials

+ Five different colors of playdough (page 72)
+ Marble or other small ball

Your challenge is to create a model of the five layers of the Earth using playdough and a marble or small ball. The easiest way to do this is to use a ball for the inner core and build the layers around it.

Once you've finished, cut a section out so all the layers can be seen.

More Fun

Can you do the same for one of the other inner planets?

*See photo insert page 30.

Mercury and Magnets

Scientific Concepts—Magnetism, how craters form

Mercury is the closest planet to the Sun and the smallest planet in our solar system.

Mercury spins very slowly, so although it is the closest planet to the Sun, the side facing away from the Sun is very cold. It also has no atmosphere to retain heat and no water, making it very unfriendly for humans.

Like the Earth, Mercury has a magnetic field, although it is much weaker than that of the Earth.

Materials

+ 10 small squares of felt
+ 2 strong magnets

Magnets attract other magnets and some metals (iron and metals that contain iron). The area over which they attract each other is called a magnetic field. You can test to see how strong a magnet's magnetic field is by putting objects between two magnets.

Start by putting one felt square between two magnets—the magnets are probably still attracted to each other. Keep adding the squares of felt one by one until the magnets no longer attract each other.

More Fun

Mercury is also covered in craters. Try dropping different size balls into a small layer of sand from different heights to see how the crater size differs.

Mars and Its Moons

Scientific Concept—Mars

Mars has two small moons called Phobos and Deimos. Both are odd, irregular shapes that look more like asteroids than a moon. Phobos is the closest to Mars and shaped a bit like a potato; it's very dark and covered in craters.

Materials

+ Red, gray and black playdough (recipe on page 72)

Use the playdough to create a model of Mars and its two moons. Phobos is about five times the mass of Deimos, and both have a lot of craters.

More Fun

Can you make a list of the things you'd need for a trip to Mars? Remember, Mars has a very thin atmosphere and almost all the air is carbon dioxide, so don't forget to take your own oxygen! It's also very cold, so pack a big, thick coat!

Learning Points

Mars is the only one of the inner planets to have more than one moon. Phobos and Deimos are the sons of the Greek god of war Ares, who was known as Mars to the Romans.

Olympus Mons

Scientific Concept—Volcanoes

Mars is the fourth planet from the Sun and the second smallest. It can be seen from the Earth as a small, red disc.

Did you know Mars is home to the biggest planetary volcano in our solar system? Olympus Mons is almost three times as tall as Mount Everest!

Olympus Mons hasn't erupted in millions of years, but you can make your own eruption using a couple of household ingredients.

Materials

+ Small empty container or water bottle
+ Sand and small stones
+ Plastic wrap, optional, but does save the sand from getting too messy
+ 2 tsp (8.5 g) baking soda
+ 1 tsp dish soap
+ A few drops of red and yellow food coloring
+ 2 tbsp (30 ml) vinegar

Make a volcano shape around the water bottle using the sand and stones. Olympus Mons is a shield volcano, which means it was created by lava flowing slowly down the sides, giving it a short, squat appearance. Carefully build up a volcano shape around your water bottle; it should be slightly sloping like Olympus Mons. If you want to really make your volcano look like Olympus Mons, mold a cliff around the outer edge.

If you want to erupt the volcano more than a couple of times without it going soggy, you can cover it with plastic wrap.

(continued)

For the eruption, first add the baking soda, dish soap and food coloring to the water bottle. When you're ready, pour in the vinegar and watch the lava flow. If it's a bit slow, add some more dish soap and vinegar, or give it a good stir.

More Fun

Olympus Mons has several collapsed craters at its summit, which stretches a massive 50 miles (80 km) across. Give your sand and stone volcano a flat summit and watch how your lava flows over it.

Learning Points

Vinegar (an acid) and baking soda (an alkali) react together to neutralize each other. This reaction releases carbon dioxide, which creates bubbles. These bubbles make the dish soap foam up to give the appearance of lava erupting from a volcano.

Red Martian Sand

Scientific Concept—Chemical reactions

Most of the surface of Mars is a hot, rocky, dusty desert with canyons, craters, plains and volcanoes. When you look at a photo of Mars, the ground looks red. This is because of iron in the soil rusting.

This activity investigates the conditions needed for metals to rust. Good metals to test are iron and steel, which do rust. Aluminum isn't a good metal to test as it doesn't rust easily (it's coated in aluminum oxide, which protects it from corrosion).

- - - - - - - - - - - - - -

Materials

+ Iron nails (bright, not galvanized)
+ Test tubes or small containers
+ Water
+ Vegetable oil
+ Steel paper clips
+ Steel paper clip covered in plastic, or steel wool

You can design this investigation in lots of different ways, but sample test conditions could be:

- Iron nail in air
- Iron nail fully submerged in water
- Iron nail half in water
- Iron nail fully submerged in water with a coating of vegetable oil on the top (this stops air getting to the nail).

Label the test tubes or small containers for each condition you want to test. Place a nail into each test tube and add water and vegetable oil for the conditions where they are needed.

Each condition can be repeated using a steel paper clip and/or a paper clip covered in plastic.

Once you've set up your conditions, watch how they change over a few days noting down if and when each starts to rust.

More Fun

To add an extra condition to your investigation, add salt to water and compare this to water alone. You should find that salt speeds up the rusting process.

Learning Points

Rust is formed when iron comes into contact with water and oxygen. When iron reacts with oxygen it forms iron oxide, which we call rust. This is an example of an irreversible reaction, which means it's a permanent change. It can't be reversed.

Give Saturn a Bath

Scientific Concept—Density

Saturn is the second largest planet in our solar system, but it's less dense than water, which means it would float if we had a tub of water big enough! Can you imagine a giant planet floating in an even more gigantic bathtub of water?

If something is buoyant, it floats in water. For this activity, you'll need a ball that floats and a ball that sinks. For an object to float, it must be less dense than the water.

Materials

+ Different balls to test
+ Tub of water
+ Bubble wrap

Check that you have a ball that sinks and one that floats by testing your balls to see if they float in your tub of water.

Wrap a layer of bubble wrap around the ball that sinks; does it float? If it doesn't float add another layer and try again.

More Fun

Lemons float on water—how do you think you could get a lemon to sink?

Hint—try removing the skin. Like bubble wrap, lemon skin is full of air, which reduces the density of the lemon, allowing it float.

Can you think of any other fruits with the same type of skin?

Learning Points

The bubble wrap makes the ball weigh a little more, but also displaces more water making the ball more buoyant. Bubble wrap is full of air pockets, meaning that it isn't very dense. The bubble wrap and ball together are less dense than the water and therefore float.

Lava Flows on Venus

Scientific Concept—Viscosity

Venus is the hottest planet in the solar system because its very dense atmosphere traps heat. Venus also has lots of volcanoes and much of the surface is covered with lava flows. Did you know the surface of Venus is covered with strange-shaped structures formed from solidified lava?

How far and fast a lava flow travels depends on its viscosity. High-viscosity lava will flow slowly and only cover a small area, whereas low-viscosity lava flows faster and can cover a much bigger area.

This activity investigates the viscosity of different liquids. Which do you think will travel faster, water or honey? Why do you think this is?

Materials

+ Warm water and towel
+ A small or large ramp (this could be a cutting board, mini white board or large sheet of cardboard)
+ Box or books to hold the ramp in place
+ Pen and paper
+ Substances to test (ketchup, honey, sugar syrup, water, ice cream, syrup)
+ Small containers
+ Timer

A viscosity race can get a little sticky so it might be handy to have some warm water and a towel nearby to wash little hands.

Set up your ramp by leaning it against a box or stack of books—think about how steep you want it to be. You don't want the liquids to flow too fast or too slowly, and remember they should all be tested with the ramp at the same slope.

(continued)

Draw a start and finish line on your ramp; you're going to time how long each liquid takes to travel between the two lines. Which liquid do you think will be fastest (least viscous)? Why do you think this is?

Pour the same amount of each liquid into a small container and get ready to test them. If you have enough helpers you could start all the liquids off at the same time, or test one at a time.

Pour each liquid onto the ramp at the start line and start the timer. Remember to record the time when each reaches the finish line.

Which liquid is the most viscous? Was it the one you expected?

More Fun
How could you make a viscous liquid less viscous? Think about what you could add to it to make it flow more easily.

Learning Points
Viscosity is a measure of a fluid's resistance to flow. Thicker liquids have a higher viscosity as there is a lot of internal friction, which slows down the flow of the liquid as it moves. The viscosity of lava depends on its temperature and chemical content.

Stormy Jupiter
Scientific Concept—Weather

Jupiter is a huge gas giant, made up mostly of hydrogen and helium gases. Did you know Jupiter is so big that all the other planets in the solar system could fit inside it?

If you have seen a picture of Jupiter, you probably noticed its Great Red Spot, which is actually a huge storm about 25,000 miles (40,000 km) wide.

You can easily create a model of a storm using just an empty bottle, water, dish soap and glitter.

– – – – – – – – – – – – – – –

Materials
+ Jar or empty water bottle with a lid
+ Water
+ Dish soap
+ Glitter

This super simple model of a storm looks really impressive. All you need to do is fill your jar almost up to the top with water and squirt in some dish soap and a little glitter.

Remember to replace the lid tightly and then swirl the jar around in a circular motion for a few seconds. When you stop, you should see a storm inside the jar! You can do this again and again once the storm settles.

More Fun
Can you find an object small and light enough to swirl around your storm?

Learning Points
When the jar is swirled the liquid inside forms a circular motion, called a vortex, which looks like a tornado.

Windy Neptune

Scientific Concept—Wind, weather

Neptune is a dark, cold gas giant with wild winds that can reach up to 1,500 miles (2,414 km) per hour, making them the strongest in the solar system.

Here on Earth a windsock (a bit like a kite) can be used to work out which way wind is blowing. If there were a windsock on Neptune, it would be flying around in all directions.

You can easily make a windsock using a paper cup and ribbons.

- - - - - - - - - - - - - -

Materials

+ Ribbons of different colors and sizes
+ Paper cup
+ Scissors
+ Double-sided tape
+ Tape

A windsock is a great way to see how air moves in the wind. First you need to think about how to attach the ribbons to the paper cup. You could make holes and tie the ribbons to the cup (ask an adult to help), or place double-sided tape inside the cup edge and attach ribbons to that.

Once you've decided how to attach your ribbons, spread them out along the inside edge of the cup. The ribbons should be long enough to blow easily in the wind. You'll need to attach an extra ribbon to the top of the windsock so you can hold it or attach it to something outside. To do this, carefully make a hole in the bottom part of the cup (ask an adult to help), then thread a piece of ribbon through the hole and tape it securely to the inside.

If it's a windy day, tie your windsock up outside and watch the ribbons blow around. If it's not windy, try running around with your windsock; you should find that the ribbons wave around in the wind. Can you tell which way the wind is blowing by looking at the windsock?

More Fun
Make a paper airplane with wide wings so they catch the wind. Try throwing it outside. What happens?

Rolling Uranus

Scientific Concept—The unusual orientation of Uranus

Uranus is a bitterly cold, windy planet, with many moons and faint rings. Uranus is unusual as it's tilted on its side. The Earth is slightly tilted but not nearly as much as Uranus. Imagine Uranus rolling like a ball as it orbits the Sun while the other planets spin like spinning tops. This means Uranus's north and south poles alternate between direct sunlight and complete darkness.

Uranus is slightly larger than Neptune, but smaller in mass. It looks to be a green-blue color because there is a lot of methane gas in the atmosphere.

This activity demonstrates the unusual spin of Uranus.

- - - - - - - - - - - - - -

Materials

+ Modeling clay
+ Skewers

(continued)

First you need to make your planets and the Sun. Use yellow clay for the Sun, green for Uranus and then pick another planet to model. It doesn't matter which you choose as only Uranus spins on its side.

Think about how big each planet should be. Remember Uranus is one of the giant planets, so if you choose to model one of the inner planets they will be much smaller if you want to make them very slightly to scale.

Once you're happy with your planets, carefully place a skewer into each one. Use the skewer to make your second planet rotate around. Remember the time it takes a planet to make one complete rotation is a day and the time taken to orbit around the Sun is a year.

Think how you can model the spin of Uranus. Try turning the skewer onto its side.

More Fun

Try adding other planets to your model—can you place them in order around the Sun on a piece of black cardstock?

Part Four

BACKYARD ACTIVITIES

(fifteen)

BEETLES, BUGS AND MORE

Do you like catching butterflies in the yard? Or do you prefer ladybugs or spiders? Maybe you like them all . . . I know I do! Entomology is the study of insects, and most entomologists specialize in one type of insect or arachnid.

This chapter is my favorite (shhh! don't tell anyone!) because you get to catch *real* bugs, worms, insects and larvae to observe and experiment with. It's seriously cool to feel the scratchy feet of a bess bug as it walks up your arm, or the cool sliminess of a worm flopping around in the palm of your hand.

To be sure that you keep them safe—whether you're outside checking out roly poly bugs, worms, butterflies or caterpillars—you need to have gentle tools to catch and keep them.

When you're making ground traps like the one on page 297, or finding roly poly bugs to observe and experiment with, it's important to be careful with them.

When you play, experiment and explore with nature, you need to be a good steward, and keep living things safe. Respect them and their natural habitats, and you'll be able to enjoy them for a long, long time.

Super Simple Bug Boxes

Great backyard explorers get to know the plants and animals they're studying by observing them closely. You'll need to catch critters and dig things up. And you'll need places to keep them temporarily, when they're not crawling up and down your arm!

There are lots of different bug boxes available in stores everywhere. My kids pick out several little plastic bug boxes from the discount store every spring. But we also love making our own from recyclables around the house—take a look in your recycle bin and see what YOU can repurpose to be a great bug house!

- - - - - - - - - - - - - -

Materials

+ Small containers, such as plastic berry crates, canning jars with lids and glass pickle or sauce jars
+ Colored duct tape
+ A nail, awl, craft knife or another sharp tool

The plastic containers that blueberries and strawberries come in can make great homes for little backyard creatures. Simply snap them closed and seal the edges with decorated duct tape!

Then, have an adult help you cut a rectangle-shaped opening in the top with a nail, awl, craft knife or other sharp tool so you can put your bug into their fantastically cool temporary home. You can use more duct tape to make a hinge on the plastic rectangle you cut out, so you can open and close the bug box easily. It's like a bug palace!

For a simpler bug home, have a grown-up drill holes in the lids of leftover food jars. Clean them out really well, get outside and find a critter, put some dirt and plants in the bottom, and let your bug friend enjoy its new digs.

More Fun

Make a portable bug box necklace. The next time you go to the grocery store with your parents, get something out of one of the toy vending machines for a quarter or two, and save the plastic container. Have an adult drill small air holes in the lid, and a bigger hole in the middle of it. Tie a necklace cord with a big knot through the middle hole. Put a little ladybug friend in the toy container and snap the lid on. Wear your friend around on your adventures for a day, then let it go free in the evening. Maybe you can even write a story about your little bug friend's adventures in your nature journal (page 343) to remember the day you had together!

The Best Bug Net Ever

You have boxes and containers, but some of those quicker critters might be a bit more challenging for you to catch. Have you ever tried to catch a butterfly with just your hands? Not too easy, is it? A net can help.

It's super easy to make the perfect bug catching net at home with things you likely already have on hand. You may need to run to the store with an adult to grab an embroidery hoop. But those are inexpensive and easy to find.

Ready? Let's get started!

- - - - - - - - - - - - - -

Materials

+ Small embroidery hoop (wooden or plastic)
+ Mesh produce bag or leftover fabric (tulle or muslin works best)
+ Scissors (optional)
+ Craft wire
+ Stick or wooden dowel
+ Duct tape

Got your materials? Great. Now head outside to your backyard. Let's go!

First, loosen the screw on the small embroidery hoop and slide out the smaller ring. Simple—now you've got two rings. Take the produce bag or fabric (we used tulle we had left over from a costume we once made) and wrap the ends over the small ring.

Slip the small, fabric or bag covered ring back into the outer ring and tighten up the screw. The fabric should form a pouch now, with the embroidery hoop holding it open. It's a net with no handle! You're almost there! If there is any excess fabric or mesh hanging over the edge once it's tightened, feel free to trim it close with a pair of scissors.

Use the colored wire to attach the stick or dowel to your net tightly. We wrapped ours around the hoop, poking it through the holes in the tulle, then around and down along the stick. It holds well (and lasts longer) if you extend down the stick a bit with the wire.

Finally, use the duct tape to cover up any sharp points sticking out, and to cover the wire completely. Since we used decorative duct tape, we wrapped ours all the way down the handle of our bug net. We love how it turned out!

You're all set to catch flying insects like butterflies without using your hands! Head outside and have fun!

The Easiest Ground Bug Trap You'll Ever Make

Catching butterflies and other flying insects is a lot of fun, but there are so many cool creatures creeping around your yard, too. What about the ones near the ground? Or the ones that come out at night?

Capturing worms, centipedes and other ground creatures is easy with this trap made out of recyclables. And it's the perfect addition to your outdoor bug collecting kit!

– – – – – – – – – – – – – – – – – –

Materials

+ Small plastic cup or yogurt container without a lid
+ Larger plastic container or carton without a lid
+ Trowel or small shovel
+ Scissors
+ Large stone
+ Your nature journal (page 343)
+ Super Simple Bug Box (page 296)

Before doing this activity, check with your parents. You'll need to dig a small hole in the yard or garden—or even under a bush—so you can catch insects overnight. It only needs to be big enough to fit the small container, and you can fill it back in once you've caught some bugs, but you should get permission first.

Once you're ready, clean and dry both the large and small containers really well.

Dig that hole we chatted about—and the one you already got permission to dig—and drop the small cup or yogurt container into it so that the container's opening is level with the ground.

(continued)

Pack the dirt tightly around it.

Now, you're going to use the larger container to protect the smaller one in case it rains. It'll be a cover for the smaller container, but you still need insects to be able to fall into the hole you dug. To make sure they can get in, but the hole stays protected, cut doors into the top lip of the larger container. When you flip the container upside down over the smaller one, the doors will give insects easy access to the trap.

Got that? Great! Now, put a stone on top of the roof to weigh it down, and leave it alone until the next day.

I know . . . waiting is always the toughest part. While you're waiting, you can draw a picture in your nature journal of what your trap looks like before any bugs fall in.

In the morning, head out to the backyard to see if any new friends decided to drop by for a visit. Scoop them into your bug box, or create a habitat for them so you can observe or try some of the activities in this chapter with them. When you check your bug trap, make sure you take a minute to identify the bugs you caught. Use an insect field guide or the Internet to figure out the identification of any unfamiliar bugs to make sure they are all safe to handle. If there are any that you can't identify, let them go without touching them. You don't want to take a chance that an unfamiliar insect could harm you. Only experiment with familiar bugs.

Make sure that you put the little creepy-crawlies back where they belong once you're done observing them.

FUN FACT

Instead of closed circulatory systems like humans, insects have an open system where their "blood," called hemolymph, flows through the body cavity, bathing the organs. Hemolymph is usually clear, but can be yellow or greenish too. The heart is chambered and runs along an insect's back, sending the hemolymph up towards the head, then sloshing back into the body. Can you imagine that? It probably feels strange to have all that fluid sloshing around inside one's body. When you catch some insects in your ground trap, hold them up to the light to see if you can observe evidence of their circulatory systems in action.

Cool Critter Choice Container

When you're testing an animal's behavior, you need to use a testing vessel that gives the animal a way to get from one choice to another.

While exploring roly poly bugs, you're going to test their preferences between several different opposite choices (light/dark, wet/dry, sweet/salty, etc.). This cool critter choice container makes choosing their favorites easy for your crustacean friends!

It's going to be so much fun!

Materials

+ Toilet paper or paper towel roll
+ Two same-sized clear plastic containers or cups
+ Marker
+ Scissors
+ Electrical, duct or masking tape

Put the tube against the side of one of the cups, as near to the bottom as you can, and trace around it with the marker. Do that again on the other cup. Get an adult to help you use the scissors to cut out each of the circles, making a tube-sized hole in each cup.

Tape the tube between the openings, joining the two cups together. Seal the openings completely by taping both the inside and the outside.

Now your roly poly bugs—and any critters you catch for the activities in this book—will be able to travel from one cup to the other through the tube. Get ready to try out some experiments now! You're going to love this next part!

FUN FACT

Roly poly mamas carry their eggs around with them in a special pouch called a marsupium. When they first hatch, roly poly babies hang out in the pouch for a few days before heading out into the world to explore. That's one of the reasons it's so important to put your roly poly bugs back exactly where you found them when you're done observing them—they want to be with their family just like you do!

Wet Bugs, Dry Bugs

What do you think? Will the roly poly bugs prefer the side of the container that has the damp paper towel? Or will they prefer the dry side? In this simple experiment, you'll test your hypothesis—or scientific guess—and see what happens when you give roly poly bugs a choice.

So, grab your roly poly bugs and head out in the yard with your choice container, find a cozy spot in the grass and see what they do!

- - - - - - - - - - - - -

Materials

+ Your Cool Critter Choice Container (page 298)
+ Paper towel
+ Spray bottle of water
+ Your nature journal (page 343)

Do you have a table in your yard? We love doing these activities on the picnic table or sprawling down on the grass. Remember to get outside and build your brain!

Get your choice container ready for the experiment. Put a paper towel flat on the bottom of one side of the container and mist it with the spray bottle so that it is damp. Leave the other side dry.

Do you remember what a hypothesis is? It's an educated guess, basically. Scientists have an idea about what's going to happen when they try out an experiment, so they write it down then see what really happens. They use their results to design new and better hypotheses and experiments, learning more and more about their world.

You can too!

Which side do you think your roly poly bugs will prefer? Make your hypothesis by writing (or drawing) it in your nature journal.

Set half of your roly poly bugs in the wet side of the container and the other half in the dry side.

Watch your roly poly bugs. What are they doing? Jot down what you're seeing so you can look back in your nature journal later and remember the experiment.

To give them a chance to show you which conditions they really prefer, leave them alone for five minutes. Take a look at the clock, and write down the time you got started.

(continued)

While you're waiting for your five minutes to go by, make a simple chart in your nature journal. Have three columns and seven rows. In the top box of the first column write Time Elapsed. In the top box of the second column write Wet. Write Dry in the top box of the third column. Under the Time Elapsed column, write 5 Minutes, 10 Minutes, 15 Minutes, 20 Minutes, 25 Minutes and 30 Minutes. It will look like this:

Time Elapsed	Wet	Dry
5 Minutes		
10 Minutes		
15 Minutes		
20 Minutes		
25 Minutes		
30 Minutes		

Once five minutes have passed, check to see how many roly poly bugs are in each side of the choice container. Write the number under the correct column. Recheck the choice container every five minutes for a half an hour to give your roly poly bugs enough time to explore.

Once a half an hour has elapsed, write down your final count and then look over the results. Was your hypothesis correct? Why do you think this was the case? What surprised you? Write down and sketch your observations and conclusions. Then transfer your roly poly bugs back into their holding container to rest up for the next activity. Even crustaceans need a break!

More Fun

If you want something fun to do while you wait, and if you're the dancing type, my kids love the song "Roly Poly" by Roger Day. You can listen to it on YouTube and dance around while the roly poly bugs make their choices.

Light Bugs, Dark Bugs

You've had the chance to check out how the roly poly bugs behave when given one choice—how do you think they'll behave this time? Will they prefer the dark side or the light side? I can't wait to find out! Let's get to it!

– – – – – – – – – – – – – – –

Materials

+ Your Cool Critter Choice Container (page 298)
+ Dark-colored paper
+ Tape
+ Your nature journal (page 343)

You're going to set up your experiment in the same way you did with experiment one from page 299, except instead of putting a damp paper towel inside of the choice container, you'll completely cover all but the bottom of one of the sides with your dark-colored paper and tape. The idea is to make one side open to the light and the other dark. You'll need to leave a part of the paper open until you put your roly poly bugs in.

On a new page in your nature journal, record your hypothesis for this experiment. Will the roly poly bugs prefer the dark side or the light side of the choice container?

Then, make a similar table to the one in the left column, but instead of labeling the columns Wet and Dry, you'll label them Dark and Light. Follow the same steps you did before—checking and recording every five minutes, and then drawing your conclusion.

Time Elapsed	Dark	Light
5 Minutes		
10 Minutes		
15 Minutes		
20 Minutes		
25 Minutes		
30 Minutes		

What happened? Why? Based on what you learned in experiments one and two together, what can you conclude about a roly poly bug's preferred habitat? Hint: think, too, about where you found them in your yard.

Roly poly bugs like habitats that are dark and damp, which is why the underside of a log or stone is perfect for them. You can find roly poly bugs around the world in grasslands, forests, rainforests—anywhere that's damp. They need to stay moist because they breathe through gill-like membranes at the base of their abdomens.

Female roly poly bugs hold up to two dozen eggs in a liquid-filled brood pouch until they're ready to hatch. Can you imagine having one or two dozen eggs sloshing around in a pouch attached to you? Strange!

Once the babies hatch, both the female and the male roly poly bugs raise their family together, often living out their lives in the burrow, only leaving to scout for food.

The whole family works hard to gather food and to clean out their waste to keep their burrow clean. Do you help YOUR parents keep your house clean like a good roly poly does? Next time you do your chores, tell your mom that you're just being a good roly poly!

Busy, Busy Ants

Usually scouts from ant colonies will head out to hunt for food, and then head back to the colony to tell others. They leave a scent trail of pheromones to mark the path back to the food source so they can find their way back and lead others along the path.

Sometimes it's fun to see if you can confuse the critters that do their work in your yard. If ants leave pheromone trails to find their way between home and food, what might happen if they suddenly can't find their original trail? It's time to play around with an ant family to find out!

Materials

+ Your nature journal (page 343)
+ Ripe fruit or another sugary treat for bait
+ A piece of wood, a book or some building blocks

Take your nature journal outside and search for an ant colony. The best place to find ants is in the dirt or sandy soil. Observe the ants for a bit, then see if you can confuse them. Place the food treat a few inches (6 or 7 cm) away from the ant hill, and watch what happens.

How long does it take for the ants to find the sweet treat? In your journal draw the path the ants took to find the bait, and make a note about approximately how long it took them to get there.

What happened?

What do you think will happen if you put an obstruction, or something to block them, in the way of that scent-marked path? Will the ants become confused? Will they eventually find their way back to the food source along another path?

(continued)

Write down your hypothesis in your journal and place your wood, book or block in the way of the ants' path. A hypothesis is a scientific guess you make based on what you know about the subject you're studying. Draw where you put the obstruction in your journal, and take notes about what you see the ants do.

Usually, it will take the ants a few minutes of confusion before they'll find their way again and mark a new pheromone-scented path. Is that what you observed? Don't forget to write down your observations and conclusions in your journal.

More Fun

Set a new piece of food down, and time how long it takes for the ants to find the new bait. Then, set another obstruction in the ants' path, and time how long it takes them to find their way around the obstruction. You can try this again and again with different foods to see if the type of bait makes a difference.

Hungry, Hungry Ants

Now that you know how ants find food and communicate with one another, do you wonder if they prefer one type over another? Scientists ask questions like this all the time.

I think it's incredible how many things you can do and learn without ever leaving your own backyard. Head back outside to the anthill with your food and nature journal. It's time to learn more about the habits of your backyard ant friends.

- - - - - - - - - -

Materials

+ Four different types of food (for example: a crushed up pretzel, a gummy candy cut up, honey and some rice)
+ Your nature journal (page 343)

Set out your four food choices near the anthill. Make sure that each food type is about equidistant (the same distance) from the ant colony.

Now watch and observe.

Which food type do you think the ants will prefer? Which will they find faster? Will they try to take all of the food types back to the colony? Or will they choose to focus on just one type? Write down your hypotheses in your journal.

What happened? Did the ants like the sweeter foods better? Why do you think the ants preferred the foods they did? Most insects are attracted to sugary foods because they provide quick energy. Write what happened and your conclusions in your nature journal.

Awesome Ant Hotel

You've probably seen the ant farms that you can buy in the stores. They come with sand or gel and a coupon to send away for a vial of ants. Here's your chance to make one that's more natural and fun to view. Seriously—this awesome ant habitat will make the ants that have to live in the yard envious! (Okay . . . maybe not, but the ants that DO live in it will love it!)

- - - - - - - - - -

Materials

+ 2 (2-L) soda bottles
+ 1 (20-oz [591-ml]) soda bottle
+ Utility knife (used with adult supervision)
+ Quick-set epoxy or glue
+ Funnel
+ Soil
+ Duct tape or an inexpensive tornado tube
+ Small patch of grass, rocks, twigs, etc.
+ Cotton balls
+ Shipping tape
+ Ants (get these last after reading through the instructions and putting together your habitat)
+ Your nature journal (page 343)

Make sure you get an adult to help you with this activity as you'll be using a razor-sharp utility knife and super strong epoxy or glue, and build this outside so you can make as big a mess as you need to.

First, take the labels off of each of the bottles and clean them out completely.

Then, have an adult help you use the utility knife to cut the bottom off of both 2-liter bottles along the ridge that's about 2 inches (5 cm) up. To make it easier, you can use the utility knife to make the first cut, and then use a pair of scissors to finish.

Once you have both bottoms cut off of the two 2-liter bottles, use the epoxy or glue to attach the small bottle (with its lid in place) to the inside of one of the bottoms you cut off. Make sure it's secured. This smaller bottle takes up the space in the middle of the ant farm bottle so that when your little workers begin to build a colony, they'll do it against the outer wall so you can see their tunnels.

Let it dry completely—this might take a while, so check the instructions on the epoxy bottle before you get started.

When the epoxy, or glue, is dried, put the top back onto that bottom and seal the seam with epoxy. Take your time on this step. You want to make sure that the seam is completely sealed so that no dirt (or ants!) comes out. It might take several applications to get this seal. Let the epoxy or glue set completely in between applications. Once the epoxy is set, you can blow gently into the top of the 2-liter bottle and feel along the seam to see if air escapes anywhere.

This is the part where you have to just be patient. It's going to feel tedious to seal the bottle, then reseal it, again and again, but it's totally worth it—trust me. This ant hotel is really great.

Now that you have the bottom of your new ant habitat in place, use the funnel to add soil. If it's possible, find an ant colony outside in your yard (you'll need them to populate the habitat in the end anyway). Use soil from near the natural ant colony in your yard. Just gently fill the bottle up using your funnel. Fill it completely to the top because you'll want the ants to be able to dig straight down once you add the foraging area on top of their habitat.

Now, take the second 2-liter bottle. If you bought a tornado tube to use in this activity, connect the two bottles by screwing them together. If not—no big deal! Duct tape works wonders. Grab some fun-colored duct tape and connect the two bottles by taping the openings together tightly. When I did this, I wanted to make sure that there were no openings, so I used a little bit of the epoxy to secure the seam between the two bottles, and then, once it set, I taped the duct tape around the two bottle tops.

In the top area, you'll create a foraging zone for your ants so they have all they need to survive in their new habitat. First, pour more soil in, pushing it down so there is a continuous flow of the soil from the top bottle to the bottom one. Fill it about half way. Then, plant the grass patch in the top and mist it because your ants will prefer moist soil. You can add some rocks or sticks to decorate the area further.

Finally, take the remaining bottle bottom, and tuck it, bump side down, into the top of your foraging area, creating a sealed habitat. If you're worried that the ants will escape, you can cut a quarter-sized hole in the bottom of the "lid" and tuck a dry cotton ball into it and attach the lid to the bottle with packing tape. This will allow air to flow into the habitat, but block the ants from escaping.

Add the ants (try to find a queen if you can) and a tiny amount of the food you discovered that they prefer in the experiment from page 302. Mist your habitat about once a week. Feed them regularly too, but don't add too much food at once. You don't want the food to have a chance to mold and contaminate your ant habitat. If you notice food sitting around, uneaten, it probably means that you're feeding them too much. Just scoop out the uneaten food and feed them less often.

(continued)

Enjoy observing your ant colony. Draw what it looks like now in your nature journal, and check back, drawing what you see every few days.

More Fun

Ants prefer the dark, so if you want to encourage them to build their tunnels and do their work right up against the walls of their habitat so you can see it more easily, cover the habitat in dark black construction paper and only check it every few days so they feel like they're really in the dark.

*See photo insert page 31.

NOTE

If you can't find an ant colony in your yard, relax. Just use any dirt or soil from your yard to get set up. You can hunt around your neighborhood once your habitat is ready. There are ants to be found just about anywhere—and there are even a few places you can order them from if you aren't having luck finding a colony in your yard.

Warm Ant, Cool Ant

Do you see many ants during the colder months of the year? Why? Let's see how temperature affects our ant friends. It's a super simple activity—and really cool. . . . (Get it?)

- - - - - - - - - - - - - -

Materials

+ Small shovel
+ Bug Box (page 296) or a clean, clear food container with a lid
+ Your nature journal (page 343)

Scoop up some ants from outside, using a small shovel, into your bug box or a see-through container. Be careful not to touch them in case they are a type that bites or stings.

Grab your nature journal and draw your container and the ants inside it. Make observations. Remember, these are your observations, so they are anecdotal, which means what you think you're seeing. You don't need to time their movements, just describe them. What are they doing? How quickly are they moving around? Are they trying to get out of the container? Do they look like they're communicating with one another? How?

Once you've written out some observations, put your container of ants into the refrigerator for ten minutes.

What do you think will happen? Write your hypothesis in your journal. Your hypothesis should answer the questions—How do you think the cold will affect the ants and why do you think that will happen.

When you remove the ant container from the refrigerator, sit and watch them for a bit. How are they acting differently than before? Describe their movements in your journal. Was your hypothesis correct? Why do you think the ants are now behaving this way?

Ants are pretty interesting to observe. They're great over-winterers. During the fall, as colder temperatures approach, they eat more food, and put on extra fat stores.

When the temperatures drop, ants become sluggish and burrow down into their colony, huddling together around their queen to protect her. Because they're not really moving around, the openings of their burrows close up, further insulating them.

As warmer temperatures arrive in the spring, the ants warm up and begin to stir. They start clearing their tunnels and opening back up their entrances. They go out in search of food, and when they find it the worker ants eat their fill, then go back to let the others know about it, starting the cycle of gathering food, mating and tending the queen and the young all over again.

Red Flower, Blue Flower

I often wonder about ladybugs (Coccinellidae) and other critters in the yard when I'm sitting outside watching. Do you? When I'm seeing ladybugs in the garden, for example, I often wonder if they have a preference about the colors of the plants and flowers I plant in there. In this activity, we'll see if we can get to the bottom of that question.

- - - - - - - - - - - - - - -

Materials

+ A large solid-colored bedsheet (optional)
+ Several flowers in different colors
+ Ladybugs in a container
+ Your nature journal (page 343)

Go to a nice open area in your yard or driveway. If you're using a sheet, spread it out and set the flowers in the middle, a few inches (6 or 7 cm) apart from one another.

Let your ladybugs loose near the flowers and have a seat nearby to observe them, while documenting your observations in your nature journal. My kids love sketching the behavior of little creatures like ladybugs. Draw the flowers and where you set your beetles down, and then write quick notes about what they're doing.

Did you make a hypothesis? Which flower color did you think they'd prefer? Why? Are you noticing that the ladybugs are behaving as you predicted? Or are they doing something different? What are your theories about their behavior?

We love doing this activity. When the kids sit still for long enough, ladybugs land on them and crawl around, tickling their arms and legs. Have you ever caught a ladybug and let it wander around on your hand?

Ladybugs eat tiny insects called aphids. Those aphids love garden plants like tomatoes and flowers like nasturtium. They also eat other small insects like mites and whiteflies. To supplement their carbohydrate needs and give them a quick burst of energy if the insect population is down, ladybugs can also eat pollen and nectar from flowers.

One of my theories is that the type of flower is more important to ladybugs than color. I think they prefer flowers that have abundant pollen and nectar, and might also house aphids. I can't wait to hear about your experience.

More Fun
Let your ladybugs go in the garden when you're done experimenting with them. They'll eat all those pesky little bugs that damage your flowers and vegetables. They're great garden helpers.

Lights Out, Lights On

Ladybug Experiment Two

What do you think? Will ladybugs react to the choice between light and dark in the same way that your roly poly bugs did? Think about how ladybugs and roly poly bugs are similar and different from one another. I wonder if they like the same conditions? . . . Let's find out!

Materials

+ Your Cool Critter Choice Container (page 298)
+ Dark construction paper
+ Tape
+ Your nature journal (page 343)
+ Small container of ladybugs
+ Clear plastic wrap

Head outside and set up your choice container the same way you did for the roly poly activity on page 300, taping dark construction paper on the outside of one side of the container, covering all but the bottom.

Create a table in your nature journal like you did on page 300 for the roly poly experiment.

Time Elapsed	Dark	Light
5 Minutes		
10 Minutes		
15 Minutes		
20 Minutes		
25 Minutes		
30 Minutes		

Write down your hypothesis. Will the ladybugs prefer the light-colored side or the dark-colored one? Why do you think that?

Gently place your ladybugs into the container—half on each side—and cover the top of the light side with clear plastic wrap so the light shines in brightly.

Check on your ladybugs every five minutes, recording how many ladybugs are on each side. Once your half an hour has elapsed, look over your results. Are you surprised? Was your hypothesis correct? Why do you think this was the case?

Super Simple Ladybug House

Now you know how important those little ladybug beetles are to your backyard. They eat the pests that would eat your tomato plants or kill your pretty flowers. Plus, they're very gentle and fun to observe.

You can attract more to your yard by building a simple ladybug house to give them shelter and a great place to hide from predators. It's easy! Give it a try!

Materials

+ Oatmeal (or other round) container with a lid
+ Paint
+ Paintbrush
+ Spray sealer
+ Utility knife
+ Wire
+ Your nature journal (page 343, optional)

Find a spot outside that's perfect for painting, then decorate the outside of your oatmeal container. Cover it completely with a base coat of paint and then add fun details. Remember that ladybugs don't seem to have color preferences, but they are definitely attracted to the light. You may want to use light and bright paint colors to cover your oatmeal container.

Let it dry and then seal the container with the spray to help protect it from the weather.

Check with an adult before using the utility knife. Cut (or have help cutting) a small window slit on the top of your container. Then, cut a small door at the bottom of the container.

Poke a hole on either side of the oatmeal container and string the wire through it to create a hanger.

Hang your ladybug home from a tree near your garden or flower bed and watch for new ladybug families to come and set up their new home. If you want, you can use your nature journal to record how long it takes ladybugs to find your house and call it their own. Check on it each day, and draw or write about what you see.

More Fun

You could kick-start your ladybug population by purchasing a bag of ladybugs. They're readily available at garden centers and online.

*See photo insert page 31.

Observing Light Patterns and Talking to Fireflies

Do you wonder why fireflies light up? Or if there is a reason they flash and flicker in the ways that they do?

Scientists believe that certain patterns of light from male fireflies attract female fireflies better. And, scientists take a lot of time studying animals they are interested in. Here's your chance to be a great scientist, too! Gather up your materials and head outside to observe and talk to fireflies. You'll learn to speak their language!

– – – – – – – – – – – – –

Materials

+ Your nature journal (page 343)
+ Small flashlight (like a penlight)

Head outside with your nature journal and find a quiet place to sit and watch the fireflies. Pay attention to the different patterns of lights in the sky and the patterns of lights in the grass. Jot down your observations or draw out the flight patterns of the lightning bugs you're observing. Remember that scientists keep track of what they're seeing in nature journals so that they can formulate conclusions about animal behavior.

Male fireflies flicker in the sky, trying to find a female mate flickering back in the grass. What do you notice about the light patterns? Are they quick? Short? Slow? Make notes about both the female and male beetles. Draw some of what you observe.

Now, pay special attention to the female fireflies in the grass or in low bushes. Choose one to watch closely.

(continued)

Is she flashing long? Slowly? How many seconds go by between flashes? How many flashes does she make in a row? Once you think you have her pattern down, find a spot on the grass and try to attract a male firefly.

Hold your flashlight so it makes a small, beetle-sized point of light right on the grass. Turn it on and off, mimicking the flashes you observed the female firefly make. Keep doing this, calmly and patiently.

If you've figured out your neighborhood fireflies' "language," the males will be fooled and will start talking back to you by flashing and moving closer to you. Hopefully, one will land near your light.

Now you can talk to insects! You're amazing!

FUN FACT

Did you know that even firefly larvae glow? It's true! They're called glowworms, and the light warns predators that they'll taste bad.

Warm Bugs, Cool Bugs

Firefly Experiment One

Did you know that a lightning bug's glow works similarly to a glow stick's light? When you bend a glow stick to break the chamber inside, two chemicals mix together and give off a glowing energy with no heat.

Lightning bugs have different chemicals, but they work in the same way, mixing together to cause a glow. You can use glow sticks to help you learn more about lightning bugs—like how temperature affects their glow, for example. . . .

Materials

+ Pitcher of hot water
+ Pitcher of ice water
+ Two identical glow sticks
+ Your nature journal (page 343)

Do this experiment outside on a dark night.

First, get two pitchers filled with water—one should be really hot (but not boiling) and the other should be icy cold.

Take the two glow sticks and activate them however the packages tell you to. Take a minute to think like a scientist. Jot down in your nature journal how YOU think temperature is going to affect the glow. Put one of the glow sticks in the hot water and the other in the cold water. Wait a few minutes.

What is happening?

The glow stick in the hot water gets gradually brighter, while the glow stick in the cold water gets dimmer. Why do you think this is? The light energy is released faster in the hot water than in the cold. Fireflies light up more, and are more active when it is hotter outside, too.

More Fun

Which of the glow sticks do you think will lose its glow sooner? The one in the hot water or the one in the cold water? Why do you think this? Jot your hypothesis down in your journal and watch to see if you were right.

Catching Fireflies Like a Boss!

One of my favorite summer evening activities is catching fireflies and observing them as they crawl around a jar. You can do that too—it's easy!

Glass jars make the perfect bug habitat for fireflies. This is a great time to use up all of those pickle, jelly and spaghetti sauce jars from the recycle bin. Just make sure you clean them well—fireflies don't mix well with jelly!

— — — — — — — — — — — — —

Materials

+ Bug net (page 296)
+ Glass jar (do NOT poke holes in its lid)
+ Grass clippings
+ A stick or leaves
+ A piece of an apple or potato

Use your bug net to head outside and gently catch fireflies without hurting them.

When you have caught one, you can get it to crawl all by itself into the jar. Simply hold the jar upside down over top of it while it's in the net. Fireflies always crawl upward.

Pretty cool trick, isn't it?

Put some grass clippings into the jar once your fireflies have crawled inside. Add a stick or some leaves for them to climb and a piece of potato or apple to the jar.

Make sure that you don't poke holes in the jar lids. Air holes dry the air inside of the jar out. Fireflies prefer damp air—which is why we see them outside on hot, humid nights. If you put a damp paper towel in the jar, and close the lid, there will be enough air for the fireflies you catch to stay alive for a day or two.

If you want to keep one or two of your fireflies for a few days to observe them, they'll be fine in your jar. Just open up the lid once or twice a day and blow across the top to displace and freshen the air. Fireflies don't eat. They did all their eating as larvae, so you don't need to worry about feeding them. But let them go after two or three days. Most fireflies only live a week or two, and they shouldn't have to spend all of their lives in a jar.

More Fun

Every summer in Japan, people collect fireflies in jars and cages, then go out on boats together and let them go (often by the thousands) at the same time. The fireflies light up the sky at the firefly festivals in Japan. Invite your friends over for a firefly festival. Have them bring their own jars of fireflies and let them go together in your yard, and then play Hide and Glow Seek by hiding glow sticks all over the yard and trying to find them as the sky darkens.

Make the Best Home for Your Beetles and Mealworms!

Darkling beetles and their larva are super cool to raise. We've raised them a few times at our house, and all the kids that come over get hooked on making mazes and obstacle courses for the mealworms and beetles. You can do that too! It's simple and fun. Check it out!

- - - - - - - - - - - - - - - -

Materials

+ Plastic or glass container with holes punched in the lid
+ Bedding (rolled oats, wheat bran, crushed cereal, ground corn or a mixture)
+ Chunk of a moist fruit or vegetable (potato, carrot, apple, etc.)
+ Mealworms and/or darkling beetles

Setting up your habitat is super simple, and you'll likely have mealworms and beetles for months. It'll be like your own little beetle farm! Grab your materials and head outside.

Make sure that your container is clean and dry, and put in about a ½ inch (1.3 cm) of the bedding you chose. The bedding will be both a place for the beetles and larva to hide in, and food for them to eat.

Set a chunk of fruit or vegetable in there to provide moisture for the beetles and mealworms. Darkling beetles don't drink water. They get their moisture from the foods they eat. So they'll munch on the fruit to stay hydrated. You'll have to change it out for a new piece every day or two. It's important that you replace it before mold grows. You want to keep your beetles healthy.

Once it's set up, introduce your beetles and/or mealworms to their new home. They're pretty hardy insects, so you can just tip them into the habitat and they'll start eating.

If you had trouble finding mealworms or darkling beetles in your yard, you can get a little tub of mealworms from a local pet or birding store for $2.00 to $4.00. When my kids wanted to learn about mealworms, we ordered a big box of them on the Internet and had a blast! A population of mealworms is easy to maintain. We've kept them going for long periods of time to have a steady supply of live larva to feed our pet red-eared sliders and the robins that love to visit our backyard every spring.

FUN FACT

Darkling beetles go through complete metamorphosis. This means that they go through all four stages—egg, larva, pupa and adult. Female beetles can lay up to 500 eggs at a time. The larva, or mealworms, hatch a few weeks later. Over the next two months, depending on the species, mealworms will molt 10 to 20 times before entering the pupal stage. About two weeks later, a whitish adult emerges. It turns brownish-black within 24 hours. They're pretty cool to observe—don't forget to draw their life cycles in your nature journal! You'll want to remember this!

Cozy Oats, Comfy Bran

What do you think mealworms prefer to be tucked in with, oats or wheat bran? Do you think it matters to them? Using a method similar to how you tested roly poly ethology (page 299), you'll see if they care one way or another.

Instead of using a choice container, though, you'll just use a flat tray. Mealworms are cool to explore, but they're not quite as curious as some of the other insects you've maybe explored. See what I mean. . . .

- - - - - - - - - - -

Materials

+ Large rectangular tray or container with high sides
+ Oats
+ Wheat bran
+ Mealworms
+ Your nature journal (page 343)

Head outside and sit on the ground or at a picnic table. Spread a ½ inch (13 mm) of oats in the left third of the container and wheat bran in the right third of the container. Place 10 to 15 mealworms in the center of the container (the third with no bedding). Write your hypothesis in your nature journal. Which bedding do you think the majority of your mealworms will prefer? Why?

Leave your mealworms alone for about a half an hour. Read a book, play a quiet game or just listen to the sounds of nature—but stay close so you can make sure your mealworms are safe from predators like backyard birds. Check back to see if all of them have made their way over to one of the bedding options. Which type has the most mealworms? Sift through the oats and wheat bran and count the mealworms in each.

More Fun

Try testing your mealworms' preference for other things—food, light, etc. You can do these same activities over again once they've metamorphosed to see if the beetles still behave in the same ways.

Getting to Know Your Mealworms and Beetles

There are so many interesting things to observe about mealworms and darkling beetles. And sometimes scientists do just that—observe. Here's your chance to get to know your mealworms and beetles better. Who knows what you'll discover!

- - - - - - - - - - -

Materials

+ Your nature journal (page 343)
+ Mealworms and darkling beetles
+ A small tray or clear container
+ Magnifying glass, hand lens or pocket microscope
+ Mirror box (page 332, optional)

Grab your nature journal, something to write with and a few beetles and mealworms on a small tray or in a shallow container, and sit outside.

Using a magnifying glass, observe them carefully. Write and draw what you see happening in your journal. Here are some questions to get you started:

Can you tell the mealworms apart? How?

What is the distance a mealworm can travel in a minute? (Start it at one side of the tray, and mark where it stops after a minute. Then measure that distance and record it.)

(continued)

What is the distance a darkling beetle can travel in a minute?

Can either the larvae or the beetles walk up a slanted surface? (Tip the tray or container to test this.)

Do the beetle's (or mealworm's) legs all move together when it walks? This is a good activity to observe using your mirror box from page 332.

What else do you observe about your mealworms' and beetles' behavior?

Often, scientists do activities like this again and again to see if the behaviors change over time. You can try this every few days to see if the beetles and mealworms act differently at different times of the day or during different seasons.

More Fun

Make a maze by gluing toothpicks to a piece of paper. Once the glue dries, put a piece of food or some shelter at the other end and time how long it takes your mealworm to find it. Test several times to see if its time got faster with each trial. We've also made fun mealworm mazes using wooden blocks on plastic trays so we can change them around again and again.

Getting to Know Your Bess Beetles

Head outside with a container and put a small layer of dirt and a chunk of rotting wood inside. Dig through the woodpile, leaf litter, under shrubs or bushes or anywhere that sticks, twigs or logs might be rotting. Pull apart the bark from the wood and look for holes inside the logs. Keep digging until you find the shiny black beetles chewing up that wood. Try to grab two or more if you can. Now, put together this habitat and watch them for a bit. They're cool to observe!

— — — — — — — — — — — — —

Materials

+ Clear container (plastic shoeboxes, pretzel containers or old plastic food storage containers work well)
+ Soil
+ Rotting wood (it should be decaying enough that you can easily break it apart with your hands)
+ Bess beetles
+ Spray bottle full of water
+ Magnifying glass, hand lens or pocket microscope
+ Your nature journal (page 343)
+ Mirror box (page 332)

Put your bess beetles in their new home. They are easy to care for, and can be kept for awhile, but it's always a good idea to release them back to the log where you found them when you're done observing them, as bess beetles need the stability of a large rotting log habitat in order to reproduce.

Since bess beetles look so intimidating with their large size and strong mandibles, this is a good time to get used to handling and observing them so that when you begin experimenting you'll have no trouble. They look scary, but they're not!

Bess beetles like humidity, so make sure to mist their habitat each day with your spray bottle. Don't get the wood too wet, though; you don't want it to get moldy.

Take your bess beetle out and let it walk on your hand. I promise that they're extremely gentle bugs. They won't bite you because, while their mandibles look like intimidating pinchers, they're made for chewing through wood. Are you daring enough to try it? Come on! You're brave . . . you can do it!

Let the beetle crawl around on your hand, and observe its movements using your magnifying glass. Draw a picture of it in your nature journal, then write about what it did while it was in your hands. Try putting it in your mirror box and see what it looks like from all angles.

What did it feel like? How quickly did it move? What did you notice about its mandibles when you looked at them through the magnifying glass? How can this help it eat through wood? Be a scientist and make detailed observations. They'll help you come to conclusions during your experiments on the next few pages.

Mighty, Mighty Bugs

This is an easy activity to do with bess beetles because they're so gentle and easy to handle. It's a great demonstration of just how strong beetles really are. You'll test how many pennies a beetle can pull—prepare to be amazed!

- - - - - - - - - - - - - -

Materials

+ Paper towel taped to a table outside
+ 10- to 12-inch (25- to 30-cm)-long piece of waxed dental floss
+ Small plastic container
+ Bess beetles
+ Pennies
+ Your nature journal (page 343)

Head out to a table in the yard with your materials and your beetles. How many pennies do you think a bess beetle can pull? Take a minute and jot down your prediction in your nature journal.

Tie a loop on one end of your dental floss with a slip knot. You'll be looping this around the bess beetle's abdomen like a lasso, so you'll want it to be easy to resize.

Attach the other end to the plastic container.

Loop the lasso around your beetle's abdomen and tighten the loop gently. You want it tight enough so that it won't fall off, but not too tight. Remember that your bess beetles are living creatures, and it's important to handle them carefully while putting the lasso around their abdomen.

Don't put it on too tightly.

Place your beetle on one end of the paper towel. The towel will provide traction so it's easier for the beetle to walk. Put a penny in the container while the beetle pulls it.

Keep adding pennies carefully until the beetle stops moving, and isn't able to pull any more weight. Record the number of pennies the beetle was able to pull. Was your guess close?

Gently remove the harness from your beetle and put it back into its habitat. Let it rest for a while before you take it out to play again.

Incredible Beetle Chariot Races

Do you want to have more fun with the pulling power of bess beetles? Let your friends rest up for a few days after you test how much weight they can pull, and then rig up two fresh lassos with slip knots and attach them to your beetles carefully.

See how quickly they can carry your little people to the finish line.

- - - - - - - - - - - - - - - -

Materials

+ Paper towel, taped to a table
+ 2 bess beetle lassos (page 313)
+ 2 small plastic containers
+ 2 small toy people
+ Bess beetles

Go outside and draw a start line and a finish line on a paper towel, and hook the beetles' lassos to two same-sized plastic containers. Tape the paper towel to a table top. Place a small plastic person in each container. Try to find same-sized, lightweight people so the race is fair.

Place your two chariot-driving bess beetles at the start line and loop the lassos around their abdomens. This is a fun activity to do with a friend. Release them and see which pulls their chariot to the finish line first. Cheer your racer on!

*See photo insert page 31.

Bright and Breezy Digs for Your Crickets

Crickets are easy to keep, and will chirp in the early evening, giving you plenty of lullabies to lull you to sleep. Real white noise for your room! Learn how to make the best home for them—they'll love their new "digs."

- - - - - - - - - - - - - - - -

Materials

+ Plastic or glass container with a vented lid (you can use one of your bug boxes from page 296)
+ Sand
+ Branches, cardboard tubes, egg cartons, etc.
+ Piece of fruit or vegetable
+ Small square of sponge
+ Your nature journal (page 343)

Head outside with your materials, and find a comfortable place to make this project. You can start making your cricket friends comfy right away by spreading a layer of sand on the bottom of your container.

Put some twigs, pieces of cardboard tubes or egg cartons, or other things on the bottom so they have somewhere to hide. Crickets love to hide!

Crickets will eat almost anything. You can feed them bits of fruit and vegetables, but you'll need to keep an eye on it to make sure it doesn't spoil. Replace the food with fresh pieces as it dries out or gets old.

Your crickets can easily drown in standing water, so place a piece of damp sponge in the container so they can drink from it. You'll love watching these little critters!

FUN FACT

Crickets have been kept as pets in China for centuries. They're considered good luck, and you can still find street vendors there selling pet crickets in little bamboo cages today. See . . . doing the activities in this book can actually bring you good luck!

First-Rate Cricket Thermometers

On a day when the temperature falls between 55° and 100°F (13° to 38°C), head outside to where you normally hear crickets or bring the pets you've already captured to a shady area in the yard.

Let them relax and start chirping. Pretty soon, they'll start to tell you what the temperature is out there.

Materials

+ Crickets (or a spot in your yard where you usually see or hear them)
+ Stopwatch
+ Outdoor thermometer
+ Your nature journal (page 343)

Pick out the sound of one cricket and use your stopwatch to count the number of chirps you hear in 14 seconds. Add that number to 40. The answer you get should be close to the temperature in degrees Fahrenheit. (To determine temperature in Celsius, count the chirps in 25 seconds, divide that count by 3, then add 4.)

It's as simple as that. Really!

You can get even more accurate if you do this several times and take the average result. Do you know how to figure out averages? Say you calculated the temperature five times, and you got 70, 71, 71, 74 and 72. You would add those results together to get 358. Then, you divide that number (358) by the number of temperatures you had added together (5). Your average temperature would be 71.6 degrees Fahrenheit.

Check the outdoor thermometer. I bet you were pretty close. Crickets are amazing at telling us the temperature of the air around us.

Pretty cool, huh?

FUN FACT

Female crickets can lay up to 200 eggs at a time. Imagine how many little cricket thermometers you could have in your yard!

Wet Sand, Dry Sand

You've made your crickets a home, but did you think about the conditions in which you found them? Do you think they'd prefer wet or damp sand to the dry sand you put in there? Let's check it out and see what they like!

- - - - - - - - - - - - -

Materials

+ Small lidded container
+ Sand
+ Water
+ Your nature journal (page 343)
+ Crickets

Grab your clean container and head outside, and then spread dry sand on one side of the container. Get some sand wet (but not too wet—you don't want standing water) and put it on the other side. You can't use your choice container (page 298) for this because the crickets would likely just hide in the center tube. They like to cozy up in small spaces.

Make a hypothesis. Write down which side you think the majority of the crickets will go to in your nature journal. Write down your reasons for thinking that, too.

Place your crickets in the center of the sand choices, and leave them alone for 10 to 15 minutes. Check back. Where are most of your crickets now? Are they on the wet or dry side? Why do you think that is? Write down your results and why you think that happened.

Depending on how damp it is, the crickets might have liked that side better. While they don't like wet ground, they do like it cool and moist. So, the next time you walk by their habitat, you might want to mist it with a spray bottle.

MORE FUN

Try testing other cricket preferences, too. What other experiments can you come up with? Maybe you can test different food choices, or whether they have color preferences or the light versus the dark. The possibilities are endless.

Together Bugs, Lonely Bugs

Do you think that crickets prefer to live alone or with others like them? Why do you think that? Write down your hypothesis in your nature journal. Then, get ready to test it out and see what your crickets do.

- - - - - - - - - - - - -

Materials

+ 1 cardboard tube per cricket
+ Container with a thin layer of sand on the bottom
+ 2 or more crickets
+ Your nature journal (page 343)

Put the cardboard tubes inside the container, bring it all outside, then set your crickets gently on the sand. Check back every 5 to 10 minutes to see what your crickets are doing. Are they together? Apart? Chirping?

Finally, after 40 minutes, write down your results in your nature journal. Draw your container and where the crickets all ended up. Most of the crickets should have decided to find their own hiding spot. They're solitary insects that prefer to live alone.

If you heard chirping, though, you had at least one male in the container, and he may have been interested in attracting one of the females.

The Most Colossal Worm Home You Can Make

If you want to keep your worms at home for a while, this is one of our favorite homemade worm habitats. Your wormy friends can live in it for a long, long time if you take good care of them. Let's go build, construction workers!

- - - - - - - - - - - - - - - -

Materials

+ Clean 2-L bottle
+ Craft knife
+ Small rocks or gravel
+ Unfertilized potting or garden soil
+ Cornmeal
+ Dry, dead leaves
+ Chopped fruits and vegetables
+ Spray bottle with water
+ Worms
+ Plastic wrap
+ Rubber band
+ Your nature journal (page 343)

Do this activity in the driveway or yard so you can brush away any spilled dirt when you're done. Take the label off your 2-liter bottle, and have an adult help you cut the top off with the craft knife.

Spread an inch (2.5 cm) of gravel on the bottom of the bottle, and place several inches (8 to 12 cm) of soil on top of the gravel.

For the top layer, mix cornmeal, leaves and food scraps together. This is the food layer for your worms. They'll eat this and break it down into compost. Lightly spritz this top layer with your spray bottle, being careful not to soak it.

Gently place a few worms in the habitat (two to four work well), and stretch plastic wrap over the top. Secure the plastic wrap with a rubber band and poke a few holes into it for ventilation.

Now you have a safe home for your worms, and a mini vermicomposting bin, too! Vermicomposting is a method of composting that uses worms to do what they do best—break down plant matter into super healthy soil. Every few days, add a little bit of food to the habitat and spray it lightly with your spray bottle.

More Fun

If you want to encourage your worms to hang out near the sides of the habitat where you can see them, then cover the outside of the bottle with dark-colored paper or cloth and put it in a cool, dark place for a few days. When you uncover it, you should see the layers and any tunnels the worms have made. You can hold tracing paper up to your habitat and trace their tunnels, then tape that into your nature journal.

Wet Worms, Dry Worms

You find worms out on the driveway and sidewalk after a heavy rain where they go to escape the flooded soil. Does that mean that they don't like moisture, though? It's interesting, isn't it? There are so many things in nature that seem contradictory. This might be one of those things.

Try it out, though. Find out just which conditions your worms really do prefer. . . . Here we go!

- - - - - - - - - - - - - - - -

Materials

+ Your nature journal (page 343)
+ Two paper towels—one damp, one dry
+ Shallow container or tray
+ Three or four worms

(continued)

What do you think? Do earthworms prefer their habitats to be wet or dry? Think about where you found your worms, and write your hypothesis in your nature journal.

Put your wet paper towel flat on one side of your container, and set your container on a table outside in the yard. Place the dry towel on the other side, making sure that they overlap a bit in the center.

Put your worms right in the middle where the paper towels meet, and leave your worms alone for about 30 minutes.

When you come back, observe where your worms are. Did they all crawl to the same side? Which did they choose? Why do you think that is?

Worms tend to like moist soil, so they probably all crawled to the damp paper towel.

More Fun
Make worm-y ice pops by putting sour gummy worms into ice pop molds, then pouring your favorite fruit drink over top of them. Freeze until they are solid and enjoy! Now you can tell friends you like to eat worms for a snack!

Light Worms, Dark Worms

Think about what you know about earthworms so far. Do earthworms prefer their habitats to be light or dark? Think about where you found your worms, and write your hypothesis in your nature journal. Once you're done writing out your hypothesis, let's work together to find out the answer!

- - - - - - - - - - - - -

Materials
+ Shallow container or tray
+ Three or four worms
+ A dark cloth
+ Your nature journal (page 343)

Set your container on a sturdy table or on the driveway. Put your worms in the center of the container and wrap one half of it in a dark cloth. Leave the other half exposed to light.

Let your worms hang out for about 30 minutes.

When you come back, observe where your worms are. Did they all crawl to the same side? Which did they choose? Why do you think that is?

Worms tend to like dark soil, so they probably all crawled to the dark side of the container. Think about where you find worms—under rocks and in the soil. It just makes sense, doesn't it?

Bright Lights, Sensitive Worms

You discovered that worms prefer dark habitats in the previous activity, but how sensitive are they to the light? And, are certain parts of their bodies more sensitive than others? Let's see!

- - - - - - - - - - - - -

Materials
+ Your nature journal (page 343)
+ Piece of cardboard that will fit over the flashlight
+ Flashlight
+ Tape
+ Lid or cloth to cover half of the container or tray
+ Shallow container or tray
+ Worms

You can make some predictions about what will happen in your journal. Which part of an earthworm's body will be the most sensitive to the light? Why do you think that? Write your answers down, then head outside to experiment.

Poke a hole in the center of the cardboard. You'll be taping this to the light on the flashlight to make a concentrated point of light. You don't want the light to be too big, but you want it to be big enough to light up a part of the worm.

Tape your cardboard over the light on the flashlight and test it by turning it on and pointing it towards the tray. Does a small point of light shine? Perfect. Put the lid or cloth over one half of the tray to create a shaded area for your worm to retreat to if it gets stressed.

Now, put a worm gently on the tray and shine your light at one of its ends. What happens? Shine your light at its middle. Does it react the same way? How is it reacting differently? What about its other end? Is that sensitive to the light? What happens when you shine your light there?

When my kids did this activity, they found that their worms were more sensitive to the light when they shined it on their ends. Was your experience the same as theirs? Remember, too, that worms are living creatures and you don't want to hurt them. If one gets too stressed by the light, let it hang out in the shaded area of your tray and grab another worm to test further. Respect your worm friends!

More Fun

Worms are sensitive to, and dislike, light. But, what about colored light? Do you think they'll react the same way if you expose them to colored points of light? You can easily make your flashlight shine colored light on your worms by gathering three colored Magnatiles toys, food container lids or another transparent colored thing you find around your house. Just put the color on the flashlight and tape it to it with the hole-punched cardboard. Do the same thing you did in the light experiment. Point the colored light to the worms' ends and middle sections. Do they react differently when different colored lights are shined on them?

Strong Smells, Weak Smells

If worms don't have noses, do they have a sense of smell? Will they react to different odors when surrounded by different choices? Find out how sensitive they are to smells in this simple experiment.

- - - - - - - - - - - -

Materials

+ Paper towel
+ Sharpie
+ Water
+ Cotton balls
+ Three different items with a strong scent
+ Your nature journal (page 343)
+ Worms

(continued)

Set your paper towel on a table outside. Use your sharpie to divide it into four quadrants. Label each section with one of the three different scents you'll be using. We used an orange slice, dish soap and mint oil. Label the fourth quadrant with the word Control. That will be your control for the experiment.

A control is something that represents the normal state of something. In this case, you'll be trying to answer the question, "Can worms smell?" By having a section with nothing in it, you're able to have a section with little to no smell.

Once you label your paper towel, get the whole thing damp and spread it out on a table or tray. Rub your three scents all over the cotton balls (one on each) and place them in whichever quadrant is labeled with their name. For example, we placed our orange juice soaked cotton ball in the section labeled Orange. Leave the Control section alone.

Draw your testing area in your nature journal so you have a record of what is happening. Do you think worms can smell? Will they stay away from certain scents? Will they be drawn to certain scents?

Gently place a worm down in the center of the paper towel. Observe its movements. What is happening? Is it just sitting there? Is it moving around? Draw and write what you're observing in your nature journal. Let the worm hang out on the paper towel for at least 10 minutes. Did it stop moving?

Put it back in the habitat and test a different worm. What did this worm do? Did it react in the same way as the other worm? You can try this with many different worms and write down your observations.

So, what is the answer? Could you tell definitively if the worms you placed on the paper towel could smell the scents? Maybe . . . maybe not. Some kids who have tried this experiment see their worms react strongly to specific scents. Others don't.

The truth is that worms don't actually smell and taste things the way we do. They have special chemoreceptors that are found in their skin. They sense both smell and taste through those chemoreceptors. While there are chemoreceptors all over their bodies, worms have a more concentrated amount of them near their heads and tails. So . . . they kind of have noses all over their bodies!

More Fun

Try to design your own experiment. Can you figure out a way to do this experiment to see where the most chemoreceptors are on a worm's body? And, do you think it matters what type of worm you test (earthworm, night crawler, red wiggler, etc.)? What about the size/age of the worm? Do you think that matters? There are so many ways you can extend your scientific study of worm chemoreceptors.

Heart to Heart to Heart: Earthworm Hearts

Imagine if you had five separate hearts beating together in your body. How quickly could your blood travel then? Earthworms have five hearts located in their anterior section. Together, these five hearts move blood to all areas of the worm's body. Most earthworms grow to be about 12 inches (30 cm) long.

Humans breathe using lungs. Oxygen and carbon dioxide are exchanged with each breath. Although earthworms have many hearts, they do not have lungs. They breathe through their skin. Their bodies must stay moist for them to be able to breathe.

In this activity, you can see a worm's hearts at work. Watch carefully—they beat quickly!

- - - - - - - - - - - - -

Materials

+ Watch or clock with second hand or a timer
+ Your nature journal (page 343)
+ Worm
+ Paper towels
+ Spray bottle filled with water
+ Petri or other clear dish (optional)
+ Magnifying glass (or a microscope if you have one)

Take your pulse by placing two fingers (not your thumb!) at your wrist and counting the beats for one minute. Record your pulse in your nature journal.

Place your earthworm on a moist paper towel or in a clear dish that has been spritzed with water.

To observe your earthworm's heartbeats, find the clitellum, or saddle area, that's the thick band on the worm's body. The anterior section is the shorter end of the body. Your worm's mouth is at the very tip of the anterior section of the worm. An earthworm's hearts lie very close together about halfway between the mouth tip and the saddle.

For a clearer view of the heartbeats, look closely through a magnifying glass and locate the hearts. My kids like to hold their worms above them in a container when they're outside so the sun shines down on it.

Notice that the hearts seem to ripple as they beat. Each ripple is made up of the five hearts beating one after another, one time. This ripple counts as one heartbeat. Make sure to spritz your worm with water if it gets dry.

Set a timer for one minute so you can count your worm's heartbeat. This is your worm's pulse. Figure out how many times the earthworm's hearts beat for every one of your heartbeats by dividing the worm's pulse by your pulse.

Here's a challenge for you—do some math to figure out whether your heart, or the worm's hearts will beat more over the course of a lifetime. On average, healthy humans live for approximately 78 years. Multiply the following:

- Your pulse (heartbeats per minute) × 60 minutes = Your heartbeats per hour
- Your heartbeats per hour × 24 hours = Your heartbeats per day
- Your heartbeats per day × 365 = Your heartbeats per year
- Your heartbeats per year × 78 = Your heartbeats per lifetime

(continued)

An earthworm can live for about ten years if it avoids becoming another animal's prey. Try this formula to determine how many times an earthworm's heart will beat over its lifetime:

- Earthworm's pulse (heartbeats per minute) × 60 minutes = Earthworm's heartbeats per hour
- Earthworm's heartbeats per hour × 24 hours = Earthworm's heartbeats per day
- Earthworm's heartbeats per day × 365 = Earthworm's heartbeats per year
- Earthworm's heartbeats per year × 10 = Earthworm's heartbeats per lifetime

Which one—you or the earthworm—will have more heartbeats over the course of a lifetime?

FUN FACT

The longest earthworm ever discovered was found in South Africa. It was almost 264 inches (6.7 m) long! That worm's hearts had to push its blood a long way!

Putting Worms to Work

You made a little worm habitat already with the activity on page 317, but did you know that worms are fabulous workers that can really help your garden grow? It's true. Vermicomposting is a great way to get nutrient-rich garden soil for your plants.

And your worms will happily work for you all year round, with very little maintenance and a bit of food scraps. You can make your own vermicomposting bin in this activity!

- - - - - - - - - -

Materials

+ Two 8 to 10 gallon (30 to 37 L) plastic storage containers
+ Drill with ¼-inch (6-mm) and ¹⁄₁₆-inch (1-mm) bits
+ Shredded newspaper
+ Water
+ Unfertilized soil or dirt and leaf litter
+ About a pound (450 g) of worms (you can hunt for them, or order some online to kick-start the project)
+ Piece of cardboard

Have an adult help you with this project. Drill about 20 to 30 (¼-inch [6-mm]) holes in the bottom of the containers. This will allow for drainage and for the worms to wriggle through when you're ready to harvest your worm castings. Worm castings are the waste left by a worm after it breaks down organic waste. They're full of nutrients that plants love.

Drill ¹⁄₁₆-inch (1-mm) ventilation holes around the top of each container about an inch (2.5 cm) apart, and about 20 to 30 on the lid. This will allow air to flow well around the top of the bin.

Remember that worms like their habitats moist, but not wet. Shred the newspaper and soak it in water. Then, wring the paper out completely so that it's just damp. Add it to one of the worm bins, and fluff it up. Put a thin layer of dirt and leaf litter on top of the newspaper. Put the worms in the bin and let them get acclimated for a few days before you add any other food.

Put the cardboard on top of the newspaper and leaf litter. Put the second, empty, bin on the cardboard and cover that with the ventilated lid.

Place the worms into the bin and find a nice shady place outside to store the bin. Put the bin on top of blocks or bricks to allow for drainage. Use the lid of the second bin as a tray to catch any moisture that may drain from the bin. This worm tea is a great liquid fertilizer.

If it gets too hot or too cold, bring the worm bin inside and put it in the basement or in the laundry room. Otherwise, they'll live and work happily outside for you.

Feed your worms slowly at first. As the worms multiply, you can begin to add more food. Gently bury food scraps (fruits, vegetables, grains, cleaned eggshells or coffee grounds—no meat, eggs or cheese) in a different section of the bin each week, under the cardboard. The worms will follow the food scraps around the bin.

About a month or two before you're ready to harvest the castings to use in your garden, add newspaper, dirt, leaf litter and a bit of food to the top bin. Stop adding food to the bottom bin. The worms will migrate up through the drainage holes to get to the food in the top bin, and then you can dump the contents of the bottom bin into your garden.

Then, place the now empty bin on top, and let the process begin again. A healthy worm bin will continue to work for you for years.

More Fun

Want to gather lots of worms at once? Take a large piece of cardboard and get it damp. Leave it out in your grass overnight and check it early the next morning. You should find dozens of worms, ready to be added to your vermicompost bin!

Super Simple Yogurt Lid Feeder

This is probably one of the easiest butterfly feeders you'll ever make. All you need is a few simple supplies from around the house and you're good to go! Let's do it!

— — — — — — — — —

Materials

+ Lid from a plastic yogurt container
+ Hole punch
+ Yarn, cut into 3 to 4 long pieces
+ Pony beads
+ Very ripe fruit
+ Your nature journal (page 343)

Punch three or four holes around the edge of the lid. You want them to be equidistant from one another because you'll use these to tie on the yarn and hang your feeder.

Tie the yarn to the holes, and thread pony beads on the yarn to decorate your feeder. Once you have your beads all strung, tie the three or four pieces of yarn together at the top, and hang it near your flowers. Put the ripe fruit on the lid once it's hung securely.

And there you go! I told you it was easy! Now you can observe beautiful butterflies enjoying the fruit in your feeder and make cool scientific notes about them in your nature journal.

*See photo insert page 31.

Groovy Garden Butterfly Feeding Center

Looking for something to give your butterfly visitors more of a reason to stay in the yard? This feeding station is just the ticket! It takes a little more energy to put together than the Super Simple Yogurt Lid Feeder on page 323, but it's so worth the extra effort! Your garden is going to look so super groovy!

- - - - - - - - - - - - - - - -

Materials

+ 2 (14-inch [35-cm]) terra cotta pots
+ Epoxy (optional)
+ 1 (20-inch [50-cm]) terra cotta saucer
+ Water
+ River rocks or gravel
+ Small potted flower or herb varieties that butterflies love (we used dill and parsley)
+ Fruit
+ Your nature journal (page 343)

Turn one of the pots upside down in the center of your butterfly garden. Place the other pot right-side up on top of it. (You could glue the two pots together with epoxy if you want your structure to be permanent—just make sure you get your parent's help because it is a permanent adhesive. We decided not to because we wanted to be able to stack it easily to store it for the winter.)

Put the saucer on top of the top pot and fill with about an inch (2.5 cm) of water. Make little islands with the river stones or gravel so that butterflies have a place to perch as they drink. Also in the water, put the herb or flowerpots on one side, and the fruit on the other. We like to put out orange slices and sideways slices of banana.

Clean out the fruit regularly, replacing with fresh, and clean and freshen the water, too, so that visitors always have fresh water to drink. Make sure you head outside regularly to observe the visitors you get. Try drawing them in your nature journal so you keep a record of the types of butterflies that stop by for visits.

FUN FACT

Did you know that butterflies don't build a chrysalis; they shed their final layer of skin to reveal the chrysalis underneath. I wonder . . . do you think a caterpillar will form its chrysalis in your butterfly garden? How cool will that be?

Spectacular Sponge Feeder for Butterflies

This is probably one of the easiest butterfly feeders ever! For real! But, just because it's easy to make, don't think it's less appealing for your butterfly friends! They'll love it just as much as the others in this chapter!

- - - - - - - - - - - - - - - -

Materials

+ Sponge (without a scrubber side)
+ Hole punch
+ Garden twine
+ Sensationally Sweet Butterfly Nectar (page 325)
+ Your nature journal (page 343)

Grab the things you need and head outside to make this easy-peasy butterfly treat! Simply punch a hole in the top of the sponge and thread garden twine through it. Tie it tightly and hang it near flowers or bushes.

Dip it into a jar of butterfly nectar every day or two days, depending on the heat and how quickly it dries out. Use your nature journal to track the butterflies that visit and how often they come.

FUN FACT

Butterflies taste with their feet. Can you imagine that? What if you had to taste with YOUR feet? Yuck!

Sensationally Sweet Butterfly Nectar

Those gorgeous garden visitors need something to fuel them up as they do the tough work of finding somewhere to lay their eggs. Sweeten their visit with this yummy butterfly treat.

Materials

+ ½ cup (96 g) sugar
+ 2 cups (473 ml) water
+ Saucepan
+ Glass jar with a lid
+ Spectacular Sponge Feeder for Butterflies (page 324)
+ Medical syringe or pipette (optional)

Have an adult help you use the stove. Mix the sugar and water together in the saucepan and bring to a boil. Stir it until all the sugar is dissolved. Pour the nectar into the glass jar and let it cool.

Dip the nectar feeder into the jar, or squirt some nectar on it with a medicine syringe or pipette. Refrigerate the rest of the nectar until you need it.

Sleuthing & Caring for Caterpillars

Butterflies and moths are easy to keep and observe at home. They're pretty awesome to watch as they eat and eat their way through different life stages. We've kept a jar of caterpillars on our kitchen table every spring since our oldest child was two years old. You can too!

Materials

+ Glass aquarium, plastic container or gallon (3.8-L) jar
+ Stick that can fit diagonally in your container
+ Host plants (for caterpillars to eat)
+ Spray bottle

Butterflies and moths start their lives as eggs. When they hatch, they eat their egg shell first, then immediately need to start munching on their host plant. That's why female butterflies and moths lay their eggs on the leaves of caterpillar host plants, usually. It ensures that their caterpillars will be well taken care of.

Aren't they such great parents?

Caterpillars are larvae of butterflies and moths. They typically molt four or five times before becoming a pupa. The pupa of a moth is covered in a protective cocoon. A butterfly pupa, called a chrysalis, does not have a cocoon covering it.

When you find a caterpillar, put it carefully in your container with a stick so it can eventually climb it to form its pupa. You'll need to keep up a steady supply of fresh food for your caterpillar. It won't eat dry or dead leaves, so you'll need to get it fresh leaves from its host plant every day. Are you a finicky eater, too?

(continued)

Mist the leaves with your spray bottle so that the caterpillars have moisture. They'll get it from the leaves as they eat. When your caterpillars pupate, your waiting begins.

Usually a pupa will get dark or clear right before the adult butterfly or moth is ready to emerge. Watch carefully because once it begins to emerge, it happens quickly. The adult will crawl out of the chrysalis or cocoon and hang, pumping its wings until they are dry. If your caterpillars were butterfly larvae, then make sure you have some nectar-soaked cotton balls or cut up fruit at the bottom of your jars. They'll need to refuel as soon as their wings are dry.

If you have a moth, check the Internet or a field guide to find out if that species feeds as an adult. Some moths, like the luna moth, only live about four or five days and don't feed at all during that time. You'll want to let it go within a day or two, so that it has time to find a mate and live some of its short life outside in the fresh air.

Other species might be okay to keep for a few extra days so that you can observe them. Remember to let them go at some point, though. Butterflies and moths are meant to flutter in the garden, and you've already created a perfect natural habitat outside.

FUN FACT

Birdwing butterflies have angular wings and fly just like birds do. I love that different species of animals often mimic each other. Nature is so cool!

Adorable Life Cycle Craft

There are lots of great butterfly lifecycle crafts, projects and printables on the Internet. Here's a super easy one, though, and you can use things you likely have in your pantry right now. Get creating!

- - - - - - - - - - - -

Materials

+ Markers
+ Paper plate
+ Dried pasta: orzo (5–6), spiral (1), small shell (1), small bowtie (1)
+ Glue

First, bring your materials outside to a table or good crafting space. Divide the paper plate into four quadrants and label them egg, caterpillar, pupa and adult. Draw and color a leaf or plant in the egg quadrant. Glue the orzo pasta onto the leaves in your plant to represent the eggs.

In the caterpillar section, draw a caterpillar munching on some leaves, and color the spiral pasta the same color with which you colored your caterpillar. Glue the pasta onto your caterpillar's back to make it three-dimensional.

In the pupa section, draw a stick and glue the shell pasta to the stick to represent the pupa stage of your butterfly or moth. You can color the shell pasta like you did the spiral pasta if you want to.

Finally, color the bowtie pasta and glue it into the last quadrant, and add a head. This is your adult butterfly or moth.

You can show that this life cycle goes on and on by drawing arrows from one quadrant to the next. Hang this near where you are raising your caterpillars inside to remind you of the stages that butterflies and moths go through.

*See photo insert page 32.

Become a Beautiful Butterfly

Butterflies are everywhere, and now's your chance to become one for a little while. Will you flutter around and play? Or, will you decorate your wings realistically and mimic the migratory path of monarch butterflies? Whatever you do, have fun and play around, imagining that you're a butterfly on its long migratory flight.

- - - - - - - - - - - - - -

Materials

+ Large sheet of poster board
+ Scissors
+ Markers, paints, pastels or your favorite art supplies
+ Ribbon or yarn, cut into two pieces

Fold the poster board in half and cut out a wing shape. Decorate the butterfly wings with your art supplies. You can make this realistic by grabbing a butterfly field guide and copying the markings of your favorite butterfly species, or you can have fun and be whimsical, making up patterns and mixing colors as you go.

Once the wings are decorated and dry, punch two holes towards the top, and two toward the middle of your wings. We just used a sharp pencil to poke our holes.

Thread the yarn through the holes to make arm bands (like backpack straps) on the back of the wings, and tie them securely. You can see how we made ours in the photo.

Now, put your wings on and flutter with the butterflies in your yard! Maybe you can even grab a great book about butterfly migration like *An Extraordinary Life* by Laurence Pringle and Bob Marstall, then act it out.

*See photo insert page 32.

A Creepy-Crawly Pet Your Parent Will Not Love

It's really easy to make your own spider home. Make sure you ask if you can bring one into the house though. Spiders are one of those creatures that are interesting, but hated by many people.

— — — — — — — — — — — — —

Materials

+ Soil or dirt
+ Small plastic terrarium (critter keeper) from a pet store or a plastic container that has a tight-fitting lid and is well-ventilated with tiny air holes
+ Twigs, leaf litter, sticks and/or pieces of bark
+ Small piece of sponge in a dish with a bit of water
+ Petroleum jelly (optional)

Head outside to where you can find some dirt for this habitat setup. Spread some soil in a layer on the bottom of your terrarium. Make sure it isn't wet. Spiders prefer their habitats to be dry. Put a layer of twigs, leaf litter, sticks and bark over top of the soil.

Arrange some of the sticks and bark so they are crossed and upright. You want your spider to have places in which to hide and weave their webs.

Place your small dish with the water-soaked sponge in the habitat so your spider has a fresh water source.

Go spider hunting.

Unlike some of the other insects you've handled during the activities in this book, spiders aren't always safe to hold. To make sure you capture a spider carefully, follow these tips:

- Grab a jar or other recyclable container with a lid and search your backyard for spiderwebs or spiders crawling around.
- When you find one, gently coax it into your container using the lid.
- Dump it into your already prepared terrarium, and place the lid on tightly.

If you want to make sure that your spider spins its web towards the bottom of the terrarium, and not the top or lid (so you can open the enclosure easily for feeding), then spread a thin layer of petroleum jelly around the edge and top of the lid.

Give your spider prey to eat once or twice a week, depending on its size. Simply put a cricket or another insect into the terrarium with it. Watch it feed—it's so fascinating. If it doesn't eat what you put in the terrarium, try other insects of varying sizes until you find things it will eat.

Spiders can make good pets, but if you ever get tired of keeping it, then make sure you release it back to the area in your yard where you found it originally.

Spider-Friendly Frames

Spiders like to weave their webs in sheltered areas of your yard, usually near plants where insects like to hang out. And while they seem creepy to some people, spiders are awesome backyard tenants. They can eat all sorts of pesky backyard pests. With this activity, you'll encourage them to take up residence in your yard.

- - - - - - - - - - - - - -

Materials

+ Old window panes, picture frames, bike tires or other recyclables that have open frame-like areas
+ Your nature journal (page 343, optional)

Make a spider-friendly area in your yard by leaning open recyclables against trees, walls and shrubs.

Check back often. You'll likely find that spiders have taken up residency in your spider shelters within a few days or weeks. You may even want to observe them, draw their web designs and jot down your thoughts in your nature journal.

FUN FACT

Tarantulas can fling tiny hairs called urticating hairs at their predators. They have small barbs on them that get in a predator's eyes and nose, irritating the soft tissue so the tarantula can get away. Ouch! They're like miniature porcupines!

Spinning Sensational Webs

Spiders are pretty amazing, aren't they? Their spiderwebs are as much as ten times the size of their bodies, and they build one almost every day.

Could you do that? Do you think you could build something ten times bigger than yourself, and have it come out as intricately designed as a spiderweb? If you were to do that, how big would your web need to be? Try it out in this simple activity.

- - - - - - - - - - - -

Materials

+ Measuring tape
+ Yarn
+ Double-sided tape

First, head outside with your materials. Measure your height using your measuring tape, and then calculate how wide your web would have to be. Remember—if you were a spider it would be ten times your height!

Stick one end of your yarn to a tree, and then try to build a web, mimicking the patterns you observed when you went hunting for a web to capture. You'll need a large area. Good luck!

Spiders create their webs by releasing a single thread of silk, just like you're doing with your yarn. The spider starts by sticking its thread to a single point, and then attaches the other end to the starting point.

Amazingly, spiders can spin two types of thread while they build their webs. Some threads are sticky to catch prey, and others are not, so they can easily walk across them.

(continued)

It's a lot harder than it seems, isn't it? How did you do? Were you able to replicate a spider's web?

Probably not, but it's fun to try things like that. My kids love when we take a skein of inexpensive yarn and make a spiderweb to play in. We've done it in the house and in the backyard.

Now . . . go find some friends and pretend to be spiders and prey this afternoon! Your web is ready!

FUN FACT
Abandoned spiderwebs are called cobwebs. Spiders were once nicknamed cobs for the Old English word for spider, attercops, which means "poison head."

Sending Spider Messages Through Vibrations

How quickly do you think a spider can detect prey on its web? This is a cool way to find out. You'll use vibration to send messages to a spider in the yard, and see how it reacts! How cool is that—talking to spiders! You can be the next spider whisperer . . . maybe even have your own reality show someday. . . . Try it now!

- - - - - - - - - - - - - - -

Materials

+ Metal bar, tuning fork or other object that vibrates when struck
+ Wooden block
+ Stopwatch or watch with a second hand
+ Your nature journal (page 343)

Look for a web outside in your yard that has a spider on it. Hit your metal bar or tuning fork against the wooden block to set it vibrating and very gently (you don't want to ruin the web) set it against the spiderweb about 6 inches (15 cm) from the spider. Time how long it takes for the spider to get to the point where you touched.

Write that down in your nature journal.

Experiment with different vibrations. Hit the metal bar harder and softer against the wooden block to change the frequency of the vibration. Each time, let the spider rest, then place the bar 6 inches (15 cm) from where it sits.

Time the spider each time and note whether or not the change in vibration affects how quickly the spider responds.

Why do you think the spider reacts as it does? Those vibrations tell it something—that dinner may have just gotten tangled in its web—and it needs to act fast. Pretty cool! Try it again sometime with a different spider and compare your results.

FUN FACT
Spiders have between two and six spinnerets on the backs of their abdomens. These are like tiny showerheads each with hundreds of holes that spray out liquid silk. It's amazing to think that those tiny showerheads create homes and food traps for arachnids. So super cool!

Stupendous Spiderweb Art

Ever see a spiderweb in the yard and wonder how such a beautiful piece of art could be created by such a tiny creature? They're amazing. And the cool thing is that they spin new webs all the time, so you can capture one to keep for yourself to study for patterns. I'll show you how!

– – – – – – – – – – – – – –

Materials

+ Talcum powder
+ Black construction paper
+ Hair spray

Now, go be a super sleuth outside and find a spider web to capture. Don't disturb a web that has a spider or prey on it. Look for a web that isn't in use. Spiders spin new webs every day or two, though, so don't worry if you accidentally take one that was going to be used.

When you find a good web, gently dust it completely with talcum powder by shaking the container so that the powder comes out in a fine shower—like it's raining on the web. The powder will stick to the web, making the spider silk look white.

Hold your construction paper underneath the web, and slowly bring it upwards towards the web until it detaches from whatever branches it was attached to.

Spray the web with hair spray and set it aside to dry.

Once it's dry, you can further protect it by taking it to an office supply store and having it laminated, or slipping it into a clear plastic sheet protector.

Enjoy your natural artwork!

FUN FACT
It is estimated that there are one million spiders in every acre of land, though it might be closer to three million in the tropics. That means that no human is ever more than 10 feet (3 m) away from a spider. Ever. Does that excite or terrify you?

Epic Mirror Box for Observing Nature

While a mirror box isn't necessary for catching and observing anything, it can make it an even cooler experience. With a mirror box, you're able to see all the different sides of a critter at the same time. Awesome!

And this one is super simple to make—especially if you have metallic scrapbooking paper leftover from fancy holiday cards or a similar project. A good quality aluminum foil might work, too. Let's go!

- - - - - - - - - - - - - - - - - -

Materials

+ Quart or half gallon (1- or 2-L) cardboard milk carton
+ Scissors
+ Silver metallic (mirror-like) scrapbooking paper or metallic tape
+ Transparent tape

Are you ready? This one's a little technical—but so, so cool. Make sure you read the directions carefully. It will be totally worth it!

Have an adult help you cut the milk carton in half across the middle so you have the bottom box-like portion and the top of the carton. You'll only need the bottom part for this activity, so go ahead and put the top part in the recycling bin.

It's easier to put the mirror tape or paper on a flat surface, so cut along the sides of the bottom half of your carton, down towards the bottom. Flatten it into one piece.

Tape your silver mirror-like paper to the inside of the flattened carton securely. Then, fold the sides back up and tape the carton together again.

Hooray! You did it!

Bring this outside with you so the next time you catch a ladybug, ant, grasshopper or another small critter, you can put it gently in your mirror box.

Isn't it amazing to see its movement from all angles? I just love being able to see an insect's underside as I look down on it.

More Fun

Want to try catching more insects to check out in your mirror box or bug box? Grab a large, light-colored sheet (white works best) and spread it out under a tree. Have an adult help you shake the branches really hard for a minute or two. Explore the sheet to see what insects, caterpillars, spiders and other creatures you had hanging out in your yard. Then, put a couple of them into one of the bug boxes you already made from the directions on page 296, and check them out one by one in your epic mirror box.

(sixteen)

SALAMANDERS, SNAKES, LIZARDS, TOADS, OH MY!

Herpetology is the subfield of biology where scientists study reptiles and amphibians. Its name comes from the Greek word *herpeton*, which means creeping creature. There are over 7,000 different species of amphibians on Earth and over 10,000 species of reptiles currently known.

Most scientists who study herpetology tend to specialize in learning about one specific species, like the scientist I met who specializes in the study of the red-sided garter snake.

I love that there are people out there that study one species of snake for their whole lives! It's fascinating how passionate people can be about things that interest them.

Is there a specific herp (the nickname for reptiles and amphibians) you are interested in learning about? Think about why you want to learn about it, and then go find out all about it!

There's a lot to learn about different reptiles and amphibians, but depending on where you live, you might not be able to find any in your backyard as easily as you could find the bugs, insects and worms in the last chapter. So, while I'll show you how to set up a section of your yard to make it "herp friendly," most of the activities and experiments in this chapter can be done without any animals in hand.

Basking Beauties: Reptiles in the Heat

Have you ever wondered why snakes and other reptiles and amphibians bask in the sun? Why they come out during the day and hang out on rocks and logs? Reptiles and amphibians are ectothermic, so instead of using energy from food to keep its body temperature regulated like we do, a snake uses the environment to warm itself up and cool itself down.

Many people think of reptiles and amphibians as cold-blooded creatures, and while their blood can be cold at times, it can also be quite warm. That's why scientists prefer the term ectothermic to describe how these animals use their environment to regulate temperatures.

Where do you think the best place would be for a snake or lizard to bask during the day? How about after the sun has set? Grab your nature journal, get the following materials, and try to find out on the next sunny day.

Materials

+ Dark construction paper
+ Light construction paper
+ Aluminum foil
+ Light-colored rock
+ Dark-colored rock
+ Thermometers (find at your local discount store)
+ Your nature journal (page 343)

Take each of the items outside and find a flat, sunny spot, then take each item's temperature with the thermometer and record the starting temperature.

Leave them alone for 10 minutes, then touch them and take their new temperature and record it. Leave the items in the sun for 2 hours, then record their temperature in your journal.

Take them inside and set them back on the table for ten minutes, then record their temperature.

Look over your results and form some conclusions by answering the following questions:

Did all the items warm up and cool down at the same rate?

If you were a snake or a lizard, which of those materials would be the best place to bask on during the day? Why?

Which would be the best place to bask on after the sun has set? Why?

Sneaky, Scent-Hunting Reptiles

Most snakes shoot their tongues in and out, up and down, and pull them back inside their mouths where there are two openings. These openings lead to the Jacobson's organ. Snakes rub their tongue on this sensitive organ, wiping off the scents they have gathered. (Many lizards smell that way, too.)

The Jacobson's organ then sends a signal to the snake's brain so it can identify the scent as prey, predator or mate. Can you imagine relying on only your sense of smell to find food and friends? Let's see how you'd do. In this game, you'll pretend to be snakes.

Materials

+ Cotton balls
+ Scented oils or extracts (peppermint, almond, vanilla, etc.)
+ Plastic zipper-top bags
+ Permanent marker
+ Blindfold
+ Friends to play with
+ Timer
+ Your nature journal (page 343)

(continued)

Prepare the materials before playing the game, then head outside.

Soak a separate cotton ball in each of the oils or extracts and place them in separate bags and zip them shut.

Choose one of the scents you've already used and soak another cotton ball in that oil, place it in its own bag, seal and write SNAKE on the outside of the bag with the permanent marker. Choose a player to be the snake.

Secure a blindfold on the snake, hand him or her their scented bag, and have the snake familiarize itself with the scent by opening the bag and smelling it.

Have all the other players spread out with a different scented bag, and have them open them up and hold them out in front of their bodies.

Turn on the timer, and let the snake try to find its mate (or friend) by finding the player with the matching scent just by using his or her sense of smell.

Once the snake finds its mate, record its time, mix the scents back up and choose a new snake. Play again, trying to beat the first snake's time.

What did you think about having to rely on your sense of smell to locate your friend? A good scientist writes reflections like these in their nature journal. Take a few minutes and write about what you did during this game and what you thought about it.

Wouldn't it be strange to flick your tongue in and out, rubbing it against holes inside your mouth in order to smell? The animal world really is amazing. And snakes and lizards might just be some of the coolest things in the animal world!

FUN FACT

Cobras are the most aggressive snakes in the world. They're so dangerous that just one drop of venom could kill 50 humans. Whoa! I'd hate to have a cobra get a whiff of me in its habitat!

Where Are All the Reptiles?

If reptiles rely on their sense of smell to find food, mates and to know when a predator is nearby, how do you think they protect themselves from those predators? Reptiles, like so many other creatures in your yard (and yes—there are probably snakes and lizards in your yard from time to time) use camouflage to keep them safe from being eaten. They're so good at hiding that I bet you've rarely seen a snake or lizard in your yard—and if you have, good for you! That's quite an accomplishment.

See just how coloring helps snakes and lizards stay alive with this simple game using colored objects to represent reptiles in your yard!

Materials

+ Colored craft sticks or pipe cleaners in different colors
+ Patch of grass
+ A friend
+ Blindfold
+ Timer
+ Other places to play—like a driveway, sandbox or garden
+ Your nature journal (page 343)

Choose ten to fifteen craft sticks in each color—making sure you have green—then head out to your backyard.

Choose a player to be blindfolded.

Once the blindfold is secure, scatter the sticks across the grass.

Set a timer for five minutes, remove your partner's blindfold, and have him or her see how many "reptiles in the grass" they can find before the timer goes off.

Once the timer goes off, sort them by color and count how many of each color your partner found. Did he or she find them all? Which color was easiest to find? Hardest? Why?

Play the game again, but this time you try to find the reptiles.

Did you find them all? Was your experience similar to your partner's?

Keep playing the game, but try it out on different surfaces like the driveway, garden, blacktop, etc.

Compare your success rate to your partner's and then compare both success rates between surfaces.

Make sure you find all of the craft sticks you started with before you head inside for the day. It's important to take care of your yard.

A reptile's coloring helps keep them from being found. That's why garter snakes tend to have greenish colors and rattlesnakes tend to be brownish. They need to blend into their unique habitats.

It was probably more difficult for you to find the green sticks in your grass because they blended in just like a garter snake would. Reptiles have amazing adaptations.

Radical Reptiles: Snake Temperature Regulation

Snakes are masters at regulating their body temperatures, or keeping themselves at the perfect temperature. Besides taking a dip in the water or moving to a more shaded area, they change the way they're arranging their bodies in order to release or preserve heat. In this activity, you'll see how different body arrangements can affect a reptile's body temperature. Grab your materials, head outside and check it out!

Materials

+ Two small hand towels that are the same color
+ Two thermometers
+ Your nature journal (page 343)

(continued)

Bring your materials to your backyard on a hot, sunny day. Roll up each of your towels into a tube shape and pop a thermometer into the center of each one. Lay them in a sunny area—one stretched out and one rolled into a coil.

Which do you think will warm up the fastest? Write your hypothesis in your nature journal.

Draw a simple chart in your journal with three columns like the one below. One should be labeled Straight Snake and the other should be labeled Coiled Snake. Record the temperature of each snake every minute. You'll want to note which snake reaches a maximum temperature the quickest (you'll know this because the temperature will stop rising each time you check it). How long does it take for the other snake to reach that temperature? You may need more rows than the sample table.

Time Elapsed	Straight Snake	Coiled Snake
1 Minute		
2 Minutes		
3 Minutes		
4 Minutes		
5 Minutes		
6 Minutes		
7 Minutes		

Once they reach the same temperature, move them to a shady spot, but keep them either stretched out or coiled. Record their temperature every minute. Which cools faster?

While a snake stretches out to absorb the sun's energy more quickly than when it's coiled, it will coil up to conserve that energy and stay warm for longer.

Sometimes, though, stretching out or coiling up isn't enough to keep a snake warm. During winter months, snakes enter a brumation period, which is similar to hibernation. They just can't keep their body temperature up enough to be actively out in the wild during the colder months.

Brumation is different than hibernation because snakes, and other reptiles that brumate, don't go completely to sleep. They eat a lot less, sometimes not eating at all for months, but still need to rouse themselves to find water to drink. Brumation, like hibernation, is triggered by falling temperatures and a decrease in daylight hours.

FUN FACT
Some snake species, like the red-sided garter snake, come together in large numbers to keep each other warm through the winter months. At the Narcisse Snake Dens in Manitoba, Canada, you can see, touch and interact with tens of thousands of red-sided garter snakes all together in one place. Amazing!

Creating Lounging Spaces for Lizards

Like all ectothermic animals, lizards rely on the sun and air to keep their body temperatures regulated. Because of this, lizards need basking areas that are safe for them to relax and soak up the sun's heat. Rock piles and walls are wonderful areas in which to watch out for these neat creatures.

They're really the perfect habitat for lizards because they can get warm and they have the little crevices between the rocks to dart into and hide if predators come. You can make one yourself!

– – – – – – – – – – – – – – –

Materials

+ 20- to 24-inch (50- to 60-cm)-diameter terra cotta pot
+ Rocks of various shapes and sizes
+ Cinder blocks
+ Bricks
+ Your nature journal (page 343)

Create the perfect place for a lizard to take up residence by filling your clay pot with different shaped rocks, leaving gaps and cracks between them. Set it up in your backyard near bushes, walls and other spots that are lit up with streaky patches of sunlight during the day. They'll sun themselves in the patches of light, but enjoy the variety of shade and shadows to hide in if they sense danger. Scatter cinder blocks, bricks and more rocks in a jumbled pile so there are lots of hiding places for lizards to get away from predators.

Check it out every few days to see if there are any signs of lizards living there. On hot, sunny days, you can sit out in the yard with your nature journal and quietly observe. If you see a lizard or even a snake sunning itself on the rocks, sketch them in your journal, then look it up to see which species visit your yard.

Toad-ally Tubular Toad House

When you are searching for backyard amphibians, toads are easy to attract. They eat thousands of insects from vegetable gardens and flower beds, so they're great to have around, too.

With this fun project, it's easy to turn old or broken flower pots into toad houses. You can use things like coffee cans, too.

– – – – – – – – – – – – – – –

Materials

+ Flowerpot or coffee can
+ Nature treasures like pebbles, rocks and sticks
+ Glue gun
+ Small shovel
+ Dried leaves
+ Dish with water (optional)

Bring your materials to a table in the backyard, and take some time to decorate the outside of your flowerpot or coffee can. Pebbles, rocks, sticks and other natural treasures are great for this. Just attach them with a glue gun.

Pick out a cool, shady spot in your yard and dig a hole. Set your container on its side, half buried in the hole. Toads love burrowing, so a dirt floor will encourage them to call the toad house their new home.

(continued)

Crumble up some of the dried leaves on top of the dirt for bedding, and wait for your new residents. You can further encourage toads to live there by keeping out a dish of water so there is a readily available water source.

Keeping Toads as Pets

Have you ever wanted to keep a toad as a pet? It's toad-ally easy to do, and if you take good care of it, your toad can be a great pet for years. We have two right now, and they hop out of their hiding places when my daughter approaches their habitat with food. Super awesome pets!

When you're looking for toads to keep as pets, go outside just before dark. The bugs are out, and toads are just becoming active. Look around wood piles and behind rocks. Catch a toad with your hands or the net you made on page 296.

— — — — — — — — — — — — —

Materials

+ Old tank or aquarium, large plastic box or other large container
+ Dirt or peat moss
+ Small terra cotta pot and saucer
+ Water

A toad habitat is easy to set up. Bring your materials to a good workspace outside. You'll need an old aquarium or another large container that has a screened lid. You can make one by laying an old screen on top of a large plastic shoebox.

Toads like moist dirt, and they like to dig, so put a few inches (6 to 7 cm) of dirt or peat moss on the bottom of your tank while you're outside setting it up. Partially bury a terra cotta saucer for water. Lay the terra cotta pot on its side in the corner and layer the bottom with more dirt or moss. This will give your toad a place to hide when it needs to.

Put your toad gently in the aquarium and set the lid on tightly. You'll need to feed your toad every other day. And, since toads don't like to eat the same things over and over again, you'll want to change things up. Catch flies to give it, dig up earthworms, find mealworms . . . there are lots of things in your backyard to feed your toad.

FUN FACT
Did you know that a group of toads is called a knot? I never knew that!

Creating a Salamander-Friendly Space

There are more amphibians than just frogs and toads. Salamanders are tricky amphibians to find in our area. My kids love going to a vernal pool nearby on the first warm rain of the spring to watch spotted salamanders migrate to lay their eggs. It's a pretty amazing sight. Vernal pools are pond-like pools of water that are only in place from early spring to the middle of summer, when they evaporate from the heat. They are home to incredible creatures like salamanders who rely on these temporary pools for survival.

You can attract some of the less finicky salamanders to your yard (along with snakes and arboreal [tree] lizards) pretty easily.

— — — — — — — — — — — — —

Materials

+ Sticks, logs, rocks, etc.
+ Your nature journal (page 343)

Like you did with your lizard habitat (page 338), find a place in your yard that has low bushes, a wall or a shady spot. Build up a brush and rock pile.

Pile the logs, sticks and rocks at the base of your wall or bush, and leave lots of cracks and hiding places. Leave it alone for a few weeks. Then, check back to see if you can spot some cool new wildlife in your yard. This is a good time for you to practice your observation skills and watch the pile, while drawing what you see in your nature journal.

FUN FACT

The name salamander comes from Greek and means fire lizard. They got their name when logs were thrown on a fire, and these teeny lizard-like creatures scurried out.

Amphibian Athletics

Frogs and toads are fun to play with, as long as you remember that they're living creatures, and you're careful to treat them well. My kids have always loved to race their frogs. It's simple to set up a frog or toad race. Come on! I'll show you how!

Materials

+ Long plastic container
+ Several frogs or toads
+ Friends

Set your plastic container on a sturdy outdoor surface like your driveway. This will be your racetrack.

Sit at the start line (one side of the container) with your friends and their frogs or toads, and set them down at the same time. See which one makes it to the other end first. You can encourage your frog or toad to jump by tapping its behind gently.

More Fun

Frog races and frog jumping contests were once a famous pastime, even being a part of county fairs everywhere. Look to see if your local county fair has frog jumping contests and how you train a frog to enter. Who knows? You just might discover a new sport!

Scurrying, Scavenging Tadpoles

If you head out to a creek or a pond during late spring and early summer, you'll probably see lots of tadpoles swimming at the edge of the water—especially if you head there in the heat of the day. Take some time before you go, and prepare a habitat for them at home because tadpoles are very easy to raise, and so fun to watch as they go through their life cycle. Let's go hunting!

Materials

+ Large container
+ Gravel
+ Water pump (optional)
+ Large, flat rocks
+ Tadpoles
+ Your nature journal (page 343)
+ Lettuce, algae, pond plants

(continued)

Get a large container and head out to your backyard. My kids use a 2½-gallon (9-L) aquarium that we ordered online. You can use jars, bins and other containers, too. Just make sure that you have enough room for the tadpoles to move around.

Cover the bottom with gravel or small rocks. Your tadpoles will scavenge for algae in between them. My kids like to add a pump to their tank and bury the line in the gravel. It's not absolutely necessary, but if you have a pump lying around from an old fish tank, it can help keep the water full of oxygen. Otherwise, you should give the water a stir to aerate it a few times each day.

Take your big rocks and arrange them in a pile on one side. Try to get the top rock positioned at a slant. When the tadpoles begin developing their legs, they'll need to be able to crawl out of the water and bask.

Fill your tank with water that's non-chlorinated or a bucket of pond water that you bring home with you when you catch your tadpoles. Your tank is ready, so add your tadpoles in whenever you find them. You can also add a frog or toad spawn, or eggs, if you find that instead. Just lay the jelly-like spawn at the top of the water.

We keep our tadpoles in the kitchen so my kids can watch them all day long. They use their nature journals to draw pictures as they change from tadpole to frog. It's so much fun.

Frogs take between six and twelve weeks to go through metamorphosis, so be patient! Use your nature journal to record observations as they grow. You'll need to feed your hungry tadpoles often. Ours like boiled lettuce. We boil dark green lettuce for ten to twelve minutes and let it cool. Sometimes we lay a leaf right on the top of the water and watch them eat. Other times we chop it up and freeze it in little clumps to feed them each day. When the frogs and toads are fully developed into froglets and toadlets, bring them back to the place where you caught them and let them go.

(seventeen)

BIRDS, BIRDS AND MORE BIRDS

Ornithology is the study of birds, and is an area of science where everyday people—just like you—can make important contributions and discoveries. There are annual bird counts around the world, and kids and adults help by counting the different species they see in their yards so scientists know where to go to study certain species.

Ornithologists study everything there is to know about birds, and most specialize in one aspect of that. So, you might find some ornithologists study how different parts of a bird work and how those body systems work together. You might find one who is interested in one specific species and its migratory path.

There are some really cool things to discover about birds and they're super easy to study from your own backyard. You'll make some feeders to encourage new birds to visit, and observe their preferences! It's so much fun to have a nature-friendly place right in your yard.

Amazing Nature Explorer's Journal

The notebooks of great scientists throughout history have been built upon in every generation. What YOU record today might be the observation that sparks a new understanding ten years from now. Seriously! You never know what will come of jotting down the strange thing you saw a beetle doing in your yard . . . or how big that anthill was . . . or how the chickadee's feet felt as it perched on your hand and ate seed from your palm.

So, start by making the best nature journal ever— all from things around the house—and record the things you do as you read this book and explore your backyard. Your observations are as unique as you are—and so they need an amazing journal to be written into!

- - - - - - - - - - - - - - - -

Materials

+ Cereal box
+ Scissors
+ Glue stick, tape runner or double-sided tape
+ Decorative paper
+ Heavy needle and embroidery floss, twine or cording
+ Button with large holes
+ Paper for the inside pages
+ Ruler
+ Awl, skewer or hole punch (optional)
+ Pen

Cut out the cereal box to create the cover for the journal. You can make it as large or as small as you want to, but my kids like to use one whole side of a cereal box, so they can use regular computer or grid paper in their journal. Fold it in half so that the blank cardboard side is facing out. Glue a piece of scrapbook or wrapping paper to both the inside and outside to make a pretty lining and cover. Trim any excess paper.

Use the needle and twine to sew the button onto what will be the front of the journal. Leave about 12 inches (30 cm) of twine hanging. You'll use that to wrap around the journal and then around the button to close it.

My kids like to use 20 to 25 sheets of computer paper or grid paper for the pages of their journals. You can make yours as full as you'd like. Lay the paper in the inside of the journal (if it is bigger than the cover, you'll need to trim it so that it is about ¼ inch [6 mm] smaller than the cover on all sides).

Using the needle and twine, stitch the paper to the cover down the spine. My kids and I like to use an awl—which is a pointy tool that's used to poke holes for crafting—to make three holes in the spine of the journal first to make it easier to poke the needles through and sew it all together. You can use a skewer or even a hole punch if you don't have an awl. Just poke a hole near the top, middle and bottom of the journal's spine.

Want it to come together even easier? Poke holes in the center of the papers, too! Then, sew it all together, and you have the most amazing nature journal ever! We love experimenting with new colors and papers to make ours!

Now, tuck your journal, some colored pencils (watercolor pencils are awesome), pencils, a portable sharpener, binoculars, magnifying glass, small containers for collecting specimens, old spoons or a small shovel for digging in the dirt, and other things you might need in your explorations into a small backpack or tote bag. You'll always have your tools ready and waiting for you.

Head out to your yard, find a comfortable place to sit and draw or write what you see. It's so fun to look back on nature and science journals like this—you can see all of the adventures you've been on! Throughout the book, I mention writing something down in your journal—this is the journal I'm talking about! Keep it with you, and document all of your amazing explorations. You'll treasure it always!

> ## FUN FACT
> Henry David Thoreau is the author of some of the most famous nature journals of all time. They were full of personal reflections, drawings and observations. Often, there was a combination like this reflective observation, "I saw a bird flying across the street with so long a strip of cloth, or the like, the other day, and so slowly that at first I thought it was a little boy's kite with a long tail." I wonder what kinds of cool observations you'll make in your journal!

Popped Corn, Unpopped Corn

Many people hang bird feeders or scatter seed in their yard to attract birds. Do you? We'll make some different types of bird feeders later in this chapter. For now, let's see some bird ethology (or study some bird behavior).

Birds like to eat seeds like sunflower and corn. Some people enjoy sunflower seeds and corn, too, but they tend to prefer their seeds toasted and the corn roasted or popped, not raw. Do you think birds would like their corn popped like people eat it? Let's see if they have a preference.

Materials

+ Your nature journal (page 343)
+ Two plastic dishes
+ Popped corn
+ Unpopped corn

Make a hypothesis in your journal. Do you think that birds will prefer their corn popped or unpopped? Why?

Place your two dishes outside in a safe place near where you've seen birds or already have a feeder set up.

Put popped popcorn on one and unpopped popcorn on the other. It's best if you can observe this experiment from far away. Birds can be skittish, and you don't want to discourage them from enjoying their snack. You can further encourage them to come near enough to the popcorn to eat by sprinkling some of the seed you already know they love around the area where you've placed your plates.

Which did the birds in your area prefer? Mine preferred the popped corn when we tried this most recently, but in the past, they've eaten the unpopped as well. Watching the behaviors of animals like birds is so interesting because we see that they have unique personalities too!

> ## FUN FACT
> Many birds kept as pets, including doves, parakeets and lovebirds, enjoy living in pairs for companionship. Do you have a pet bird?

The Sweet Sound of Birdsong

Birdsong is important if birds want to survive. It tells others what species it is. It announces whether it is male or female. It scares intruders away from a nest.

Birds can sing different songs just like instruments can produce different notes. Each one tells a different story. Interestingly, birds don't have a larynx like people do. They have a bony structure called a syrinx for making sounds. This is controlled by special muscles that vibrate to make different songs and calls.

See if you can listen to and record some of the bird songs in your yard with this activity!

- - - - - - - - - - - -

Materials

+ Digital recorder (from a phone or tablet works well, too)
+ Field guides and Internet access
+ Your nature journal (page 343)

Find a spot in the backyard where a lot of birds hang out like low-hanging trees, bushes and shrubs. Secure your recorder near a nest or feeder. Now, go sit somewhere a bit away from the recorder where you can watch without disturbing the birds' activity.

Close your eyes, be very still and listen for several minutes.

Write down the sounds of the birds that you hear in your journal. Try to replicate those sounds as closely as you can. For example, a chickadee makes a chick-a-dee-dee-dee sound. Spend as long as you can, quietly listening and recording the sounds that you hear. You might even want to sketch some pictures of the birds you see in the journal, too, or make notes of what they look like.

When you're finished, use bird books, the Internet, your sound recordings and your notes to identify the birds that you saw and heard. Write the common names of the birds you hear in your journal near your written interpretations of their sounds. Keep a running list of birds you see and hear in your yard in your journal.

More Fun

There are lots of birdsongs recorded online. With an adult's permission, find some clips of birds that are local to you. Listen to them and get to know their songs. Then, go to the yard and close your eyes, trying to figure out what birds are around you.

Exploring Feathers

Every bird has feathers—they're very important to a bird's survival. They provide insulation, keeping the bird warm. They also allow birds to fly because they have a hollow shaft in the center that gives structure without adding weight.

Each shaft has a vane made up of many barbs projecting from it. These barbs cling to each other using their barbules. Feathers are fascinating structures. As you observe them in this activity, note how these seemingly simple objects are amazing examples of nature's wonder. Look closely and draw what you see in your journal!

- - - - - - - - - - - -

Materials

+ Your nature journal (page 343)
+ Feather (if you can't find one in your yard, the feathers you can find at craft stores make a great substitution)
+ Magnifying glass (and a microscope if you have it)
+ Scissors

(continued)

Bring your materials outside and record observations in your nature journal by drawing what you see as you study the feather and all its parts.

Using the magnifying glass, examine the feather from top to bottom. Carefully cut through the center shaft of the feather. What do you notice? How does this help flight?

Look carefully through your magnifying glass at the surface of the feather. What do you notice about the vane? If you have a microscope, look more closely at the barbs that make up the vane of the feather.

Brush backward against the barbs to separate them. Look through your magnifying glass. How might this affect flight?

While looking through the magnifying glass, smooth the barbs back into place. Do you see the tiny hooks called barbules catching each other to keep the feather in this smooth state?

Feathers are important for different things besides flight. They also help birds show off to attract a mate, keep warm, stay dry or to blend into their surroundings.

Finding and Identifying Bird Nests

Birds are amazing engineers. They create intricately woven homes out of hard materials like twigs and bark. They make their homes among branches that twist and turn in heavy winds.

These homes come in all shapes and sizes, too. From the tiny ping-pong ball–sized nest of a hummingbird to the 10-foot (3-m)-wide nests of bald eagles, birds can build incredible structures. See if you can discover how they do it by carefully dissecting a nest in this activity.

Materials

+ Binoculars
+ Bird's nest
+ Your nature journal (page 343)
+ Tweezers
+ Magnifying glass

In the late fall or early winter, go outside with your binoculars and search for abandoned bird nests. Most birds migrate and abandon their nests during this time of year, so it's a great time to find unused nests. You can find them in lower branches of trees, shrubs and even among rocks and tall grasses. If the nest you find is up high, ask a grown-up to help you get it down.

Gently take the nest from the tree after you've made sure that it is no longer occupied. Set up a workspace at home in your yard that has room for you to spread out. Make sure you have your nature journal opened up so you can draw what you're doing.

Use your tweezers to separate the pieces of material making up the nest. Examine them closely with your magnifying glass and separate the materials into like piles.

Make a list of materials and analyze how the nest was constructed. Was there a pattern to the materials used? Did the materials give you any clues as to when the nest was built or where the bird flew to gather supplies? Write down any of these observations in your journal.

More Fun

Save scraps of colorful yarn and ribbon throughout the year from your craft projects. Hang it from trees in recycled strawberry cartons or in suet bird feeder cages in the springtime. Birds will pull the pieces out and use them in their nests, and you'll be able to see them when you hunt for abandoned nests next fall.

Become a Feathered Architect

Birds build their nests everywhere, from the tops of some trees to ditches on the side of the road. Some shore birds even build nests of rocks surrounding a clutch of eggs. Others build intricate woven cups of grasses, twigs and down.

Think about the bird nests you've seen or the one you recently dissected. Could you do it? Could you build a secure nest from materials you find in your yard? How do birds make it seem so easy? Let's see if you're as talented as the birds in your yard!

- - - - - - - - - - - - - - -

Materials

+ Twigs
+ Leaves
+ Dried grass or plants
+ Paper scraps
+ Yarn
+ String
+ Your nature journal (page 343)

Walk around the neighborhood, take a hike in the woods or search the Internet to find bird nests of all shapes and sizes. Observe them carefully and try to discover how the nests have been constructed. If you are looking at real nests, try not to disturb any bird families.

Gather a variety of materials from the list, and any additional nest-building supplies you think would be useful, then head outside to get building.

Using just your fingers—no glue or tape—try to build a nest that mimics one of the nests you observed. Make sure your nest would be able to hold two or three eggs.

How did you do? Are you a master nest builder? Or is that task for the birds? Write about your experience and thoughts in your journal.

Pointy Beaks, Stubby Beaks

You can tell a lot about birds just by looking at their beaks. Beaks come in different sizes and shapes because they do different jobs. Insect-eating birds, like the bluebird, have pointed beaks with large mouths. Cardinals and other seed-eaters have a stubby, sharp beak. Worm-eaters like the robin have pointed beaks for digging. Woodpeckers have a long, thin beak that is perfect for drilling into trees.

In this game, become a sparrow or a swallow, and use your beak to eat your food. Notice how important it is to have the right tools for the job!

- - - - - - - - - - - - - - -

Materials

+ A friend
+ Paper clip
+ Dried fruit
+ Clothespin
+ Nuts
+ Timer
+ Your nature journal (page 343)

You need a friend, parent or sibling to play this game with. Head outside and set up your game.

Stretch the paperclip out so that one end is straight and the other is still bent. This is the sparrow beak. Put a bowl of dried fruit in front of the player using the paperclip sparrow beak. The other player is the swallow, and is using the clothespin as a beak. Place a bowl of nuts in front of the swallow player.

Set the timer for 3 minutes. Each player tries to get as much food out of their bowl as they can using only their beak. When the time is up, compare the food each player was able to remove from their bowl.

The player with the most bird food in front of them is the winner.

Was the challenge of removing your food easy or difficult? Why do you think that is? Write your thoughts in your journal.

Try the game again, this time switching food. The sparrow should have the nuts and the swallow should have the fruit. Will this change the results of the game? How?

Sparrows in the wild have thick beaks to eat seeds and nuts, while swallows have thin beaks to eat soft creatures like insects. So, in the game, the paperclip is the perfect beak with which to spear soft insects like the soft pieces of dried fruit and the clothespin is perfect for pinching and picking up seeds and nuts.

Oil-Slicked Feathers

What do you think will happen if a bird gets wet? When the feather is smoothed, it creates a solid wall to push against the air. When the barbs are messed up, there are holes for the air to come through, making it tough for a bird to fly.

When a bird gets wet, the water rolls right off that solid wall. That's why ducks are able to swim all day, but take off quickly if they're threatened. But, if oil gets on a duck's feathers, they can't do their job now—just like if there are holes while they're flying.

Take a new feather and see for yourself how oil can hurt birds—especially ducks. You can make observations and drawings in your nature journal.

－ － － － － － － － － － － － －

Materials

+ Feathers
+ Magnifying glass (and a microscope if you have one)
+ Water
+ Paper towels
+ Your nature journal (page 343)
+ Pipettes or medicine droppers
+ Cooking oil
+ Plastic gloves
+ Dish detergent

Set up your outdoor workspace. Choose one feather and study it carefully. Look at it under the microscope or magnifying glass and notice how the barbs overlap. This provides a waterproofing effect for the bird.

Dip your feather in a glass of water. Pull it out and look carefully. What happened? Did the water soak in? Bead up? Roll off? Dry your feather by pulling it through a paper towel gently. How quickly did it dry? Write your answers in your journal.

Now, use a pipette or a medicine dropper to add a few drops of oil to the water. Put on your gloves and dip your feather again. Pull it out and look carefully. What happened? What did the oil do to the surface of the feather? Dry your feather by pulling it through a paper towel gently. Does the oil come off? How does the feather look now?

Try to find the best way to clean oily feathers. Dip two more feathers in oil. Clean one with cold water, one with hot water and one in soapy water. Which substance do you think will clean the oil off the best? Why? Write down your hypothesis before you begin.

Which one worked best? The dish soap is able to cut through the oil and get the feather the cleanest. Environmentalists who clean up large scale oil spills often use dish soap to bathe the wildlife that gets trapped in the spill.

Egg-cellent Chemistry

Do you know what a bird's eggshell is made up of? Bird eggs are made up of a hard calcium carbonate shell. On the membrane that surrounds the yolk and albumen inside the egg, there are points where columns of calcite form. These columns continue to form side by side until a shell is made. The shell does not get hard until it reaches the air right before it leaves the bird's body. Calcite is a form of calcium carbonate and the necessary ingredient for forming hard eggs.

It's possible to remove the calcium carbonate and have the egg stay intact through a simple chemical reaction using simple white vinegar. Have you ever made a naked egg before? Try it now!

- - - - - - - - - - - - - - -

Materials

+ Chicken eggs (you'll want several in case any break, and so you can have a control)
+ Two large glass jars
+ Water
+ Vinegar
+ Your nature journal (page 343)
+ Corn syrup
+ Food coloring

Bring the materials outside and set up your workspace for the experiment. Put one egg in a jar of water. This will be the control egg to remind you what the egg was like at the beginning of the experiment.

Place another egg in a jar of vinegar. What's happening? Jot down your observations in your nature journal. For the best results, you'll want to leave the egg in the original vinegar for 24 hours, then carefully drain the old vinegar out and re-cover the egg with fresh vinegar. Leave that alone for a week.

What happened? You should have seen a chemical reaction almost immediately. The vinegar started bubbling around the egg's shell. Those bubbles are carbon dioxide. The vinegar is made up of acetic acid and water. The acetic acid in the vinegar reacted with the calcium carbonate in the eggshell.

This made calcium acetate along with the water and carbon dioxide bubbles you saw on the surface of the egg. That reaction left behind only the semi-permeable membrane covering of the egg.

After a few days, take the egg out and carefully handle it. What do you notice? Draw and describe your observations in your nature journal. Try bouncing it gently on the table.

The egg is slightly bigger than it was because that membrane is semi-permeable, meaning that water can pass through it. The process of osmosis is a natural process that works to keep things balanced. There was more water outside the membrane in the vinegar than inside the egg, so through osmosis water passed into the egg, swelling it but making it balanced with the water molecules outside the egg.

What do you think would happen if the egg were in a solution that had a lower concentration of water than what was inside the egg?

Since the process of osmosis works to balance systems out, water should pass back out through the membrane into the other solution, shrinking the egg.

Try it—rinse the vinegar off the egg and place it in a cup of corn syrup and let it sit overnight. Did it work? Do you now have a smaller egg?

That hard shell is an important part of what keeps a baby bird developing and healthy while it grows inside its egg. It covers that semi-permeable layer so harmful chemicals and liquids can't get inside.

More Fun

There are lots of ways to extend this activity and have more fun with naked eggs.

Try putting the egg back into colored water after it has gotten smaller in the corn syrup. Does the color travel through the membrane into the egg?

Make a new naked egg. Try bouncing it from a few inches (6 to 7 cm) above your patio or driveway (covered in a cloth). Keep holding it farther and farther away from the ground. From how high can you drop it before it breaks rather than bounces?

Ask a question, make a hypothesis and test it. Here are some ideas to get you started: Do organic eggs react more or less than non-organic eggs? Are brown eggs less reactive than white? How do eggs react in different liquids?

Blue Feeder, Green Feeder

Like most animals, birds have eyes with two types of cells. These are called rods and cones. Rods help them see light. Cones help them see color. Birds have more rods than cones, but don't have any blood vessels in their eyes. This helps prevent shadows and the scattering of light as it enters the eye. Images enter without being diffused and birds' eyes are able to get to work processing light and colors.

Humans have three types of cones, each able to see a specific color. When the cones combine, we see all the colors in our world. Birds, though, have four types of cones. Some even have five! Besides these colors, they can also see ultraviolet light, which is invisible to humans. This means that birds can see red, green and blue like we do, but they can also see two additional colors. Amazing!

With their special color-detection ability, it would be interesting to see if one color is more appealing to birds than another. Try this experiment to find out!

- - - - - - - - - - - - -

Materials

+ Four small wooden or wire bird feeders, unpainted
+ Squirrel cones or feeder poles (optional)
+ Large bag of birdseed or bird suet
+ Paint in three colors (red, blue and green)
+ Scale
+ Your nature journal (page 343)

Find a place in your yard to hang the birdfeeders clustered near each other, taking precautions against squirrels. (Hang them on poles or trees with squirrel cones or some other type of deterrent.) Fill them with seed, and leave them for a one to two week period so birds recognize the feeders as a food source and begin to frequent the location.

Following the initial feeding period, take your feeders down and paint three of them—each a different color. Leave the fourth unpainted.

Do you think color will matter to the birds? If so, which color do you think will be most attractive? Why? Write your hypothesis in your nature journal.

Fill each feeder to the top with seed and weigh each, recording the weight in your journal. Date all entries in your journal. Put your feeders back out for 48 hours, then bring them back in and weigh them. Record the weight and refill each.

Weigh the feeders again and record the new full weights. Replace the feeders outside and leave them for another 48 hours. Repeat the procedures every two days for two weeks.

After two weeks, subtract each end weight from the start weight and average the amount of birdseed eaten from each feeder over a two-day period. Remember that to find an average, you add the amounts eaten all together, then divide that answer by the number of things you added together.

(continued)

Revisit your hypothesis. Did color matter? Which color feeder was most attractive to the birds that visited your yard? Why do you think you saw these results? Is there something you could do differently the next time you perform this experiment?

Terrific Terra Cotta Bird Bath

It's easy to make a yard appealing to birds of all types. Just like you were able to plant and make a few things to encourage butterflies and other animals to move into your yard, you can do the same with birds.

It's just a matter of figuring out what types of things they like and need and providing it for them. Birds need a lot of the same things you and I do. They need food, water and a cozy place to raise their babies safely.

If you have a variety of trees and shrubs in your yard, you're already part of the way there. If you have feeders, nesting boxes and water sources, your bird friends will help you keep the insect population under control.

Here is a fun and easy way to get started attracting birds to your yard.

— — — — — — — — — — — —

Materials

+ 18- to 20-inch (45- to 50-cm) terra cotta saucer
+ 16-inch (40-cm) terra cotta pot
+ 14-inch (35-cm) terra cotta pot
+ 12-inch (30-cm) terra cotta pot
+ Silicone adhesive, epoxy or caulk
+ Tiles, shells, gems or other decorative items
+ Acrylic paint
+ Paintbrush
+ Acrylic sealer
+ Water
+ Your nature journal (page 343)

You can unleash your creativity with this project and maybe even make a few bird baths as gifts for friends.

First, head outside, and turn your terra cotta pots upside down, stacking them on top of one another from largest to smallest. Secure each with the adhesive of your choice (whatever strong glue you have), but have a grown-up help you. Attach the saucer right side up tightly to the top of the stack.

Now it's time to get creative. You can glue on the tiles like a mosaic or add the gems and stones. You can also paint it. Whatever you choose to do, seal it with acrylic or another type of sealer so it's weather proof.

Fill the saucer with water and put it in a sunny spot near where birds visit regularly. Then set up somewhere discreet and observe your visitors, noting which species visit, and draw observations in your nature journal.

FUN FACT

The penguin is the only bird that walks upright. It can also swim really well, but cannot fly. It uses its wings like flippers.

Magical Milk Carton Homes for Your Bird Friends

Did you know that there are specific requirements depending on the type of birds you want to attract to nesting boxes and bird houses in your yard? You can make several inexpensive custom nesting boxes using the chart below to help you with your dimensions.

Which bird do you want to attract first? Let's get started!

- - - - - - - - - - - - - - - -

Materials

+ Empty, clean half-gallon (2-L) milk carton
+ Masking tape
+ Dark-colored paint
+ Paintbrush
+ Scissors
+ Wire
+ Your nature journal (page 343)

First, bring all your materials outside to set up your crafting station. Then, take the clean half-gallon (2-L) milk carton and cover the entire thing with masking tape so that none of the carton shows through. You may need to overlap a few times.

Paint the entire carton with the dark-colored paint. We've used black, brown and have even covered nesting boxes like this with black shoe polish! Let it dry completely.

Decide what type of bird you want to attract to your yard. Check a field guide or the Internet to make sure that they are likely to be in your area before you take the time to make the box. Look at the chart to determine where your cuts need to be:

First, cut the entrance hole and make several small holes in the bottom of the carton to allow rainwater to drain out.

Make a few holes in the top of the carton to allow condensation to escape, too.

Finally, use the wire to hang your nesting box from a tree at the correct height for the species you chose. Make sure you hang this in the early spring so birds have time to find it and build their nests before it's time to lay eggs. Watch and wait! Your new friends will come home soon!

Species	Height of Entrance	Diameter of Hole	Height from Ground
Bluebird	6 inches (15 cm)	1½ inches (38 mm)	5 to 10 feet (1.75 to 3 m)
Chickadee	6 to 8 inches (15 to 20 cm)	1⅛ inches (28 mm)	6 to 15 feet (2 to 5 m)
Titmouse	6 to 8 inches (15 to 20 cm)	1¼ inches (31 mm)	6 to 15 feet (2 to 5 m)
Robin	8 inches (20 cm)	1 side open	6 to 15 feet (2 to 5 m)
Barn swallow	6 inches (15 cm)	1 side open	8 to 10 feet (2.5 to 3 m)

Pinecone Feeders

Making pinecone feeders is one of those activities that is so simple and fun that most people try doing it at sometime in their life. Make it a science experiment, though, with this simple twist. . . .

- - - - - - - - - - - - - - - -

Materials

+ 4 large, open pinecones
+ Purchased bird suet or lard
+ Cornmeal
+ Rolled oats
+ Peanut butter
+ Yarn or twine
+ Birdseed
+ Dried fruit
+ Your nature journal (page 343)

This can get a little messy, so head outside to make up these birdfeeders.

Mix each of the following four recipes until well blended:

- ½ cup (67 g) suet with 2½ cups (426 g) cornmeal
- ½ cup (67 g) suet with 2½ cups (201 g) rolled oats
- ½ cup (130 g) peanut butter with 2½ cups (426 g) cornmeal
- ½ cup (130 g) peanut butter with 2½ cups (201 g) rolled oats

Tie your yarn or twine to your pinecones and cover each with a different mixture.

Roll them in birdseed and dried fruit and tap off any excess. Hang them outside in a tree for the birds. Which one do you think the birds will eat clean first? Make your prediction in your nature journal. Check back every few hours each day until the first is picked clean and record your results. Why do you think the birds preferred that choice? Was it the one you predicted they'd like best?

More Fun

Robins lay eggs that are pretty blue with sandy speckles on them. You can make a simple craft by painting a piece of construction paper light blue, and then sprinkling sand in the wet paint. Let it dry, then cut out an egg shape and hang it up!

Magnificent Milk Carton Bird Feeder

Here's another fun thing to do with all of those used milk cartons you have each week. You made a birdhouse on page 352, now give those new feathered residents a place to eat with a simple bird feeder.

- - - - - - - - - - - - - - - -

Materials

+ Ruler
+ Half-gallon (2-L) milk carton, cleaned and dried
+ Scissors
+ Yarn or twine
+ Birdseed
+ Your nature journal (page 343)

Head out to your favorite workspace in the yard with all of your materials. Using your ruler, mark a line 2½ inches (6 cm) up on two adjoining sides of the carton. Mark a line on those same two sides 2½ inches (6 cm) down. Cut the sides out along your lines so that your carton looks like the one in the picture on photo insert page 32.

Decorate your bird feeder in any way that you want to.

Punch a hole in the top of the carton and tie your yarn or twine through it and around a tree branch. Fill the feeder with birdseed. Hang out in the yard with your nature journal and wait for your new feathered friends to discover the buffet. Record the birds that come to eat.

More Fun

Think about what other things you can repurpose around your house to make bird feeders. Try to make some unique feeders to hang in your yard.

*See photo insert page 32.

Tasty Fruit and Veggie Feeders

Bird feeders can be made with just about anything. Even fruits and vegetables. . . . Once you gather the different supplies listed below, you can head outside and make a bunch of different types of feeders to have outside for your bird friends to enjoy. Check it out!

- - - - - - - - - - - - -

Materials

+ Ears of corn—dried or fresh
+ Yarn or twine
+ Apples
+ Oranges
+ Peanut butter
+ Birdseed
+ Wooden kabob skewers
+ Small cut-up pieces of fruit (apples, oranges, grapes, peaches, nectarines, etc.) and dried fruit (raisins, cranberries)
+ Your nature journal (page 343)

To start, bring all the materials outside to your workspace.

For the Corn: Peel the husks downward, leaving them attached. Use the yarn or twine to tie the husks together and hang them upside down in the trees.

For Apples and Oranges: Cut the fruit in half. Spread peanut butter on the peel side and roll it in birdseed. Stick a wooden skewer all the way through the fruit so it sticks out on either side. Tie yarn or twine to the skewer and hang it in a tree.

Bird Kabobs: Thread pieces of dried and fresh fruit on a wooden skewer. Tie yarn or twine to it and hang it in the trees.

Garden Garland: Tie your string or yarn to a wooden skewer and thread chunks of fresh and dried fruit onto the yarn. Tie off the ends. Drape it in shrubs and bushes.

Once you have made a few different fruit and vegetable feeders, put them out in your yard and observe. What types of birds come to eat? Do other animals like them too? Which type seems to be the most popular? Record your observations in your nature journal.

FUN FACT
An owl can turn its head almost in a complete circle, but it cannot move its eyes. Pretty cool!

Radical Recycled Log Suet Feeders

Some birds like woodpeckers and starlings prefer eating bird suet, which is a birdseed and lard mixture. You can make a super awesome bird suet feeder out of a log. It's easy, just try it!

- - - - - - - - - - - - - - - -

Materials

+ Thick branch or a small log (between 4 and 8 inches [10 and 20 cm] thick)
+ Drill with a 1- to 1½-inch (2.5- to 4-cm) diameter bit
+ Large eye screw
+ Bird suet, homemade (right) or store-bought
+ Rope
+ Your nature journal (page 343)

Have an adult help you drill several 1-inch (2.5-cm)-deep holes around the log to make wells for the suet. Then, screw the eye screw into the top of your log feeder.

Fill in each of the holes with suet feed.

Hang your log feeder with rope from a sturdy branch on a tree outside. Which birds come to this feeder? Are they different species than those you've seen at other feeders you've made? Why do you think that is? Record your observation in your nature journal.

Peanut Butter Suet

Can't get to the store to buy bird suet to fill the log feeder you made on this page? Try this easy-peasy recipe using things that are right inside your kitchen. You'll have flocks of birds visiting you in no time!

- - - - - - - - - - - - - - - -

Materials

+ 1 cup (260 g) peanut butter
+ 1 cup (220 g) lard
+ Saucepan
+ 2 cups (322 g) quick cooking oats
+ 2 cups (341 g) cornmeal
+ 1 to 2 cups (125 to 249 g) flour
+ Small containers

Melt the peanut butter and lard in a saucepan. Add in the other ingredients, stirring in flour just until it's no longer runny. Pour it into small containers like recycled yogurt or margarine containers. Store these in the refrigerator until you're ready to use them.

You can hang this feed in mesh bags (like produce comes in), suet cages (sold at most big box stores) or stuff it into the holes in your log feeder (left). Observe which birds come to enjoy the suet in different containers!

Stuffed Bird Loaf

This just might be the easiest bird feeder you'll ever make!

- - - - - - - - - - - - - - - -

Materials

+ Large loaf of stale bread (set it out overnight to harden)
+ Peanut butter
+ Cornmeal
+ Dried fruit
+ Nuts
+ Your nature journal (page 343)

On a table outside, cut off one end of the bread loaf and hollow it by scooping the soft insides out. You can crumble the heel and the insides and spread it out in your garden for the birds to eat. Mix peanut butter, cornmeal, fruit and nuts together and stuff the mixture inside the loaf until it's overflowing. Set the bird loaf out on a table, platform or rock pile in your garden for the birds to snack on.

Watch and see which types of birds like eating this loaf. Make observations in your nature journal.

FUN FACT

Birds can eat twice their weight in food every day! So, when someone tells you they "eat like a bird," you can tell them that it doesn't really mean what they think it means, since most people say that to mean they don't eat a lot.

Happy Hummingbird Feeder

Hummingbirds are one of my favorite things to attract to my yard. I just love watching them dart back and forth. Their movements are so cool.

It's easy to make them simple feeders so you can attract more of them using things from around your house instead of buying the globe feeders most people buy when they choose to feed hummingbirds. These are colorful and enticing to the little speedsters.

- - - - - - - - - - - - - - - -

Materials

+ Hammer
+ Nail
+ Clean baby food jar
+ Colorful plastic pieces
+ Hot glue gun
+ 1 cup (192 g) sugar
+ 4 cups (946 ml) water
+ Saucepan
+ Yarn or twine
+ Your nature journal (page 343)

Using the hammer and nail, poke several small holes in the metal lid of the baby food jar—having an adult help you if needed. Hot glue colorful plastic petals around the holes to decorate the feeder and make it more appealing to the birds you're trying to attract. Hummingbirds seem to like bright colors, so I like to use reds, oranges and yellows.

(continued)

Mix up some simple nectar by combining the sugar and water in a saucepan (with adult help) over medium heat and stirring until it comes to a boil and the sugar dissolves. Let it cool and store it in the refrigerator.

When the nectar is cool, pour it in the jar and tighten the lid securely. Tie a piece of yarn or twine on your jar and hang it near a window. Watch and see if hummingbirds find it. Watch how they sip. They'll stick their long beaks into the holes you've made and lap up the sweet nectar with their super-fast tongues. In your nature journal, keep track of how many hummingbirds start to visit once they discover you're feeding them.

*See photo insert page 32.

FUN FACT
Hummingbirds can fly at speeds higher than 33 miles per hour (54 km per hour) and are the only birds capable of flying backward.

Footprint Robin

We love doing crafts and art outside when the weather is nice—especially projects like this that celebrate the things we're learning about. After studying the birds that come to all of your new feeders, you'll be able to recognize the markings on the different visitors you host. You could make lots of different paintings to show who's visiting.

- - - - - - - - - - - - - -

Materials

+ Paintbrushes
+ Brown, red and orange paint
+ Heavy paper
+ Black marker
+ Nature treasures like sticks, leaves and pebbles (optional)
+ Glue (optional)

First, bring the materials to your favorite outdoor workspace. Paint the bottom of one of your bare feet completely brown. Step onto the center of a piece of art paper. Try to set your foot down evenly and firmly.

Lift your foot and clean it off while the footprint dries.

Using your red paint, add the robin's red breast. Add feet and a beak with your orange paint (or mix a little orange and brown together), and add an eye with your black marker.

That looks great, doesn't it? But, maybe you can make it look more like the robins that hang out in your own yard. Take some time to observe your feathered friends and add some of their unique markings to your painting. You could even gather some nature treasures to glue on to the background to make the painting look more realistic.

More Fun
What other types of footprint birds could you and your friends make? Make a flock of different bird types using a field guide for inspiration.

FUN FACT
Male birds tend to have the prettiest colors, most elaborate dances and attractive songs. Female birds choose them based on those characteristics.

(eighteen)

FLOWERS, MOSSES, FERNS AND FUN

There are so many different plants, flowers and trees to study in your yard! Botany is the study of plants—from the smallest duckweed to the largest redwood trees. Because there is so much to cover in this field (algae, fungi, lichens, trees, ferns, flowering plants, etc.), most botanists focus on one major area of study. You'll focus on things most of you can find in your own backyard or near your home in this section.

That includes how plants work, what they look like, where they grow and how people make use of plants. Plants are essential to life. They provide food—either directly or indirectly. They also give us oxygen.

Plants also provide medicine, fibers for making clothes and other things we use to live. They're such an important part of our ecosystem, and can be found everywhere. Let's learn all about them!

Crazy Capillary Action

First, spill a little bit of water into a tray on the table. The water pools up because it is sticky. The forces of cohesion make water molecules stay close together, and the forces of adhesion make some of those molecules stick to the table tray.

Capillary action happens when adhesion is stronger than cohesion. So, first, you can thank cohesion for keeping that water in a nice neat puddle. Then, you can thank the adhesion forces that cause capillary action as you take a paper towel and dip it into the puddle on your tray.

Do you see the water climbing the fibers and moving to the spaces between and inside of them? Plants wouldn't be able to live without capillary action.

To see capillary action in, well . . . action, try this fun activity!

- - - - - - - - - -

Materials

+ 4 clear glass or plastic cups or jars
+ Water
+ Food dye in four colors
+ Three white flowers (this is one you might want a little outside help for—you can ask an adult to buy three white carnations from a florist for you)
+ Scissors
+ Paper towels
+ Your nature journal (page 343)

Fill each jar two-thirds full with water. Color each one differently with the food dye. Then cut the bottoms off the stems of your three carnations.

Put one flower in the jar of your choice. Then, put another flower in a second jar of your choice. Take the last flower and slit the stem of it up to about an inch (2.5 cm) from the top with scissors. The last flower should seem to have two stems now.

Put one of those stems into one of the two remaining jars and the other stem into the other jar. Place those flowers in the house in a sunny window so you can watch what happens. Over the course of the next few days, you'll see how capillary action works as the colored water moves up each stem into the flower petals. It's especially cool to see that the flower with the split stem takes on both colors.

So, what does this mean for taking care of your backyard plants? How should you water them? Since plants pull both water and nutrients from the soil, it's important to water them at their base so the water soaks into the ground by their roots.

More Fun

Try this with other plants. Celery in colored water is a common demonstrator of capillary action. What about other plants, though? Roses? Ferns? What else could you experiment with?

Leaf Chromatography Fun

You might know that leaves contain chlorophyll—the chemical that makes them look green—but did you know that there are other pigments in there?

Carotenoids (yellow and orange pigments) and anthocyanins (red pigments) are in there, too. The chlorophyll hangs out in the leaves, doing its photosynthesis thing, until autumn when it begins to break down. The other colors are left for all to see once that happens.

This fun activity will help you find the hidden colors in the leaves around your yard.

- - - - - - - - - -

(continued)

Materials

+ Green leaves
+ Small glass jars
+ Rubbing alcohol
+ Plastic wrap
+ Hot water
+ A glass bowl
+ Tape
+ Coffee filters, cut into 1-inch (2.5-cm)-wide strips
+ Pencils
+ Your nature journal (page 343)

Break up the leaves you've gathered into separate jars (one leaf type per jar), and cover them with rubbing alcohol. Label the jars with the type of leaf you have in them. Cover the jars with plastic wrap so the alcohol doesn't evaporate.

Set the jars into a bowl of hot water, but don't submerge them. The alcohol will start to turn green after about a half an hour. When this happens, tape one coffee filter strip to a pencil for each jar you have. Rest a pencil on the opening of each jar so the filter strips just dip into the pigment and alcohol mixture.

Let those sit for an hour to an hour and a half.

Come back and check on the pigments. You should see that the colors began to creep up the filter strips and separate. Which type of leaf had colors that separated the most drastically? Which had bright pigments? Which were more subdued? What color do you think each tree's leaves will become in the fall? Write your observations in your nature journal.

> **FUN FACT**
> It is estimated that there are about 50,000 edible plant species in the world, but that most humans only eat about 20 of them. Think about all of the foods you are missing out on!

Photosynthesis Action

Photosynthesis happens when a plant harnesses the energy from the sun to produce food. Chlorophylls are found in the leaf and absorb the energy from the sunlight. This energy splits water molecules in the plant into hydrogen and oxygen.

The oxygen is released through the plant's leaves into the atmosphere. The leftover hydrogen mixes with carbon dioxide that comes in through small pores, called stomata, in the plant's leaves and makes glucose. Some of that glucose gives immediate energy to the plant for growth and development. Some is stored in the fruit, leaves and roots for the plant to use later.

This is a simple demonstration of what happens when light can't reach the leaves of a plant to trigger the process of photosynthesis in your own backyard.

Materials

+ Two identical plants with large leaves
+ Heavy cardstock
+ Paper clips
+ Your nature journal (page 343)

Explore in your backyard to find two identical plants that have large leaves. You can plant them if you don't have any—just have your parents help you get some inexpensive potted plants at the garden center. You can also do this activity on a house plant. It won't do any long-term damage to your plant.

Make sure that both plants are in an equally sunny location. Clip heavy cardstock on several of the large leaves of one of the plants. The second plant will be your control plant. What do you think will happen if you leave the plant's leaves covered for a week? Make a hypothesis in your nature journal.

Gently uncover the leaves after a week of sunny days. What do you notice? Without the energy from sunlight, the plant was not able to photosynthesize and the plant's leaves have probably begun to change color and die. Write down your results in your journal. Was your hypothesis correct?

Beautiful Nature Patterns

Although nature often appears to be random, there are actually patterns everywhere. In fact, there is a lot of math found in nature! Can you believe that? It's true!

For example, the Fibonacci number pattern occurs so often that some scientists consider it a basic law of nature. The Fibonacci sequence is a series of numbers in which each new number is the sum of the two numbers before it. 0, 1, 1, 2, 3, 5, 8, 13. . . .

You can see the Fibonacci sequence in flowers, shells, plants, leaves and so much more. If you count the spiral pattern you see in flower petals, you'll notice that the number of petals is usually a number from the Fibonacci sequence. The same thing can also be found in seed arrangements on flower heads. Go check it out in your yard!

Materials

+ Your nature journal (page 343)
+ Camera
+ Nature materials (sticks, rocks, shells, etc.)

Head outside and observe carefully. What examples of growing patterns can you see in your yard? Draw some of what you see in your journal. Or, you can take photos of nature patterns and tape them into your journal.

When you feel inspired, try creating a Fibonacci sequence or another pattern using natural materials. This is often called land art. Find an open area, and build a pattern with rocks, sticks, flower petals and anything else you can find.

Groovy CD Case Bean Plant

Have you ever planted seeds before? This is a fun way to plant, watch the growth cycle of a bean plant unfold and identify the parts of a plant. Plus, it's easy to plant your seedlings in a sunny place in your yard once you're done observing it in its case.

Materials

+ Empty CD cases
+ Soil
+ Variety of vegetable seeds (try to have at least one lima bean as they grow well in this setting and you can really see the parts of a plant when looking at a bean seedling)
+ Permanent marker
+ Droppers
+ Your nature journal (page 343)

(continued)

Do this activity outside so you can enjoy nature and don't make a mess in the house. Open up the CD cases and make sure the hinges are at the top. Put about 1½ inches (3 cm) of soil in the bottom. Plant one seed in each of your CD cases. Close the cases and label them with the permanent marker so you know what type of plant is in each. Stand your CD garden in a bright sunny window, watering each case every day by dripping water with a medicine dropper at the hinge on the top.

In your nature journal, draw what you see every few days to help in your observations of a plant's growing cycle. Remember that roots pull water and nutrients up from the soil. Do you see them growing downward and spreading through the soil to search for nutrients?

Remember that leaves need to pull energy from sunlight to make food for the plant. Do you see the leaves reaching upward towards the sunlight? Once your plants have started growing nice big leaves to replace the baby leaves, called cotyledon, that first sprout from the seed, you'll know that it's time to transplant your garden outside. You can grow these seedlings in a garden or in large containers.

More Fun

What else could you grow your seedlings in? My kids had fun growing five different types of seeds in the fingers of a plastic glove that they had hung on the window this year. You could try that or grow it in something else.

Fantastic Flower Dissection

This is a cool way to see all of the different parts of the inside of a flower, but you need to ask an adult for permission to use the craft knife or have them make the cuts for you. Be safe, and you'll be able to discover lots of amazing things as you explore the insides of the flowers in your yard!

- - - - - - - - - - - - - - -

Materials

+ Several flowers with big blooms
+ Tray or white piece of paper
+ Craft knife
+ Your nature journal (page 343)

Bring the materials to your favorite workspace in your yard. Set one flower on a tray or a white piece of paper to make it easy to see all of the parts. (You have several flowers just in case you make a bad cut on one. Just put the extras in water and enjoy them as a decoration until you need them.)

First, take a minute to identify the flower, stem and leaves of your flower. These are the outside parts of the flower that most people pay attention to. Once you've identified those, it's time to check out the inside of your bloom.

Take your craft knife (with adult supervision), and gently press it into the petals, pulling it through the top layer of petals, the base of the flower and all the way down the stem. Be careful not to cut all the way through—you'll want to be able to open the flower up and lay it flat to look inside.

Begin at the top of the flower. Gently pull the petals apart on either side of your cut. First, you'll see the male parts of the flower. Those are called the stamen, and are the long tubes that have the powdery pollen on their tips. The tips with the pollen are called anthers.

When you keep pulling apart the petals and separating the stamen, you'll find one long tube in the middle. This is the female part of the flower and is called the pistil. The pistil is usually taller than the stamen and has a sticky tip called the stigma.

Look at those parts closely. For a flower to be pollinated and reproduce, pollen from the anthers of one flower needs to be transferred to the stigma of another flower. Bees are great pollinators. They get pollen on their feet when they visit one flower, and it rubs off on another flower when they switch.

If you take a look at the base of the flower where the stamen and pistil come together, you'll see a bulge. This is another female part, called the ovary. Slit that open really carefully. There are little ovules in there—small eggs. When a plant is pollinated, fertilization takes place and those eggs will develop into seeds. Pretty cool, isn't it?

FUN FACT

Some plants are carnivorous, which means that they get their nutrients by eating small insects and spiders. The Venus flytrap is one of my favorites.

Pizza Garden

Do you like homemade pizza? We love it here at our house. Here's a fun way to grow your own pizza during the summer—and a fun recipe to use the ingredients once they're mature. Cooking is science, too!

- - - - - - - - - - -

Materials

+ Soil
+ Seeds (or seedlings) for pizza ingredients: basil, oregano, parsley, thyme, tomatoes, peppers
+ A circular place in the yard for a garden or a large pot for a container garden
+ Your nature journal (page 343)

Decide if you're going to plant a large container garden or one in the ground. If you are planting a container garden, get your pot ready by filling it with soil. Divide your container or plot of land into six wedges like pizza slices. Plant your seeds or seedlings—one type of plant per "slice."

Label your garden sections. We like to use craft sticks that we decorate with permanent markers.

Make sure your garden is in a sunny spot, and water it every day. There's so much science involved in growing gardens like this. How much water is not enough? How much is too much? Are the plants getting enough sunlight? How quickly are they growing? You can make all of these observations and answer all of these questions in your journal as you take care of your pizza garden.

When it's ready to harvest, you'll just need an adult to help you make the pizza sauce using your garden ingredients and buy a store-bought pizza crust and cheese. Yum!

Pizza Garden Pizza Recipe
Ingredients

+ 6–8 tomatoes
+ 1 clove garlic, minced
+ 2 tbsp (5 g) chopped basil
+ 2 tbsp (5 g) chopped oregano
+ 1 tbsp (2.5 g) thyme
+ 2 tbsp (5 g) parsley
+ 1 tsp salt
+ ½ tsp pepper
+ Prepared pizza crust
+ Mozarella cheese
+ Chopped peppers

(continued)

Put the tomatoes in a pot of boiling water for 30 seconds, and then put them into a bowl of ice water. Use a paring knife to remove the tomato skins once they've cooled down. Cut out the core and seeds of the tomatoes and dice them up.

Bring your tomatoes, garlic, herbs, salt and pepper to a simmer in a pot over medium heat for 30 minutes. Spread the sauce on a prepared pizza crust, then sprinkle lots of cheese and chopped peppers on top. Bake it in a 350°F (177°C) oven until the cheese is warm and bubbly. Yum! Enjoy!

Magical Fairy Garden

We make fairy gardens every single summer. Each year looks different than the year before, but each one is just as great as the last one. They key to a beautiful and fun fairy garden is that it's meant to be interacted with and played in.

- - - - - - - - - - - - -

Materials

+ A large container or small area of the yard
+ Soil
+ Brightly colored flowers and small plants
+ Fairy houses (store-bought or handmade)
+ Pretty stones, gems, shells and other fun things to decorate with
+ Your nature journal (page 343)

For our fairy garden, we blocked off a small plot of ground near our garage. There's a brick wall and brightly colored flowers planted in a rainbow pattern—this has been named Rainbow Woods. Behind Rainbow Woods is a rock structure my kids built.

Coming out of Rainbow Woods, fairies (or the dollhouse people my kids play with in the garden) can follow a path made out of shells that leads to Fairy Village. The village is made up of birdhouses we found at a garage sale and one fairy house made out of an unfinished wooden birdhouse with a bark and stick ladder. Surrounding the homes are gardens full of plastic and glass gems (because fairies like shiny objects) and more small plants.

Fairy gardens are fun because you can plant whatever you have on hand, and use old toys, logs, rocks, sticks and other scraps to make homes and play structures out of. They important thing is to have fun with nature and your imagination.

You can hang out and see the new critters that come to join the fairies in their garden. Tiny tree frogs, worms and insects might make their homes there, too. It's fun to sketch the changes in your nature journal as the garden grows throughout the summer.

More Fun Fairy Lore

- Fairies range in size from tinier than a firefly to bigger than a giant.
- Laughter and imagination attracts them.
- A ripple in the air or water, or a sudden chill indicates they're there.
- They love music, bells and rhymes, and they love to dance.
- If you're missing small objects, there might be fairies around.
- Their favorite things to eat are milk, honey and nectar.

Juice Pouch Garden

Want to add a little fun and whimsy to your yard? Try this simple garden idea with some of those juice pouches left over from lunches or trips to the zoo.

- - - - - - - - - - - - - -

Materials

+ Empty juice pouches
+ Scissors
+ Soil
+ Several types of garden seeds
+ Craft sticks
+ Permanent markers
+ Your nature journal (page 343)

Cut off the tops of the pouches and clean them out really well. Poke a few holes in the bottom so water can drain out. Fill them up with soil and plant a few seeds in each by poking a hole in the soil with your finger, dropping the seeds in and covering them with soil. Make sure each pouch has a different type of seed.

Label each pouch with the type of seed you planted with a decorated craft stick and the permanent marker.

Make a prediction in your journal. Which type of seed do you think will grow the quickest? Why? Every day, water the pouches a little and draw what you observe in your nature journal. Even if you don't see any changes, draw that. You'll use those observations to come to conclusions about how quickly plants grow and can use that information in the future when you plant again next spring.

More Fun: Try these other fun garden ideas, too!

- Shoe Garden—Plant flowers in old shoes. This is fun and quirky and adds whimsy to a fairy or container garden in your yard.
- Edible Flower Garden—Chose edible flowers like lavender, thyme, chives, nasturtiums, daylily, dill or basil and plant those in a garden to eat in a salad.
- Purse Garden—Line old bags and purses with plastic bags and plant flowers and herbs in them. You can hang those from a fence in the yard for a fun backyard garden.

(nineteen)

BACKYARD ECOLOGY

Ecology is the study of the relationships between living organisms and their environment. It's how we understand the connections among us, the plants, reptiles, insects and anything else in our backyards. It includes how those living things interact with each other and their own physical environment—the climate, water, soil and more.

Ecologists tend to specialize in a specific type of ecosystem—and you are going to be an ecologist that studies your own backyard ecosystem!

Mysteries Found in a Square Yard: Your Ecological Survey Site

Here's a chance for you to do a little ecological field work in your own backyard. Random sampling is when ecologists make an estimate of the populations of different species in an area by calculating what they see in a small section.

It can be really interesting to see the biodiversity, or variety of life, that is living right in your own grassy backyard. You're going to section off a square yard (square meter) of land in your backyard where you can do some of the experiments in this chapter. A yard is the same as 3 feet (1 m), and a square yard is a square section with four equal yard-length (meter) sides.

- - - - - - - - - - - - - - - -

Materials

+ Tape measure
+ Wooden stakes or sticks
+ Twine or string
+ Your nature journal (page 343)

Measure a square yard (square meter) of land, and mark each corner with a wooden stake or stick in the ground. Wrap twine or string around the stakes, creating an enclosure. This is your ecological survey site.

The first thing you'll do, once you set up your site, is to sit quietly with your nature journal and observe. Then, after you've sat awhile, write down any initial observations you have about the site. Draw it, adding in as many details as you can. Scientists need to know what normally happens in observation sites so that they know when there is a problem. You're observing to figure out what usually happens in your yard when you're able to sit quietly.

More Fun

Use a piece of paper or cardboard and make a sign so others know not to disturb your scientific test site. Our sign reads, "This is an ecological survey site. Please do not disturb the area or any equipment." You can staple it to the twine wrapped around the stakes, or attach it to another stake and put it in the ground next to your survey site.

Animal Populations in Your Ecological Survey Site

Ecologists need to know the distribution of animals in the ecosystem they are studying. This helps them discover the biological and physical factors that are important to an animal's survival. They can compare this information to historical data for the area.

When scientists study areas and their data over time, they can identify patterns and see how populations might be changing in the future. This is great information that can help them potentially save endangered species in the future.

While you don't have enough data to identify and protect endangered species in your backyard, you can get some pretty good information about what is living there. Head out to your ecological site to watch and learn!

- - - - - - - - - - - - - - - -

Materials

+ Ecological Survey Site (left)
+ Your nature journal (page 343)
+ Watercolor pencils (optional)
+ Magnifying glass

(continued)

Choose a time when you won't be bothered and head outside to your backyard. Make a checklist in your nature journal with the following categories: mammals, reptiles, amphibians, insects and birds.

Find a quiet spot near your Ecological Survey Site and watch. Make a tally mark on your checklist every time you see an animal in each category. Since it sometimes takes a long period of silence and calm for animals like squirrels or rabbits—if they're around your yard—to come back, try to stay quietly observing for as long as possible. An hour is great.

You can try your hand at some nature journaling during this time. I like to use watercolor pencils and sketch the animals I see. You can do this around your checklist.

After awhile—as long as you can handle—waiting for the bigger animals to stop by, use your magnifying glass to look down into the grass in your survey site. Mark all of the insects you see.

What species surprised you? Was there anything you expected to see, but didn't? Write the answers to these questions in your nature journal, too.

More Fun

Try visiting your site at different times of the day. Do you see different animals at different times? Why do you suppose that is?

Plant Populations in Your Ecological Survey Site

Just like ecologists need to know the different animals in a given area, they need to know about the plant life found there, too. When you go out to your ecological survey site this time, arm yourself with field guides to help you identify the plants you see. If you don't have time to go to a library, just take good notes or cut a leaf from each plant you see to press into your nature journal to look up later.

- - - - - - - - - - - - - -

Materials

+ Ecological Survey Site (page 367)
+ Watercolor pencils (optional)
+ Your nature journal (page 343)
+ Plant and wildflower field guides
+ Magnifying glass

Go over the entire Ecological Survey Site carefully and take note of every different type of plant you see. Draw them in your nature journal. My kids love using watercolor pencils so they can use brushes and water to blend the colors later.

Were there any types of plants that looked unfamiliar? Did you find anything cool or unusual? My son found a four-leaf clover the last time we did this. Lucky kid!!

More Fun

You can preserve your plant leaves by pressing them into the pages of your nature journal. Arrange them on a page how you'd like, and close the journal. Put the journal underneath stacks of heavy books and leave it alone for a week or more. When you open it back up, you can glue your pressed leaves onto the page where you arranged them so you have them forever.

Texture Test
Part One

This first soil experiment will help you determine the physical makeup of your soil.

‑ ‑ ‑ ‑ ‑ ‑ ‑ ‑ ‑ ‑ ‑ ‑ ‑

Materials

+ Ecological Survey Site (page 367)
+ Shovel
+ Glass jar with a lid
+ Water
+ Your nature journal (page 343)

Go out into your yard and dig up a small sample of soil from your Ecological Survey Site. (Make sure this is okay with your parents first.) Fill your jar one third full with your soil sample. Add water until the jar is about two thirds full and put the lid on tightly.

Shake the jar as hard as you can (but don't let go—that would be a mess!) and then let it settle somewhere on a shelf overnight. We have a shelf near our garden outside that my kids leave experiments like this on.

The next day, draw what your soil sample looks like in your nature journal. The coarse sand in your sample should have settled first, followed by the silt and then the clay. Can you see the layers?

Sand is the looser, more granular part of your sample. Silt is the superfine clay and sand pieces that settle as sediment. Clay is the densest part of the soil sample.

FUN FACT

One cupful of soil can contain over six billion bacteria!

Texture Test
Part Two

This test will tell you how heavy the clay content is in your soil. Heavy clay means the soil won't drain well. If the water doesn't drain out of the soil, then plants will get too much water and die.

‑ ‑ ‑ ‑ ‑ ‑ ‑ ‑ ‑ ‑ ‑ ‑ ‑

Materials

+ Soil sample from your Ecological Survey Site (page 367)
+ Water
+ Your nature journal (page 343)

Moisten a small handful of soil. Squeeze it as hard as you can, then open your hand, set it down and draw what it looks like in your nature journal. Though . . . you might want to rinse and dry your hands first.

If your soil sample holds together, forming a cast, then it has a high percentage of clay in it. Write down your observations in your nature journal.

FUN FACT

It can take over 1,000 years for healthy topsoil to form on its own.

Humus Test

This test will give you information on how well the soil will grow plants. Rich humus is better for growing than weak humus. It's more nutritious for your plants.

- - - - - - - - - - - - - - -

Materials

+ Shovel
+ Ecological Survey Site (page 367)
+ Your nature journal (page 343)

Use your shovel to take a one-foot deep by a few inches wide (30 cm deep by 6 cm wide) sample of soil from your Ecological Survey Site, and look closely at its color. Humus is the nutrient-rich organic component of soil. It's the part where decomposed leaves, worms and microorganisms are found. If your soil sample is dark—the darker the better—then it's rich in humus and is a great place to grow a garden.

Write and draw your observations in your nature journal. What did the humus content look like? Rich or weak? Would your ecological site be a nutrient-rich place for plants to grow?

Chemistry Test (pH)

Depending on the makeup of soil chemistry, farmers and gardeners consider which nutrients to add in and which plants to grow. You can test the soil chemistry of your ecological site with this simple activity.

- - - - - - - - - - - - - - -

Materials

+ Water
+ Soil sample from your Ecological Survey Site (page 367)
+ Glass jars with lids
+ pH test strips OR baking soda and vinegar
+ Your nature journal (page 343)

Knowing the chemical makeup of your soil can help you make good choices when you are trying to figure out what to plant. Ideally, you want your soil to have a pH reading of around seven because that's neutral and just about anything can grow.

And, while pH test strips make it super easy to test the alkalinity, or how acidic the soil is, you don't have to have them to figure out what your soil is like. If you want to be official, you can order pH strips inexpensively online or even find them at the drugstore.

If you do get pH strips, mix equal parts water and soil in your jar, put the lid on, and shake it well. Dip your test strip into the water and record your results in your nature journal. Your paper will change colors, and you should compare the color to the chart that comes with your strips. That will tell you the pH level of your sample.

What Do the pH Results Mean?

pH Reading	Meaning
< 5.6	Strongly acidic
5.6—6.2	Moderately acidic
6.2—6.7	Slightly acidic
6.7—7.3	Neutral
7.3—7.9	Slightly alkaline
7.9—8.5	Moderately alkaline
> 8.5	Strongly alkaline

You can find out the chemistry of your soil sample with things found around your house, too. Put 2 tablespoons (11 g) of soil each in separate jars. In the first jar, add ½ cup (118 ml) of vinegar. If it fizzes, your soil is alkaline with a pH somewhere between seven and eight.

If it doesn't fizz with the vinegar, then add water to the other jar to make the 2 tablespoons (11 g) of soil slightly muddy. Add ½ cup (102 g) baking soda to the mud. If that fizzes, then you have acidic soil, probably between pH level five and six.

If your soil didn't react at all, then it's neutral and you're super lucky! You can plant just about anything! We love trying those fizzy mud experiments. If that was fun for you, you might want to test soil samples from different areas.

Record the results of your chemistry test in your nature journal so that you have the details of the alkalinity along with the results of the other tests you've been conducting.

Earthworm Test

When there are a lot of worms in your soil sample, you'll know that the soil is healthy. Check out your ecological site and find out how healthy it is!

- - - - - - - - - - - -

Materials

+ Shovel
+ Ecological Survey Site (page 367)
+ Old sheet or another drop cloth
+ Your nature journal (page 343)

Dig up a large square (1 square foot [30 cm], if you're able to) in your ecological survey site. Try to dig at least 6 inches (15 cm) down.

Spread your soil sample on your cloth. Record the measurements of the sample you dug up in your nature journal—make sure to record the width and depth.

Sift through the soil, carefully removing and counting the earthworms and other creatures you find. Earthworms are very important for the health of your soil, so the more there are, the better your soil is for growing.

FUN FACT

Worm tea is the liquid that collects in the bottom of the worm bin you made on page 322 in the Putting Worms to Work activity. You can dilute it with water and spray it on your lawn or house plants. Try it and watch them grow!

An acre of healthy farmland will likely have over one million earthworms in it.

Breathe Right: Know the Quality of the Air

Air pollution has been around in some form or another since the first humans built fires. Smoke from those fires rose up in a haze and blocked the view. It wasn't a problem then. As time went on, air pollution reached high levels. During the Industrial Revolution, thick smoke and soot from factories clung to buildings and hung in the air of major cities. People clued in to the health issues caused by this type of pollution. Since then people have been trying to reduce the pollution in the air.

You can find out which areas in your yard and neighborhood have the highest concentration of particle air pollutants with this simple activity. It's a bit more challenging to test for chemical pollutants, but this is a good start.

- - - - - - - - - - - - - - -

Materials

+ 5 × 7-inch (13 × 18-cm) index cards or cardstock
+ Scissors
+ Transparent tape
+ Black marker
+ Magnifying glass or microscope
+ Your nature journal (page 343)

Take your materials and head outside to your favorite workspace. Cut a 1-inch (2.5-cm) square out of the center of two index cards. Cover the opening with tape, so that on one side of the index card, the sticky part is exposed, and choose two spots in your yard in which to place your cards.

Write the name of location #1 on one card next to the opening with the marker. Do the same thing with the other card for location #2. Tape your cards to a play structure, building, post or something else stationary in the locations you have chosen.

Make sure the sticky side of the tape faces out. Take them down after an hour and observe the particle matter stuck on each sticky square with a magnifying glass or microscope.

In your nature journal, write down what you found. What do the particles look like? Which area had more particles in the air? Was there anything that surprised you about these results?

What could you do to clean up the air in those locations? Anything? Maybe you could plant a garden to get more oxygen in that area. Or, could you put up a fence to block things from blowing into your yard? See what ideas you come up with, then go for it!

FUN FACT

People cause much of the problems we have with air pollution with things like factories, cars, airplanes, chemicals, methane from landfills and so much more. Poor air quality causes illness and environmental damage.

Nasty Deterioration: Find Out What Acid Rain Does

Air pollutants can cause rainwater to become polluted with chemicals that can cause further problems. We call polluted water acid rain. Acid rain is dangerous because the pollutants in the rainwater can ruin freshwater, and damage crops and food sources.

The erosion, or wearing down, of limestone and marble can result in lost artwork like statues and monuments that can't be replaced. Ecosystems like lakes and rivers can be destroyed when they become too acidic, killing birds, fish and plants. See the effects of an acid on a substance for yourself.

- - - - - - - - - - - - - -

Materials

+ Sidewalk chalk
+ ½ cup (118 ml) vinegar
+ Glass jar
+ Your nature journal (page 343)

Crush up a few pieces of sidewalk chalk. Pour ½ cup (118 ml) of vinegar in the jar and add a tablespoon (8 g) of the crushed chalk. What's happening? Record your observations in your nature journal.

The chalk is made up of calcium carbonate, and it reacts when it comes into contact with an acid like vinegar. Keep adding chalk until the reaction stops. By adding more calcium carbonate, you've neutralized the reaction, using up all of the acid from the vinegar.

One of the reasons water is so clean and fresh in mountain streams is because limestone and other minerals that make up the rocks lining them neutralize the acids in rainwater before they can fill the streams!

FUN FACT

Acid rain is made when gasses get into the air. The wind blows these gasses for miles. Then, they get washed out of the air when it rains.

About the Authors

Holly Homer is the co-author of *101 Kids Activities That Are the Bestest, Funnest Ever!* and *The 101 Coolest Simple Science Experiments*. She runs KidsActivities.com and the Quirky Momma Facebook page. It was love at first smell for her and playdough. Making salt dough was one of her earliest memories and her family's Christmas tree still holds her homemade creations.

Jamie Harrington is the creator of the blog Totally the Bomb, co-author of *The 101 Coolest Simple Science Experiments* and author of *The Unofficial Guide to Crafting the World of Harry Potter*. She has always had an appreciation for the way playdough squishes in her hands, but she never, ever, ever mixed the colors together. She is now pro color-mixing and encourages everyone to mix the heck out of them!

Brittanie Pyper is the author of *Adorkable Bubble Bath Crafts*, writes SimplisticallyLiving.com and fell in love with playdough when she was a little girl. What started with pretend cooking and baking has turned into a DIY obsession for all things ooey and gooey, which doubles as entertainment for her kids.

Rachel Miller is a lifetime learner and educator. She is a specialist in non-traditional learning techniques and has taught classes in history and sociology, as well as integrated STEM classes for grades K–8, using only common office supplies. She is a mom to a van-full whose favorite moments are exploring the world hands-on with her kids. She is the creator of the website and Facebook Community, QuirkyMomma, and can also be found on her blog, One Crazy House.

Colleen Kessler is an explorer, tinkerer, educator, creator and a passionate advocate for the needs of gifted and twice-exceptional children. She has a B.S. in elementary education, a M.Ed. in gifted studies and is the founder of the popular blog Raising Lifelong Learners. You can always find her online at RaisingLifelongLearners.com and on social media @ColleenKessler. Get in touch with her at RaisingLifelongLearners.com/Contact

Emma Vanstone, creator of the award-winning blog Science Sparks, has a degree in microbiology and virology and is passionate about making science fun and accessible for kids.

Amanda Boyarshinov is a National Board certified teacher with oodles of experience in early childhood education. She holds a bachelor's degree in elementary education and a master's degree in reading for grades K–12. You will often find her in her backyard exploring nature with her kids or doing a hands-on science project at the kitchen table.

Kim Vij is a certified teacher with over 20 years of experience teaching in early childhood education. She transitioned from classroom teaching to have a wider and stronger impact on early childhood education through advocacy. Her live and online appearances have helped her spread her message and become one of the leading experts of early childhood developmental activities. When she's not advising clients on developmentally appropriate strategies you can find her on Pinterest at www.pinterest.com/educatorsspinon.

Tonya Staab is an online content creator, photographer and partner specialist for Kids Activities Blog, who also runs her own blog tonyastaab.com.

Index